1
ts of ramparts next to Bådsmandsstræde open up for public use

1965
Sofiegården in Cop

1967
The militar

1968
The r ... drawing up plans for public housing on former barracks area

1969
Sofiegården assaulted by police and cleared

1970
The Thy Camp is arranged in Jutland

1971
In the summer people from neighbouring area start using the old barracks
The Freetown Christiania is proclaimed
A new Social Democrat (Socialdemokraterne) government

1972
The 10-point agreement with the government
Christiania Alternative is published
Cooperative TV channel launched

1973
Bossernes Befrielses Front (Gay Men's Liberation Front) moves to CA and Bossehuset is established
The Sun Chariot (Solvognen) moves to CA
The government establishes action plan and declares CA a social experiment
The Academy Board announces ideas competition
A new Liberal government

1974
CA obtains seat on Municipal Board
First major CA debate in Folketinget (the Danish parliament)
Nils Vest's movie *Law and Order in Christiania* is released

1975
LP record for CA is released
The Sun Chariot presents the play *Elverhøj*
CA summons against the State

1976
DR broadcasting of Poul Martinsen's *Diary from a Freetown*
Government decides on 'soft landing'
The National Museum publishes *Christiania – Metropolitan Community*

1977
Verdict against CA in Eastern District Court of Appeal (Østre Landsret)
CA exhibition *Love and Chaos* at Charlottenborg

1978
Verdict against CA in Supreme Court
The Sun Chariot moves from CA
Government sets up planning committee to establish local plan

1979
The Junk Blockade

960

1970

Continued on back endpapers

Space for Urban Alternatives?

Christiania is a squatted area in the district of Christianshavn in Copenhagen, located less than one mile from the Royal Danish Palace and the Danish parliament. It stretches over 49 hectares (32, excluding the water in the moats) and consists of old military barracks and parts of the city's ramparts dating from the seventeenth century; as well as a number of buildings constructed after 1971 (when the Freetown was proclaimed). The area offers city life as well as life in the countryside. Today approximately 900 people live in Christiania. According to the latest public census (2003), 60 per cent of these were male and 20 per cent were under 18 years old. Further, 60 per cent had elementary school as their highest level of education. While there is a group with a substantial registered income, two-thirds of the population either receive social assistance or have no registered income. The Freetown is divided into 14 self-governing areas and all decisions affecting the whole of Christiania are taken by the Common Meeting, which is ruled by consensus democracy.

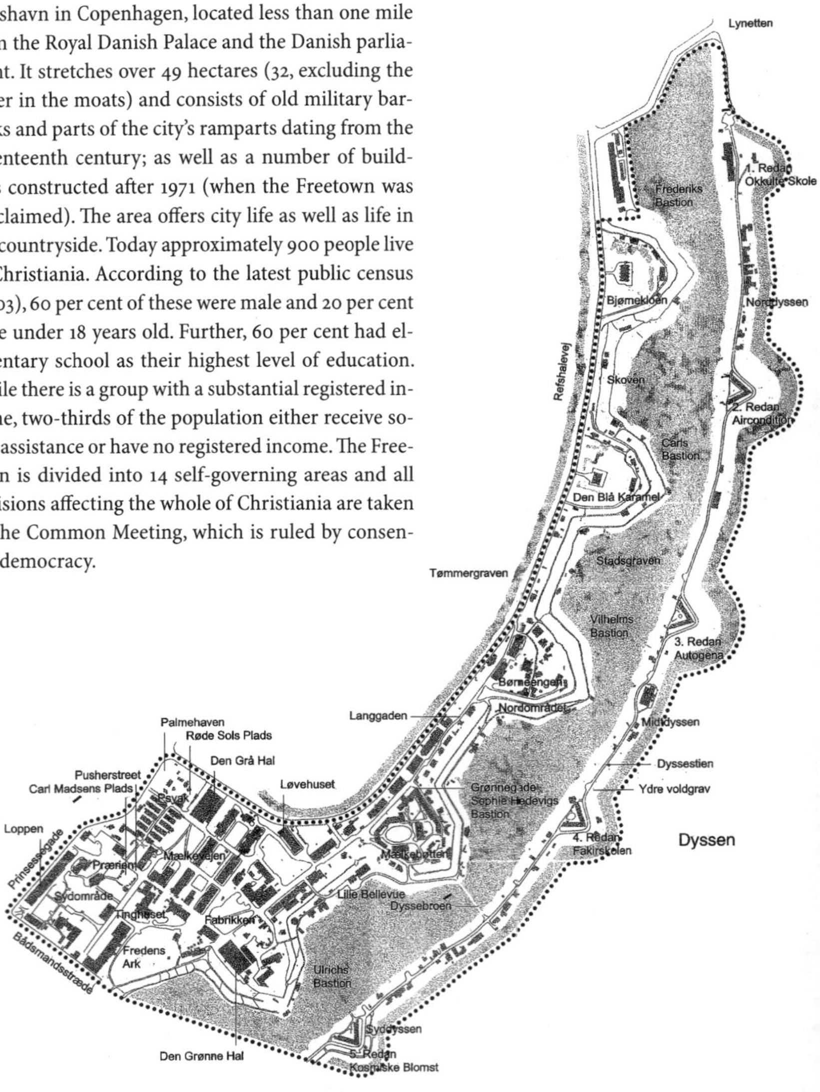

1:7000

Map: Hasløv & Kjærsgaard.

Space for Urban Alternatives?

CHRISTIANIA 1971–2011

Editors:
Håkan Thörn, Cathrin Wasshede
and Tomas Nilson

GIDLUNDS FÖRLAG

This book is also available for free download at Gothenburg University Publications Electronic Archive (GUPEA), www.gupea.ub.gu.se

Cover: Leah Robb

ISBN 978-91-7844-830-2
Printed by BALTO print, Vilnius 2011

Contents

INTRODUCTION: FROM 'SOCIAL EXPERIMENT' TO 'URBAN ALTERNATIVE' — 40 YEARS OF RESEARCH ON THE FREETOWN

Håkan Thörn, Cathrin Wasshede & Tomas Nilson

Introduction

On 26 September 1971, a group from the alternative newspaper *Hovedbladet* were photographed as they staged a symbolic takeover of the abandoned Bådsmandsstræde Barracks, a military area in Christianshavn, a centrally located working class district in Copenhagen, Denmark that had been squatted by young people. Over the following weeks, images and reports from the proclamation of the 'Freetown Christiania' were published by mainstream national media around the country. Soon people were travelling to the Danish capital from all over Europe to be part of the foundation of the new community, located no more than a mile from the Royal Danish Palace and the Danish parliament.

In 1973, the Social Democratic government of Denmark gave Christiania the official (but temporary) status of a 'social experiment'. A 'Christiania Act' passed by a broad parliamentary majority in 1989 legalised the squat and made it possible to grant Christiania the right to collective use of the area. This was however reversed under the Liberal-Conservative government in 2004, when the parliament (again with a broad parliamentary majority) passed significant changes in the 1989 Christiania law. As Christiania refused to give up its collective use of the property, and negotiations finally broke down in 2008, the Freetown took the Danish state to court to claim their right to the use of the property. The case was taken up by the Danish Supreme Court in 2011, the year of the Freetown's 40th anniversary. Christiania lost the case, but the Freetown's legal status remains ambiguous and contested. In april 2011, the Freetown closed everything down and blocked the entrances, to protest and to gain time to consider an offer from the state to buy and rent the buildings of Christiania. After three days and three Common Meetings Christiania decided to take part in negotiations regarding the state's offer, which also has a number of strings attached.

Around 900 people today live in Christiania. It is governed through a de-centralised democratic structure, whose autonomy is highly contingent on the Freetown's external relations with the Danish government, the Copenhagen Municipality, the Copenhagen Police — and organised crime linked to the sale of hash in the Freetown.

From its early days, Christiania has attracted significant attention from social scientists and architects. A significant proportion of Christiania's core political activists have been students or researchers, devoting academic work to different aspects of the Freetown. Those who have been public spokespersons for Christiania from positions outside of the Freetown have also constantly referred to research when arguing that the Freetown's claim to the area was legitimate, and should be made legal. For example, during the first major Christiania debate in the Danish parliament (Folketinget) in 1974, those who defended the Freetown several times referred to academics. For example, Social Democrat Kjeld Olesen quoted criminologist Berl Kutchinsky's argument that Christiania was a social experiment that was internationally unique, as the Freetown was a place where a significant number of individuals who had previously been in the care of public institutions, because of criminal activities or drug addiction, had regained their self-esteem and lived a life integrated into the community. Olesen further referred to the grand old man of Danish architecture, Steen Eiler

Rasmussen, who at the time claimed that Christiania promised to deliver everything that modernist urban planning had failed to achieve.[1]

Rasmussen's *Omkring Christiania* (*Around Christiania*), published in 1976, is a key document for understanding the extent to which Christiania in the 1970s attracted attention from Danish academics and public intellectuals — and how they perceived 'the issue of Christiania'. It includes statements from scholars in the fields of criminology, economics, sociology, architecture, urban planning, psychology, psychiatry, theology, and medicine (see further below). In different ways, they all regarded Christiania as an opportunity to explore possible alternatives to the capitalist economy and/or the social institutions and urban planning of the Danish welfare state. As is evident in a government report from 1973, it was such a perception of what Christiania fundamentally was about that led the Social Democratic government to give the Freetown the status of an official social experiment.[2]

Christiania never acknowledged this status but according to their pragmatic politics, they were willing to accept any outside definition that made it possible to continue what they were doing without too much interference. As there have always been numerous contesting definitions *within* Christiania regarding what the Freetown really is about, Christianites have also always been reluctant to accommodate serious attempts to define the Freetown in particular ways, whether by authorities or researchers. Nevertheless, Christiania has always been open to, and even warmly welcomed, researchers.[3] Since 2004, the locally supported and driven CRIR (Christiania Researcher in Residence) programme has offered residency for artists and academic researchers who are interested in generating important knowledge about Christiania. The programme has sponsored more than forty projects on a variety of themes.[4]

Organised by a group of researchers at the University of Gothenburg, this book brings together 10 scholars who have done research on Christiania in the 2000s in the context of various disciplines: sociology, anthropology, history, geography, art, urban planning, landscape architecture and political science; and who are based in Denmark, Sweden, the USA and Britain. Although this is a book written by academic scholars, we have asked the contributors to write in a style that makes it as accessible as possible to non-academics with an interest in urban politics and culture in general, and Christiania in particular.

As a background to the chapters in this book, the following pages are devoted to an overview of previous research on Christiania, from the early 1970s and on. Over the years, a great number of books and articles on Christiania have been written by non-academics, including journalists, authors and Christianites, and many of these publications have been valuable resources for academic research.[5] This overview will however be delimited to publications written by authors based in, or with links to, academia. Two questions have guided the overview: What is the main focus of the research? What are the most important conclusions? We have divided our account into three parts, which represent three periods in Christiania research, each of which has been dominated by a particular focus on Christiania. In each of these periods it is also quite clear that the main research works reflect, interact, and sometimes even also articulate, the themes and issues that dominated public debates on Christiania — in the media, and in parliament.

The first period, from 1972 to 1979, is clearly dominated by a focus on Christiania as a *social* issue, as in social problems, social institutions and social experiment. When the roles of hash and crime, themes which are always present in public debates on Christiania, are investigated they are embedded in a social context, defined primarily as social problems not unique to Christiania, but prominent in Denmark as a whole. When Christiania is discussed as an issue of planning at this particular time, there is an emphasis on the *social* dimensions of urban planning.

As the 1970s ended, Christiania had gone through its pioneering period as well as its first fundamental crisis. But as the Supreme Court's verdict in 1978, which ruled that Christiania had no legal right to remain, actually came to nothing, and as the campaign to get rid of hard drugs in 1979 was successful, the Freetown entered the 1980s with renewed strength. As the early 1980s were defined by a polarisation in Danish politics, when the emergence of neoliberalism was countered by a wave of new social movements, led by feminist, peace, green, squatter and solidarity movements, Christiania now became a relatively established counterpublic sphere and a political and cultural space in which these movements often interacted. This is also clearly reflected in the *second period* of research on the Freetown (1979–2002), which largely focused on Christiania as *a space for alternative culture*. In spite of recurring and violent raids by the police, as recounted in a report from Amnesty in 1994 (see René Karpantschof's chapter in this book), the period following legalisation in 1989 was characterised by relative political stability for Christiania. This is reflected in the fact that for 10 years (1994–2003) academia was rather silent on Christiania.

The third period (2004–) of research begins in connection with the changes in the Christiania law that were passed by the parliament in 2004 and focuses on Christiania as *an urban question*. This shift had however already started to emerge after Christiania was put on a path to legalisation in 1989, something which involved the presentation of a local plan for Christiania in 1991. In Christiania's counter-plan, *Den grønne plan* (*The Green Plan*, 1991), Christiania's alternative status was no longer defined in social, but in *environmental* terms, linking up with the discourse of sustainable urban development. The research started in 2004 did however approach the urban question in a slightly different way. It was part of an inter-disciplinary renaissance in urban studies, including an emerging new critical urban theory, focusing on 'the right to the city'. The strong interest in issues of urban development also meant that Christiania's aesthetic dimensions were emphasised and analysed to an unprecedented extent by researchers from different disciplines.

On the most abstract level research on Christiania in the 2000s has responded to, and critically examined, an intensified globalisation process, which has brought an increasing economic, political and cultural significance to big cities. Focusing on the concept of 'gentrification' (in its broadest sense referring to an upgrading of urban districts, socially and culturally),[6] the new urban research is mainly concerned with processes of social exclusion, as cities worldwide have embarked on urban restructuring projects, linked to a competition to attract capital, tourists and a new, 'creative' middle class. In this context Christiania started to attract attention from academics worldwide, and leading urban scholars such as David Harvey and Neil Smith visited the Freetown. How is it, they wondered, that for forty years an almost completely de-commodified space has existed in the central area of a European capital?

Christiania as a Social Issue (1972–1979)

That architects have found the Freetown exciting comes as no surprise — from the very beginning Copenhagen's leading architects and urban planning scholars closely followed what happened in Christiania. The first book written by an academic on Christiania — *Fristaden Christiania som samfundsexperiment* (*The Freetown Christiania as a Community Experiment*) — was published as early as 1972. The author, Per Løvetand Iversen, one of the leading Christianites during the 1970s, was a member of a research group at the Architectural School in Copenhagen that studied Christiania with a focus on how norms and behaviours were challenged by new ideas and alternative ways of living.

Løvetand Iversen viewed the forming of Christiania as a logical consequence of very deep running feelings of dissatisfaction with the dominating social order amongst people from various social backgrounds. For that reason, Christiania came to harbour a wide mix of people, with different reasons for settling there. Further, Løvetand Iversen put Christiania into the context of the contemporary left-wing critique of the consumer society, where materialism, alienation and commodification had to be replaced by, 'a practical socialism that enables participation and self-determination to the individual person'.[7] Løvetand Iversen's text combined parts analysing the emergence of Christiania, the current situation and the making of a collective consciousness within Christiania with parts that accounted for Christiania's present state according to various internal and external sources.

In 1975 the Danish journal *Arkitekten* (*the Architect*) published a special issue on Christiania and the recently completed architectural competition on how to develop the Christianshavn area.[8] The competition was part of a larger plan on how to better integrate (and also better protect) the scattered and random buildings in Christiania into a more regulated city landscape. Such alignment had grown out of the 'social experiment status' that had been granted to Christiania in 1973, and was one of the absolute conditions for that decision. In *Arkitekten* the winning plans were commented on and dissected by the three judges from planning-, architectural- and social pedagogical perspectives. The whole issue was very sympathetic towards Christiania, and both of the winning proposals had tried both to incorporate and develop the current social organisation in their plans.

In one of the proposed plans, submitted by Niels Herskind, Susanne Mogensen and Douglas Evans, the foundations of Christiania would remain the same: a small-scale society where the inhabitants had absolute say on matters concerning housing and ownership, and where production was collectively owned and collectively run. Christianite Richardt Løvehjerte was given space to elaborate on Christiania's own plans for the future. He suggested that Christiania would be given to the Christianites so that they could plan for a future without risking eviction — it ought to become a true Freetown, acknowledged and secured by the state. The social situation in Christiania, where drug addicts, homeless and runaway children were provided shelter and an ideological context, should constitute a good argument for a continuation of the Freetown — not the opposite. And at neighbouring Holmen, Løvehjerte wanted to create an autonomous ecological experimental community.

Architect Steen Eiler Rasmussen, in his later days one of Christiania's staunchest supporters, wrote extensively on Christiania. *Omkring Christiania* was published in connection with the campaign to defend Christiania in 1976, as part of Rasmussen's engagement in the Støt Christiania (Support Christiania) movement.[9] It contains texts Rasmussen had written earlier — but also extensive documentation of opinions on Christiania by leading authorities from different fields. The credo of Rasmussen's own writing was not to overly idealise Christiania — he could clearly see the many built-in problems, such as crime, drug abuse and unhealthy sanitary conditions — but rather to contemplate Christiania as a good example, an alternative society, created out of chaos but nevertheless a place for others to learn from. He viewed Christiania as the true sustainable society as compared to contemporary consumer societies: old buildings being re-used and preserved and where people on the fringes of society became accepted and useful parts of a greater whole. Basically, Christiania meant freedom to Rasmussen. He wrote, for instance, that it stood in contrast to the regulated and normalised but 'pretty heartless' flagship of modernity — Tingbjerg — the model estate on the other side of town, once planned by Rasmussen himself (see Signe Sophie Bøggild's chapter in this book).[10]

The last part of the book is an account of several expert opinions on the Freetown as a social experiment. This strategy of engaging opinionated people sympathetic to the cause of Christiania had been used before — and would be used again. In the book Rasmussen picked persons from a wide range of academic fields at the University of Copenhagen, Denmark's Technical School and the School of Architecture, but also from other fields of expertise, including policy, medicine, culture and even religion; such as Social Minister Eva Gredal, social advisor Tine Bryld, Copenhagen's Director of urban planning Kai Lemberg, the bishop Thorkild Græsholt; and statements from 26 medical doctors and 24 'cultural personalities' in Copenhagen. Among the results from research on Christiania presented in the book, two stand out: first, criminologist Flemming Balvig concluded from his research on Christiania that it had 'both a regulating and a mitigating effect on criminality in Copenhagen', and that the Freetown therefore 'for the moment is the most important "test case" in the area of criminal policy'.[11] Second, a group based at Denmark's Technical School, led by Professor Erik Kaufmann, presented a strictly economic cost-benefit analysis regarding the options of closing down Christiania or letting it continue. It was concluded that, considering the expenses for a number of inhabitants of Christiania that would need the care of public institutions should Christiania be closed, the additional costs for closing down the Freetown would be 6 million Danish kroner for the state; and 32 million for the Copenhagen municipality.

Flemming Balvig's contribution in Rasmussen's book was based on a research report written together with Henning Koch and Jørn Vestergaard, titled *Politiets virksomhed i Christiania-området* (*Police Activities in the Christiania area*). The aim of the report was to look at the development of criminality in Christiania during the period between 1972 and 1975 — accounting for statistics on crime as well as analysing how the police reported on and handled crime in Christiania. The main finding was somewhat surprising — the authors concluded that the crime rate in Christiania was no higher than in other parts of Copenhagen and that it even showed a downward tendency in comparison to the rest of Copenhagen. Numbers also showed that there was 20 per cent less risk of getting robbed in Christiania, and 25–30 per cent less risk of facing violence, than in the area around Istedgade (an area next to the central train station). The criminologists' study thus effectively proved that both public prejudice, and the police force's own statements about Christiania as a place with unusually high criminality, did not have much substance.

On 10 February 1977, the same day that the Eastern Court of Appeals in Copenhagen stated its verdict on Christiania's court case against the state (refuting Christiania's claims), Steen Eiler Rasmussen held a lecture at the School of Architecture in Copenhagen. It was later published as a book entitled *Fristeder i kulturhistorisk og kulturpolitisk belysning (Freetowns in the Light of Cultural History and Cultural Politics).*[12] It dealt historically with the growth of a number of regular 'freetowns' but also with 'free spaces' in ordinary cities. The historical development of Christiania was an important example of such a 'free space' within the city, according to Rasmussen. In the short introduction, Børge Schnack saw Christiania as a counter-weight to bureaucracy: made up of people who would not, or were not able to, adjust to a bureaucratic class society. Christiania was an alternative to that, inhabited by 'happy people' who outside of Christiania would be classed as deviant.[13]

In 1977, the Swedish *Arkitekttidningen* (*Journal of Architecture*) devoted a large part of an issue to Christiania, making ample reference to Rasmussen's books. In *Arkitekttidningen*, Christiania was portrayed both as a social and ecological experiment. Lena Karlsson, the author of the long reportage on Christiania, found the integration of people deemed as deviant as perhaps the most important task for the Christianities. Karlsson cited the calculations of Danish social advisor Tine Bryld, stating that the Danish state had saved the costs of around 100 places at public institutions because of Christiania. However, according to Karlsson, Christiania needed long-term security to be able to succeed with this important task; and that had been lacking since the beginning, which meant that the unique conditions of such an alternative society had never fully been allowed to develop. Regarding the ecological aspects, Karlsson saw Christiania as an independent small-scale model community; its way of life geared towards re-use and recycling, alternative ways of cultivating crops and making use of wind and sun as sources of power.

From the perspective of urban planning, Kai Lemberg, director of the Copenhagen General Planning Department, wrote the article 'A Squatter Settlement in Copenhagen: Slum Ghetto or Social Experiment', published in *International Review* in 1978. The article provided a historical background to the origins of the Freetown and accounted for the social profile of its inhabitants and the reactions of the state. Lemberg also listed arguments supportive of, or against, Christiania. Lemberg mainly focused on social issues: the governmental response to inadequate housing and the lack of water and electricity in Christiania were thoroughly treated, as well as the social responsibility Christiania had taken upon itself concerning the 'resocialising' of individuals who for different reasons had left (given up on) traditional society.

In 1976 the ethnographer Jacques Blum of the National Museum of Denmark published a study on Christiania (in English, 1977) titled *Freetown Christiania: Slum, Alternative Culture or a Social Experiment?* (with cooperation from Inger Sjørslev). The idea for the study had come from the Liaison Committee for Alcohol and Narcotics, and the research was funded by the Danish Social Science Research Council. Blum had been contacted in August 1975 and had been asked to conduct the study, which had to be completed before 1 April 1976 because of the planned closure of Christiania on that date. Blum's research was not undertaken without difficulties. Despite initial support from individual Christianites, the Common Meeting in December 1975 declared that Christiania would not participate in a study that was organised by the Social Research Institute and the Social Science Research Council, at least not before 1 April. Blum as an individual was free to interview Christianites though.

The main aim of the study was solely to convey experiences the inhabitants had of the Freetown and their surrounding reality. Blum used what he called 'untraditional' social science methods — firstly because of the resistance and scepticism from the Christianites themselves, and secondly because Blum considered his research subject to be 'so untraditional that to do otherwise would have prevented the implementation of our study'.[14] Instead he tried to act as an interpreter of the way the Christianites thought and talked, translating his findings into 'a language that is more familiar to the world outside Christiania'.[15] The main findings in Blum's study concern the consequences of trying to live without norms; Blum pointing to problems with the use of drugs, a commitment to unlimited self-realisation and an 'everything is permitted' approach to life.

Two years after the publication of *Freetown Christiania* Blum and Sjørslev edited an anthology on alternative lifestyles — *Spirer til en ny livsform: Tværvidenskabelige synspunkter omkring alternative samfundsforsøg (Seeds For a New Life Form: Interdisciplinary Perspectives on Alternative Social Experiments).* The publication of this book, which included contributions by scholars from a wide range of disciplines, including Kai Lemberg and internationally well-known Swedish sociologist Joachim Israel, was symptomatic of the genuine interest in alternative ways of living so common in the 1970s. Even though Christiania was not the prime subject, Blum and Sjørslev nevertheless focused on the Freetown, one of their main points being that even though there was a tendency towards a deep polarisation between Christiania and mainstream society, the two were deeply interrelated.[16]

In 1978 a collaboration between German and Danish researchers resulted in an anthology in German entitled *Christiania. Argumente zur Erhaltung eines befreiten Stadsviertels im Zentrum von Kopenhagen* (*Christiania: Arguments for Preservation of a Liberated District in Central Copenhagen*). Two of the editors, Heiner Gringmuth and Ernst-Ulrich Pinkert, wrote on subjects firmly framed in a social context: children in kindergarten, work in Christiania, life in Christiania — as well as on music and culture (Christiania's music and theatre group Solvognen/the Sun Chariot). Steen Eiler Rasmussen, Kai Lemberg, Flemming Balvig and Per Løvetand Iversen also made contributions, the first three roughly along the lines of what they had written in Danish (see above), while Løvetand Iversen contributed a personal history of Christiania up until autumn 1977, concentrating on social conditions and the legal battles.

In 1979 Flemming Balvig published a study on media reporting on Christiania — from April 1975 to February 1978. The study addressed the question: to what extent did the media report on Christiania and in what ways did the media manage to influence public opinion? To find out, Balvig analysed 15 national opinion polls on Christiania, conducted during the period of the study. While a majority of the Danish population had been negative towards the Freetown during its first years, the trend was now one of increasing support for Christiania — in 1978 more than half of the population wanted Christiania to remain. According to Balvig, the influence of the mainstream media in changing opinion was less than expected: information and experiences that changed opinions were rather horizontal than vertical — 'it is not the experts or the large papers that converted people' Balvig argued.[17] Instead peoples' own direct experiences counted more, as well as information exchange with people of similar social status, and that which was to be found in local papers or local radio stations.

Space for Alternative Culture (1979–2002)

In this period of research Christiania's social dimensions were still very present. They were however most often discussed in the context of a kind of evaluation of the Freetown's first decade as an alternative society. Many research questions focused on the class structure that existed even within an alternative society such as Christiania. Another connected theme during this period was the relations between Christiania, social movements/alternative cultures and surrounding society, especially the authorities. Strategies concerning freedom from government and co-option by the authorities in order to survive were central.

In 1979 Børge Madsen, a Christianite as well as a student of political science, wrote a master's thesis that attracted a lot of attention; *I Skorpionen halespids — et speciale om mig & Christiania* (*In the Scorpio's Tail Tip — a Thesis About Me and Christiania*). Two years later, in 1981, he published a book, based on his thesis: *Sumpen, liberalisterne och de hellige. Christiania — et barn af kapitalismen* (*The Trash, the Liberalists *and the Holy Ones: Christiania — a Child of Capitalism*). Madsen's focus was an analysis of the social structure in Christiania, composed of three main groups: the activists (the Holy Ones), the underclass (the Trash) and a middle strata (the Liberalists), a group enjoying the 'civil liberties' of the Freetown, but who were relatively indifferent to Christiania's political struggle.[18] According to Madsen, this social stratification, which had been established during Christiania's first decade, was an important explanation of the Freetown's crisis. To be able to reach a deeper and more complex picture of the Freetown's social structure, Madsen elaborated with two concepts; 'social deroute' and 'social dissociation'. *Social deroute* is a concept aimed at describing how people get lost (alienated) in modern individualist society and often take their refuge in alcohol, drugs and medication. Madsen argues that the Liberalists, often originating from the middle class, were hit by this process. A smaller part of the middle class activists, the Holy Ones, was more characterised by *social dissociation*, which in Madsen's analysis means a *conscious* dissociation from society, founded on political ideologies such as anarchism, socialism and utopianism. The lowest of the lowest was according to Madsen the Trash, including groups that were involved in both social deroute and social dissociation. Belonging to the Trash were for example the Greenlanders, described as an isolated group that in Danish society was the object of colonial oppression.

Because of the high tolerance in Christiania, everyone could more or less do as s/he wanted to, according to Madsen — even drug her/himself to death. Madsen however claimed that this was not primarily a result of tolerance, but of powerlessness, capitalism and individualisation. Madsen also discussed the 1979 Junk blockade in detail — and how Christiania's own organisation for social work, Herfra og Videre (Upwards and Onwards), was established in connection with this.

In the book *The Poverty of Progress: Changing Ways of Life in Industrial Societies*, published in 1982, Christiania was discussed in the chapter 'Alternative Ways of Life in Denmark'. It was authored by five

Danes; Steen Juhler and Per Løvetand Iversen, both architects; Mogens Kløvedal; author and filmmaker; Dino Hansen, sinologist and Jens Falkentorp, translator. Except for Hansen, the authors were also described as activists in one or another way. The main purpose of their chapter was to investigate significant attempts to build alternatives to the dominating ways of life in Denmark. In addition to Christiania, they also discussed the Tvind Schools, various communes, the Thy Camp and Island camps,[19] accounting for differences as well as similarities between these alternative communities. Christiania was portrayed as an alternative to the 'contemporary norm of unrestrained consumption'[20] and as demonstrating the principles of the right to *use* rather than to *own*. Most striking with Christiania though, according to the authors, was that it had shown the strength of the strategy of 'holding together'. According to the authors, conflicts with opponents on the outside, mainly the authorities, had helped to create solidarity and sustain a collective identity in Christiania. When discussing the future of Christiania, they were however ambivalent. On the one hand they claimed that social and criminal problems in Christiania were 'nearly out of control'.[21] On the other hand, they speculated on an integration of Christiania with the surrounding society, which would include an elaboration of Christiania's social and cultural functions. Thy Camp was the only one of the other cases in the chapter that was said to be directly related to Christiania, as many people were said to move between the two places. One important difference was that Thy Camp owned the land they used.

The book *Sociale uroligheder: politi og politik* (*Social Disturbances: Police and Politics*), published in 1986, contained a chapter on Christiania titled 'Befolkningen, Christiania og politiet' (The Population, Christiania and the Police), written by Flemming Balvig, and jurist Nell Rasmussen. Balvig and Rasmussen accounted for a growing polarisation between the police and Christiania. Christianites, on the one hand, felt that they were living in a police state, fearing the police more than the criminal community. They perceived that the police considered them criminals or potential criminals, and that the police had exceeded their rights during actions in the Freetown. Further, Christianites felt that the police officers often expressed a politically and ideologically biased attitude towards Christianites. The police, on the other hand, viewed Christiania as pure anarchy, defined by illegal activity. They felt that they had been viewed as enemies in Christiania and that Christianities often had sought confrontation. They further recounted how police officers had been wounded in the Freetown. Two contrasting pictures of reality — who has the right to have right?, the authors rhetorically ask. The authors concluded that the police strategy in Christiania had failed; it had led to big confrontations and created more problems than it had solved.

In 1993, AKF (Anvendt Kommunal Forskning/Applied Municipal Research), an independent research institute, published a report called *De offentlige myndigheder og Christiania* (*The Public Authorities and Christiania*). The authors of the report were Olaf Rieper, sociologist and organisation theorist, Birgit Jæger, science and technology/sociologist, and Leif Olsen, sociologist. The aim of the project was to answer the question: What can the public authorities learn about governance through the critical case of Christiania, with its self-administration? Through detailed description of the processes in the negotiations concerning the legalisation of Christiania, preceding the 1989 law and the 1991 Framework Agreement, the authors tried to investigate if the authorities had begun to use a new praxis and/or if they had gained new values. The Framework Agreement of 1991 was central to the analysis, since both Christiania's contact group and the authorities had subscribed to it. Even though there were problems with the accomplishment of some of the issues on behalf of Christiania, the authors highlighted all the things that worked out well, for example big payments and taxes from Christiania, especially from the restaurants, removal of buildings and environmental protection. According to the authors both parts were hampered by internal differences. The main problem was however the radically different political cultures that were intrinsic to the two parts; function, bureaucracy and short-termism (the authorities) contra integrated roles, wholeness and long-termism (Christiania). This was solved by the authorities through engaging in a specific flexibility and in informal relations, things that put unusual demands on the individual official, requiring, for example, sensitivity and devotion. The authors summarised their study by claiming that dialogue and agreement were central, as were mutual trust, concrete agreements and reflexivity concerning interpretation of the law.

The International Institute of Social History in 1996 published a report written by Adam Conroy, *Christiania: The Evolution of a Commune*. Conroy's main interest concerned the evolution of Christiania's structure and identity over its 25 years of existence. His aim was to analyse how Christiania had reacted to external political changes and how external and internal pressures had influenced its overall development. Conroy highlighted the classificatory model of Christiania's inhabitants discerned by Blum and Sjørslev, slightly different from the one worked out by Madsen: a) *active sympathisers* — a group made up of commuters; people with jobs outside the Freetown, those on social welfare and students; b) *passive dependants* — social claimants, petty criminals and social casualities; people who live in Christiania because of 'dire need'[22] and c) *passive opportunists* — occasional foreigners, people with no financial support, criminals, pushers, bar owners and middle-class people who just wanted a cheap place to live. According to Conroy it was the existence of the *passive dependants* that made Christiania a 'valuable experience rather than an elitist or a controlled "social experiment"'.[23] *The passive opportunists* were according to Conroy regarded as the biggest problem in the Freetown by its activists (who belong to the *active sympathisers*). Conroy however regarded the activists as the major problem: they were critically pictured as self-righteous; their activism even described as a danger to the Freetown's internal democracy.

In 1996 Bjarne Maagensen, a Christianite with a master's degree in history, published a book called *Christiania — en længere historie* (*Christiania — a Longer History*), in honour of the Freetown's 25th birthday. It was a historical narrative written in a personal style focusing on Christiania's efforts to survive through the years. Maagensen divided the history into three periods: the first period (1971–79) was the 'beginning and fame'. The second period (1979–89), was defined by the Junk Blockade, the conflicts around the biker-gang Bullshit, den Gule streg (the Yellow Line on Pusher Street, drawn to limit the hash market) and the closing of the old main entrance. In the third period (1990 and onward), Christiania according to Maagensen became bourgeois, which was related to the legalisation process. In the concluding chapter he discussed the 1990s legalisation process and the agreement with the authorities in ambivalent terms; it gave the Freetown the right to continue, and at the same time it tied the Freetown down — limiting its autonomy.

As part of a public investigation on democracy and power, initiated by the Danish parliament, the book *Bevægelser i demokrati: Foreninger og kollektive aktioner i Danmark* (*Movements in Democracy: Associations and Collective Actions in Denmark*) was published in 2002. One of the chapters, written by sociologist René Karpantschof and political scientist Flemming Mikkelsen, analysed squatter movements in Denmark from 1965 to 2001. The main part of the text concerned the BZ movement, but Christiania and the Slumstormer movement, which preceded the establishment of the Freetown, were also analysed. Young people were already squatting buildings in Christianshavn in 1965, and 'Sofiegården' was the name of one of the most well-known squats. As the Slumstormer movement disbanded in 1971, a group of activists moved to Christiania.

One of the authors' major points was that the creation of alternative urban spaces by the Slumstormers and Christiania was partly made possible by the relative indulgence of the authorities. The latter acted much harder on young activists appearing in the 1980s such as the BZ squatter movement, because they did not want 'another Christiania'. Even though the authors highlighted Christiania as one of the achievements of the squatter movements, they concluded:

> If the movement, and here we think especially on Christiania, succeeded in mobilising big external support in the form of alliance partners and common support from the population, it could survive as a living alternative culture, but not as a political movement.[24]

Urban Planning, Aesthetics and the Right to the City (2004–)

Similar to the first wave of research on Christiania in the mid-1970s, the current period began in connection with a mobilisation to defend Christiania's existence. In 2004, the Freetown was according to the new Christiania law to be the subject of urban development. When the government's Christiania Committee organised an open competition for a plan for the future development of Christiania (before the law had been passed), many of Denmark's leading architectural offices refused to participate as an act of solidarity with the Freetown.[25] Instead, a number of well-known Danish architects and urban planning scholars published articles and book chapters, which analysed both the ongoing Normalisation Plan and recent developments in Christiania. These scholars were generally critical of the government's new plan, concluding that it would most probably soon lead to a loss of everything valuable and unique about Christiania. This did not however mean that they were uncritical of Christiania's recent development and state of affairs. In *Christiania's lære/Learning from Christiania* (originally a special issue of the Danish journal *Arkitekten* and with parallel text in both Danish and English), two of the contributors, architect Merete Ahnfeldt-Mollerup and urban planner Jens Kvorning, argued that Christiania needed to develop if it was to be able to resist demands for normalisation. In the chapter 'Christiania's aesthetics — You can't kill us / we are part of you' Ahnfeldt-Mollerup boldly stated, contrary to established images of Christiania, that the Freetown's aesthetics reflected cultural values deeply embedded in Danish society. In this sense, the statement in Christiania's anthem, quoted in the title, has a lot more truth to it than most people imagine. Considering this, the aversion many conservatives feel in relation to Christiania is according to Ahnfeldt-Mollerup a bit strange: 'Perhaps the point is actually that it should not be torn down, but instead the bourgeois Denmark wants to buy Christiania and is displeased about it not being for sale'.[26] More specifically, Ahnfeldt-Mollerup argued that both Christiania's ideas and aesthetics have their roots in the traditions developing from late 18th century bourgeois romanticism and its critique of a highly organised and rationalistic version of modernity. This is a tradition that emphasises individual experience and perception while at the same time celebrating 'the communal spirit'. This is why the most profound conflicts in Christiania, on every level, have most often expressed a tension between individual and community. While Ahnfeldt-Mollerup first and foremost was interested in Christiania's building culture, she argued that the key to Christiania's originality lies in the material conditions under which these buildings have been constructed: 'they must be realised within a scavenger-economy'.[27] The fact that the pusher area aesthetically diverges from the rest of Christiania confirms this: the pushers' economic wealth means that their buildings have not been constructed on the basis of scarce economic resources. This also led Ahnfeldt-Mollerup to the conclusion, contrary to the Normalisation Plan, that no private ownership of housing should be introduced in Christiania, as it would mean the end of Christiania's aesthetic specificity.

Jens Kvorning's chapter in the same book, entitled 'Christiania and the borders in the city' placed Christiania in the wider context of global urban development. Drawing on contemporary urban studies, Kvorning pointed to how cities, as they participate in a global economic competition, increasingly are hunting for *cultural specificity*. In this process, great efforts are made to reshape inner cities in order to make the turally exciting' and attractive as dwelling places for *the creati* whose presence according to urban planning guru Richard Florida is a key to urban economic growth. Cities are thus involved in a contradictory development that as a crucial element involves the construction of physical and cultural borders; on the one hand they need to be open to the world, on the other hand they must erect, or protect, borders in order to defend their cultural uniqueness against the homogenising processes of globalisation. Relating this to Christiania, Kvorning argued that at a first glance, Christiania in a sense fits quite well into the concept of a 'creative urban milieu'. However, according to Kvorning, Christiania in the 2000s no longer had the cultural edge and impact on the Copenhagen cultural scene that it had in the 1970s. Further, Christiania hardly fits into the social profile preferred by today's city planners. While a group of the Freetown's inhabitants undoubtedly belongs to the creative middle class, a significant number belongs to the less well off in Danish society.[28] Considering this, Kvorning emphasised that in Christiania, Copenhagen has something important to preserve; a social, political and cultural alternative to the streamlined 'cultural specificity' promoted by urban planning gurus and gentrification processes. Christiania should therefore maintain its borders, including its physical fence, in relation to the surrounding city, while at the same continuing to keep its gates open to anyone who wants to visit.

Kvorning had also discussed Christiania in relation to the gentrification of Christianshavn in a previous article, titled 'Copenhagen: Formation, Change and Urban life', published in 2002 in the book *The Urban Lifeworld: Formation, Perception, Representation.* According to Kvorning, Christiania unintentionally had impacted the character of the gentrification of Christianshavn, one of the first inner city districts in Copenhagen selected for restructuring in the 1970s:

> Christiania had become a compression chamber of alternative lifestyles in Copenhagen. But the alternative by its very nature is impermanent, and this status became the springboard for the special form of gentrification that now began in Christianshavn.[29]

This special form of gentrification was according to Kvorning the district's 'alternative profile' (of which the closeness to Christiania was an important part), something which attracted students who returned to the district after completing their degrees, and the 'so-called creative professions', such as advertising bureaus and architectural firms.[30]

In an article entitled 'Rumskrig, nyliberalism och skalpolitik' (Space Wars, Neoliberalism and the Politics of Scale), published in 2005, Danish geographer Anders Lund Hansen discussed Christiania in an urban perspective similar to Kvorning's. Hansen however showed that in the early 2000s, Christiania was hardly a facilitator of gentrification, but rather an obstacle to the continuing upgrading of Copenhagen's inner city, as manifested for example in the area of Holmen (next to Christiania) with its new opera house.

Artist and design theorist Maria Hellström's dissertation on landscape planning, *Steal this Place: The Aesthetics of Tactical Formlesness and 'The Free Town of Christiania'*, published in 2006, provided a comprehensive analysis of Christiania from the perspective of urban planning.[31] Drawing on a wide range of perspectives, including urban theory, architecture, philosophy and sociology, Hellström's work situated Christiania in the context of a contemporary urban aestheticisation, occurring on a global scale. This is a process that in urban studies is associated with the increasing commercialisation of social life and commodification of urban space; driven by an expansion of the market mechanisms that ultimately obscure political conflicts, as inner cities are turned into Disneylands, where everyone is assigned a role to play in the grand spectacle. While Christiania's urban experiments and cultural politics, which emphasise an aestheticisation of politics, have reflected this process, the Freetown has also according to Hellström offered a different and radical interpretation of this process — a 'critical aestheticisation'. In the book, Hellström set out to examine and analyse how a critical urbanism such as the one performed by Christiania could 'affect more general urban planning and design discourse'.[32] In the following quote Hellström brings forth her main conclusion, focusing on a 'principle dilemma of urban planning', related to its difficulties in handling reality's 'abundance and unpredictability':

> What Christiania has made clear is the fact that in the in-betweens, surplus spaces, passages and vacancies, there is a profusion of life that cannot be submitted to planning but that, nevertheless, constitutes a necessary leeway for creative consideration. As such, these relational spaces become public spheres in the deeper, non-proprietary sense; spaces that have no properties and no forms and therefore, on a very distinct level of action, are experienced as *free*.[33]

A similar interpretation of Christiania, informed by urban theory and French philosophy, was made by French artist Gil M. Doron in 'Dead Zones, Outdoor Rooms and the Architecture of Transgression', published in 2006 in the book *Loose Space: Possibility and Diversity in Urban Life*. Doron, founder of Transgressive Architecture, a group of artists and architects, made Christiania one of the stops in a global odyssey, during which he searched for 'dead zones' or 'gap spaces' in urbanised areas. Dead zones are according to Doron 'also endless openings. They are also pure possibility; hence the utopian sentiment that is attached to them'.[34] In a similar manner, British cultural theorist Malcolm Miles made Christiania one of nine cases in his book *Urban Utopias: The Built and Social Architecture of Alternative Settlements*, published in 2008. Among the other examples of self-organising societies around the world that according to Miles are 'demonstrating plural possibilities for alternative futures' are Ufa-Fabrik in Berlin, Auroville in Tamil Nadu, Uzupio in Vilnius and Ecovillage at Ithaca (USA).[35]

The editors of the special issue of the journal *Nordisk arkitekturforsk-*

ning (*Nordic Architectural Research*) in 2005, Tom Nielsen, Jørgen Dehs and Pernille Skov, also regarded Christiania as an oppositional force in relation to dominant trends in contemporary urban development. They even suggested that Christiania's qualities may be considered as metaphors for the architectural profession, understood as a critical exercise: something that neither represents petrified visions nor opportunism, but a 'negotiating opposition'.[36] In the article 'Christiania/*Christiania*', art historian Signe Sophie Bøggild explored the space between on the one hand Christiania as 'real urbanity' and on the other hand as an infinite space of urban imagination ('urban imaginary'). She defined Christiania as a 'porous enclave', which at the same time is part of, and separate from, the surrounding society.[37] Bøggild further argued that the ambiguity and porosity that characterise Christiania's spatiality, make it a suitable point of departure to rethink the concept of public space, beyond the exclusive categories it is associated with. Bøggild also discussed the government's new emphasis on cultural conservation, focusing on the old military buildings; and Christiania's counter-strategy in relation to this, as they have argued that it is the countercultural historical heritage that must be preserved, an approach also expressed in the slogan 'Bevar (Preserve) Christiania' (printed on T-shirts and stickers for sale in the Freetown).

This theme was further discussed in another article in the same issue, 'SAVE som æstetisk og politisk praxis — med udgangspunkt i Christiania' (SAVE as Aesthetic and Political Praxis — with Christiania as a Point of Departure), by art historian Kasper Lægring Larsen. The cultural environment assessment protocol SAVE (Survey of Architectural Values in the Environment), developed by the Danish Environmental Office, and even exported to Eastern Europe, has listed 400,000 buildings 'worthy of conservation' and 9,000 of national significance. In the article, Larsen critically analysed SAVE's practice in relation to Christiania, concluding that although according to SAVE's own criteria it would have been possible to list a number of Christiania's self-built houses, they were almost completely absent from SAVE's list, which prioritised the monumental, nationally recognised military buildings.

Perhaps a bit surprisingly, a comparison between Christiania and the famous Copenhagen amusement park (Tivoli), located next to the central railway station, was made by several researchers in the 2000s. It was not only pointed out that Christiania and Tivoli, according to the Copenhagen Tourist Agency, are among Denmark's three top tourist attractions; they are also two highly aestheticised spaces in the city, and places that a significant number of people visit each weekend for amusement. Such a comparison was actually the main theme in the introduction to the special issue of *Nordisk arkitekturforskning*. The editors also pointed out that Christiania itself has made this comparison in the public debate on the government's demands for a complete restoration of the old military barracks (dating from the 17th century), which would be the end of Christiania. As Christianites have pointed out, this implies that Tivoli also has to be closed down, as it similarly occupies a part of the historical military ramparts that ran all around the city centre. The editors did however also emphasise the fundamental differences between Tivoli and Christiania, most importantly the fact that Tivoli is completely uncontroversial politically. In Hellström's terms, their argument was that while Tivoli is a symbol of the contemporary aestheticisation of everyday life, Christiania represents the critical, political counter-version of aestheticisation.

The most ambitious attempt so far to explore and analyse Christiania's aesthetic dimensions in the context of urban restructuring is provided by the anthology *Forankring i forandring: Christiania og bevaring som resource i byomdannelse (Anchoring in Change: Christiania and Preservation as a Resource in Urban Restructuring)*, published in 2007. The book, the product of a research project led by Anne Tietjen and Svava Riesto at the Department of Art and Cultural Science at the University of Copenhagen, has 14 chapters written by 16 researchers from various disciplines.[38] The purpose of the book was according to the editors to explore how the past can be thought of as a resource in the development of a future city, using Christiania as a case study. The choice of Christiania was obvious, since the ongoing debate on the Freetown according to the editors is 'a laboratory for a renewal of the praxis of conservation'.[39] They emphasised that their interest did not primarily concern the Freetown as a social experiment or as a political alternative, even though they admitted that these aspects cannot be separated from Christiania's aesthetics. The chapters in the book specifically focus on the many historical identities that have unfolded in Christiania, and particularly how they have changed over time. It is according to the editors a hypothesis of the volume that an investigation of the physical and socio-cultural changes that have turned the Bådsmandsstræde Barracks into Christiania, can make an important contribution to the discussion of what in the area is worthy of preservation and how it may be further developed in the future. In a concluding remark to the book, architect Jens Arnfred echoed Steen Eiler Rasmussen's writings on Christiania's importance for urban planning in the 1970s (see above), as he stated that Christiania openly has challenged 'our over-regulated society' with its 'strident, intrusive normality'.[40] To Arnfred, any attempt by architects or urban planners to intervene in Christiania must be deeply anchored in the peculiarity of the place, while at the same time be in command of an 'insane patience'.[41]

The Danish authorities' attempts to steer and control Christiania, with a particular focus on the massive police actions launched in the Freetown in the 2000s, have been the topic of works by North American social anthropologist Christa Amouroux and by René Karpantschof and Flemming Mikkelsen. In 'Normalizing Christiania: Project Clean Sweep and the Normalization Plan in Copenhagen', published in the journal *City and Society* in 2009, Amouroux analysed the 2004 police raid to clear out Pusher Street and the 2004 Normalisation Plan, using Michel Foucault's theory of power. Karpantschof and Mikkelsen discussed and analysed the interaction between the Copenhagen police and Christiania in two chapters in a 2009 book on the Youth House revolt, *Kampen om ungdomshuset: Studier i et uprør (The Struggle over the Youth House: Studies of an Uprising)* — a theme that Karpantschof further develops in his chapter in this book.[42]

Finally, the justifications put forth by Christiania and its defenders, as they have claimed the Freetown's right to exist, have been scrutinised from the viewpoint of moral philosophy by Danish political scientist Søren Flinch Midtgaard in the article '"But suppose everyone did the same" — the Case of Danish Utopian Micro-Society of Christiania', published in *Journal of Applied Philosophy* in 2007.[43] Midtgaard tested three moral theories to find out whether Christiania's claims can be justified. He argued that both Kantian constructivism and rule-consequentialism deny Christiania's right to exist, while the theory of act-consequentialism endorses 'the exceptions made by Christiania, in so far as these exceptions are of a kind which does not tend to spread and they seem to produce some good'.[44] Considering this, Midtgaard concluded that moral theory cannot really 'give rise to a clear verdict with respect to Christiania or other similar cases'.[45]

The contributions in this book thematically link up with all of the three periods of Christiania research accounted for above; analysing Christiania in a historical context and focusing on the Freetown as a social issue, a space for the construction of alternative cultures and a site for urban political struggles. When inviting contributors to the book, we however emphasised that we wanted to have texts that highlighted issues and aspects that had not been given significant attention by previous work.

Structure of the Book

The initiative for this book was taken by a group of researchers at the University of Gothenburg in Sweden, in the context of a research project titled *The Inner City as Public Sphere: Urban Transformation,*

Social Order and Social Movement. The project looks at urban restructuring processes in Denmark and Sweden, using Christiania and the district of Haga in Gothenburg as cases.[46]

In the first chapter, *Bargaining and Barricades — the Political Struggle over the Freetown Christiania 1971–2011*, René Karpantschof deals with the political history of Christiania, departing from the question: How did Christiania survive this far against such powerful and resourceful opponents as the Danish state and the Copenhagen Police? Karpantschof highlights important elements in the struggle over Christiania's very existence and makes visible the complex web of actors and their relations with each other and Christiania itself — governments, the police, the public and external sympathisers.

In the second chapter, *Governing Freedom — Debating the Freetown in the Danish Parliament,* sociologist Håkan Thörn deepens the investigation of how the government has handled the 'Christiania issue' through an analysis of the debates in Folketinget (the Danish parliament), between 1974 and 2004. Thörn shows how the shifting definitions of 'normalisation' are linked to fundamental changes in the Danish parliament's understandings of Christiania as a 'problem' to be dealt with by the government. Comparing two debates in 1974 and 2003, Thörn shows how the meaning of 'normalisation' has shifted from being linked to the notion of Christiania as a social problem/social experiment in the 1970s, to be associated with the notion of urban fear, security and privatisation in the 2000s. Further, Thörn argues that the significant attention paid to Christiania by the parliament as well as various Danish governments, is related to the fact that Christiania early on was given the status of a highly *symbolic issue*, which fits well into an emerging pattern in mainstream politics, through which the left-right conflict gained a new 'value-political' dimension.

In *Happy Ever After? The Welfare City in between the Freetown and the New Town*, Signe Sophie Bøggild approaches the strategy of 'normalisation' from another perspective: the relation between the planned and the unplanned city. Looking through the glasses of Steen Eiler Rasmussen, Bøggild analyses the post-war Social Democrat New Town utopia (Tingbjerg) and the anarcho-socialist utopia (Christiania) as two contrasting embodiments of the welfare society and welfare city — emerging when re-conceptualisation of urban spaces were crucial to frame transformations of lifestyle. Bøggild further examines how they relate to current developments of the old capital, marked by gentrification and segregation, and ambitious urban renewal initiatives under the slogan 'Joint City' (*Sammen om Byen*). In this context Tingbjerg and Christiania are regarded as 'urban others', 'the ghetto' and 'the freak', containing the poor, the immigrants and those off the norm, claimed to be in need of integration into the normal, and into law and order through the strategy of urban planning/regeneration.

In the following chapter, *The Hansen Family and the Micro-Physics of the Everyday*, Maria Hellström Reimer analyses the documentary films *Dagbog fra en fristad* (Diary from a Freetown) from 1976 and *Gensyn med Christiania* (Return to Christiania) from 1988, in which an 'ordinary family' — the Hansen family — are filmed during their visits to Christiania. Hellström Reimer discusses the relationship between 'the social experiment', everyday life and documentary film practice. With the help of Michel Foucault's notion of a 'micro-physical' power dynamics, she shows how the films, far from simply documenting daily life, also contributed to the public perception and evaluation both of the experiment and of 'normality', and how they in this way actively intervened in the further course of events.

In the fifth chapter, *Alternative Visions of Home and Family Life in Christiania: Lessons for the Mainstream*, human geographer Helen Jarvis focuses on one of the core practices in an alternative community: the organisation of the family. Jarvis investigates how 'fulfilling long-standing feminist family-friendly ideals' are practiced in the Freetown. By focusing on single mothers and children she analyses phenomena such as 'fluid families' and 'junk playgrounds'. Jarvis provides a gender perspective on Christiania's social organisation, and argues that the hostile milieu and the late evenings that define many of the Common Meetings are not suited for women and single mothers. Instead women often gather in women-only groups where they can take care of each other and make decisions about their daily lives.

In the following chapter, *Bøssehuset — Queer Perspectives in Christiania*, we move into one of the Freetown's important 'institutions'. Sociologist Cathrin Wasshede analyses Bøssehuset's role in Christiania as well as its relations to lesbians and the Danish gay movement LGBT Denmark (earlier Forbundet af 1948). She shows how the identity of the gay *male* character has been intrinsic to Bøssehuset since Bøssernes Befrielses Front (the Gay Men's Liberation Front) established Bøssehuset in the beginning of the 1970s. At the same time, they have used femininity as a strategy to oppose traditional masculinity and patriarchy, for example in the form of Christiania's Pigegarden (Girl's Guard) and Frøken Verden (Miss World Contest).

In chapter seven, *Weeds and Deeds — Images and Counter Images of Christiania and Drugs*, historian Tomas Nilson tackles Christiania's relations to drugs, one of the most debated — and infected — political issues associated with the Freetown. While providing an overview of Christiania's history of drug controversies from 1971 to 2011, Nilson focuses on a specific case; the events of 1982, when there were strong demands from the outside to close Christiania because of the sale of hash on Pusher Street; and how the Freetown responded with the 'Love Sweden Tour'. Through this, both internal and external images of Christiania are made visible, as well as the major ambivalences that are imprinted in those images.

In the chapter *Normalisation within Christiania*, Christa Amouroux takes up the thread that Børge Madsen left in the late 1970s — namely the internal conflicts and tensions in Christiania. Amouroux focuses mainly on two conflicts: between activists and pushers and between older and younger people — the first as old as Christiania itself and the second more recent, since many of those who built up Christiania now are getting older and there is not enough space for the young generation. Through the example of young Christianites squatting a house in (the squatted) Christiania, Amouroux clearly brings out the generational tensions and their relations to the authorities' idea of normalisation.

The theme of inner tensions and conflicts are continued in chapter nine, *Consensus and Strategy: Narratives of Naysaying and Yeasaying in Christiania's Struggles over Legalization*, by anthropologist Amy Starecheski, who analyses the Common Meeting and the practices of consensus democracy. At times, Christiania has been deeply split between 'naysayers', who reject the terms being offered by the government's representatives, and 'yeasayers', who want to move ahead with legalisation as proposed at that moment. However, a decision has always somehow been reached. Using a series of oral histories the chapter analyses Christianites' accounts of their decision-making process around legalisation issues. The sending of the flute player in 2006, as an answer to the Danish government's proposition regarding legalisation, works as an illuminating example in Starecheski's analysis, as does 'the miracle meeting' in 2008 where the Christianites finally agreed on saying no to the state ultimatum.

In the final chapter, *Christiania and the Right to the City*, Anders Lund Hansen discusses Christiania in the context of the struggles over space that go on in cities all over the world. He focuses on the case of the Cigar Box (Cigarkassen) — a house in Midtdyssen in Christiania — that in 2007 was demolished by the police and then immediately rebuilt by activists. Collective activism, dedication, humour, art, improvisation and politics of scale are highlighted as important aspects of such direct actions. Lund Hansen shows that the concept of 'the right to the city' can be understood in very different ways and he places this discussion in relation to the international debate on gentrification.

BARGAINING AND BARRICADES — THE POLITICAL STRUGGLE OVER THE FREETOWN CHRISTIANIA 1971–2011

René Karpantschof

Once upon a time the author of this chapter was a young and militant Copenhagen squatter eager to support other comrades such as my fellow squatters in the Freetown Christiania. One day in 1986, I was told by some insiders that Christiania was ready to revolt, so my like-minded friends and I expressed our solidarity by building barricades outside the Freetown's entrances waiting with expectancy for scores of combat-ready Christianites to join us. In fact some excited Christianites did turn up, that is a group of hash pushers with stones who we believed were dedicated to our common enemy, the police. Yet, soon the stones were flying in our direction putting us to a disgraceful flight. After that I had to rethink my way of helping Christiania. Confusingly though, on other occasions I have seen these very same types of pushers carrying boxes of Molotov cocktails to these same entrances to supply a veritable bombardment of approaching riot police. So, is there any logic at all in Christiania's relations to the police and the rest of the surrounding society? Yes, a clear logic, and in this chapter I will reveal and explain it by using my later-gained skills as a PhD specialist in social movements.[1]

Strange Vibrations and the Birth of Christiania in 1971

The story of Christiania begins in the 1960s when young people in the USA, Italy, France, Germany and elsewhere started to move in, sit down and take over classrooms, university departments, abandoned houses, factories, parks etc. to create free spaces for alternative ways of being together. It was all part of the international youth revolt whose strange vibrations were also felt across the Danish capital of Copenhagen.

In these days of the late 1960s, the baby boom after the Second World War, the expansion of the educational sector, and the moving-out of families to the suburban districts had all altered the demographic profile of Copenhagen. Scores of young people now crowded the inner city, many of whom were looking for a place to live, and at the same time the municipality implemented an urban renewal plan that left many houses empty and thus ripe for occupation.

Partly for the simple reason to have a roof over their heads, many youngsters therefore started to squat abandoned apartments and whole buildings in the inner parts of Copenhagen. But there were also ideological dimensions such as the collectivity and Do It Yourself culture of the youth revolt. Thus the early Danish squatters — known as Slumstormers (Slumstormere) comprising a mix of students, leftist activists, drug offenders and other young people — took over not only houses but also outdoor land to form autonomous 'republics' and hippie-inspired, utopian communities that in the language of the day were perceived as 'a revolutionary island in a capitalist ocean.' Figure 1 illustrates the most sensational squatting actions throughout Denmark 1945–2005 and leaves little doubt that 1969–71 were the breakthrough years for this form of action.

One of the actions that hide in Figure 1 is exactly the squatting of Christiania. It started in the autumn of 1971 when local inhabitants tore down a fence to establish a playground in a newly abandoned military area in the neighbourhood of Christianshavn. On 26 September 1971, now the official birthday of Christiania, a handful of activists went on exploration in the rest of the 85 acres of barracks, workshops and halls, all built from brick or solid old ships' timber, beautifully situated among renaissance ramparts and moats. No wonder the explorers were excited,

Figure 1. Squatting actions in Denmark 1946–2005.

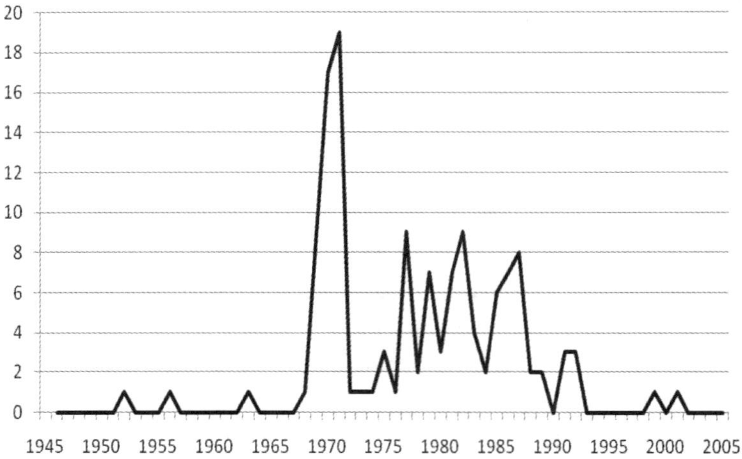

Source: Database by Flemming Mikkelsen: 'Collective action in Denmark 1946–2005.'
Note: The database compiles collective actions from the Danish Newspaper Yearbook (Avis Årbogen), that retrospectively refers to only what is rated as the most important news published in Danish papers. Minor incidents are therefore not recorded.

and one of them immediately called for the establishment of a Freetown in what he at the same time described as 'the forbidden city of the military.' The call was announced in the alternative magazine *Hovedbladet* that was widely distributed among the Copenhagen youth. The phrase 'forbidden' had an irresistible effect, and soon the Christiania area was invaded by young people.

A decisive circumstance was the generally irresolute attitude of the authorities who were puzzled by the new phenomena and consequently often met the squats with a wait-and-see policy. Thus, the owner of the Christiania area, the Ministry of Defence (Forsvarsministeriet), was caught by surprise and since it had itself no plan for the ground, the ministry refrained from action against the illegal trespassers. Nor had the Danish parliament (Folketinget) or the municipality of Copenhagen reached any conclusion about the future of the area; and for such reasons representatives from the municipality and the Copenhagen police in November 1971 decided to give up ineffective attempts to prevent youngsters from settling in Christiania (see also Håkan Thörn's chapter in this book).

At the same time the new Freetown came up with a, handwritten, mission statement declaring: 'The aim of Christiania is to build a self-ruling society, where each individual can unfold freely while remaining responsible to the community as a whole'.[2] By the beginning of 1972 that society encompassed a population of 300 that soon reached around 500 residents.

Now this tale could end with an afterword on how the people of Christiania continued to build their utopian community of direct democracy, alternative business and experimental social and cultural life based on ideals of freedom, collectivity and universal love to humans and nature. Yet, however hippie-like and love-praising Christiana represented itself, it was for several reasons an intolerable provocation and challenge to the established order of Danish society.

First of all, Christiania had challenged a cornerstone of capitalism: the private ownership (in this case, the state's ownership) of land and buildings. Second, it challenged the sovereignty and jurisdiction of the state by replacing official rules and regulations with the claim of autonomy and Christiania's own self-governing praxis. Third, the whole lifestyle in Christiania, not least the obvious use of drugs, was a thorn in the side of traditional bourgeois virtues of the hard-working, law-abiding, nuclear-family citizen life. And fourth, Christiania was not any obscure phenomena in some remote part of the countryside. Quite the contrary, Christiania was, and of course still is, highly visible situated right in the centre of Copenhagen on lucrative ground of high financial value, just next to the most important commercial and administrative facilities in the country and no more than one kilometre from the Danish parliament.

For these reasons Christiania was bound to encounter the state again and again throughout the years.

The General Strategic Situation

How did it come about that the squatting of Christiania was not just accepted as a *fait accompli* by the authorities? And what has kept the state from successful use of its impressive power to force its will upon the illegal squatters?

One reason why Christiania was not simply left alone is that, whenever led by governments of one or the other orientation, authorities in a strong-state nation like the Danish have an inherent inertia to seek to administrate, regulate and control all important spheres of social activity. The new inhabitants of the alleged autonomous and seceded area of Christiania had to realise early on that they could not escape contact with the authorities nor would be left in peace by political circles. Though sometimes years went by without much sign that the state bothered about Christiania, any illusion that the Freetown had been forgotten forever would occasionally be broken by police campaigns and political decisions. Thus the utopian self-governed society had to face the fact that the state is a durable counterpart, which cannot be ignored.

On the other hand, that same state has proven far from all-powerful and not that fatal a menace. One reason is the many alternate governments with shifting agendas about Christiania. In the first three decades after 1971, Denmark was ruled by minority governments and political coalitions with heterogeneous and most often cautious attitudes towards the Freetown. Usually it was therefore difficult to mobilise a parliamentary majority behind any dramatic decision on the issue.

Nor was a 'military' solution provided by the forces of law ever any easy task. Faced with a situation on the ground with around 1,000 settlers unwilling to give up the area voluntarily, a full-scale police attack would inevitably provoke sensational scenes of tumult. And that would be the least of the problems for the police, as an eviction would just as inevitably trigger reactions from the growing numbers of regular visitors and sympathisers of Christiania in line with what happened in other free-space conflicts in Copenhagen such as The Battle of Byggeren in 1980, a big squatter-uprising in 1986 and the Youth House (Ungdomshuset) Revolt in 2007.

Yet, the real problem for the state is, that all this would just be the beginning. What would follow, nobody knows, except that it without any doubt would mobilise and engage very significant societal, cultural and political communities, groups, organisations and parties. In short: A full-scale police attack to clear Christiania was always a very risky business with so uncertain an outcome that such an action hardly was any option.

As we will see, the whole issue of Christiania vs. the surrounding society should not simply be perceived in such bellicose terms. Nevertheless, at its core, the question of power — or the *balance* of power — as presented above is a fundamental strategic background with continuous importance to the relations between Christiania and the state.

From Acceptance to Death Sentence 1972–75

Back in 1972 the authorities were left with the choice between a violent police solution and a deliberative approach; and the latter was preferred. In April and May 1972 various ministries under the Social Democrat (Socialdemokraterne) minority government met together with the likewise Social Democrat led municipality of Copenhagen and set up a contact group to negotiate with representatives of Christiania. In particular, the Ministry of Defence, the formal owner of the area, expressed its desire for 'one or the other form of normalisation and legalisation of the conditions in Christiania.'[3]

Besides the fact that the authorities were already amply occupied with the spreading squatter activities (Figure 1), this helping hand of the state towards Christiania was prompted by the absence of official plans for the future use of the disputed area. Furthermore, despite the unlawful methods, the purpose of the Freetown itself was not without resonance and legitimacy in a society influenced by the New Left and communitarian visions that spread in those rebellious days about people's right to local influence, self-determination and own choice of lifestyle.

On 31 May 1972, then, the first treaty between Christiania and the state was signed. There were still many unclarified questions, e.g. about rent, registration of residents and relations with the police, but with the governmental approved status of a 'social experiment' in 1973, Christiania had come a long way towards being accepted as part of the Danish society.

The idyllic start, however, was soon broken by a dramatic political turnaround. In the 'Earthquake Election' of 1973 three brand new right-wing parties, the Progress Party (Fremskridtspartiet), the Centre Democrats (Centrumdemokraterne) and the Christian Democrats (Kristeligt Folkeparti) stormed into the parliament with a full 28 per cent of the votes. These parties were in part a counter-reaction to the political-cultural left turn in Denmark bearing on the youth revolt, and the new-right parties carried with them an agenda of hostile attitudes towards Christiania. As one of its last acts, the right-wing government led by the Liberal Party (Venstre) declared their denunciation of Christiania's status as a tolerable experiment; and though a Social Democrat minority government once again was formed in 1975, a proposal by the Progressive Party to shut down Christiania by 1 April 1976 at the latest was passed by a majority in parliament.

Becoming a People's Movement 1975–78

Christiania responded to the political death sentence by raising an army of followers, which under the banner of names like the Santa Claus Army and the Rainbow Army, and reinforced by a so-called Peasant Army from the rural region of Jutland (Jylland), carried out spectacular happenings, street theatre and parades. Furthermore scores of visitors were attracted to the Freetown by events such as a Barricade Fiesta, various rallies, musicals and concerts; not to mention one of Christiania's most popular traditions: the free Christmas Eve dinner, which began in 1975 and since then annually has been attended by hundreds of poor and homeless Copenhageners.

Obviously, the hippie community was becoming a place of great, in fact existential, importance to many outsiders as well; a free space offering a palette of alternative social and cultural experiences and, especially in the summertime, a recreational area for informal being together frequently used by thousands of people from the surrounding city. Some of them established a Support Christiania committee in 1975; and in 1976 a series of the most popular Danish rock and folk musicians of the day released a support album including the number 'You cannot kill us, we are part of you' (I kan ikke slå os ihjel, vi er en del af jer selv) that would become a truly Danish evergreen.

Then, when the appointed day of Christiania's end came on 1 April 1976 the threat was opposed by a gathering, impressive in Danish terms, of 20,000 people in front of the Copenhagen town hall. Faced with this whole mobilisation and a parallel Christiania summons against the state,[4] the parliament decided to postpone the scheduled eviction; and on 8 February 1978 a majority in parliament even decided to preserve the Freetown for another 2–3 years.

This political U-turn away from the parliamentary decision of 1975 to close Christiania was in good agreement with the development in public opinion. In April that year the first opinion poll on the issue had resulted in a clear majority of 59 per cent in favour of a closure, which would prove to be the strongest popular aversion to Christiania ever (Figure 2). But just next year, shortly before the announced closure by 1 April 1976, a new poll showed a dramatic increase in the support for the Freetown; and, especially considering the error margins in such polls, there was an almost equal split in 1976–78 between opponents and sympathisers of Christiania.[5]

This shift in opinion towards Christiania was influenced by the whole support mobilisation of 1975–76, which also activated many educated people, specialists, professionals and not least cultural figureheads who had easy access to, and significant impact in, the media. One media event especially, the broadcasting of filmmaker Paul Martinsen's 'Diary from Christiania' on national Danish television in January 1976, is believed to have moved many common Danes (see Maria Hellström Reimer's chapter in this book). At the same time, media attention culminated with on average two or three articles a day in the most important national newspapers, and the young hippie community went from being obscure to something that practically every Dane (99 per cent of the population) by 1976 knew about.[6]

Public attention in itself, of course, was not equal to support. Instead, opinions polarised into conflicting perceptions of Christiania as either a space for a legitimate and societally desired alternative lifestyle or as an area inhabited by antisocial, work-shy scroungers and criminals; perceptions that formed along existing political boundaries with the voters of New Left parties like the Left Socialist Party (Venstresocialisterna) and the Socialist Party (Socialistiskt Folkeparti) as the absolute most Christiania-friendly and voters of new-right parties like the Progress Party, the Centre Democrats and the Christian Democrats as by far the most hostile.[7]

Still, by the late 1970s the support for Christiania had become so widespread, that a prominent criminologist, Flemming Balvig, referred to it as 'a people's movement.'[8] And having attracted the attention of the whole population to the extent that Christiania would never again slip the minds of the Danes, the new Christiania anthem, 'You cannot kill us, we are part of you', made its point.

Figure 2. The Danes' opinion about Christiania 1975–2003 (per cent).

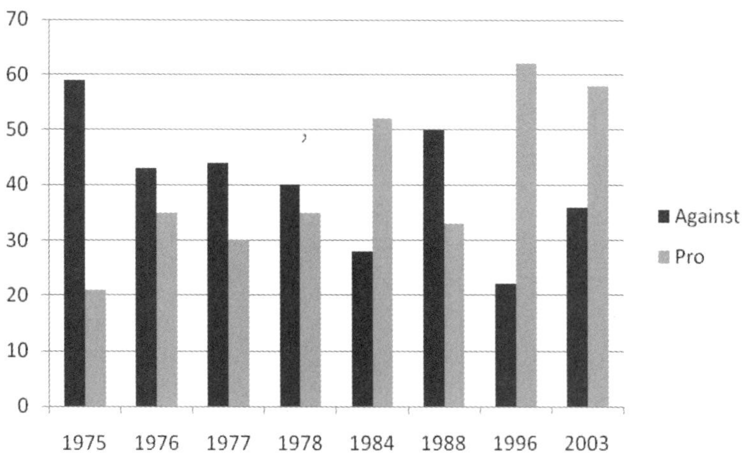

Source: Gallup surveys Apr. 1975, Feb. 1976, Jan. 1977, Jan. 1978, Aug. 1984, 1988, Sep. 1996, Mar. 2003.
Note: The Gallup institute has performed the most frequent and thorough opinion polls about Christiania throughout the years, asking Danes, in varied ways, about their attitudes to a continuation/preservation or a clearance/closure of Christiania, and other more detailed questions.

New Vibrations 1978–86

The literally most deadly threat to Christiania, though, came from inside in the form of heroin and other hard drugs that claimed ten lives in 1978–79 and in general threatened to stagnate the whole Freetown. In light of the seriousness of the problem, some anti-junk Christianites went so far as to rely on cooperation with the police to stop the drug kingpins. But their experiences with the police turned out to be a big disappointment as the forces of law carried out indiscriminate raids that also targeted small dealers and the common use of hash, which was considered a legitimate toxin and a cornerstone of the hippie lifestyle (see Tomas Nilson's chapter in this book). In the autumn of 1979 a faction of Christianites took matters into their own hands and set up the so-called Junk Blockade to rid the area of hard drugs. The blockade was successful and ever since dealers of hard drugs have not been welcome in Christiania.

Thus, the Junk Blockade helped Christiania to survive, but relations with the police went from bad to worse, and in 1981 the first real street battle around the otherwise peace-loving hippie community took place. It happened during the celebration of Christiania's tenth anniversary, when inhabitants and followers of the Freetown reacted to what they perceived as police harassment by building barricades and fighting the police with bricks and Molotov cocktails. For their part, officers in Copenhagen police stations in those days were striking up choruses of 'Clear Christiania — Just tear the damn thing down — They shall never, never, never smoke again!' to the tune of Rule Britannia.[9]

These mutually hostile attitudes were formed in the context of a more general struggle around the city. In the spring of 1980 a conflict about another free space, Byggeren, a large self-governed playground and recreational area in the neighbourhood of Nørrebro, turned into an urban uprising. Many thousands demonstrated and built barricades to resist the riot police and bulldozers that were sent to clear the contested ground. During the conflict, people from Christiania arrived as a conspicuous support unit with their own flag, and were welcomed with cheers by the local playground defenders. The activists lost, but only after a fortnight of extensive unrest still remembered as the Battle of Byggeren.

The dramatic event was a sign that the official attitude towards Copenhagen's squatters was shifting. Unlike the reluctant and dialogue-seeking measures of the 1960s and 1970s, a less tolerant policy and a more heavy-handed deployment of police forces became the norm in the 1980s. For that reason a second generation of squatters, gathering in the autumn of 1981, soon developed a distinctly militant style quite unlike the predominant hippie culture of the first generation of Slumstormers and the like. Times were a-changing, and though the squatters of the 1980s did carry elements from their hippie predecessors with them, they were accompanied by the hard-core rhythms of punk and gloomy slogans such as No Future.

The new squatters emerged as part of a wave of squatter revolts in European cities in 1980–81 and named themselves the BZ-movement, whose activities are reflected in Figure 1.[10] Throughout the 1980s, the Danish BZ-movement controlled a series of fortified strongholds around Copenhagen — including the later legendary Youth House at Jagtvej 69 — and engaged themselves in escalating clashes with the police during which the BZ activists developed into militia-like street fighters equipped with black helmets, catapults and Molotov cocktails.

The striking difference between BZ and the Christiania culture would sometimes make cooperation difficult or even, as illustrated by the intro to this chapter, lead to collisions and quarrels. Yet these were rather like family quarrels, as BZ and Christianites shared important core visions about free space, alternative lifestyles and the whole Do It Yourself culture. In fact, youngsters from Christiania had been among the initiators of BZ, and in many cases, such as when a conflict about a BZ stronghold in 1986 escalated into a nine-day-long barricade revolt, the young BZ activists could rely on support from Christianites.

Politics and Bargaining 1986–91

In 1986, relations between Christiania and the state took a decisive turn. In May an alternative parliamentary majority of Social Democrats, New Left Socialists and Social Liberals urged the Conservative minority government that had come into office 1982 to find a way to legalise Christiania, and almost simultaneously people from Christiania presented their own proposal about the future of the area. With such signals a political dialogue with real intentions of a mutually acceptable agreement was set in progress. The good intentions were supported by the establishment of an administrative body in 1987 with members who had close relations with many Christianites and thus were able to function as mediators and brokers between the Freetown and the authorities.

Among the substance of the negotiations were issues such as building maintenance and regulations, payment of rent, unlicensed pubs and criminality, and not least the sale of hash. Though progress was made difficult by factions on both sides — by right-wing politicians who continued to introduce bills for the closure of Christiania, and by those Christianites that were annoyed by any interference in their customary autonomous lifestyle — the so-called Christiania Act was passed in parliament in 1989 and it resulted in the Framework Agreement (Rammeaftalen) in 1991.[11] The latter was the result of classical bargaining. Christiania gave in the idea of being totally seceded from all authorities and official laws, e.g. by accepting licenses, taxes and payment for renovation, consumption of electricity etc, and in return the state, as worded in the 1991 agreement, 'confirms the right of Christiania's inhabitants to use the buildings and the area as a whole' and committed itself to 'secure maximum self-administration for Christiania.'

It was historic. The until now outlaw hippie community and the state had actually come to terms; and for the first time a broadly-based majority in parliament accepted a legalisation that preserved the special self-administration and collectivity within, and thereby the uniqueness of, the Freetown.

Paradoxically, the successful 'peace process' was accompanied by the most serious clashes in the streets so far. The situation began to escalate in earnest in February 1989. Hundreds of riot police raided Christiania to close the unlicensed pubs and thus put pressure on the Christianites to bow to the ongoing legalisation plan. The limited objective notwithstanding the police intrusion provoked heavy fighting inside and in the streets around the besieged Freetown.

The fighting was not a sign of any united front of Christianites, among whom there were intense discussions. Many felt the need for some kind of legalisation due to the judgment that the Freetown could not withstand 'a concentrated attack by the state and its forces of law', as one Christianite put it in January 1990, but on the other hand there was a fear whether Christiania could survive in acceptable terms if 'cooperating with the authorities,' as that same person continued.[12] In addition, a fundamental scepticism towards the state together with the consensus democracy of the Freetown made it hard to form any quorum in favour of binding agreements, and the climate for discussion was not made easier by more police actions and hence also more clashes. During 1990, though, important Christiania pubs such as Woodstock, Nemoland and Loppen gave in and accepted licenses under relatively easy terms. The legalisation had begun.

Police and Barricades 1992–93

The ongoing legalisation process didn't prevent the police from continuing their actions, not even against some of the now licensed pubs, on grounds of hash-smoking customers. The result was a perception of the police as being eager to attack the Freetown no matter what. That perception was confirmed by a massive police campaign in 1992–93 with a series of media-exposed scandalous police behaviour such as physical sexual harassment of women, tear gassing of playing children and the classic: severe beating of arrested people — a behaviour that, unusual to the Danish democracy, caused serious criticism in an Amnesty International report in 1994.

The background was a radicalisation of factions of the Copenhagen police due to years of fighting, especially with the BZ squatters who just like Christiania had become a kind of 'police enemy number one.' In particular one unit, the so-called riot squad (uro-patruljen) based at Copenhagen police headquarters, caused trouble. In Christiania and around the city the squad officers were feared for their brutal behaviour and irregular methods that proved increasingly uncontrollable even by the rest of the police force. The last straw was the conspicuous part played by the riot squad in the shooting of 11 protesters and bystanders (who miraculously all survived) during a clash with BZ militants and other youngsters on 18 May 1993 in connection with protests related to the Danish referendum on EU membership. Right after this, the controversial police unit was ordered to stay away from demonstrations as well as Christiania, and finally the unit was completely disbanded in 2001. Also in 1993 the Minister of Justice (in Denmark the political head of the police) also called a halt to the police campaign against Christiania, partly due to more media exposures, this time as a result of a police unit named the Christiania Rangers that voluntarily sought out action in the Freetown.

The minister represented the Social Democrats who had come into power in January 1993 after a decade of right-wing and usually Christiania-hostile government. With the new government and the passing of the Framework Agreement in 1991, much seemed to show that the Freetown and the authorities finally had found a way of peaceful co-existence. The police then withdrew and practically stayed out of the Freetown for four years.

It was all a very regrettable development in the eyes of the right wing such as the conservative paper *Berlingske Tidende*, which commented on the Freetown's 20th anniversary 1991 by describing 'The history of Christiania' as 'one long series of defeats for parliament, which since

1975 by turns have decided to clear the area or to legalise it.'[13] Or the tabloid paper *BT*, which promoted the opinion that Christiania 'shall not be allowed to celebrate either 25 or 30 years anniversary. The Freetown must be removed.'[14] No such thing happened; on the contrary, Christiania entered a period of consolidation and a bright prospect for the future.

Legalisation and Détente 1993–2001

Despite some debate, e.g. due to the 1994 Amnesty International report about police ill-treatment, public interest in the Christiania issue as such was declining as the new détente relation between the Freetown and the state developed (Figure 3). Inside Christiania itself activities flourished with various social and cultural projects supported by the now legal self-administration. Together with the government, a 'green' development plan for the area was agreed to and pubs, cafés, restaurants, shops and many other facilities were renovated just as yet another kindergarten was built for the growing number of Christiania children, and a ramp was constructed for yet another subculture, the skaters, who thus mixed into the motley crowd of Christianites and followers.

Throughout the 1990s visitors flocked to Christiania to an almost unbelievable extent. In 1996 a poll revealed that every second Dane (47 per cent) had visited the Freetown at least once. Among Copenhageners separately as many as 76 per cent had seen the place with their own eyes, and 24 per cent were even regular visitors (been there 10 or more times) to whom the existence of Christiania therefore was of concrete personal importance.[15]

These people participated in the most varied events, such as the Christiania Christmas-market, NGO conferences and meetings with Native Americans and Eskimos, concerts from blues to techno raves, theatre, outdoor festivals and drag parties by the gay community that performed 'the most hysterical beauty contest in Denmark' to a likewise absolutely overexcited audience (see also Cathrin Wasshede's chapter in this book).[16] Also the Christiania performance of Bob Dylan and his 'how many years can some people exist, before they're allowed to be free?' made perfect sense. Added to all this, the recurrent anniversary celebrations offered performances by a number of the most outstanding Danish musicians and artists who themselves obviously enjoyed the special Christiania atmosphere.

Even the sale of hash had become more regulated since action by Christiania women in 1989 had removed the pushers from the main entrance, after which the sale zone was limited to what is now known as Pusher Street at the centre of Christiania. In the following years up to forty roofed hash stalls mushroomed in the street, which for this reason attracted not only many hash-smoking Danes (and other Scandinavians) but also tourists who simply wanted to see the somewhat odd sight of a fully undisguised shopping centre for the otherwise forbidden toxin.

Furthermore, one Christiania invention especially, a three-wheeled cargo bike, was gradually embraced by many Copenhageners as a welcome alternative to cars. By the 1990s thousands of these low-speed and eco-friendly vehicles were seen all over the city carrying young people, groceries, music gear and not too big families. Even today the cargo bikes, colloquially referred to by the Danes as 'Christiania bikes', work as rolling advertisements for the special Christiania culture and as confirmation that the Freetown had met some of the intentions in the 1971 manifesto: 'to show that the psychological and physical pollution can be prevented.'[17]

Yet, behind the seemingly perfect idyll, there were various problems. Some of them concerned the implementation of the legalisation and the thereto related cooperation with the authorities, which still was met with scepticism by quite a few reluctant Christianites, just as there were unsolved questions, such as development plans and how to finance maintenance of buildings in the Freetown. And then there was the whole hash sale issue that caused not only external troubles with the authorities but also internal stress among Christianites (see Christa Amouroux' and Amy Starecheski's chapters in this book).

While the consumption of hash may be an integrated element in the hippie culture and lifestyle of many Christianites, the very sale of hash had been everything but a hippie-like business for years. Even in the 1980s biker gangs and criminals were attracted to the Freetown with which they shared a certain outlaw style; but such groups were also attracted by the profitable hash market, for which reason they muscled themselves into the Christiania area. To some Christianites this new breed of pushers represented an egoistic culture that not only was indifferent to the original sense of solidarity and responsibility to the community but also a culture that carried with it aggressive behaviour and a not very alternative materialism. Furthermore, some pushers caused continued turmoil in the Christiania consensus democracy especially when there were attempts to reach conclusions about the legalisation, which was of no interest to the pusher community, who clearly profited from the absence of usual law and order.

The pushers represented a strong group that was hard to control, not to mention get rid of, and the issue was confused by the fact that many Christianites were themselves hash smokers or even activists in the Free Hash movement. For such reasons the issue was never settled, and some Christianites found the whole pusher situation so unbearable that they actually chose to leave the Freetown.

Nevertheless development in the Freetown was still steered by ongoing cooperation with the authorities within the framework of the 1991 Agreement, and after many years of tension and sometimes open hostilities between Christiania and the state, it was tempting to think of the détente situation in the 1990s as the 'end of history' as regards serious confrontation between the two parts.

At Christiania's anniversary in 1996 the hippie community was supported by 62 per cent of the Danes (Figure 2); and the social-liberal paper *Politiken* was delighted that 'For 25 years the Freetown has lived and survived' and celebrated the place as 'a free space for fantasy and different lifestyle, a crevice in the state-authorised cage in which most people voluntary let themselves be kept.'[18] With more regret the conservative *Berlingske Tidende* noted that 'The so-called Freetown Christiania can celebrate its 25th anniversary showered by progressive pats on the back and tearful applause.'[19] And as the paper resignedly accepted, there was apparently nothing more to do about it: 'That the Freetown is built on an unprecedented unlawfulness affects by now only a few' — in line with another most Christiania-hostile right-wing paper, *Jyllandsposten*, which by the next milestone anniversary, the 30th in September 2001, soberly remarked: 'it is still there. The Freetown for better or worse.'[20]

Thus by autumn 2001 the large majority of Danes, from the left to the right, seemed to have submitted to the inevitable: Christiania had come to stay. Only a few would imagine that within a short time the existence of Christiania would once again be at stake with renewed and furious street battles as a result.

Right-Wing Marching 2001–2004

Christiania was in some sense hit by the repercussions of the 9/11 terror attack as anti-Islamic sentiments in the aftermath of the attack favoured the xenophobic Danish People's Party (Dansk Folkeparti) and thus contributed to an absolute majority for the right at the Danish parliamentary election in November 2001. This party was a successor to the most Christiania-hostile Progress Party; and when the two other victorious parties, the Liberal Party and the Conservatives, formed government, the Danish People's Party took up the position of influential support party. Very unusually in Danish political history, the right-wing was then free to rule without regard for the political centre and left wing.

The leader of the Danish People's Party, Pia Kjærsgaard, quickly realised the opportunities of the situation and proclaimed it 'shocking and absurd that the Freetown Christiania has not been levelled to the ground long ago' followed by a reminder to the government, that they were now actually capable of executing what supporters of law and order like themselves had demanded for decades: 'Clear Christiania!'[21]

Pia Kjærsgaard didn't speak to deaf ears. Just one month after his inauguration the new Prime Minister, Anders Fogh Rasmussen (Liberal Party), had opened the so-called cultural struggle (kulturkamp) that developed into a general showdown with all kinds of leftist positions. Now Danish society was to be restored under the banner of traditional right-wing values, which for Christiania implied a showdown with the idea of collective use, just as 'tough on crime' principles, fed by anti-terror sentiments, indicated a new politics of 'zero tolerance'. Furthermore, around the year 2000 the Danish police had been heavily rearmed due to a whole new crowd control strategy, so that they were now able to raise an unprecedented force of protected vehicles carrying well-trained, body-armoured anti-riot officers. Finally, the left wing was not only on the retreat in the parliament but also in the streets, where the era of collective action and significant movements seemed to be a thing of the past.[22]

In all, by 2002 the strategic balance of power between the Freetown and the state clearly had tipped to the advantage of the latter, and against that background it was a confident government that then began to tackle one of the banes of the right-wing: Christiania. First step was the preparation of a preliminary governmental *Report about Christiania* presented in May 2003, followed by the final *Future of the Christiania area — general plan and action programme*. In March 2004 this then formed the basis for a bill passed in June as *Law about the change of law about the use of the Christiania area* (see also Håkan Thörn's chapter in this book).[23]

The Christianites were in disbelief. The government had actually cancelled the state's own Christiania Act of 1989 and denounced the hard-won result of years of dialogue, the Framework Agreement of

1991, which for more than a decade had regulated the coexistence and cooperation between the Freetown and the authorities. The fact that 'Christiania has since 1994 punctually paid expenses for electricity, water, taxes and duties regarding property, renovation etc.' and that 'the pubs and restaurants have the necessary permissions and licenses', as acknowledged by the government's own 2003 report, didn't satisfy the new right-wing in office.[24] Instead, a sweeping transformation of Christiania was now the objective.

While the Framework Agreement of 1991 preserved the self-governing practice and collective use of the Christiania area, the new Act of 2004 and thereto-related plans implied an introduction of the usual authority-controlled procedures in areas such as accommodation-assignment, individual contracts, new building of private apartment blocks and demolition of numerous Christiania buildings, especially along the old ramparts, which instead should be restored to their original 17th century state. In short, while the 1991 Agreement represented a *legalisation* of the uniqueness of Christiania, the 2004 Act obviously aimed at *normalisation,* that is to bring Christiania 'in line with the rest of the society that surrounds the so-called Freetown', as worded by *Jyllandsposten.*[25]

The 2004 Act was not the signal of an immediately all-out police-attack in the way the Danish People's Party had called for. After all, such an attack was still too risky. Nevertheless, an accomplishment of the governmental plan would deeply affect and therefore represented a menace to the special Freetown culture.

Christiania of course reacted to this development. In the summer of 2003, after the government's first report, the Christianites arranged a series of people's festivals including 'open door' days during which tens of thousands crowded not only the Freetown but also the streets in the surrounding neighbourhood of Christianshavn. On 31 August 15,000–20,000 people marched through Copenhagen in a 'People's procession for the right to be different', and having passed the parliament the participants joined an 'orgy of culture' around Christiania. Besides one of Christiania's most faithful foreign supporters—German punk icon Nina Hagen—Kim Larsen, Sort Sol, Steppeulvene, Savage Rose and other legendary Danish musicians filled 22 stages.[26] In the following year, Christianites, local sympathisers and leftist activists established the 'Defend Christiania' support committee, which alongside continued protests produced various support articles, including the popular Christiania T-shirts that since then have been an unavoidable sight in the streets, concert halls and schools around Denmark. In other words, Christiania blew the mobilisation trumpet within a well-known repertoire that proved effective once again.

Public Discourses and Popular Opinion After 2001

When the government and Christiania mobilised against each other, it sparked an unusually intense public debate in 2003–04 (Figure 3) that polarised along two different discourses. As for the right-wing, attitudes towards the Freetown were traditionally antagonistic: 'Normalisation must mean that the Freetown of Christiania is closed', 'that Christiania, as we know it, is ended. Completely ended.'[27] Recurrent themes in right-wing editorials were the self-appointed status of the Freetown as an open provocation to all law-abiding citizens: 'Christiania lies there as a state within the state. Superior to common legislation with its own rules for right and wrong', as noted by *Jyllandsposten,* which was confident though, that the time was ripe to bring an end to 'more than 30 years of lawlessness and self-help.'[28]

The leftist and social-liberal counter-discourse equated 'normalisation' with 'dullisation' and presented the view that if Christiania is closed 'not only the Christianites will be losers. We will all be more poor and everyday life more gray without this anarchistic lung of the city.'[29] To this the right-wing tabloid paper *BT* broke the camp of Christiania enemies and opposed the 'savage, petit bourgeois indignation towards Christiania' that the paper instead declared a 'symbol of Danish broad-mindedness.'[30]

The loser of this discursive battle was the government, which despite the marked political right turn, failed to change the overall public opinion in a decisive way. One reason was that the normalisation discourse in some respects didn't fit reality very well. For example, governmental arguments such as Christiania 'should be a recreational green area for all citizens, and [...] open itself up'[31] was perceived as a joke in Christiania, which had already been overrun by half the Danish population, as citizens in their thousands regularly flowed to the existing 'open' spaces, grassy lakeshores, fireplaces, playgrounds and other indeed 'recreational' and 'green' facilities in the Freetown.

Christiania had not only become a very frequented but also an indisputably popular place with a cemented proportion of support (Figure 2). Unlike the 1970s and 1980s when the support was highly dependent on the most leftist Danes, the Social Democrat voters had been moved and were now clearly in favour of Christiania. The earlier categorical aversion towards the Freetown by right-wing voters had also crumbled and divided the bourgeois Danes into two almost equal parts on the issue.[32]

Not surprisingly, the opinion polls further revealed that younger people were more Christiania-friendly (in fact, only the age group of 60+ was against Christiania), and among Copenhageners (of all ages) the support was overwhelming with 70 per cent (1996), 72 per cent (2003) and 70 per cent (2006) in favour of the Freetown.[33] In other words, the vast majority of all young Copenhageners were on the side of Christiania and among them plenty of leftist youngsters with a tradition of political activism, which altogether should worry any Christiania-hostile government.

Figure 3. Newspaper editorials about Christiania 1990–2010.

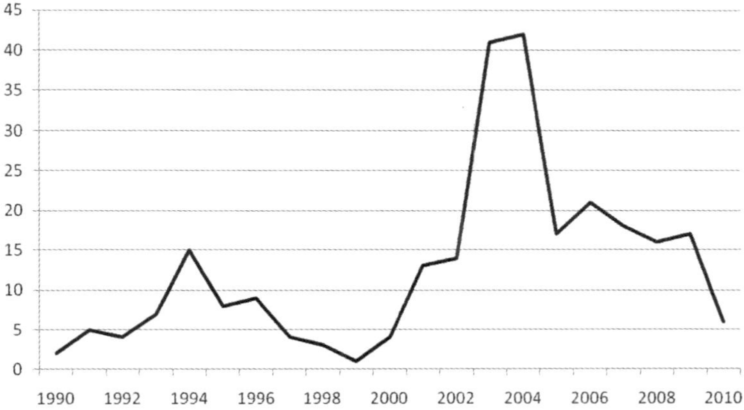

Source: Editorials in the six most important national Danish newspapers: *Information*, *Politiken*, *Ekstrabladet*, *BT*, *Berlingske Tidende* and *Jyllandsposten*.
Note: The figure counts the early number of editorials that discuss or mention Christiania.

On the Warpath Again 2004–11

In 2004 tensions rose, when the police pursued an important objective in the governmental normalisation plan by carrying out a major offensive against hash sale in Pusher Street. The offensive sent many pushers behind bars, but otherwise it didn't help the government much. The effect on the very target, hash sale, was soon disputed as new pushers stepped in to replace the missing, and within a few years the hash market in Christiania was back in full bloom and as visible as ever. Besides it was a widespread opinion that the Freetown as such was not to blame for the criminal pushers as 'hash is being sold and smoked all over Denmark, in every setting, in every city.'[34] By October 2003 as many as 70 per cent of Danes would like to keep Christiania as it is, just without Pusher Street.[35]

Furthermore the campaign against the pushers signalled a new period of massive police presence in the Freetown followed by the usual exposures of police behaviour that made even a conservative journalist concede that 'It is sad to have to write so [...] but the conditions in Christiania seem to bring out the worst in some policemen.'[36]

Meanwhile the full implementation of the normalisation plan was about to begin. Having desisted from a frontal police clearance, the government was compelled to make the Christianites give their voluntary consent to the plan. If not, a police solution of course lurked as the government's last resort. Yet, the immanent question was: would the government dare to play that hazardous card of no return? The Christianites were not unaffected by the threat; but then again: with Christiania more in line with the population than the government, they themselves had their usual joker of unpredictable sympathy reactions lurking in the back hand.

As the government had decided on the cautious approach, the normalisation began slowly and bureaucratically. Not until September 2006 was the Palace and Properties Agency (Slots- og Ejendomsstyrelsen, SES), which was the new administrative body that had taken over responsibility for the Christiania area, ready to present the final governmental offer to the Christianites, who at the same time were faced with a deadline of 15 November to accept the plan. 'Overrunning that deadline will be regarded as a rejection of the offer', the Christianites were warned.[37]

Christiania did overrun that deadline by five days and with an answer that was either, or both, yes and no. Yes to some elements in the governmental offer, and no to the induction of private ownership, individualistic profit-making, conversion of the rampart area into a conventional park and other elements that the Christianites feared would destroy the Freetown as a 'housing experiment' with 'self-administration and direct decision-making process.' The answer ended with the poem 'Dear sister Denmark' and the slogan 'Let dreams live!' as a sign of how Christiania resisted the political-bureaucratic game.[38]

Though the Christianites thereby formally had refused the government, they were given another chance as the Palace and Properties Agency entered into a renewed dialogue that resulted in a revised offer and a new deadline of 8 February 2007.[39] Once again Christiania responded neither nor, but asked for more clarification, upon which the responsible minister regretted the fruitless talks and stated that 'there will be nothing of any renegotiation.'[40] Parallel to this the Christianites had taken legal action against the state in which they claimed a prescriptive right to the collective use of the area due to more than 30 years of existence and various forms of acceptance by alternate governments. The minister threateningly but vainly demanded that the Christianites cancel their legal action, and on 31 March 2007, he concluded the Christianian conduct to be 'a no to the deal.'[41]

On that same day 10,000–15,000 people marched off from Christiania in a most colourful parade with a spectacular pirate ship on wheels and a cacophony streaming from several rolling stages. The background was less amusing. On 1 March a joint force of police and military elite units with helicopters had attacked and cleared the old cultural centre of the BZ movement, the Youth House at Jagtvej 69, which was subsequently torn down. The immediate response was days of all-out riots in which the Copenhagen night sky was marked by columns of smoke from big fires in the streets, burning cars and rounds of tear gas. Unaffected by around 1,000 arrests, the protests continued on a daily basis throughout the month; and due to the simultaneous tense situation around Christiania the Youth House sympathisers and Freetown followers, who to a large extent were the same people anyway, obviously united; or as it said on the front banner at the 31 March parade: 'Free spaces for everybody! Defend Christiania! More Youth Houses now!'

The whole situation about free spaces literally became a frontline in the more general cultural struggle in which traditional leftist and social-liberal ideas in this period increasingly collided with harsh right-wing attitudes represented by the government and its supporters from the Danish People's Party. As a representative of the oppositional camp, *Politiken* took the position that 'It is a dull city, and in a wider sense a less creative society, that cannot see anything but problems in alternative communities like Christiania and the Youth House' and warned that 'the bourgeois plainness has gone too far.'[42]

In the streets the struggle continued and, as with the Youth House conflict, with an outcome unexpected by many observers of a victory to the activists. After the March 2007 revolt the protesters carried on with seemingly unending demonstrations including more clashes fuelled by a profound anger at the loss of the house at Jagtvej 69 and incited by a spreading sympathy and understanding of the need for such free spaces in a city like Copenhagen.[43] When 5,000 activists overran the otherwise well-prepared forces of law in a squatting action of unprecedented scale in October 2007, police leaders and politicians seriously began to fear where this apparently uncontrollable situation was going. The persistent protests had simply exhausted the police, who on several occasions had mobilised reinforcements on a national scale. Consequently the responsible politicians on the Copenhagen City Council resumed what they had long refused: talks with the protesters, and in June 2008 they finally gave the activists a municipal building as compensation for the old Youth House.

Two weeks later a newspaper expressed the widespread view that 'If the government does not accept the invitation by Christiania to dialogue [...] things can turn out much worse than when the Youth House was evicted'; or as made clear by an anonymous Christianite: 'We have many friends in the autonomous community and all over the world. If the police move in, I promise you there will be fighting.'[44] Earlier also the right-wing *Jyllandsposten* had warned the authorities to 'take possible aggressions into account and be cautious.'[45] There was little doubt, the strengthened free-space movement in Copenhagen had once again tipped the balance of power between Christiania and the state and this time back in favour of the Freetown.

Nonetheless riot police were sent into Christiania in 2007–08 to demolish two minor, and according to the governmental plan illegal, constructions named Cigarkassen and Vadestedet. These feelers to force the normalisation process through led to furious battles in the streets during which most of the Freetown and a great part of the surrounding neighbourhood was shrouded in tear gas, but with no other result than that the retreating police could almost hear the sound of the rebuilding work on the just demolished constructions (see also Anders Lund Hansen's chapter in this book). Even so, Christiania was permitted still more talks that however repeated the pattern of former rounds of negotiation and came to nothing.[46] What also repeated itself were clashes with the police as their patrols in Christiania occasionally exploded in fighting that besides more wounded rioters and officers didn't change anything in the deadlocked talks between the Freetown and the state.

The 'how many times must the cannon balls fly, before [...]?', so often heard in Christiania homes, still made its sad sense. Even more so as these homes by 2005 were inhabited by people among whom 68 per cent were 40–65 years old and who for that reason alone were most unlikely to be found among the combat-prepared rioters. With no common approved Christiania plan for how to react to 'intolerable' police intrusions, the occasional clashes instead seemed to be a kind of automatic and learned reaction by various Copenhagen groups such as left-radical youngsters, indignant Christiania visitors and the usual pushers, to some extent in sympathy with the younger generation of Christianites. Usually the role of the older Christianites was to act as spokesmen who afterwards tried to prevent the riots from causing irreparable damage to the public image and political situation of the Freetown — which the dramatic events in the streets, looking back on Christiania's long history, in fact never really did.[47]

40 Years of Bargaining and Barricades

The faith of so-called free spaces has in modern western metropolis depended on many things, but above all the relation to one other actor: the state. It is the state and its many authorities that sooner or later tend to get involved when people take over other people's property to form autonomous societies and thereby challenge the principle of private ownership and the state's right to rule its territory.

This is also true of the Freetown Christiania as proved by its 40-year-long history of dramatic interaction with the Danish state. A state that was never *per se* an uncompromising enemy. In a democracy like Denmark it all depends on the head of that state: the successive governments — and sometimes, in the case of a minority government, alternative parliamentary majorities. Yet, as we have seen, some of these governments and majorities were indeed hostile to Christiania, so how did the Freetown manage to survive all these years with recurrent political claims for its end? In the extremes: by bargaining and barricades.

Bargaining. Due to the immanent pressure on the politicians to settle the unsolved question, Christiania has had to try to come to terms with the authorities. Realising that, the Christianites have engaged themselves in negotiations, just as they have made use of another way of talking: legal action against the state. In part the Christiania rationale was to gain time and thereby wait for a better political situation or for the state to lose its focus. But it must also be said that to the Christianites these negotiations were always a delicate balance between a desire to bring an end to the everlasting precarious situation and stressing troubles with the authorities and a desire to preserve the unique Freetown culture of collectivity, self-administration and unrestrained creativity. The Christianites also realised that their strongest negotiation card was popular support to legitimise their existence, so every round of talks usually was accompanied by various mobilisation efforts to influence the public. Yet, airy sympathy alone would not have saved the Freetown that long.

Barricades. If a closure of Christiania had been an easy and costless task, it almost certainly would have been completed by one of the Christiania-hostile political majorities that actually have existed. So the fundamental reason why Christiania still exists begins with the pioneer Christianites who by their unwillingness to give up the area voluntarily raised the cost of a forceful police clearance and thus made the authorities hesitate to claim the state's rightful ownership to the area. Later on, a series of most comprehensive free-space battles with the Youth House revolt in 2007–08 being the latest, underlined that a full-scale police attack on Christiania would ignite possibly uncontrollable protests in the rest of the city followed by a long-lasting society-wide mobilisation and engagement with an altogether very uncertain outcome — including a probability that it would look like civil war more than anything else in recent Danish history. This nightmare scenario is exactly why successive governments have refrained from such an action.

The Freetown's survival capacity was not least put to the test during the 10 years 2001–11 of the most lasting Christiania-hostile political majority ever. And notwithstanding internal stress the Christianites once again pulled through using the well-known repertoire of delaying tactics and mobilisation of sympathisers, after which the right-wing offensive against Christiania lost momentum. By the turn of 2010–11 that offensive had in fact not achieved anything on the ground; and when the Freetown lost its lawsuit against the state in the Supreme Court (Højesteret) on 18 February 2011 the government, despite earlier warnings, allowed the Christianites more time and yet another revised negotiation offer — exactly as had been the case when the few attempts to force the normalisation through in 2007–08 had been met with street battles, which then caused a halt to further such police manoeuvres. Even the barricades still proved their logic as an element in the crucial balance of power between the Freetown of Christiania and the state.

GOVERNING FREEDOM — DEBATING THE FREETOWN IN THE DANISH PARLIAMENT

Håkan Thörn

Freedom is nowhere as big as in Christiania, and nowhere as frightening.
Jean-Manuel Traimond, Christianite[1]

The government wishes a normalisation of the Christiania area.
Prime Minister Anders Fogh Rasmussen in the Danish parliament, 2003

Challenging the Danish State

What distinguished Christiania in the context of the 1970s squatter movements and counterculture, was the declaration that an autonomous Freetown had been constituted in the centre of a European capital. Thus, Christiania challenged the sovereignty of the Danish state, whose major institutions, including the parliament, the offices of the ministries, and the Royal Palace, are situated more or less a kilometre away from the Freetown. The sign 'You are now entering the EU', above the main exit from Christiania to Prinsessegade, confirms that this challenge four decades later continues to play a key role in the Freetown's political identity.

Important for the fact that the Christianites managed to get away with this, both in the short term and the long run, was their creative use of 'empty' spaces, both politically and materially. First, when the Bådsmansstræde Barracks ceased to exist as a military area in the summer of 1971, the centre-right government had no plans for the area.[2] Second, when activists proclaimed that they had founded the Freetown

Christiania on 26 September 1971, the space of the sovereign was empty, as Denmark had no functioning government. In the national election five days earlier, the centre-right and the left coalitions got 88 mandates each. It was only on 10 October, after the votes from the Faroe Islands had been counted, that the Social Democrats, with the support of the Socialist Party (Socialistisk Folkeparti), could put a government in place. According to Jacob Ludvigsen, one of the Freetown's founders, the chaotic political situation that lasted for almost three weeks gave Christiania an important lead in relation to the government.

As accounted for in a government report, a meeting on Christiania that included representatives from the Ministries of Defence, Justice, Housing, Culture, the Copenhagen Municipality and the Copenhagen Police was held in November 1971. Here, it was concluded that it was not 'practically possible' to clear the area of its inhabitants and prevent 'a new intrusion' through fencing the area off.[3] In a sense, this meant that the Danish government regarded Christiania ungovernable — at least from the point of view of sovereign power; and through the use of coercive force (police action). Instead, it was agreed that 'one should attempt to reach a normalisation of the relationship between the inhabitants and the authorities'.[4] This was manifested in the agreement made in 1972 between Christiania and the state, and in the latter's declaration in 1973 that Christiania could remain for three years in the form of an officially sanctioned 'social experiment'.

How should one understand this initial response to Christiania's challenge from the government in terms of the exercise of state power? As one observer noted: 'The traditional liberal Danish government allowed the settlement at first [...] Then it spent the next three decades trying to reclaim the area'.[5] To be more precise, its most serious attempt to reclaim the area came after 33 years, through a new law in 2004 that was meant to enforce a normalisation of the area. Initiating a debate on this in 2003, the Socialist Party asked: 'What can the government inform regarding the plans for Christiania's "normalisation" seen in the light of the government's thoughts on freedom?' The first speaker addressing the question was the Prime Minister, Anders Fogh Rasmussen, of the Liberal Party (Venstre), who a decade earlier had published a book that can be characterised as a neoliberal manifesto celebrating the concept of freedom and the idea of 'the minimal state'.[6] In his five-minute-long response, he not only frequently used the word 'freedom' (twelve times), but also the word 'law/s' (ten times):

> Freedom is about society making space for diversity and difference, and that the individual has the best conceivable possibilities to develop her abilities and talents [...] But at the same time, it is important to underline, that freedom has some common frames, constituted by the laws of the land.[7]

The simple argument in Rasmussen's speech is that if the goal of politics is to maximise freedom for the individual, freedom also has its limits, as manifested in the law. And in the case of Christiania, there is simply too much freedom, and too little law. This is a rather different conception of 'normalisation' than the one expressed in the above quoted governmental report from 1973. How should one understand this shift? To what extent, and how, have the government's strategies to 'reclaim' the area changed during the period? And more important: on which perceptions of Christiania as a 'problem' to be solved, have these strategies been based? Further, I will address the question that the parliamentarians repeatedly asked themselves during 30 years of Christiania debates: Why has the state and the parliament devoted so much time, energy and administrative work to govern such a small area (49 hectares) with no more than 900 inhabitants? This chapter will attempt to answer these questions through an analysis of debates on Christiania in the Danish parliament (Folketinget) between 1974 and 2004. The analysis puts Christiania into a wider political context and intends to shed some further light on the interactions between Christiania and the government. I will highlight how the political actors participating in these debates in some respects represent conflicting perspectives; and in other respects share certain understandings, of what is good, normal and desired. Basically, I will make two arguments. First, in relation to the question of the significant attention paid to Christiania by the parliament, I will argue that Christiania early on was given the status of a highly *symbolical issue*, which fit well into an emerging pattern in mainstream politics to focus on 'value politics'. Second, I will show how the shifting definitions of two key, interlinked, concepts in the Christiania debates, 'normalisation' and 'freedom', are linked to fundamental changes in the Danish government's strategies to govern the Freetown.[8]

As a background to the analysis of the parliamentary debates, the two following sections will provide a conceptual discussion of 'governing freedom' and 'Christiania's public-ness'. I will then take a close look at the first big Christiania debate in 1974. Here, many of the themes that would define the next 21 debates that were held in the coming 30 years were established.[9] The following section discusses Christiania as a highly symbolical issue in the context of the emergence of 'new politics', quoting from several debates between 1974 and 2004. I will then move on to a close look at the 2003 debate. The reason for paying special attention to the 1974 and 2003 debates in this chapter is that they provide contrasts that make a shift in the Danish state's approach to Christiania between the 1970s and 2000s clearly visible. Finally, I will discuss this shift in the wider context of the emergence of neoliberalism and a new form of urban governance.

Governing Freedom

In a series of lectures, dating from 1976 to 1983, French philosopher and historian Michel Foucault refined his theory of modern power, distinguishing between three modes of government: sovereignty, disciplinary power and bio-power — which he also termed 'regulatory power' (the term I will use). *Sovereign power* is connected to the founding of the modern state in Europe, its fundaments being the monopoly of violence and the 'law of the land' — ultimately 'the right to life and death' within the borders of a particular territory.[10] As an important driver in early capitalism, *disciplinary power* emerged in the form of various techniques to control the individual and his/her body, in order to 'increase their productive force through exercise, drill'.[11] *Regulatory power*, finally, is directed at the population as whole, which from the viewpoint of government is defined as a statistical entity. Consequently, in order to impose regulations to steer the population in a particular direction, the activities of certain expertise, such as collecting statistical data and making probability calculations, are crucial.[12]

The establishing of regulatory power in Europe is the beginning of the era of governmentality, in which the management of social life through the imposition of various regulations is the dominant form of power. A key to understanding variations between, and changes in, different regimes of power, is however to look at how government is performed through different *combinations* of sovereign, disciplinary and regulatory power.

As pointed out by British sociologist Nikolas Rose in his book *The Powers of Freedom*, the emergence of regulatory power in Western Europe was part of the rise to dominance of capitalism and liberal government, based on the philosophy of classical political economy. This meant that government in its most basic sense was understood from an economic perspective — and that the principles of laissez-faire and individual freedom were considered as fundamental. Further, an emphasis on *the security* of the population now became instrumental. This did not just refer to the forming and strengthening of national armies. If liberal government on the one hand ultimately seeks to maximise freedom as circulation, of goods, and of people, too much circulation, or too much freedom, may ultimately be perceived as a threat to social order. Therefore, liberal government always involves a distinction between 'good' and 'bad' circulation, the latter defined in terms of threats to the security of the population.[13] Foucault argued that there is a dark side of liberalism, because in order to 'produce freedom', liberal government needs to establish a series of new forms of disciplinary and legal measures: 'limitations, controls, forms of coercion and obligations relying on threats'.[14] This is quite clearly expressed in Anders Fogh Rasmussen's Christiania speech quoted above — freedom is only possible through 'normalisation', meaning the enforcement of the law and the possibility 'to exercise normal police activity in the area'.[15]

When discussing disciplinary power, it is also necessary to make a distinction between 'soft' and 'coercive' disciplinary measures. In relation to social movements or oppositional political communities such as Christiania, 'soft' disciplinary power refers to various forms of conditioned co-operation, established through practices such as dialogue and negotiation. From the horizon of state power these practices are part of the various attempts to gain legitimacy through consensus formation; or in the words of Antonio Gramsci, the production of cultural hegemony as *consent*, something which every liberal government is fundamentally dependent on. However, as Gramsci also emphasised, liberal cultural hegemony also ultimately needs to be 'protected by the armour of coercion'.[16] In our case, coercive disciplinary measures refer to the policing of political movements, political communities or protest.

In a Scandinavian context, the degree of political violence in the form of clashes between demonstrators and police is relatively low seen in an international perspective.[17] This is undoubtedly related to the political consensus culture that was established in connection with the Scandinavian welfare state and that has defined relations between social movements and the state since the 1930s.[18] As an important dimension of the Scandinavian social model, the consensus culture was established through the practice of creating procedures for consultation, negotiation and dialogue with movement representatives.

The case of Christiania and especially the process through which the Freetown was given the status of an official social experiment is a clear example of the workings of the political consensus culture in Denmark. According to the government report cited above, the Ministry of Defence in 1971 appointed a 'contact group' who 'through negotiations with representatives of "Christiania" — would seek to reach an agreement regarding the actual use of the area'. The report further accounts for a process in which the inhabitants of the Freetown had worked out an internal structure for democratic decision-making; and that it had instituted a Common Meeting (fællesmøde), which in turn had appointed a group that should represent Christiania in talks with the authorities. The 1972 agreement did however also involve conditions for 'normalisation' which could clearly be regarded as a manifestation of the exercise of soft disciplinary power. It included demands on Christiania such as performing 'an internal registration of the inhabitants', to organise individual payment for electricity and water, improvement of sanitary conditions (i.e. availability of toilets, showers and baths). Further, the demands included a requirement that the Freetown engage in a conditioned co-operation with municipal authorities. This included demands that Christiania should appoint a group to perform social work in co-operation with the Copenhagen municipality's various departments of social work; and that its relationship with the Copenhagen police should be further discussed with the Ministry of Defence's contact group.[19]

The basic assumption in my analysis of the parliamentary debates is that to pass decisions to make Christiania the subject of government action, it must be characterised as a more or less urgent problem. So what kind of 'problem' is Christiania, according to the parliamentarians? Using Foucault's notion of three interacting forms of power, this question can be further specified: Is it a problem of failed sovereignty, to be dealt with by making existing laws effective, as suggested by Rasmussen in the 2003 debate; or by passing new laws, such as the 1989 Christiania law? Is it a disciplinary problem, to be dealt with through negotiations to establish conditioned co-operation, such as those in 1972;

or through coercive means such as when the infamous so-called 'uro-patruljen' (riot squad) patrolled Christiania in the 1990s? Or is it a problem of regulatory power, to be dealt with through registration and regulation, as in 2004, when the government demanded that the Christianites individually register their claims to property in the area? The government's attempts to govern Christiania have always involved a combination of these three forms of power. As will be made clear however, the combinations have changed, as governments and authorities have shifted emphasis and strategies in their exercise of power.

These strategies share the assumption that new measures should be taken in order to ensure that Christiania is properly governed by the state; and consequently that the Freetown should *remain* in *some* form. Up until 2002 however, an additional, and frequently expressed, position in the parliamentary debates was that Christiania should be evacuated, its dwellings demolished (except for the old military buildings). In this case a particular framing of 'the problem', dense with stigmatising metaphors, was presented. In order to evacuate a populated space, an image of the area must be established that portrays its buildings as indecent dwelling places, and/or, often more important, its current inhabitants and their way of life as abnormal, or even inhuman. The space must in this sense be made to appear as a place already outside, or as a fundamental threat to, the social order. In this form of discourse, a particular place is *primarily* associated with human misery, crime and drugs. Sociologist Loïc Wacquant has used the concept *territorial stigmatisation* to signify the process through which such images of an area and its inhabitants are established publicly.[20] The fact that this form of discourse has appeared in connection with demolition plans in different parts of the world, testifies to the power of language, and of metaphors.

As a space of counterculture and radical social movement politics, Christiania is however also associated with *utopian place* images, challenging the process of territorial stigmatisation. Consequently, public debates on Christiania have in many cases been defined by a radical bipolarity. Characterisations such as 'a rats nest [...] a lawless district [...] a mecca of hard drugs, that makes Sodom and Gomorra look pale in comparison' / 'an unbelievably disorderly, hackneyed and untidy city district, where junk pieces float between waste, glass splinters and dog poop', have been pitted against images of 'a place where people get inspiration to new forms of life' / 'an experiment with many forms of democracy [...] a district of exciting dwellings of urban renewal [...] of areas of freedom'.[21]

Christiania's Public-ness

The parliament is one of the physical spaces (enlarged to a national scale by the media reports) where the debates and conflicts defining the Danish public sphere are articulated. The debates on Christiania are not only about the Freetown itself. The frequency, the length of the debates, and the degree of passion and conflict expressed, indicate that something more than the destiny of 900 people and 49 hectares is at stake. What then, is the concern? I would argue that the debates in their most profound sense are dealing with the question of how to govern urban life in a society driven by a capitalist economy. Beyond ideological differences between Social Democrats, Liberals, Conservatives and Populists, an ideal of modern liberal government is expressed in the debates: to maximise circulation of people, of commodities, of traffic and air, while at the same time suppressing, or at least taming, 'bad circulation' in order to achieve the perfect equilibrium, or social stability. This actually points to another aspect of Christiania's uniqueness. Few, if any, other utopian communities of this size have existed in the centre of a big city that, importantly, is also a capital.[22] Here, the impact of different forms of circulation and the pressure from estate developers (at least during the last two decades) are more intense than in most other places. Defining and defending the area not just as a dwelling place for Christianites, but also as an urban space open for everyone, means that the Freetown has constituted itself as *public space*. Further, the Freetown could also be regarded as a material manifestation of *the inner city as a public sphere* because of its symbolic and highly contested character; its status as a recurring reference point in Danish debates on urban planning and urban life, urban government and urban freedom. Maria Hellström argues that the public-ness of Christiania is constituted by its unplanned, relatively un-defined, and non-commodified spatiality—and that this makes possible an experience of freedom of agency.[23]

The First Christiania Debate

The first major Christiania debate occurs in 1974 under a government led by the Liberal Party. It departs from a written account by the Minister of Defence, Erling Brøndum, who declares that he does not recognise the previous government's act to declare Christiania an official 'social experiment'. Brøndum further states that while he will not break the previous government's agreement that Christiania can remain until 1976, he nevertheless asks for permission to demolish sixty buildings that cover 20,000 square metres in the area.[24]

The *sovereignty theme* is immediately established in the debate as a member of the populist Progress Party (Fremskridtspartiet) argues that the 'occupation' of Christiania must be discussed in terms of shortcomings of Danish national defence. Referring to events on 24 October 1971, when Christianites 'stormed the military buildings' at Bådsmandsstræde, he asks if the Military Ordinance of 1952 was not applied 'for this special occasion'?[25] When the speaker goes on to compare the event with the surrender to the German occupiers on 9 April 1940, the transcription records 'merriness' in the parliament. Although it is quite clear that this statement is not taken seriously by the other participants in the debate, Christiania's critics in the parties to the right of the government nevertheless agree that Christiania poses a challenge to the sovereignty of the Danish state. The Conservative Party expresses great concern that 'half of the population, who live out there [...] are foreigners' and that representatives of the Danish state make themselves allies with 'lawbreakers'.[26] The Socialist Party argues that the governing Liberal Party shares this view, as they have 'chosen to perceive Christiania in a law-and-order context'.[27] This is implicitly confirmed by the Minister of Defence, as he states that although liberal politics are all for 'social innovation [...] it cannot act in open opposition to those laws that the parliament has passed'.[28] The theme 'law and order' is to the right also *a problem of disciplinary power*. Most important, according to the Conservatives, is that Christiania's existence may open up for a problem with the discipline of the whole population, as it undermines the Danish population's confidence in the law ('retsbevidstheden') and its trust in the police, who are hindered from doing their job in Christiania.[29]

Taken as a whole however, Christiania is during the debate *first and foremost discussed in terms of a container of social problems*. When drugs are mentioned, they are mainly associated with numerous 'social problems'. As pointed out by a Social Democrat, the debate is first and foremost preoccupied with 'the problems of children and youth'.[30] I would add that the greatest concern is the existence of orphans in the Freetown; and the fact that they even have an organisation, called Børnemagt (Children's Power), which is housed in two buildings. Depending on the speaker, this is either considered as a problem of disciplinary or regulatory power, or used as a key reference point in a strategy of territorial stigmatisation of the area.

To the Centre Democrats (Centrumdemokraterne), this clearly is a disciplinary problem, as children are allowed to dwell in the Freetown

> without supervision neither of parents nor of authorities [...] How can one support that children are allowed to take care of themselves in an environment of slum, hard drugs and criminality?[31]

The argument from the Social Democrats that Børnemagt and Christiania's own social workers actually co-operate with Copenhagen's social authorities, implying that a governmental disciplinary power is not absent in the area, are by their opponents deemed illegitimate.

In the posts where the right is most clearly engaging in territorial stigmatisation, children are claimed to be not only exposed to drug use in Christiania, but also to immoral (and illegal), even incestuous, sexual relations. A member of the Progress Party claims that he has asked 'one of the wealthy' inhabitants of Christiania to comment on 'the situation prevailing in the wooden barrack called Algar, where minor boys and girls hang out with homosexual men'.[32] The single post in the debate given most attention by the Danish media was however an account by Inge Krogh of the Christian Democrats (Kristeligt Folkeparti), who claims to have visited the Freetown '15–16 times'. She repeatedly assured the parliament that the people of the Freetown are 'very kind', but that 'the dwelling circumstances are miserable', and that it is extremely difficult to keep up personal hygiene in the Freetown. It was however the following account that got the attention of the media:

> It was one day, I entered one of the small houses [...] When I came in through the door, I wanted to draw back, but I was prompted to come further. There were three people in a bed, one man 30 year old, and one approximately 20 year old woman and a 12 year old child. It seemed, as it was a quite natural thing.[33]

The debate on the situation of children, youth and other 'social problems', is however also broadened when it centres on the concept of 'social experiment'. While the Christian Democrats argue that Christiania 'multiplies our social problems',[34] the main argument in defence of Christiania by the Socialist Party and the Social Democrats is that its social problems are not specific to Christiania, but are widespread in Danish society. And it is according to the Social Democrats precisely in the light of the fact that the institutions of the Danish welfare state, in spite of 'an intensive effort of social pedagogy', cannot manage this problem, that 'Christiania enters the picture' as 'an alternative opportunity'.[35] Considering this, the critique of Christiania put forth in the parliament is according to the Social Democrats a sign of

> a complete ignorance about what social reality looks like in this country, what social reality looks like in Copenhagen [...] They think they can manage some problems by running out a bulldozer and say: get out, without considering what the Social Board points out: that the problems will appear at some other place.[36]

The Social Democrats then put forth an argument, which would later be repeated many times by Christiania's defenders in parliament: that the demand to close the Freetown because of its social problems becomes absurd considering that such problems are also common in other districts in Copenhagen; but nobody would even think of the idea of 'closing' or 'demolishing' the Vesterbro district, for example.

A number of experts and public intellectuals are referred to in the debate, all of whom have advocated the idea of Christiania as a 'laboratory' for the development of alternatives to the existing forms of state regulation of social problems.[37] Neither the governing party nor the parties to the right of the Liberal Party are impressed. For the Progress Party, this is actually an indication of what is fundamentally wrong with Denmark, as 'it is a big and serious problem for the country' that Christiania has got 'protection from the government, the Social Board, social pedagogues of all kinds, with criminologists, with professors of law'.[38] The Danish Communist Party criticises the idea of a social experiment from another angle:

> They call Christiania a social experiment. We would rather call it a social emergency solution, because the experiment in living on the threshold of starvation, that is an experiment that the underclass has felt on its bare skin in decades and centuries.[39]

The discussion about social experiment/social politics also makes clear that regulatory power involves as fundamental elements registration and public census, and ultimately rests on a cost-benefit analysis. Several critics of the idea of Christiania as a social experiment point out that the Freetown simply has not agreed to take part in such an experiment. As a sign of this, it is pointed out that the Freetown has not fulfilled its promise in the 1972 agreement to carry out a registration of its inhabitants. According to the Minister of Defence, 'only recently has Christiania let us know how many inhabitants there are; and they refuse to tell us who they are, or where they live'.[40]

The economic issue regarding to what extent Christiania presents a cost or actually a benefit to the Danish state (see the introductory chapter in this book) is also linked to the idea of Christiania as a social experiment. As the critics point out that the Freetown is in debt to the state due to its declining payments for water and electricity, the Social Democrats argue that this debt is negligible compared to the amount of money that Christiania is saving the Danish state by caring for a significant number of individuals, who would otherwise be in care of public institutions. They are supported by the Socialist Party, who argues that the sum of the Danish state's expenses for Christiania in the budget year of 1972–73 would only cover care for two persons in public institutions in the same time period.[41]

While several posts in the debate argue that the attention being paid to Christiania by the parliament is disproportionate in relation to the issue's actual significance, two of the debate's most important antagonists, Simonsen of the Conservative Party and Olesen of the Social Democrats — actually agree that the attention paid to Christiania is justified. According to Simonsen, the concern with Christiania shown not just by the parliament but by the population as a whole, has risen because 'it concerns some fundamental principles in society' and because 'many people feel insulted by the leeway that the Freetown has got'.[42]

Olesen on the other hand comes as close as anyone in the debate to representing Christiania as a utopian place:

> Christiania is neither the realisation of the happy existence we all dream about, nor a showcase of all the sins in the world. It is not something that can be translated to money or be valued in an objective manner [...] It is the place where other people seek inspiration to new forms of life, values, norms, if you wish; it is also the place from which you can get arguments if you want to address people's prejudices, the last thing something which has defined the debate.[43]

While deeply disagreeing on what the Freetown represents, Olesen and Simonsen thus still agree that the attention given to Christiania is not undeserved, since it concerns some of the profound values that govern political ideologies, and presents a test to what extent politicians are prepared to put them into practice.

Christiania as a Symbolic Issue and the Emergence of New Politics 1974–2004

An obvious feature of all of the parliamentary debates on Christiania is that the Freetown is an issue that divides the left and the right. There is however much more to say regarding how the issue of Christiania has been framed in the context of Danish parliamentary politics.

The confusion in the Danish parliament at the time of the birth of Christiania in September 1971 was only the beginning of a turbulent period in Danish politics. In 1972, the populist the Progress Party (the forerunner to today's Danish People's Party/Dansk Folkeparti), was formed, its major issue being the lowering of income taxes. Opinion polls soon showed that one out of five Danes supported the party. In the same year, Denmark decided to become a member of the EEC (today EU) after a referendum on the issue. The following election, occurring in December 1973, has been called the Earthquake Election ('Jordskredsvalget'), because its results turned the world of Danish party politics upside down.[44] For decades, the parliament's seats had been proportionally divided between five or six parties, which formed a left and a right block. After the 1973 election there were suddenly ten parties in the parliament, five of them newcomers; and the Liberal Party formed a minority government. Although the change in Danish politics did not become as dramatic as first expected, it threw the parliament into a state of slight disorder that lasted until the end of the decade. The Earthquake Election was also the first strong indication of a deep-going structural shift, bringing new conflict and voting patterns to Danish party politics. This shift perhaps made its final breakthrough only in the 2001 'Second Earthquake Election', when a right-wing coalition won its greatest victory ever in Denmark.[45] The Liberal and Conservative Parties formed a government under the leadership of Anders Fogh Rasmussen, with the support of the Danish People's Party, who had built their support base through aggressive xenophobic rhetoric.

In certain respects, the birth of Christiania and the results of the 1973 election could be seen as particular and different responses to the same global process: the transformation (and emerging crisis) of the capitalist economy, which in the Nordic countries came out as a crisis of the Scandinavian welfare state. At this particular time, sociologists launched the term 'post-industrial' to conceptualise a shift in the organisation of production and the patterns of consumption in the Global North. In connection with this, political scientists started to argue that a 'new politics' was on its way, as 'class voting' was gradually being replaced by 'issue voting'.[46] Importantly, this political shift was not only, or perhaps primarily, occurring in the context of the party system. The emergence of 'new politics' in the parliamentary context could actually be seen as an effect of the pressure of the extra-parliamentary wave of new social movements, which manifested themselves globally in the 1960s, in Europe initially led by the New Left, which gave birth to Christiania.

'New politics', referring to 'issue voting' or 'single issue movements', is often mistakenly associated with a new emphasis on narrow individual self-interest in political life, gradually replacing the role of (class-based) ideology in political debates, protest action and voting behaviour. On the contrary, research on both new social movements and changing voting patterns shows that new politics is highly *value-based*; it is often publicly articulated as a principled protest politics in which both morals and ideological commitments play a significant role.[47] In Europe, this shift not only includes the so-called new social movements, but also new populist movements, which had an early debut in Denmark, compared to other European countries.

It is further sometimes argued that 'new politics' means a declining importance of the left-right conflict. It is however more accurate to say that while the political map has been supplemented with new co-ordinates, the line of conflict between left and right remains, although it has been redrawn. In the Danish case, it may even be argued that new politics at several moments has meant an increasing polarisation between left and right. In 1968, the Socialist Party, a political party close to the New Left, and the Conservatives, both had their best election for decades.[48] In addition, two of the new parties entering parliament in 1973, the Progress Party and the Centre Democrats, had an anti-communist profile. Furthermore, Danish political scientist Ole Borre argues that the period between 1975 and 1984 actually was defined by increasing left/right 'ideologisation' of Danish election politics, linked to the new tendency of 'issue voting'.[49] And, in the absence of a Green Party, in Denmark it was primarily the already established parties to the left of the Social Democrats that linked up with the new social movements, while established parties to the right had to face negotiations with new coalition partners — populist parties, who had built their support base mainly on an anti-tax and anti-immigrant rhetoric.

It is in this context we should understand the main logic of the conflict lines and rhetorical figures of the Christiania debates. The leading roles in the fiercest verbal battles over Christiania in parliament between 1974 and 2004 were played by parties who were closely associated with the new value politics and who, for radically different ideological reasons, regarded Christiania as an important symbolic issue, through which they could project their ideologies and utopias, their stereotypes and stigmas. With the exception of the Danish Communist Party, the strongest voices in defence of the Freetown came from the left — the Socialist Party, the Left Socialists (Venstresocialisterna) and the Red-Green Alliance (Enhedslisten, a left wing coalition entering parliament in 1994).[50] These were parties with links to the new social movements, for whom Christiania was of great significance as a space for counterculture. Leading the attacks on Christiania from the side of the right was the Progress Party and (from 1998) Danish People's Party, who were the driving forces in the territorial stigmatisation of the Freetown. For the populists, Christiania presented a perfect opportunity to illustrate what was profoundly wrong with the Social Democratic welfare state, as they painted an image of the Freetown as an embodiment of urban decay, populated by scroungers, parasitising on decent working people's tax money. In the 1987 debate, the small left-wing party Common Course (Fælles Kurs), quite accurately pointed out that the Progress Party had two 'whipping boys' — Christiania and the refugees.[51]

In spite of the numerous attacks from the parliament's right-wing, it might actually be argued that the political opportunity structures were in favour of the Freetown during its early decades because, in addition to the turbulent situation in the parliament in the 1970s, 'the issue' or 'problem' of Christiania was framed in a manner that made it fit into the increasing emphasis on 'value politics'. It is also important to underline that Christiania's existence has been more or less parallel with the emergence of a 'media society', which has further supported an emphasis on 'symbol politics'. Christiania's own cultural politics is a good example of how this practice has been articulated by the new social movements (see Cathrin Wasshede's chapter in this book).[52] In parliamentary politics, mediatisation means that public debates to a larger extent than before are turned into theatre, into spectacle, where political conflicts are staged as drama. In such a context, ideologically dense and highly charged symbolic issues such as Christiania are often paid significant attention. In several Christiania debates, parliamentarians have interrupted the debate about the Freetown simply to point out that they regard the attention paid to the issue heavily disproportionate in relation to more important political issues and decisions, affecting far more people. For example, in the 1974 Christiania debate the Liberal Party Minister of Defence, Erling Brøndum, commented on the fact that five ministers in the Social Democrat government had been involved in Christiania, stating that it 'would almost make you believe that Christiania was a whole country to govern and not just a military area'.[53] Such an observation was not inaccurate. In 1976, the parliament engaged in three long Christiania debates in less than three months. The last one was actually not announced as a Christiania debate. It spontaneously broke out in the midst of, and took over, the debate on the government's proposition for the yearly state budget. The 1975 debate makes the issue of Christiania as a political 'happening' explicit. Referring to the fact that the state's Art Fund had given money to Solvognen (the Sun Chariot), a theatre group based in Christiania who staged a series of public happenings, the Progress Party ironically states:

> 4 1/2 years ago a happening started which has not come to an end, and which is of such overwhelming format, that it is completely unbelievable that the Art Fund has remained blind to its qualities.[54]

By the end of the debate, the Socialist Party turns the table around, by suggesting that the Progress Party actually had organised a happening in the parliament by initiating another debate on Christiania: 'how much will the Art Fund give the parliament, or perhaps the Progress Party, for the happening we have had today?'[55]

The relative stability in the Danish parliament in the 1980s, compared to the turbulent 1970s, came with a turn to the right, as Denmark 'followed the international conjunctures that brought Reagan, Thatcher and Kohl to power'.[56] As in these countries, the first clear steps towards a liberalisation of the Danish economy were taken in 1982 by a right-wing government under the influence of the neoliberal free-market ideology.

The 1980s is often described as a decade completely defined by a heavy right-wing political dominance, but this is not the case in Scandinavia (and perhaps neither in other parts of the world). What is often forgotten is that in parallel with the rise of neoliberalism, the early 1980s brought a new wave of new social movements — including the new women's movement, the peace movement, the environmental movement, the squatter movement and the solidarity movement. After a couple of difficult years in the late 1970s, this also charged Christiania with new energy, and the Freetown reassumed its status as a space for urban alternative culture in Denmark. In the Danish parliament, the 1980s is perhaps best described as a period defined by deepened polarisation in Danish voting patterns. The left-right division also became increasingly gendered as the turn to the right to a large extent reflected a male-dominated voting pattern.[57] From the mid 1980s a strong opposition emerged against the cuts in public spending introduced by the government, something which made the Socialist Party the third largest party in the 1987 election. Nevertheless, the centre-right wing coalition managed to stay in power.[58] It was in this context that a broad parliamentary majority voted for the 1989 Christiania law, which was regarded as highly favourable for the Christianites, as it gave them the right to collective use of the property; and the Freetown legal status. The Liberal Party Minister of Defence Knud Enggard called the 1989 Christiania law a 'parliamentary innovation', referring to the fact that it was supported by a broad left-right parliamentary majority.[59] The parliamentary debates in 1989 and 1991 do however make clear that the legislation allowed for different interpretations. To the Social Democrats and the

Socialist Party the law secured Christiania's existence, something which they had supported since 1972. Legalisation also satisfied some of those to the right who had always framed Christiania as a problem of law and order. Thus, to the left, the law meant making Christiania legal, while for the right it meant enforcing the law on a territory that for almost two decades had remained outside of sovereign control.

So far, Christiania had, both in expected and clearly unexpected ways, been favoured by the shifting political opportunity structures provided by Danish parliamentary politics. Even when an elite consensus on market liberalism was established in the late 1980s, its emphasis on (a regulated) *self-regulation* could be used to promote Christiania's self-government.[60]

It was only after the Second Earthquake Election in 2001 that the tide would finally turn with force against Christiania. As the importance of the value-political dimension of the left-right division has increased, it could be argued that the dominance of the right-wing in the 2000s has been due to its successful cultural strategy, with its emphasis on anti-immigrant and anti-expert rhetoric. In the 'cultural war' launched by Anders Fogh Rasmussen in his first New Year's Speech, Christiania was an obvious target. Positioned in Copenhagen's inner-city, it is a powerful cultural symbol: of the continuing influence of the 1968 generation and of the following countercultural currents, such as punk and hip-hop; and of the cultural politics of the 'social state' that once, and under the strong influence of leading Danish social scientists, architects and public intellectuals, baptised the Freetown as a 'social experiment'.[61] Consequently, as the new government declared that they now once and for all would solve the issue of Christiania, attention to Christiania intensified in the parliament, with four big debates between 2002 and 2004. As pointed out by the Christian Democrats, the first of these debates presented the parliament with rather surprising news. The Danish People's Party, whose mandates in parliament the Liberal-Conservative government was dependent on, had changed their position on the Freetown. While the Danish People's Party (and their forerunner the Progress Party) had always demanded immediate eviction of the Christianites, it now recognised the 1989 Christiania law.[62] Soon it became clear that this was hardly good news for Christiania, as the government proposed changes in the Christiania law that in practice meant a reversal of its content.

While assuring that the Christianites would not be evicted, the last debates are imprinted by the right-wing parties' ideologically driven determination to put an end to everything that makes Christiania a symbol of (leftist) alternative culture. In the debates, the Liberal Party, leading the government, not only declared that it was time to put an end to Christiania's collective use of property, but also to its consensus democracy, which had been an obstacle to the government's attempt at governing Christiania through the years (see Amy Starecheski's chapter in this book).[63]

Of the last debates, the one held in 2003 was the most intense and ideologically driven. The two following debates, held in spring 2004, were much less heated as the parties in parliament were approaching the agreement to adopt significant changes in the 1989 Christiana law. Just like in 1989, there was a broad parliamentary majority, as all of the parties except the Red-Green Alliance, voted for the new law in May 2004.

The 2003 Debate

What perhaps is most striking when comparing the 1974 and the 2003 debates, is that the discussion of Christiania in terms of a 'social problem' and/or a 'social experiment' that dominated the first debate, is more or less absent in 2003. The term 'social experiment' is only used once in the debate, when the Christian Democrats state that the position of the party is that 'the social experiment, which Christiania once was claimed to be, has turned out to be a decidedly failed experiment'.[64]

The only post portraying Christiania as a successful 'experiment' is the opening statement by the Socialist Party. It actually relatively closely resembles Social Democrat Olesen's opening statement in the 1974 debate:

> Of course there are problems in Christiania; there are few places on earth where Utopia exists [...] Christiania is a fantastic plurality of things: an experiment with many different forms of democracy; a district with large space also for those with significant social problems; a district with a great diversity of age groups; a district buzzing of entrepreneurs with over 80 enterprises; a district consisting of exciting dwellings expressing urban renewal, together with dwellings of poor quality; areas of freedom, that should make an impression on every liberal minded person; one of Denmark's largest tourist attractions — and a very comprehensive hash market. [65]

Interestingly, the most frequent argument put forth by parliamentarians defending Christiania in the debate (representing the Social Democrats, the Socialist Party and the Red-Green Alliance) is Christiania's status as a major tourist attraction. It seems to be an argument difficult to contradict, as the only response put forth is a remark from the Danish People's Party that it would be interesting 'to know how many tourists come a second time, when they have seen what it really is out there'.[66]

The debate, however, centres first and foremost around the sale of hash on Pusher Street. While drugs in 1974 primarily were discussed in relation to social problems, to be dealt with through the regulatory power of social policy and the soft disciplinary power of conditioned cooperation; they are now defined as a problem of law and order, *demanding the exercise of sovereign power (new laws) as well as new strategies of coercive disciplinary power*. Although the issue of law and order was also present in the 1974 debate, there is in 2003 not just a heavier emphasis on the theme, but it is also clearly framed in a discourse of *urban fear*, linked to a praxis of *zero-tolerance policing*. The argument that the Copenhagen Police do not regularly patrol Christiania, because they fear for their security, had been a recurring theme since 1974. In the 1990s, Christiania's critics had started to emphasise that police presence was also an issue of the security of Christiania's visitors and neighbours.[67] In his first statement in the 2003 debate, the Conservative Minister of Defence, Svend Aage Jensby, argues that 'the most beautiful area we have in Copenhagen, lies frightfully situated'. He even goes a step further as he argues that the 'inhabitants of the nice part of Christiania do not dare to send their children into the streets' because they fear[...] dealers or similar criminal elements'.[68] Then he goes on to give an account of a new police strategy in relation to Christiania, and what it had achieved in 326 actions over the last 6 months, according to a report from the Copenhagen Police. It is clear that this strategy is not simply intended to strike at hash dealers, but in the prescribed manner of zero-tolerance policing, to crack down on the slightest offence to the law:

> More than 5,700 cars have been checked, over 1,500 individuals have been frisked, and around 300 legal searches (ransagninger) have been carried out. There have been 850 cases of drug-related offences; 7 offences against Penal Law paragraph 191 regarding serious drug crime, almost 1,300 offences against Traffic Law, 1,100 parking tickets, and around 100 individuals have been arrested. And I can add that in these 6 months 695 kilos of hash and almost 1.6 million kroner have been confiscated — or more than was confiscated between the years 1998 and 2001 [...] As earlier stated, the intensified police action will be continued up until the eviction from Pusher Street.[69]

In the cases when Christiania is territorially stigmatised in the 2003 debate, it is not through using images and concepts of 'social misery' or 'slum', but by associating it with 'biker-gang criminality' ('rockerkriminalitet') and ordinary citizens' fear for their personal safety when moving in, and in the neighbourhoods of, the Freetown. Christiania's defenders however use the same strategy for 'de-stigmatisation' as in 1974, arguing that whatever problems with hash sale and use there are in Christiania, they are nothing specific to the Freetown. For example, the Social Democrats refer to an investigation showing that '20 per cent of the Danish population regularly use [...] hash'.[70] The Red-Green Alliance, which advocates the state-controlled legal sale of hash, asks whether the fact that substantial amounts of hash have been confiscated in Hellerup, an upper middle class suburb of Copenhagen, implies that 'the police should be deployed to normalise Hellerup?'[71]

The Socialist Party chooses a different strategy as they repeatedly question whether a more important driving force lies behind the government's concern for law and order — an exercise *in neoliberal regulatory power in the form of privatisation of state property*, something which is indicated by the fact that the main responsibility for the area has been transferred from the Ministry of Defence to the Ministry of Finance:

> If it is correct that it is the hash trade and the difficulties to perform police action that are the government's main reasons, how can it be, that it is the Ministry of Finance that is chairing the Christiania Committee?[72]

As neither the two parties of the government (the Liberals and the Conservatives), nor the Danish People's Party, state that they want to close Christiania, the opposition tries to get the government to openly state what it actually has in mind for the future of the Freetown. They also criticise the government for not inviting Christianites to take part in the planning process, as the Freetown is not represented in the government's Christiania Committee. Regarding the actual plans, the responses are rather unspecific, but put a strong emphasis on the claimed recreational and conservational value of the area — and that it should be of gain to all citizens of Copenhagen. The Minister of Defence claims that the area 'has got the country's most important historical relics'.[73] The Prime Minister even argues that the new 2004 law on Christiania has been introduced not just to guarantee law and order but to protect both the nature and 'the outstanding ancient relics' in the area. The issue of the conservation of the old buildings, which was only a sidetrack in 1974, has been presented as a major concern by the government since it came to power in 2001 and is clearly connected to the right-wing's intensified emphasis on a nationalist discourse in the 2000s. It is also quite obvious that this particular discourse of urban conservation, emphasising the historical value of buildings in inner cities, links up with a trend in European city planning, related to processes of gentrification and the global marketing of cities in order to attract tourists and capital. The conservation argument does not however impress the Social Democrats as they by invoking the changing conjunctures of urban planning relativise the claims of the 'unique value' of the military buildings:

> They talk so much about the beautiful military buildings out there. Honestly, those of us, who represent a couple of parties, the Liberal Party, the Conservative Party and the Social Democrats — how many kilometres of military area have we not devastated? Where is the Tivoli Gardens located? It is situated in an old military area. Where is the Central station? It is situated in an old military area. Worthy of conservation? Is it not true, Mr. Minister, that it is very much worthy of conservation, only that it is an impossible mission?[74]

The Shifting Meanings of Normalisation

Since November 1971, when the Danish government had its first meeting on Christiania, 'normalisation' has been the key concept in the Danish state's attempts to govern the Freetown. In this chapter I have however showed that the meaning of 'normalisation', as defined in the Danish parliament, has changed in a profound way between the 1970s and 2000s. In the 1970s, the meaning of 'normalisation' was linked to the idea that Christiania represented a 'social problem/social experiment'. On the most abstract level, *Christiania was made into an object of the regulatory power specific to the project of social engineering*, a term often used to designate the Scandinavian welfare state with its pro-active policies to balance and compensate for negative effects of the capitalist economy. As expressed in the 1974 debate, even the strongest advocates for social engineering in Denmark, the Social Democrats, argued that the welfare state's institutions for social care to some extent had been shown to be too costly, 'non-efficient' and even inhuman. It was in this context that Christiania, by being adopted and baptised as a 'social experiment', was regarded as a laboratory to 'test' new strategies in the field of social policy.

Another important part of Scandinavian social engineering was the consensus culture that was a source of legitimacy for the government, but also provided a certain space of agency, through which autonomous urban movement spaces like Christiania could be constructed. From the perspective of government, the consensus culture involved a *soft disciplinary power*, based on conditioned co-operation. In the case of the 1972 agreement, this meant that the Freetown's self-governance was allowed on a number of conditions, the most important being that it actively dealt with its social problems in co-operation with the Copenhagen social authorities.

This attempt to govern Christiania through a combination of social liberal regulatory power and soft disciplinary power was phased out in the 1980s, when a new form of liberal government, heavily influenced by the doctrine of neoliberalism, began to emerge. When the definition of Christiania as a social problem/social experiment faded out in the parliamentary debates at this time, a consensus on *legalisation* moved in, interpreted differently by the left and the right. Actually, the 1989 Christiania law, and its different interpretations by the left and the right, may be seen as a point of intersection between the previous social-liberal government and the emerging new form of liberal government, which would take an increasingly stronger neoliberal turn in Denmark during the coming decades, particularly in the 2000s.

This new form of liberal government involves a particular constellation of Foucault's 'triangle of power'. The dominant form of *regulatory power* now emphasises measures to facilitate capitalist circulation — liberalisation as 'de-regulation'. In practice this means re-regulation to support privatisation and 'self-regulation'. Further, new forms of *sovereign* (legal) and *disciplinary power* are mobilised to deal with what in Foucault's terms is perceived as 'bad circulation'. From this way of looking at contemporary power regimes it follows that the mix of radical conservatism and neoliberalism that characterised the Thatcher and Reagan/Bush administrations, mimicked by the Liberal-Conservative government under Anders Fogh Rasmussen, is not a strange hybrid of contradicting political doctrines. Instead it may be seen as a 'logical' ideological attempt to make a certain version of liberal government legitimate.

In relation to the government of city life, urban research has paid attention to how this new power constellation has brought an *increasing privatisation* of urban public spaces, new laws linked to a *discourse of urban fear/security* and an increasing *emphasis on zero tolerance/coercive policing* measures. As highlighted by a group of Danish urban scholars, the aim of such strategies in the case of the Danish capital, now marketed as 'Beautiful Copenhagen', has by a Municipal Head of Planning been described as taking 'the trash' out of Copenhagen (see Anders Lund Hansen's chapter in this book).[75] In 2006, a new law gave the police the unlimited right to stop and search a person within certain 'frisking zones' — Christiania being one of these zones. And just before the Climate Meeting in 2009, the Danish Parliament passed a new law, called 'lømmelpakken' ('the rascal package'), which allowed the police to detain people for 12 hours without arrest, a measure intended to provide the police with improved capacity to prevent urban riots.[76]

While zero tolerance policing was introduced in Christiania as early as 1981, the account by the Minister of Defence in the 2003 debate (quoted above) testifies to a quite remarkable coercive police activity in the area.[77] As pointed out by the Socialist Party in the 2002 debate, it is also in a Scandinavian context quite extraordinary that the government exercises direct control over the police authorities in the manner that the Liberal-Conservative government did when they ordered the police to take measures to increase their activity in the Freetown and to 'evict' Pusher Street.[78] The increasing police activity in Christiania coincides with a displacement of the meaning of 'security' in the Christiania debates. In the 1970s, 'normalisation' was a concept linked to the notion of *social* security, while in the 2000s, it was first and foremost a matter of *private* and *professional* (the police) security.

The Danish state's direct, face-to-face interaction with Christianites has always been a mix of dialogue and coercive policing (see René Karpantschof's chapter in this book). However, while dialogue was still on the state's repertoire in the 2000s, in the 2003 debate the opposition argued that the government was no longer taking it seriously. And when negotiations completely broke down in 2008, it was clearly a result of a shift in emphasis from the soft disciplinary power of the consensus culture (in the 1970s) to discipline through 'the armour of coercion'.

Freedom of What?

Freedom was a key concept in the left-wing and countercultural critique of capitalism in the 1960s. As the early Christiania debates make clear, this critique was also directed at the Scandinavian welfare state, which was perceived to administer late capitalism through an over-regulation of social life (see Signe Sophie Bøggild's chapter in this book). In the ideological battle that laid the ground for a decomposition of the social liberal welfare state, neoliberalism clearly incorporated elements of this critique in connection with their successful campaigns to take the concept of freedom back to (the new) liberalism. Some observers have noted that Anders Fogh Rasmussen's definition of freedom in his book *From Social State to Minimal State* (*Fra socialstat til minimalstat*) is quite close to the notion of freedom expressed in Christiania's 'mission statement': 'to build a self-ruling society, where each individual can unfold freely'.[79] There is however an important difference. Perhaps fearing that his ideas about freedom may be misinterpreted, Rasmussen devotes a couple of pages to criticise anarchism. In the final paragraph he concludes: 'We should say to the anarchists: There is a need of state power in order to protect man's rights of freedom'.[80] He then goes on to argue that the minimal state's 'mission of protection' concerns three things: the individual's life, freedom and *property* (my italics). This underlines the fact that when the Liberal Party-led government in the 2003 debate demands *normalisation as legalisation*, it is not just in order to impose law and order to deal with what is perceived as 'bad circulation'. It is also a legislation to support the exercise of regulatory power in order to make way for capitalist circulation through a privatisation of the property.[81] While the demands on Christiania to register its population in 1972 were linked to its cooperation with the social authorities, the demands for registration in 2003 were first and foremost an issue of registering individual claims to property. Christiania's official position when faced with an ultimatum in 2008 was however that the key issue of the Freetown's future is its collective use of property. Undoubtedly, this is a constitutive element of Christiania as a Freetown.

HAPPY EVER AFTER? THE WELFARE CITY IN BETWEEN THE FREETOWN AND THE NEW TOWN

Signe Sophie Bøggild

> 'From Tingbjerg at one end of Copenhagen, where everything is quite heartlessly regulated and normalised and forced into the right shapes, one can follow the no. 8 bus route to the other end of Copenhagen to Christiania, where everything is free, many think *too* free.'[1]

The above quote from 1976 is a description by Danish urban planning's grand old man, Steen Eiler Rasmussen, of the difference between his own totally planned New Town Tingbjerg and the squatted, self-organised Freetown. Condensing post-1968 planning scepticism, it introduces the individual/user/inhabitant to alternative aspects of urban welfare, inspired by a new discourse of the social.

Using the occasion of Christiania's 40th birthday to rethink past experiences to imagine the future, I will examine the relationship between Tingbjerg and Christiania in a retroactive cultural-historical perspective: How they were created from planned and unplanned conditions, lost control over their own narrative, and are currently being reconfigured by new policies, plans and actors fighting with narratives to redefine them.

The New Town and the Freetown are conventionally regarded as contrasting phenomena within recent urbanism. Yet, their historical development — individually and mutually — makes it productive to study contact zones where they overlap and affect each other. The former is planned from tabula rasa, the latter superimposed on an urban palimpsest, yet both embody radical changes since the post-war period, still marking Copenhagen/Denmark as frontiers for construction and reconstruction, definition and redefinition of the welfare city. Searching for new urban communities and ideals of 'the good life' with diverging strategies and points of departure, Christiania and Tingbjerg emerged with the welfare society when reconceptualisation of urban spaces was crucial to frame transformations of lifestyles. Today, the social democratic utopia and the anarcho-socialist enclave are treated as urban others: 'the ghetto' and 'the freak', containing the poor, the immigrants and those off the norm, needing to be reintegrated into society's law and order via urban planning.

Tracing a story, unfolding between the two Copenhagen districts, of a modernist welfare city, contested by postmodernists in the broadest sense and a homogenous welfare state, marked by globalisation processes, I will analyse relations between the planned New Town and the unplanned Freetown, through transformations of the built-up environment (the physical spaces) and the narratives about it (the mental/discursive spaces). Since the cases constitute contested urban spaces and debates over Danish urbanism, I will first introduce the becoming of Tingbjerg and Christiania, mirroring social engineering and social movements respectively. Second, I will examine post-1968 planning ambivalence through Eiler Rasmussen's perspective on the Freetown as a corrective to his vision of the New Town. Third, I will relate the general disappointment with the planned welfare city to alternative strategies for urban welfare, adding softer social values to urban planning while introducing the actor of the individual/user/inhabitant, beginning with the Situationists. Writing at a time when the welfare city and welfare society are being renegotiated, I will lastly examine how urban planning is reintroduced as a political instrument, disciplining cities and citizens, in current plans for normalising the Freetown and anti-ghettoising the New Town.

Squatting the Freetown Christiania: Imagining Alternative Aspects of Urban Welfare

When Tingbjerg was completed in the early 1970s, Copenhagen still suffered from a housing shortage. Together with post-1968 practices and discourses, promoting social issues and individual emancipation, this produced unplanned phenomena, exploring new models for welfare and organisation in alternative communities: island camps, communes, the Thy Camp (1970), and most famously Christiania (1971). While planning more suburban tabula rasa New Towns, Copenhagen Municipality executed slum clearance. As old tenements were condemned, young Copenhageners took matters into their own hands, squatting houses like Sofiegården on the island of Christianshavn in central Copenhagen. After the eviction of Sofiegården's bohemian 'pre-Christiania' (1969), 'Slumstormers' transgressed the fence surrounding Bådsmandsstræde Barracks, also on Christianshavn.

A few months earlier the military had abandoned the area, but the state owner had neither executed future plans, nor formed a new national government. Exploiting the power vacuum, the trespassers proclaimed the squatted territory as the Freetown Christiania on 26 September 1971. As a performative act the event *took place* without a regulating master plan, yet like Tingbjerg it was a social experiment, testing new lifestyles of the welfare society.

Whereas Tingbjerg developed generically from scratch, Christiania is characterised by process and human activity — existing structures, mutating into something else: Historical buildings appropriated for new purposes, nomadic caravans becoming increasingly permanent houses, crafted self-builder villas reinventing environment-friendly vernaculars. As a romantic landscape garden, quirky names like Mælkebøtten (the Dandelion) and landmarks like a Tibetan stupa mark local places, while the infrastructure consists of paths, trod by Christianites. Cars are prohibited on the territory, indicated by a graffiti-covered fence with open gates.

Copenhageners and tourists can visit, but need permission to settle. Joining consensus democracy and private initiative, Christiania is a porous enclave with cultural venues, enterprises, independent institutions and 14 self-administrating neighbourhoods with local committees, maintaining basic facilities. An offspring of 1968 counterculture and social movements, organising alternatively and mobilising nonconforming identities, the Freetown is a toleration zone for individuals who do not fit into the public welfare-system. Having outreach to Greenlanders, the homeless, orphans, etc. Christiania collaborates with the municipality, providing space for unconventional production of subjectivity, e.g. hippies dropping out of society's rat race or gays, creating a community centre in Bøssehuset (see Cathrin Wasshede's chapter in this book). Accommodating around 900 people, some on welfare, others well-off, Christiania is thus more diverse than most Copenhagen districts. Everybody pays the same 'rent' to the joint moneybox plus basic facilities, regardless of whether they inhabit a self-builder villa on the waterfront or a ramshackle caravan. Before the present building stop, Christianites could put as much effort as they liked into their dwellings, but they can neither own them, nor take the property's value with them when leaving.

Although Christiania is a social grassroots phenomenon, it is also a product of failed normalisation attempts through urban planning and legislation. While Copenhagen Municipality first lobbied for planning a New Town on the site, unresolved negotiations with political parties and ministries, taking turns at administering the area, allowed the Freetown to develop in a permanent state of exception for over 40 years. Initially, the Christianites named themselves 'settlers' (*nybyggere*), sharing a destiny with Tingbjerg's first inhabitants, often called 'pioneers'.[2] In both places, 'old rats', experiencing radical changes since the pioneer period, have a special status. Aging with their neighbourhood, their life is intertwined with the trajectory of the New Town and the Freetown respectively.

Beginning from Tabula Rasa

Aspects of the planned New Town and the unplanned Freetown, official and unofficial narratives about them, still influence contemporary discourses and practices of the urban. Storytelling is a key when initiating urban projects, but has always worked to justify decisions, implement solutions, and frame values.[3] Plans are adjusted and architecture shifts functions. Likewise, planned stories about them change and mix with unplanned physical transformations and narratives. Like the city's shape or image, you can loose control of its narrative. It acquires its own logic and develops through self-generated narratives, based on certain incidents: political events, cultural change, crises, and autonomous cultural developments like the Slumstormers proclaiming Christiania on former military ground. Nevertheless, people once had high hopes of managing society through master plans and narratives, as in the planning of Tingbjerg from scratch.

Making his 'Iron Curtain Speech' on 5 March 1946, Churchill drew the Cold War's geopolitical map, dividing the world into two main spheres of interest. After the calamities of World War II, urban planning and social engineering became political instruments to make cities and citizens, acting crazily, urban again. Planners from around the globe gathered at the urban planning congress in Hastings, arranged by The International Federation of Housing and Planning in 1946. Cleaning the slate, New Towns multiplied in the footsteps of Congrès Internationaux d'Architecture Moderne (CIAM) and Le Corbusier's modernist codex of hierarchical, rational zoning, ordering of functions, and Howard's garden city.[4]

These fresh-start cities look alike. Planning methods were similar — even between ideologically opposed systems. Scandinavian welfare cities, American suburbs, socialist workers towns and new postcolonial capitals were based on the same planning scheme, but varied at the narrative level, because they wanted to tell different stories of future happiness, underpinned by political interests. Not the intimacy of home, but a community's 'public happiness', taking place within the public domain. Planners staged icons, supporting promises of happiness, defined by clients, politicians, developers, marketing experts, etc. These icons aimed to shape people's minds, while realising the imagined prospects. Influenced by cultural-historical conditions and political contexts they became stories: Urban landscapes reflecting ideals and ideologies, e.g. Marxist narratives of history's culmination in communism, or American economist Walt Rostow's capitalist story about stages of economic development, leading to self-sufficient growth.[5]

Social Democratic Utopia

The Danish welfare city's social democratic utopia developed between planned economy and capitalism. Urban planning worked as a disciplining tool to regulate what the governing Social Democrats (Socialdemokraterne) welfare programme (1945) designated as a latent conflict between public and private economic interests.[6] Entitled *DENMARK OF THE FUTURE*, it proposed a politics of egalitarianism, justice, and redistribution, supported by a moral foundation of social indignation and solidarity. Envisioning full employment, social security and democratisation of business, social engineering was indispensable:

> Everybody agrees that a new and better world — a new and better Denmark — must be built. However the new and better does not come independently — not automatically. Someone must have the will to create it — someone must have worked through plans for how this can be done.[7]

This dream of a modern welfare Denmark produced a lubricated urban planning machine within the growing public sector, based on Keynesian economic policies of state-regulated capitalism, constituting the Ministry for Housing and Construction (1947) and the Building Regulation Law (1949).[8]

Documenting life in dark, unhealthy tenements, Jørgen Roos and

Bror Bernild's photo book *Can We Allow Ourselves This?* (1946), raised debates on slum-like housing conditions. Like Jakob Riis' images of New York, it reaffirmed the need for urban planning. Consolidated in 1947, Copenhagen's *Finger Plan* was initiated during the German occupation of Denmark. Due to mounting urbanisation, industrialisation, and rural-urban migration, this regional plan intended to release pressure on Copenhagen's medieval core. It redirected urban development to semi-independent satellite districts along 'fingers', with housing and public transport connecting these New Towns with the capital.

The name refers to this layout of a hand with built-up areas and green wedges between the fingers. Co-planner Steen Eiler Rasmussen, Royal Danish Academy of Fine Arts, the Copenhagen School of Architecture's first urban planning professor (1924), called the Finger Plan 'the glove for the hand'.[9] Unlike Stockholm's metropolitan network of satellite towns, the Finger Plan was only partially realised, but simultaneously he began planning one of Copenhagen's first New Towns with the landscape architect Christian Sørensen.

Planning the New Town of Tingbjerg: Imagining the Welfare City

Constructed between the mid-1950s and early 1970s, Tingbjerg is an icon of the cradle-to-grave welfare city (developing between 1950–80) with its ensemble of housing, public institutions and modern lifestyle within the neighbourhood.[10] Situated 10 km northwest of Copenhagen Town Hall this 'model city' was inspired by Mumford's neighbourhood planning and the English New Towns.[11] Committed to creating welfare and community for future inhabitants, schools, collective laundrettes, library, sports facilities, kindergartens, home for the elderly, church and shopping street, etc. were fixtures of the urban design, echoing the social democratic/modernist Zeitgeist of progress, collectivism and egalitarianism.

Tingbjerg was planned on old farmland, bought by Copenhagen Municipality around 1900, and later parcelled into allotment gardens. Embraced in the natural setting of Vestvolden and Utterslev Mose, it comprised a green pocket, safe from the city centre's decaying tenements. Rose pergolas, trees and berry bushes completed the healthy environment, with its clean air, meeting places and common activities. Accessibility to downtown Copenhagen was reduced to one public bus line, although the Finger Plan suggested a local train station. Path systems protect children, whereas converging streets stimulated contact between locals.

Most dwellings are located in long, low blocks in yellow brick with characteristic white shutters. As a local landmark a 12-storey high-rise block overlooks the district. Intending to provide housing of equal standards, Tingbjerg's rental apartments are administered by the public housing organisations FSB, KAB and SAB, with eight independent housing departments. As elsewhere in Scandinavia, public housing was labelled as 'common housing' (almennyttigt boligbyggeri) for everybody, regardless of class, income and education, rather than blue-collar 'social housing'.

...Still Something Important is Missing

Although Tingbjerg was designed as a semi-independent New Town, it belongs to Copenhagen Municipality. Starting from tabula rasa Eiler Rasmussen recognised the difficulties of creating a lively social environment: something less hands-on than designing institutions, entertaining teenagers or nursing the elderly, yet crucial for a happy living environment. Using captions like 'A Social Programme', 'The Human Society of Tingbjerg' and 'The Inhabitants' Wellbeing', he proudly explains how his master plan uses the site optimally, while fearing qualities lacking:

> If you examine a modern residential area, you will often find that even if there is all that must be there according to various rules, then there is still something important missing. With all respectability, with all friendly gardens and decent houses the town can still be sad and dead boring to live in. It becomes a place that people inhabit, but they don't live there. You must set as your goal the creation of human surroundings that can enable every inhabitant to unfold in the most harmonic and richest way. There can indeed be extreme differences in the skills people have and desire. However, if they feel that there are not conditions for them to develop they become cowed. Some become sluggish and dead, others can seek an outlet for their energy in more or less asocial undertakings from simple destruction to romantic gangster groups' hustling and all kinds of youth crime.[12]

Before planning Tingbjerg, Eiler Rasmussen researched different neighbourhoods, including Saxogade in the city district of Vesterbro. He learned that Saxogade residents, like Sonja and her single-mother Norma, portrayed in a social-realist children's TV show (1968), preferred a crossbreed between small town intimacy and urban buzz to CIAM-like skyscrapers in park environments. Hence, Tingbjerg combines greenery with the historical city's density that Le Corbusier called 'cancerous' in Paris' case and the street's meeting place, hated by this grey eminence of modernism.[13] Materially, Tingbjerg was luxurious to pioneers swapping Vesterbro tenements with well-equipped homes. Regenerated in the 1990s, Vesterbro has become a creative class favourite while Tingbjerg is now seen as society's new slum, stigmatised as an 'immigrant ghetto' and used as the location for Per Fly's film *The Bench* (2000) about society's backside.

Confident in Tingbjerg's double attraction of nature and closeness to central Copenhagen, Eiler Rasmussen still warned about the risk of creating a 'ghetto', if public housing developed into allotted social housing, containing poor inhabitants of Copenhagen's slums, awaiting renovation.[14] He imagined a diverse population, integrating various segments into the New Town. To stimulate community and break the monotony of 'deserts of identical streets and houses [...] where the inhabitants have trouble feeling any belonging to the quarter', Tingbjerg was divided into neighbourhood units.[15] Mirroring social democratic ideals, single-family houses were absent and apartments relatively uniform, however close to gardens and playgrounds. Moreover, he opted for optimal conditions for children to socialise into well-educated/behaved citizens. Sørensen's invention — adventure playgrounds — became free zones for playhouse construction, cave making, gardening, animal care, etc.

Envisioning Tingbjerg's architecture as adaptable for later generations, a district satisfying requirements of a happy, modern lifestyle and social contact, Eiler Rasmussen recognised the New Town's handicap in competition with the historical city's cultural diversity.[16] Substituting authenticity with artificiality, he identified different needs and desires, subdividing future residents into categories: 'the infant', 'the kindergarten child', 'the school child', 'the half-grown', 'the adult', and 'the elderly'. Tingbjerg was bursting with good intentions, but was there space for everyone, considering the ritualisation and norms of lifestyles implied by the master plan, based on sociological surveys? Primarily designed for families, ten percent of the dwellings were earmarked for disabled and elderly people, while young adults had few options.

Rediscovering the Welfare City in Christiania

Perhaps surprisingly, Eiler Rasmussen was among the first professionals to recognise Christiania's potential. In the book *Around Christiania* (1976) he describes how plans to demolish 18 buildings to 'normalise' the 'social experiment' had left him sleepless. Remembering Denmark's undefended German annexation during World War II, Tingbjerg's architect feels inclined to speak up. Emphasising his point with the evocative memory image of bombed Warsaw, he questions the creation of a new tabula rasa in a thriving urban space, adding new cultural layers and alternative models of organisation:

> When you know how many solid houses there are, you must presume that dynamite will be used. It is going to look like when the Germans left Warsaw, so everybody can understand that there is no mercy. *You do not want to put up with people wanting to live in a freer society.*[17]

According to Eiler Rasmussen, Christiania emerged from a specific condition, caused by 'lack of planning' *before* the Slumstormers' arrival: After the military exit, Bådsmandsstræde Barracks was ravaged because no future plans existed. Thus, he regards the squatting of the territory as an act that saved preservation-worthy buildings from decay or deliberate destruction. Echoing 1970s' urban planning discussions, embedded in discourses of the social, as in social politics, social experiment, social state, social problems, etc., he proposes the counterfactual scenario whether Christiania would be necessary, if society was better arranged and geared to contain difference. *Through the Freetown*, however, he discovers the potential of a new actor in urban development — the user/inhabitant/individual, co-designing the framework of his/her life:

> For me, who has been occupied with the planning of dwellings and housing areas, Christiania has been a strange experience. Not in my wildest imagination could I have imagined that anything would come out of such chaos. It has not only been strange, but also uplifting, to see which positive forces there are in people — even those standing weakest — when you offer them the possibilities [...] You should not tear it down. You should build up our society, so there will not be need for any Christiania in the future![18]

Answering Copenhagen's Social Democrat mayor, Urban Hansen, anchorman behind the New Town Urban Planen near Christiania (likewise completed in 1971), Eiler Rasmussen defends the Freetown as a learning laboratory: For better or worse, Christiania is a more successful welfare city than Tingbjerg although the former is less comfortable than the latter. Putting forward an agenda to replace Christiania with an Urban Planen replica, Hansen mocks Eiler Rasmussen. How can the planner of Tingbjerg — a welfare city icon planned from tabula rasa like

Urban Planen — protect or even romanticise this enclave of squatting misfits, disobeying law and order?[19]

Juxtaposing Christiania and his pet project Tingbjerg, Eiler Rasmussen's response is branched. He stresses that people have chosen to live in Christiania whereas most inhabitants in Tingbjerg have landed there randomly: many are allotted to flats by public housing organisations out of need rather than by active choice. Due to a will of participation, the democratic ideal of tight local communities around the neighbourhood also seems more unfolded in the unplanned Freetown, organising itself into 14 self-directed, local areas, than in the New Town. Tingbjerg is an instant community where everything was in place from the beginning, planned and administered from above and outside (top-down). In contrast, Christiania is a process-driven community, growing gradually from below and inside (bottom-up), generated by local forces.

Thus, Eiler Rasmussen does not consider Tingbjerg, programmed to predict residents' needs, inclusive enough compared to Christiania, integrating or at least tolerating people beyond categorisation: Although the Freetown is 'no Sunday school' and some are outsiders, many Christianites are resourceful. It thrives by its multiplicity because of general solidarity between strong and weak, 'outweighing' each other. In Tingbjerg, people either enjoy (Eiler Rasmussen's daughter) or dislike (six-children families squeezed together like canned sardines in two-room flats by the municipality) living there.[20] Witnessing how teenagers with the 'right' conditions ravage youth clubs with healthy activities, well-meaning personnel, educating workshops, etc., he regrets the master plan's lack of openness towards reinterpretation and innovation.[21]

Installations and equipment are spartan, but unlike Tingbjerg's pampered urban space, Christiania's old buildings are adaptable for new purposes. Eiler Rasmussen compares the kindergartens he 'designed according to all the rules of the authorities' with Christiania's Children's House, a military wooden house without basic facilities: the latter is 'a real environment, friendly and familiar' — English experts even estimate it to be 'better and more interesting' than the former.[22] This fascination with the process, the slow and the self-organised also involves Christiania's anti-consumerism, its commitment to non-growth, sustainability and recycling of things dumped as waste material in Tingbjerg. The contrast repeats in the Freetown, superimposed on an urban palimpsest and reactivating historical architecture, and the New Town's context alienation, demolishing the existing to restart from scratch.

Planning Ambivalence — A Green Plant Between Cobblestones

From the above self-criticism or re-evaluation of Tingbjerg through lessons learned from Christiania, Eiler Rasmussen seems to rediscover his ideals of the welfare city, integrating life, architecture and nature, allowing people to come together and unfold happily in the Freetown. Christiania's new models/ideals of urban welfare still belong to a utopia of 'the good life', not necessarily actualised. Yet, the Freetown's counter-image permits him to indirectly formulate some of the unplannable *je-ne-sais-quoi (I don't know what)* qualities, he was searching for as the missing link in Tingbjerg's master plan. Reminding us that everything *could be* different from the status quo, the Freetown's utopian space — real or imagined — still affects the city as 'urban imaginary'.

Influenced by decrease and stagnation after the welfare society's golden age, relativising official plans and narratives, Eiler Rasmussen describes his broken dream of creating the welfare city in Tingbjerg:

> It had been my dream that people in Tingbjerg would move out of straitened conditions in the city to bigger space and *more freedom*. And now I saw a delusion of the plan: human beings left in institutions according to timetables, where you could control them from cradle to grave.[23]

Perceiving the unplanned, experimental Freetown as a 'corrective' to normal planning practice in a welfare society, managed by a strong municipal and state apparatus, turning individuals into clients and consumers, he describes Christiania through an organic metaphor:

> Correctly understood, Christiania can be an important corrective to a consolidated consumer society running wild. You could say that if you did not have Christiania you would have to invent it. Yet it cannot be done artificially because Christiania is a living budding life like a green plant between cobblestones. No paragraphs can create it. But they can crush it. Do not let it happen![24]

The image of a plant growing from the underground, following other logics than those institutionalised by society, recalls a famous statement of the avant-garde group of the Situationiste International (1957–72): 'under the pavement, a beach', a May 1968 motto, reversing instituted ways of creating welfare and community. Related to new agendas on how to be singular in the plural, it also affected Christiania's formation.

Attentive to unplanned places, buildings designed without architects, and industrial design, situationism believed that transformation would originate in appropriation and alteration of the urban environment. Their recipe for reorganising cities was simple: let citizens decide which spaces they want to inhabit and how they wish to live in them. Revolutionising practices of everyday life, this would undermine powers of state, bureaucracy, capital, and imperialism. Fearing modernist urban regeneration, Left Bank Parisian bohemians therefore introduced strategies of direct intervention in the human environment: *psychogéographie* (psychogeograhy), *détournement* (diversion), *dérive* (drift), and *urbanisme unitaire* (unitary urbanism).[25]

The subversive event of the Slumstormers penetrating the fence and proclaiming a Freetown, grafted on to the abandoned Bådsmandsstræde Barracks, and the 'urban imaginary' of an unplanned, non-consumerist city within the city, transgressing norms and regulations, evoke such situationist strategies. The same goes for the happenings of the Christiania-based performance-cum-activist collective Solvognen (the Sun Chariot), momentarily occupying Copenhagen's public space, and the reprogramming of the old military Field Magasin building (Loppen) by Christianites, becoming a veteran car museum, flea market, jazz club, exhibition space, printers and workshop, all admired by Eiler Rasmussen.

Planning Megalomania and Downscaling

As early as 1947, the Danish situationist artist Asger Jorn questioned the post-war period's 'planning megalomania', circling about aspects of the unplanned city, while defending the individual/user/inhabitant's creativity and freedom of agency. Under the provocative title 'Human Dwellings or Thought Experiments in Armed Concrete' he criticised the 'formalistic aesthetics', 'life-hostile' Platonic idealism, and rationalism, 'neglecting the individual human being's manifold development'. He further blamed the urge to construct 'private singular buildings', expressed in Le Corbusier's *The Home of Man* (1945).[26] Rather than designing for real human beings with idiosyncrasies and desires, modernist town planning was based on a human ideal, in Le Corbusier's case the *modulor*, a standard measurement equally workable in Chandigarh, India or Marseille, France. Jorn's countermeasure somehow anticipated the Slumstormers' squatting of the Christiania area, adding new layers of urbanity to the historical city without regulations or plan:

> [S]omeday Man will not anymore let houses, cities or areas etc. be constructed for him. Man will grow — and let grow, *Man will live — and let live*. The architecture of style confusion was a living architecture, constructed of ruined bits of earlier periods. The functionalists saw the dead and lifeless in the ruined bits, but they did not see the living and creative use of them and therefore they annihilated everything.[27]

While the impulse of New Town planners was to destroy and replace the existing with tabula rasa master plans, Jorn regarded the reprogramming of existing structures as a creative act, echoing Eiler Rasmussen's fondness of Christianites reinventing Bådsmandsstræde Barracks as Freetown. Both addressed the problem of bridging the gap between the individual's freedom to mark his/her living conditions and collective urban planning, underpinned by minimum standards and master narratives.[28] Needs, values and ideals of the good life differed, and urban welfare encompassed other aspects than the material comfort of the welfare city and society: freedom of expression, individuality, lifestyle, passion, identity, etc. If urban planning had future justification, it would give people space to experience this. Disagreeing with Le Corbusier about human instinct, Jorn downscaled the perspective on the urban from large-scale master planning to the scale of everyday human reality:

> What use however are these real visions when Corbusier himself thwarts Man's basic joys and when he reads Nature like the Devil reads the Bible. Human beings have become sterile because the order of society is sterile [...] Man's 'basic joys' are not 'sun, air and green trees', *but the possibility to build up, use and exercise his creative force and ability for the benefit and joy of his surroundings.* This presupposes that he gets full yield of his work, food, clothes, house, light, air and instead of the aesthetic pleasure of a bird's eye view of green treetops from 50th floor, *an active relationship with Nature*, and this demands that he can mark his surroundings unhindered as a free man, to form them according to his needs, also the architecture, if he so wishes.[29]

Originating in different contexts, Jorn and Eiler Rasmussen's planning ambivalence condenses into three key issues, characterising (postmodernist) urban discourse since the early 1960s, challenging modernism in its rationalist, functionalist forms, taking inspiration from new discourses of the social, and inspiring Christiania's proclamation: the individual/user/inhabitant's possibility of free expression and marking of the physical framework of his/her life, relations between the planned and the unplanned city, and 'the natural community'.[30]

Jorn, Eiler Rasmussen and postmodernist planning sceptics in the broadest sense thus emphasised how the production of urban space is always already related to the lives of human beings, taking place within it. In the precise formulation of an intellectual of the Situationiste International, Henri Lefebvre said: '(Social) space is a (social) process.'[31] From this perspective (urban) space is never stable, empty or Euclidian, but develops organically as an open process *with* the social in various guises.

Don't Panic it's Organic — Counter-Functionalist Discourse

In the same way as Eiler Rasmussen, godfather of Danish welfare city planning, felt inspired by Christiania's unplanned urbanism, the situationist artist Jorn was ambivalently fascinated by urban planning and its intention to provide human happiness. 1937–38 Jorn worked in Le Corbusier's studio, executing murals for the Pavillion des Temps Nouveaux. He even defended the principle of the neighbourhood, on which Tingbjerg was based, against the German sociologist Geiger, calling the neighbourhood a nest of crime and reactionary thinking at an urban planning meeting in Århus (1948) — not unlike 21st century critics calling Tingbjerg a ghetto, blaming the architecture for social problems. Replying that the local community was the best political bulwark against totalitarianism, it is the premises of urban planning based on rationalism and functionalism Jorn queries.[32]

Here, Eiler Rasmussen's metaphor of the green plant between cobblestones, acquires a new meaning of the multiplicity, inclusiveness and open-endedness of organic urbanism, transgressing the uniformity, stability, and one-dimensionality of the grid plan, loathed by situationists as metaphor for state regulation, beloved by Le Corbusier, aiming to make the city a reflection of a single, rational plan like Descartes.[33] At the Bauhaus, in Le Corbusier's manifestos, and through CIAM's constitution (1928), modernism had purified its image, marginalising unruly, eccentric elements for a functional, rational programme of universal, clean living. Originally strategies to offer normal people good design, functionalism and standardisation became synonymous with 'productivist' values of freewheeling capitalism or state communism, reducing Man to attachments of the machine rather than its drivers.[34]

From being a humanist leftist project, creating social progress and democracy, functionalism had the opposite effect on mass consciousness to that promised by modernists, believing that only reason could solve problems. Yet, for situationists like Jorn and other planning sceptics like the Christianites and, in his later years, Eiler Rasmussen, the bitter price for progress (e.g. the cradle-to-grave welfare city) was that collective interest overruled individual concerns.[35] The rationalisation of human environments produced passive submission, whereas 'real' social progress maximised the individual's freedom and potential.[36] To quote Eiler Rasmussen:

> Industrialism, which brought about a widely specialised division of labour and, indeed, attained great effectiveness by utilising and developing men's various abilities, also produced towns mechanically divided up into uniform sections, each one of them homogenous within its boundaries [...] In such uniform residential areas the inhabitants have little opportunity to develop fully and harmoniously through intercourse with many kinds of people. On the contrary, they become prejudiced and spiritually crippled.[37]

This counter-functionalist discourse was part of a bigger political project, overturning current practices of history, theory, art, politics, architecture and everyday life. Undressing the consumerist 'society of spectacle', Guy Debord wanted to emancipate the individual from the humdrum grind of work and consumption. Forwarding a self-realising lifestyle of creativity, freedom, inspiration and urban activism, the situationists inspired the countercultural 1968 student movements, fostering the Freetown Christiania, the squatter movement (BZ-bevægelsen), punk, and other postmodernist phenomena. Simultaneously, new social movements claimed that everything — including the personal — is political, questioning issues of identity, representation, civil rights, instituted systems, patriarchal structures, hierarchies, etc.

Learning from the Freetown

Hence, Christiania and the conception of urban spaces, transgressing society's norms and regulations, while pushing boundaries of urban welfare definitions, did not come out of the blue. Aesthetically and ethically, the Freetown shares similarities with the bourgeois revolutions, artistic avant-garde and the individual's emancipation since Romanticism. Not just artists and activists were influenced by the situationists' 'counter-functionalist' discourse and Christiania's alternative to rationalist urban planning. Like Eiler Rasmussen, architects more or less closely associated with the welfare society's planning machine were susceptible to radical ideas embedded in a new discourse of the social: Team Ten's break with CIAM and interest in the vernacular, Superstudio and Archigram's organic social structures, Jane Jacobs' defence of the historical city, Rudofsky's writing on architecture without architects, Gordon Matta-Clark's creatively destructive 'anarchitecture', Reyner Banham's planning-sceptical architectural history, Colin Rowe's fascination with Rome's 'collage city', Venturi's iconoclast learning from Las Vegas, Koolhaas' retroactive manifesto *Delirious New York*, and other postmodernist projects. In Denmark, Jan Gehl authored the classic *Life Between Buildings* (1971) simultaneously with Christiania's conception, shifting perspective from objects to social interaction. Experimenting with mapping the relation between life and architecture with his psychologist wife, Gehl now heads a successful office, facilitating post-planning projects, (re)animating life in cities worldwide: cultural layers in Copenhagen's 1990s New Town Ørestad, often criticised as lifeless, meeting places and bicycle lanes on Manhattan, etc.

Post-war New Towns like Tingbjerg were planned according to ONE master plan and narrative, dictated by public authorities. In the subsequent decades Copenhagen lost control over its narrative and experienced unplanned interventions, most noticeably Christiania. Today, more stakeholders (including the individual/user/inhabitant, private developers, real estate agents, NGOs, etc.) are renegotiating the city. Influenced by post-1968 and postmodernist practices and discourses, architects have thus incorporated aspects of the Freetown into contemporary planning culture: participation of the individual/user/inhabitant, values of individuality, innovation, creativity, multiplicity and empowerment; mixed functions, site-specificity, sustainable solutions, local democracy, small-scale, re-use and preservation of historical structures; focus on the urban process, culture, communication, dialogue and identity (branding); storytelling and impermanence as methods to initiate urban projects, etc. You can still discuss the premises and degree of democracy, openness, right of decision and veto, question formulation, disjunctions of power/knowledge, etc. Some also claim that architects know what is best, are better at being visionary-creative than populist-pedagogue, and that the modernist urban planning process was more transparent (who did what when?), although more hierarchical than today's flat urban networks, penetrated by new scales, actors and blurring of public/private, urban/rural, local/global, etc.

Nonetheless, Danish offices like ZARK, Metopos, Witraz and NORD, backed up by social sciences and humanities consultants like Hausenberg or 2+1 Idébureau, plunge into this morass of moderation and negotiation, offering services of outreach, communication and process facilitation — again full of good intentions. One of their good clients, Copenhagen Municipality, brands itself with slogans like 'cOPENhagen — Open for you' and 'Joint City', invites people to participate in socially engaged urban regeneration schemes such as *Områdeløft* ('neighbourhood lift'), and intends to develop Copenhagen's future New Town of Nordhavn organically over 50 years, rethinking the old harbour's urban palimpsest.

Welfairytales

Examining Tingbjerg and Christiania, we have seen how attitudes towards the planned and the unplanned city have changed on physical and narrative levels. While Tingbjerg's welfare city provided material comfort and public services to Copenhagen's house-hunting 'slum-dwellers', Christiania's Slumstormers opened people's eyes to more relative aspects of urban welfare. The paradigm shift from an overall goal of egalitarianism to a determining goal, focusing on the individual/user/inhabitant's right to self-realisation, produced new perspectives on the role of urban planning.[38]

As society transformed towards more individuality, narratives of public happiness were substituted with stories of private happiness, e.g. Christiania's enclave or the suburban single-family house. From the mid-1970s Tingbjerg's walk-up flats were voided of resourceful Danish families, choosing the building boom's private ownership. The predicted local workplaces never came, whereas unemployment, interest deduction and immigration grew. Public housing organisations allotted empty rental flats, increasingly subsidised, to those who could not afford to choose address. Suddenly, the 'unresourceful' and immigrants inhabited the welfare city that was designed for working Danish families. Crime rates and social problems grew while architecture decayed. Explaining Tingbjerg's master plan in 1963, Eiler Rasmussen prophetically wrote:

> Reality will probably form itself somewhat differently than the idealists have intended [...] Still it is important to avoid too much uniformity. If a housing estate or part of a housing estate becomes a sort of ghetto for one particular, less estimated, group of society, it can cause great harm for the inhabitants, not least the children. The housing corporations have experienced material damage to buildings in a town with a uniform bad clientele. It is something tangible that can be measured economically.[39]

This resembles contemporary media representations of Tingbjerg. The already difficult task of creating identity from scratch faced further challenges. After the utopias that defined their programme are faded or forgotten, New Towns are difficult to communicate and relate to current ideals. Contemporaries have trouble understanding why Tingbjerg was designed like it was, whilst various actors battle with narratives to redefine it in a state of 'representational crisis'.

When Denmark was more homogeneous, collectivism implied *lighed* = likeness and equality, but in an increasingly globalised world, the country and the capital city have diversified. Since the social democratic Scandinavian welfare model became the subject of dispute and lost hegemony — in Denmark around EU membership (1972), the Earthquake Election (1973) and the right-wing Foursome Government (1982) — two positions have dominated: Some nostalgise it as a golden past, associating progress, modernity and equal opportunities with ONE party. Others celebrate internationalisation and openness, replacing stagnation and social democratic dominance. Reflecting contemporary political quarrels more than historical scholarship, both perspectives are one-sided. Lately, more nuanced discussions of the welfare model's drawbacks and achievements appear in a complex field, renegotiating representation, ideology, identity, production of subjectivity, etc.[40]

Swedish geographer Lisbeth Söderqvist traces a new politicisation of welfare city discourse where social democratic policies and modernist principles are but obstacles for private initiative, economic development and 'Swedish values':

A political discourse has been transported into the field of architecture and urban planning. According to that, squares should be planned and built with the needs of corporations as point of departure. To more and more people, the publicly financed built-up environments articulate indeed another political discourse where the intervening state allows visions of equality and safety to overshadow economical realities.[41]

This shift is clearer in Denmark where the (neo-)Liberal Party (Venstre) and Conservatives (Det Konservative Folkeparti) supported by the nationalist Danish People's Party (Dansk Folkeparti) have governed for a decade. Using strategic urban planning to promote new narratives of public happiness, this also affects Christiania's future.

Cities in Treatment — The Freak and the Ghetto

A city marketing film presents Tingbjerg as an idyllic 'village within the city', recalling positive receptions of Christiania.[42] Once both represented radical utopianism, reinventing 'the good life' and local community. As ideals of the social democratic welfare model, modernist urban planning, artistic avant-garde, and anarcho-socialist 1968 counterculture are exhausted, forgotten, disillusioned or absorbed by mainstream culture, most contemporaries distrust such 20th century utopianism. After the Cold War era's confidence in master plans and narratives, utopias are continuously associated with authoritarianism and restriction, conceiving attempts to construct perfect societies or cities as something inherently repressive, even totalitarian.[43] Today, storytelling is crucial to initiate urban projects, but because planned and unplanned, official and unofficial narratives coexist, there is an ongoing struggle to decide who is 'master'. People know more about the functions of narratives and there are numerous ways to construct and use them under a meta-narrative about improvement and growth.

Sceptics criticise Christiania and Tingbjerg as (out)dated utopias becoming heterotopias[44] in society's margins — or even dystopias, nests for crime, drugs, social destitution, conspiracy, asocial behaviour, etc. Both serve as 'urban Others' through which normal people can identify themselves by observing 'the freak' or 'the ghetto' with every projection possible. In this process, the New Town and the Freetown are demarcated as outside spaces or non-places where socio-economic problems can be identified and contained although they concern society as a whole.[45] Moreover, both can seem provokingly exclusive or separate from society due to their strong sense of local community around the neighbourhood, expressed by Christiania's flag, fence and yearly birthday celebration, rap by Tingbjerg kids, showing affection for their 'hood' or Babylonian Tingbjerg dialect.[46]

Politically, the aging New Town and the middle-aged Freetown are treated as special cases in need of special laws — treatment and adaption. The general election on 27 November 2001 confirmed that the welfare debate is still contested ground, affecting the urban spaces, framing our lives. Both Tingbjerg and Christiania became political frontiers in the 'cultural struggle', announced by then Prime Minister Anders Fogh Rasmussen, echoing 1968 counterculture, yet opposing it as he now saw its legacy becoming consensus culture. Replacing the Social Democrats, the new (neo-)Liberal/Conservative government fused the Ministry of Housing with the new Ministry of Integration, Immigrants and Fugitives.

As in previous attempts to control Christiania through urban planning and social engineering, contributions to an ideas competition for a master plan for the area (2003) were shelved. The police cleared Pusher Street, while the parliament changed the 1989 Christiania Law in June 2004, again implying 'normalisation' (see Håkan Thörn's chapter in this book). Driving from pillar to post within a ramified bureaucracy for decades, Christiania is still soaring in a permanent state of exception, fostering lively public debates and, since 2006, a court case, Christianites versus the state. Christiania's manifesto reads:

> The aim of Christiania is to build a self-ruling society, where each individual can unfold freely while remaining responsible to the community as a whole. The society is to be economically self-sufficient, and the common goal must always be to try to show that mental and physical pollution can be prevented.[47]

Although much seems lost in translation in current negotiations between government bureaucrats and Christiania's collectivists, values underpinning this programme resemble Fogh Rasmussen's 1993 neoliberal manifesto *From Social State to Minimal State: A Liberal Strategy*. Both criticise the social democratic welfare state, defending the individual/user/inhabitant and his/her life world over general principles of egalitarianism and justice. Still, Christiania becomes object for integration like Tingbjerg, similarly playing a key role in the cultural struggle, as announced in Fogh Rasmussen's above-mentioned book:

> Actually a cultural struggle is needed. Perhaps this sounds slightly drastic. And I don't think about armed resistance. Yet, I use cultural struggle to underline the comprehensive character of the necessary position change. From the root we shall do away with collectivist norms, we have been drinking in with mother's milk, as it were. It will be a struggle against inherited habitual notions and decrepit, alleged truths.[48]

Then in his New Year Speech as Prime Minister (2002) he stated:

> We want to put Man before the system. The individual shall have more freedom to form his or her life. We want to do away with rigid systems, disempowerment and regimentation. We believe that human beings are best at choosing for themselves. We don't need experts and arbiters of taste to decide on our behalves.[49]

The (neo-)Liberal-Conservatives came into power shortly after 9/11, joining the Iraq and Afghanistan Wars, tightening security, anti-terrorism and immigration laws, while waking up to global connectivity with the Cartoon Crisis.[50] Against this background the cultural struggle became embedded in a new discourse of societal cohesiveness and Danishness, defining itself against societal fragmentation/segregation, globalisation and post-1968 culture/discourse. Located outside capitalist market forces, Tingbjerg's public rental housing, accommodating many immigrants, and Christiania's squatted enclave with collectivist ownerships and considerable autonomy, are treated as territories, lacking integration. As in the post-war period, urban planning becomes an instrument to (re)instate law, order and cohesion, now serving agendas of securitisation, zero tolerance, preservation, gentrification etc. — in our case normalisation and anti-ghettoisation.

Normalisation

Protecting patrimony via the Financial Law (2004), a national 'cultural canon' and instituting a national 'value commission' (2011), the cultural struggle's promotion of a certain narrative of Danish culture and values, included facts on the ground. Resisting 'red hired guns', 'circle pedagogy', 'arbiters of taste', 'cultural radicalism', windmills, etc., the fulcrum of debates on whether to clear or preserve Christiania shifted from social concerns to urban planning. Yet, as when Eiler Rasmussen wrote *Around Christiania,* the apple of discord in current normalisation efforts concerns demolition of architecture, new construction and ownerships: additional housing, openness towards the market and new segments, change of allotment rights, official registration at individual addresses replacing co-habitation of Bådsmandsstræde 43, street naming, and the clearance of self-builder houses on the embankment.

The latter mobilised the cultural struggle's competing fractions in discussions of patrimony, heritage and cultural history. The government's manager of the normalisation process, the Palaces and Properties Agency (Slots- og ejendomsstyrelsen) under the Ministry of Finance, wanted to clear self-builder villas, erected without permission, to restore the listed sea-and-land fortifications.[51] Christianites and supporters defended the houses, incarnating Christiania's history and architectural tradition. Explaining the preservation of 11 military buildings rather than 58 recommended by the Ministry of Culture's Special Building Inspection, or listing the entire area as a cultural environment, symbolising the history of alternative living with self-builder houses, hippies and Pusher Street, the Heritage Agency of Denmark's former director remarked:

> It is primarily the Heritage Agency of Denmark's task to list historical buildings more than 50 years old. Meanwhile, it is Copenhagen Municipality's role to deal with newer buildings worthy of preservation. Hence, it is the municipality's task to designate Christiania as a complete cultural environment.[52]

Once more it was complicated to categorise and place the responsibility for Christiania, too young to become protected heritage according to current law although many see it as a cultural institution of Copenhagen/Denmark. Together with hash dealing the government used the assumed 16 per cent increase in the built-up environment as an argument for normalisation, judging Christianites incapable of self-management. 130 cases of illegal construction motivated the majority of votes for changing the Christiania Law (2004). When the cases were put forward, October 2010, the Palaces and Properties Agency gave 92 permissions, 15 cases were dropped due to registration errors, 9 were terminated because the object had been removed, one is pending, whereas orders — or warnings about orders — have been issued in 13 cases. Regarding building cases, the Christiania Law is therefore founded on 90 per cent fictitious illegalities, as it were.[53]

Since then, the Palace and Properties Agency has raised new building cases. At the time of writing (February 2011) Christiania has decided to buy The Peace Ark (Fredens Ark) for one symbolic Danish krone, while losing its court case against the state (see René Karpantschof's chapter in this book). Reflecting the flux in Danish politics, the Social

Democrats and the Socialist Party in 2004 voted to change the Christiania Law, and now even demand more law and order, while the 1968 rebel attitude has become part of the consumer society.[54] After the trial, members of the (neo-liberal) corporate world defended Christiania, echoing the 'Think different' of Apple's hippie founder, Steve Jobs, and Richard Florida's mantra of the creative class/city, stressing the importance of innovation and identity in urban/global competition. In the service/knowledge economy Copenhagen's 'freak' adds more value to the city than say the hyper-discount markets, currently launched as economical magnets. After Tivoli and the Little Mermaid, Christiania is Denmark's biggest tourist attraction, making Wonderful Copenhagen's director warn against normalisation:

> Christiania is incredibly important for Copenhagen's brand internationally. If Denmark is to keep its brand as a cool, tolerant and broad metropolis it is crucial that Christiania can still call itself a Freetown.[55]

Listing commercial advantages, the advertising bureau Mensch launched a pro-Christiania campaign under the headline 'Danish trade and industry can still learn something from Christiania':

> It is easy to tear down. To demand adaption and normalisation. It is more difficult to jump out of normality. To think the unthinkable. Say the unutterable. But curiously it is the ability of Danish trade and industry to think differently that is our most important competitive factor.[56]

Jens Arnfred of the architectural firm Vandkunsten remarks: 'With Christiania's disappearance yet another of our national symbols of tolerance and diversity crumbles'.[57] Hence, cultural history with the narratives and structures we choose to tell, preserve (remember) or demolish (forget) is the wildcard in plans because cities develop differently than intended.

Anti-Ghettoisation

While planning Christiania's future, the newly elected government in 2001 focused on its inherited stepchild of the post-war welfare city when replacing the Social Democrats. On the narrative and strategic level the agenda altered from social engineering to 'anti-ghettoisation'. In May 2004, a programme committee against ghettoisation was instituted and this was followed in autumn 2010 by an 'anti-ghettoisation strategy'. The socialist opposition also introduced its own contra-solution. As the welfare society's new slum, the welfare city reappears as political spearhead — now linked to integration and promotion of 'Danish values' as new plans are superimposed on and in opposition to 'old failures'.

At the opening of the Danish parliament (Folketinget) in October 2010 the Prime Minister announced plans to tear down the high-rises in order to open up 'ghettos', mainly populated by people with immigrant backgrounds. He argued that these New Towns constituted 'black spots' that had developed into parallel societies without belonging to Danish Society.[58]

As with Christiania's normalisation, sticking points include demolition of architecture, new construction, allotment rights and ownerships. Currently, one of the 29 'ghettos' appointed by the government, Gellerup Planen near Århus, is a guinea pig for Danish history's largest makeover. For the first time locals have voted for the demolition of three housing blocks to open up the district and construct a shopping street. Århus calls Gellerup's master plan 'a historical opportunity', while the Social Minister gives assurances that this anti-ghettoisation will 'be a good inspiration for the comprehensive plans that are going to be prepared elsewhere'.[59]

To upgrade identity and quality, Tingbjerg has undergone all kinds of revitalisation initiatives in the early 1990s and the early 2000s, including a 'neighbourhood lift', rebuilding 165 one-room flats into 70 bigger family apartments, optimising lighting, while adding playgrounds, bicycle paths, squares and new balconies for the high-rise block. Yet, like most of the 28 remaining 'state-authorised ghettos', the director of Tingbjerg's tenant association dislikes Gellerup's renewal through demolition:

> I don't believe in it. We already have the arrangement that one family member must be employed to settle [in Tingbjerg]. This means that you get stronger inhabitants out here. What could make a difference was if you could find jobs for people and create some leisure activities.[60]

After the urban regeneration of the 1990s and the real estate and construction boom of the 2000s, generated by prospects of individual happiness for those who can afford to choose where to live, New Towns like Tingbjerg attract attention as containers of socio-economic problems. Like Thatcher, the government allowed renters to buy their homes in 2005: So far, 45 out of 550,000 public dwellings have been sold, whereas demand for public housing has snowballed since the global recession.[61]

Although outsiders mostly know Tingbjerg's bad stories, four out of five of the 6,000 residents are 'very satisfied or satisfied' with their district, fulfilling many requirements of the good neighbourhood through many associations, clubs and Denmark's first local resident TV station, while regretting its negative reputation. As one local explains: 'you get [negatively] branded, when you live in a ghetto'.[62] Since Tingbjerg's 'neighbourhood lift' it has been difficult to attract the more resourceful to Arkaderne's refurbished family dwellings in ground floor apartments with their direct access to common green spaces and private terraces. The public housing organisation, KAB, expected these apartments to 'become the most attractive, but the negative mention of Tingbjerg, burglary and other crime have created insecurity, and therefore it is harder to rent them out'.[63] Thus, it seems relevant to consider whether resourceful families will pull up stakes and locals integrate more if Tingbjerg is reaffirmed as a 'ghetto' or 'black spot', undergoing *anti*-ghettoisation.[64]

Negative discourse obscures the activation of inherent potentials, communication of stories of inclusion and of the 'public happiness' Eiler Rasmussen intended. By promoting values and strategies that deliberately oppose modernist principles and social democratic policies, remotely connected to socio-historical contexts — both the master plan's 'master narrative' and unplanned, multicultural layers grafted on to it — there is a risk of reproducing present predicaments, creating a new tabula rasa, while the ghetto image sticks.[65]

The Joker of History

Embodying two approaches to the urban, the New Town and the Freetown have marked the welfare society's recent history, framing new lifestyles in the cradle-to-grave welfare city's material security/comfort and Christiania's alternative model for urban welfare. City life has been reinvented by post-war period's years trust in urban planning and social engineering, promoting official narratives of public happiness, and the planning-scepticism and social discourse of the post-1968 era, proliferating into self-generated cultural layers and narratives of the city. Interwoven with minor narratives of shifting inhabitants and major narratives of the neighbourhood, the city, the country, and the world at large, Christiania and Tingbjerg have thus developed differently than contemporaries could have imagined.

Occupying attractive land in central Copenhagen near water, but outside market forces, Christiania's collectivist ownership displeases the government in the same way as Tingbjerg's public housing, inhabited by immigrants and the 'unresourceful'.[66] Continuing to affect the city as debated territories, politicians aim to (re)integrate 'the ghetto' and 'the freak' into society, using urban planning as problem solver. While (re)staging them ideologically as urban icons through anti-ghettoisation and normalisation, the city has learned from the unplanned Freetown and is now renegotiated by more stakeholders, including the individual/user/inhabitant, ideally participating in shaping the frameworks of his/her life.

Like other New Towns, Tingbjerg is still often described as an unhistorical district, lacking identity — perhaps it concentrates 'too much' culture and history, imported from more 'exotic' regions of an increasingly globalised world: a large immigrant population diversifies Tingbjerg in other ways than Eiler Rasmussen intended. While the negative reputation sticks, few visit the New Town's architecture, classified as 'highly preservation worthy'. The international press has written more about the Freetown than all the region's other districts together. Christiania's identity is strong, like its presence in the heart of Denmark's capital. Unlike the 'urban oases' of the 2000s, such as Tuborg Havn and Islands Brygge, it is open to outside inputs, as a heterotopia or urban imaginary where you can envision things being different.

Proclaiming their right to mark their own life's framework, Slumstormers appropriated Bådsmandsstræde Barracks, reversing existing orders and hierarchies, including those governing the modernist welfare city (see Anders Lund Hansen's chapter in this book). At 40, the Freetown is neither controlled by a public planning apparatus, nor by a private real estate market, escalating before the global recession. Yet, Christiania both faces inner and outer challenges: hash-selling rocker tycoons, associated with an ethos of violence and trafficking, incompatible with hippie ideals of peace, love and harmony, and the losing of the trial against the state about user rights in the territory. Some compromise, involving urban planning, will probably be reached between Christianites and politicians, perhaps thinking twice in light of current support by industry and trade for Christiania as a value-adding brand. Some even suggest *planning* more Christianias — leaving plots open to develop organically without regulations or profit-driven developers.

It is harder to imagine Tingbjerg's tabula rasa plan overtaken by squatters, although many 'third world' cases of New Town appropriations exist, e.g. *bidonvilles* becoming bazaars in Candilis-Woods' Casablanca grid-plan or slum-dwellers' adaptation of an ex-dictator's abandoned prestige project, 23 Enero in Caracas.[67] The Copenhagen municipality and the Danish state with its tradition of top-down planning are still robust. Nonetheless, the last two decades have encouraged user-driven innovation and public private partnerships, stimulated by post-1968 discourse/culture and a neoliberal political shift, both affirming individual emancipation.

It might be in its criticised anonymity that Tingbjerg is open to reinterpretation, such as when Eiler Rasmussen admired the adaptability of Christiania's historical military architecture. Re-examining the global repetition of a modernist planning scheme, framing different narratives of public happiness and experiencing different afterlives, the New Town becomes the place where everything can happen. You cannot preserve everything with a story, but like post-war master plans and narratives, present plans for Christiania and Tingbjerg rely on values, ideals and choices affecting many people. Embodying the welfare society's cultural history and today's globalised world, discussions over which works in the 2010s are therefore important. Rethinking the city, one objective must thus be to identify principal stories locally to expand on them and re-use qualities.[68]

As Popper argued in *The Poverty of Historicism* in 1957, you cannot predict everything although claiming a position at the height of history, enables you to plan ahead through general regularities.[69] From plan to city, history is the joker, because things never go as planned. Popper's early reply to the claimed authority of master plans and narratives, points towards a seed of resistance within the New Town as socio-cultural phenomenon. Reminding us of this unplannable 'je-ne-sais-quoi' quality and transgressing normal orders, the self-generated Freetown still works as 'corrective' to the planned city, as it did for Eiler Rasmussen. History will show the effects of Christiania's normalisation and Tingbjerg's anti-ghettoisation. Either way, changing narratives of the welfare city — planned and unplanned — testify to how Danes relate to the past, present and possibly the future of the welfare society in Denmark, presumably the happiest country in the world.

THE HANSEN FAMILY AND THE MICRO-PHYSICS OF THE EVERYDAY

Maria Hellström Reimer

One of the dates of faith in the history of Christiania is 1 April 1976. After some years of vacillating on the so-called Christiania question, in the spring of 1975 the Danish parliament had finally set the deadline for the clearance of the Freetown. Some three months before the planned clearing, however, a documentary entitled *Dagbog fra en fristad* (*Diary from a Freetown*)[1] was broadcast on national television. This documentary by Danish filmmaker Poul Martinsen followed the 'typical' Danish family Hansen from Hedehusene, a suburban city between Copenhagen and Roskilde, on their visit to Christiania. Featuring Eli Hansen, an unemployed construction worker in his forties; Lise Hansen, a home helper in her late thirties; and their two sons, Morten, eleven and Jesper, sixteen years old, as they agreed to spend a week in the Freetown, the documentary provided a combined insider/outsider perspective of the contested area. While the family initially held the view that the community should be closed, by the end of the week Mr and Mrs Hansen and their two sons had changed opinion. Having shared the daily life of the Christianites, the family was much closer to the view that Christiania presented an alternative that should remain. Transmitting a shift in attitude, the televised stay of the Hansen family eventually made the government understand that a clearance was politically impossible, and only two days before the planned closure, the government launched the idea of a 'soft landing', changing the demand for immediate closure to a closure 'without unnecessary delay.'[2]

When the Danish broadcasting company through Poul Martinsen twelve years later staged a revisit, *Gensyn med Christiania* (*Return to Christiania*), the Hansen family was confronted with an equally contested, yet perhaps even more precarious situation. While everyday life in the mid-seventies was a self-evident public and political concern, it had by the late eighties become harder to locate and picture. Taking the point of departure in Martinsen's project about the Hansens' sojourns in the Freetown, this chapter will address the composite relationship between social experimentation, documentary practice and the ambiguous and yet politically charged notion of 'everyday life'.

The *Diary*: Emergent Patterns

The Hansen family is 'an ordinary family', at least by seventies' standards. An exceedingly ordinary family, one would say, were it not so contradictory. When we first encounter the family members, sometime in the late autumn of 1975, they are gathered in the living room of their standard apartment — Eli, the father and husband, a sturdy construction worker, comfortably reclining in what seems to be his favourite armchair; the two more or less lanky and blond boys, Jesper and Morten, crowded together in the sofa with their mother Lise, a bit less comfortably positioned, although in her stocking feet. The atmosphere is homely, warm and cosy; the colours neutral to natural, a brownish wall-to-wall carpet emphasising the snug feeling. Placed against the wall are some scatter cushions, on the teak table in front there is an empty bowl and a ceramic vase of Scandinavian design, and in the corner we catch a glimpse of what seems to be a reasonably new TV set.

A stereotypical social constellation in a stereotypical setting; yet, the frontality of the camera in relation to its ordinary motif stresses the peculiarity of the situation. As representatives of the average Danish nuclear family, the four individuals have been selected and invited to pay a week's visit to the controversial fringes of Danish society. And somewhat hesitantly, they have accepted. In a week's time, they are going to break with their normal routines in the drowsy municipality of Hedehusene, exchanging them for the certainly much more exposed and much more exigent everyday whereabouts of the Freetown Christiania in Copenhagen.

This staged change of location was part of a documentary film project initiated by the Danish Broadcasting Company and the filmmaker Poul Martinsen. The aim was to actualise one of the most burning questions of Danish domestic politics at the time; that of urban everyday life and how to shape it. The Freetown had offered a radical and agitating do-it-yourself answer, which the authorities, after four years of pondering, now had dismissed. The time had come, however, for ordinary people to have a say too.

Dagbog fra en fristad (46 min), the initial documentary, starts off with the ordinary family's expectations of their visit to the infamous squatter community. As the camera by way of introduction zooms in on the family, the neutral voice-over introduces the issue at hand and poses the opening question. Eli, the father, gives a self-assured impression.

'My immediate opinion about Christiania,' he says, 'is close the shit-hole.'

As he continues, he does not moderate his statement.

'What you hear from there is about hash problems, thefts, criminals and on the whole asocial behaviour.'

At the same time, he recognises the political dimensions of the situation. To a certain extent, the responsibility belongs to society. As a politically conscious manual worker Eli means that society also has to do some work before they say 'shut it'.

The focus shifts to Jesper, the teenager. He is a bit more hesitant as regards the Freetown.

'It's possible that it's crummy, but that goes for many other places as well.'

Morten, on the other hand, the eleven year old, is more than happy in his practically furnished boys' room, which he shares with his brother. He cannot imagine moving long-term to a place like Christiania. Lise, his mother, is even more explicitly dismissive.

'I know it's grimy in there and I reckon we will have to burn our clothes once we get back.' The close-up shot of Lise's face sustains the impression of a veritable, bodily repulsion.

As the family pulls in by the Freetown, the imagery of ingrained dirt is somehow lingering. The visit takes place in November, and the ramshackle old barracks area certainly gives a rough and gloomy impression, emphasised as the red taxi disappears out of frame. Even though the film is in colour, the range of nuances is narrow. From a contemporary point of view this could be read as a kind of historical marker, a trace of the aesthetic preferences of the time. Yet, the roughness also has a situating effect, paradoxically reinforced as the catchword 'FREE' appears on the derelict wall—a reminder of the grand expectations that, despite everything, hover in the air.

While the arrival in the Freetown is depicted as a precarious passage on to unknown territory, the reception of the family is represented as overwhelmingly cordial, the camera following close in the footsteps of the family members as they are being embraced by a motley crew of long-haired people of different sex and age. These initial, fumbling scenes of kinship are, however, soon replaced by more hands-on acts of fraternisation, as Eli has to step into the breach to fix a collapsed sewage pump. While Eli's strong and experienced arms in this way immediately come in handy, Lise cannot but confirm her sensory unease. After a first sleepless night in the Nova housing cooperative, the anonymous storyteller behind the camera again asks her to give voice to her reactions.

'It really smells out here, they have dogs and horses and pigs and I don't know what… That is to say it smells all the way, I can hardly stand that smell, I had to lie underneath the quilt all night in order to keep it out.'

Later, we are presented with yet another close-up of Lise, now a visitor in the kitchen of a young mother of four, who lets the pony reside in the corner. In dialogue with the young women, she continues to object to what she sees as an unworthy way of living, at the same time defending her own everyday skills.

'Understand me right — surely I am capable of judging whether it is dirt from today, yesterday or from fourteen days ago. I can indeed.'

As the second day continues, the battle with the elements goes on, yet on a different scale. One of the family's assignments during the week is to join the garbage tour. From one of the rooftops, the camera surveys Eli, Lise and Jesper as they travel around the area perched on an old red tractor decorated with a white heart. The framing of the landscape is obvious. Tracing their meandering route, the camera zooms in on different sorts of heaps along the way. Everywhere they go, there are stacks and lots with more or less identifiable content: along the road a pile of paving stones; on an old house plot a rusty old bike and some other metal scrap; outside the houses, stacks of old planks and pieces of furniture, all in different degrees of decay. As they drive over to the outer part of the moat, the neck of land called Dyssen, a bleak sun breaks through and wraps the littered landscape in a forgiving and favourable haze.

Commenting on the people he meets along the way, Eli gives voice to a reflection.

'They are simply people who have a very relaxed attitude towards the entire existence and they live more or less as we did in farming society a hundred years back, without heating and without electricity.'

During the course of the tour, a deeper understanding of the landscape develops, including its heap economy. As Eli points out, the stacks of scrap are not just a sign of negligence.

'It has something to do with the way Christiania is being heated; with the use of tiled stoves and iron stoves, and the agreements with demolition entrepreneurs in the city, who dump combustible material here for use.'

As the days go by, the family seems to merge with the landscape, the passages from one day to another represented by overview shots. When Thursday comes, we see Eli in his chequered pompom hat (which by now has become somewhat of a symbol for the hybridisation of the ordinary and the alternative) as he is contentedly crossing Mælkevejen (The Milky Way). He is on his way back to the Nova cooperative, and on his shoulders he is carrying a substantial bundle of wooden bits and pieces. Heavy and sprawling, the package would not immediately go through the entrance door, but after some grubbing, Eli manages to get his pickings inside. As the door closes, we can follow the familiar sound of clogs climbing the stairs.

If the outdoor environment of the Freetown in 1975 provided one important theme, the interiors, withdrawn from public view, provided another. And while the public spaces stand out as decaying yet allowing, cluttered yet open-ended, unpruned but thriving, the interiors are as ambiguous. Having complained about unpleasant odours, on the very first evening Lise joins in the preparations in the common kitchen of the Nova cooperative. Provisional but homey, the kitchen is crammed with well-used cooking utensils and quite outdated equipment, and in the limited and narrow space, the hand-held camera follows the hectic activity closely. On the tiny gas stove, several large cauldrons are simmering, and in the little oven below, carrots and Jerusalem artichokes are being baked. While watching the intensive activity, Lise comments on the lack of planning.

'We were supposed to have dinner at eight but it was almost half past nine before the food was on the table'.

Yet, dinner is well attended. Children and adults throng around the table, and some even have to stay to the sides, along the walls of the dining room, informally reaching out over the table in order to serve themselves.

Wednesday's dinner is even more intense. It is being prepared in Mælkebøtten (The Dandelion), another of Christiania's housing cooperatives, also the home of Christianias aktionsteater (Christiania's Action Theatre). After rehearsals, a figure in a black hat enters the frame, theatrically calling to dinner, banging on a cask. Meanwhile, today's chef-in-charge, the young mother we met before, puts the finishing touches to the meal she has created. Lise is impressed, and the camera takes her curious perspective. In an old baking stove, the young woman has prepared four ducks. She has also made red cabbage and salad, and she has, as Lise points out, also gathered the required wood for the heating of the stove herself, while taking care of four kids at the same time. Around thirty people have gathered; everyone in the best spirits as the golden brown ducks are brought to the table. Eli rises from his chair and takes on the responsibility of the husband, carving the steaming ducks. Lise, now acting as storyteller, certainly sees the advantages of the arrangement. Having planned and prepared one dinner for the whole group of people, you may eat for free the next twenty days. As the camera localises Morten and Jesper, they also seem to enjoy the food and the ambience.

Despite the positive experience, Lise is, however, not prepared to bring the custom of common meals back to Hedehusene. In a commentary after the dinner, she expresses her doubts.

'It is probably only within this kind of environment such an arrangement could work.'

Beside the themes of scrap and food, which concerned the inner routines of Christiania, the *Diary* touches upon two additional topics, both rather concerning the relationship of the Freetown to the rest of society. The first of these is the issue of activism and negotiation with authorities, and the other is the issue of drugs and social maladjustment. In the *Diary*, the transition from laborious scrap collecting, via joint suppers to activist, political life is smooth. In one central sequence, we get to follow the family as they attend one of the Freetown's Common Meetings. The meeting is well attended, with most people sitting on the floor. As the camera pans around, we see Lise and Eli, attentively following the argumentation. The factual matter of the day is how to do deal with the conflict that has flared up with the municipality concerning the maintenance and security of some of the buildings. While Christiania has presented certificates showing that it has attended to listed problems, the municipality has raised new demands. The meeting is chaired by one of the Freetown's 'intellectuals';[3] his orange sweater and scarf emphasising the alarming message delivered. Many other speakers also give voice to their opinions; the speeches evoking both applause and happy barking. Having run through the situation, the whole group sets off in order to pay a common visit to the Ministry of Defence, the official owner of the area. In this sequence, the perspective expands again, as the Christianites — as a body — stroll through the streets of Christianshavn to Amalienborg, the seat of the Danish government. And at the head of the group, we find the teenager Jesper and his newly found Christiania friend Jonny.

A crowd of around hundred, the Christianites fill out the courtyard as they arrive, most of them taking a seat on the ground. After a little while, the ministry spokesman steps out. Dressed in a trench coat, he receives the ironic greetings and answers with a smile. There is still four and a half months to go before the final clearance of Christiania, he says, a time period that should be used for constructive collaboration. While the reaction from the already chastened Christiania inhabitants is one of sarcastic exhilaration, Eli and Lise seem more doubtful. As the camera finds their faces in the crowd, we clearly see their worries.

The younger half of the Hansen family, Jesper and Morten, largely seem to find their own way about the Freetown, attending school and making friends. Yet, they are also confronted with the darker sides of Christiania. As the documentary approaches the end, this perspective is given more scope. Looking up from his work in the shoe maker's workshop and facing the camera, Jesper expresses his concerns.

'There are places, he says, where they absolutely don't want to participate in anything at all; places like Fredens Ark (The Peace Ark), where you cannot get in… and I think they also ought to expose the bad sides.'

In the documentary, this remark by Jesper is taken *ad notam*. The dislocation from the small-scale and undisturbed working community of the shoemaker's shop, to the most violent of Christiania's settings, Fredens Ark, presents something of a peripatetic transition. By the end of the week, the adults without their sons are granted access to the rough four-storey brick building with the slightly deceptive name. And the picture presented is not favourable. Accompanied by a number of youngsters and dogs, they enter what used to be one of the most imposing buildings of the area. The staircase is dark and rugged, the handheld camera zooming in on doors and walls showing numerous traces of police raids and other violent disputes. In one of the 'apartments' — more den than dwelling — they meet with three teenagers; all pale and rugged against the obscure and worn-out backdrop. Here, all of a sudden Eli and Lise are the ones directing the scene, asking questions. What they want to know is why these young individuals have chosen to live under such circumstances. A young girl feels provoked by their normality and takes a defensive stance as she slides further into the shadow behind the doorpost.

'What circumstances? Are your circumstances better than mine?'

One of the boys explains his choice a bit more in depth.

'I have tried all the other circumstances including institutions and they were not good, and so I've come to this.'

On the question of why they keep all the dogs, they answer more vaguely. Why do you keep dogs? It is not because they are afraid, they claim. It is simply nice to have something to hold on to when walking around the town.

The final transition of the documentary diary is the logical return back to Hedehusene. In the film this last changeover is represented by a clip of the regular road sign, showing the rectilinear route to Hedehusene's main street. A week after the homecoming, the family members are once again neatly gathered around the coffee table. The set-up is exactly the same as in the beginning of the film, as is the anonymous voice coming from behind the camera, all of which renders the scene with some kind of scientific validity. And in between now and back then, a week or so ago, lies a fresh, untainted, first-hand experience.

Having initially rejected the Freetown as nothing but 'a shithole', the family now in different ways defend the initiative. From their living-room position, all of the family members in different ways express their support for the Freetown initiative, and this despite the more depressing aspects. Eli, the concrete worker, is still convinced there is something 'ravingly bad' with the situation, but he is not at all sure that Christiania is the problem. Lise is equally affirmative, and in a close-up she emotionally explains her change of opinion.

'I met so many people, and they helped each other... as they said themselves, they acted together... they did things together, they tended to the children together... and all the status objects that people are so fond of, all that is non-existent out there... the people, they just want to be together, they just want to be something for each other, and that I think we ought to pay more attention to...'

The *Return*: Crackled Grounds

The direct motive for the *Diary* had been the decision taken by the Danish parliament in spring 1975 to set an absolute time limit for what had somewhat reluctantly been accepted as 'a social experiment' (see Håkan Thörn's chapter in this book). The cut-off date was set as 1 April 1976, and the broadcasting of the film on Danish TV happened on 6 January 1976. Commissioned by the national broadcasting company, which at this time totally dominated Danish televised mass-mediation, the impact of the film was significant. And even if the film was not the only mass-mediated event featuring the Freetown during this period,[4] it still played a major — if not *the* major — role in the significant turn in public opinion registered during the spring of 1976.[5] An experiment within the experiment, the film presented a popular assessment; ordinary Danes obviously identified themselves with the Hansen family and similarly started to take personal interest in 'the social experiment', eventually making it politically impossible for the government to enforce its decision to put an end to it. And so Christiania remained even after 1 April 1976, now with a reinforced, experimental legitimacy.

Over the next decade, the status of the Freetown would nevertheless remain unclear, and in 1988 Poul Martinsen decided to produce a follow-up documentary, *Gensyn med Christiania* (*Return to Christiania*, 52 min). In the film, screened on Danish TV, we get to follow the Hansen Family as they return to the contested neighbourhood.

Twelve years have passed, and many things have happened, both in the life of the Hansens and in that of the Freetown. The return therefore starts off with a black-and-white summary of the initial visit before it continues in colour. More than a simple time marker, this chromatic transition draws attention to the fact that what was in 1975 not much more than an assemblage of fumbling attempts is now a diversified yet to a certain extent organised urban neighbourhood. Even if the initial crane shot over the entrance area still conveys a somewhat ragged image, colourful façades and playful architectural additions tell another and more charming story, further reinforced by a relaxed and jazzy soundtrack.

Time has obviously also passed in Hedehusene. Eli and Lise are now middle-aged, Jesper and Morten are grown up with lives of their own, and in the living room an increased number of family photographs, little ornaments and souvenirs give evidence of the fact that a considerable amount of time has passed. Yet, many things remain the same. The rental flat is the same, the basic furniture has not been replaced, and the decorative cushions are still there, as markers of the simple, habitual and continuous.

While the family prepares for their second stay in Christiania, the question hovering in the air is obviously 'what happened with the social experiment?' Since their first visit, Christiania has continued to be an issue, its existence constantly contested. And although the community has gained a certain legitimacy, it has also suffered from severe internal conflicts and violence. Consequently, the Hansens are quite pessimistic.

'I have read many terrible things in the press about what has happened out there', says Lise. 'For example the story about the guy who was murdered and cast into the concrete floor. These bikers… if they are still there… it's not very good, but hopefully we'll manage somehow.'

Even though these are serious concerns, the family is more confident when it comes to basic requirements. They know what daily life in Christiania is about.

'I'll take my thermal gear, says Eli while packing the suitcase. And then I believe… if I have my thermal gear and my underwear and the big coat and my cap, it'll be OK.'

Right from the start, the themes from twelve years back resurface. The strict diary structure is also replicated. Again, the focus on the very basics of life renders to the second documentary the same kind of anthropological touch. What we are confronted with are familiar, everyday endeavours. The first day is dedicated to social life in the cooperative, now a cooperative at Dyssen, the outer part of the Freetown; and to the raising of kids in an environment like this. The second day is devoted to the issues of how to keep warm and clean, and how to establish a decent infrastructure, and the third day to the public and commercial facilities of the Freetown. The focus of the fourth day is Christiania's social welfare work, and that of the fifth, the transformation of the former drug den, Fredens Ark. The sixth day is spent at Nemoland, one of Christiania's shady bars; and finally the seventh and last day of the week is assigned to culture, to captivating cabaret and stirring satirical theatre.

Despite a colourful and melodious start, it soon becomes evident that the atmosphere has changed. If the initial sequences in the first documentary showed hesitating yet curious welcoming ceremonies, the opening scenes of the revisit are of another kind. From an early stage Christiania is presented as a contested space, a mass-mediated battlefield, torn between utopian visions of people and chickens and cycling policemen and an increasingly militant clash of different urban interests. 'From the very delicate beginning, Christiania has been an unruly phenomenon,' claims the voice-over solemnly; an understatement in line with the slogans of the Freetown walls: 'Better swinging kids than singing canons'; and the classic 'You cannot kill us; we are a part of you'.[6] The context of the *Return* is presented as a fragmented montage, an ambiguous mix of clips of vibrant carnival processions as well as pulsating riots, of dancing drummers and stone-throwing young men, of laughing kids and agitated dogs, of mothers on bikes and gun-waving civil agents. In the second film the two faces of Christiania are directly juxtaposed.

After twelve years the Freetown is in many ways running more smoothly, with a renovated bridge over to *Dyssen*, a new kindergarten, many decorative wall paintings and increasingly neatly renovated façades, homey living rooms with pot plants in the window sills, and an increasing stream of tourists and school classes paying organised visits. At the same time, the internal bonds, as well as the relationship between the Freetown and the surrounding society, are explosive. The hash commerce is intense, and police raids everyday fare. As such, Christiania has become strategic urban territory, further underlined through an added sequence of amateur footage from the early eighties, which in grainy images depicts violent street battle scenes, with close-ups of indignant and agitated Christiania inhabitants as well as nervous policemen reloading their guns.

While in the first documentary Christiania was described as a community-in-the making, it is described in the follow-up in much more entangled terms, as a neighbourhood simultaneously under construction and in decay. Organised crime, police brutality and social maladjustment are now both physically and structurally present, braided into the story as secondary narratives, repeatedly interrupting the main plot. Although the family's repeated tractor tour through the Freetown represents a kind of homecoming, it is an impression violently overthrown as the scene is being hijacked by a Greenlandic drunkard, craving camera attention. Similar interference takes place as Lise later in the week returns to the grocery store, where during her first visit she worked for a day. Here, by the counter, all kinds of people gather, including the alcoholics, one of whom shows off in front of the camera; slurringly asking Lise for a kiss.

Chunks of harsh reality wedged into the storyline, these minor events add to the revisit an unsettling dimension. Daily life is still the main topic, yet now perhaps less of a fresh challenge. The garbage tour, now running on a regular timetable, provides a kind of geographical overview, this time featuring Jesper as a bin man volunteer. Even though the heaps are fewer and the buildings better maintained, the infrastructure is still improvised. At the cooperative, where the family is accommodated, there is still no running water or sewage system, and in order to relieve oneself one has to use the outdoor dry privy. Yet, as the revisit proceeds, we learn that after seventeen years, the infrastructure has improved and a number of social facilities have been established. In one sequence, we get to follow Lise as she visits the hairdressers. In Christiania as much as in her own home town, this is a social event, and all the more so for Lise, as she realises that her young and fashionably styled Christiania hairdresser originates from Hedehusene.

While Lise gets a haircut, Eli visits the bath house, where he gets a real, healthy rub. In combination with a dive into the invigorating cold-water barrel, it makes him feel like a new person.

The gatherings around the table are equally recurrent. On the very first day, the Hansens are invited to a fiftieth anniversary. Cream cake is served and the atmosphere is cordial. Lise is happy to be back, and with a friendly gesture she pulls Thorkild, one of the main characters of the first film, by the beard, joking about him still being 'a savage'. Yet, as the small talk is settled, the conversation turns to more serious matter, more specifically the biased and very negative image of Christiania given in the press. Although murders are more frequently committed in Nørrebro and other parts of the metropolitan area, they never get the same kind of media attention. After the party, while the camera oversees the washing of dishes, the dialogue inevitably gears towards similar topics. The new cooperative day care centre seems to work very well and the number of kids is growing. But are they not worried about their kids, growing up in an environment that is so utterly stigmatised by violence and drugs? While drying a teacup, Henrik, a young father, answers.

'Yes, of course I am afraid of that. How is your situation in Hedehusene? Aren't you a bit worried about what could happen to your kids when they reach the age of fifteen?

Lise's boys are beyond the critical age, but as they continue to discuss the topic, she admits that their suburban home town, far from being a paradise, suffers as much or perhaps even more than the Freetown from teenage binge drinking, drugs and street violence.

Stereotypical or not, the image of the Freetown is now a topic, the documentary itself offering a persistent example. And the idea is, at least according to the neutral voice-over, that 'it has begun to crackle', a statement further underpinned as the nostalgic clips of bicyclists, prams, ponies and imaginative houses are being pushed aside by sequences of storm troops, stray dogs and barricaded crowds. The violent spiral is also directly addressed in a dialogue between Eli, Morten and one of the guys running Nemoland, an infamous bar where a biker 'captain' was shot to death. The young man himself was also hurt in the incident, the bullet touching the left side of his head. Nevertheless, he plays down the episode as 'simply bad luck'. Despite this unpleasant occurrence, he considers his everyday environment to be peaceful enough, although Eli and Morten are not convinced.

The family's second stay in Christiania does not end in one of Nemoland's obscure corners, however, but in the hustle and bustle of one of Christiania's many cultural events. The last evening of the revisit, the family attends a cabaret with an abundance of song and dance acts, including satirical sketches addressing the eternal threat of eviction. As the cabaret girls are performing their engaging turns, accompanied by the gay tunes of the accordion, the camera zooms in on Eli and Lise Hansen, as they enthusiastically beat time with their hands.

Eventually, another intense week has come to an end, and the Hansens are back in their living room sofa. Again — and despite a crackled rather than composite image — all of the family members express their sympathy with the Freetown. Violence and drug-related criminality exist in many places, not least in their own somnolent Danish municipality. Comparing Hedehusene to Christiania, the family revises the media image of the Freetown as lawless territory posing a direct threat to society at large. Backed up by the voice-over, the family reminds the general public of the fact that, safe and provincial as it may seem, Hedehusene a few years back showed a top record in crime. And even though Morten, the youngest in the family, is reluctant to talk about it, he mentions that he is one of the victims of the increased street violence. Accidentally, he had happened to be in the wrong place at the wrong time, and so got a knife in his stomach. 'But it was simply a bit of bad luck'.

And that is where the documentary ends and where we as spectators leave the Hansen family. Bad luck, it seems, is more evenly distributed than one would think.

The Social Experiment and the Norm

When the Danish Broadcasting Company decided to assign to Poul Martinsen the task of making a documentary about Christiania, the notion of 'the social experiment' was vital. The idea was to offer the general audience some inside information from 'the laboratory', on the one hand shedding light on the question of what an experiment in the field of social life could be, and on the other hand initiating a discussion about the potential value of such an experiment. In this respect, the documentary mission was quite delicate, as it inevitably, within the discourse of the 'experiment', would be understood as a kind of evaluation, and as such would have to deal with both deviating alternatives and established norms of everyday social reproduction.

The first film was made as a direct contribution to the political debate and in direct response to the first serious threat of eviction. Since its establishment some four year earlier, the around seven hundred inhabitants of the Freetown had managed to hold on to the old barracks area, and this to a large extent due to the indecisiveness of the authorities. During the first year of the Freetown's existence, the Social Democrat government had been pushed hard by the right-wing opposition to take measures against what they saw as illegal seizing of property. As a concession, the Social Democrats presented an action plan, which granted Christiania the status of 'a social experiment'.[7]

For the Social Democrat government, the idea of the social experiment came in handy as a way to demonstrate efficiency before demands to remodel the social welfare system; an ambition clearly articulated in the following quote from the ministry's report:

> An increasing number of groups cannot or do not wish to accept the demands put forward by society. This is particularly true of the numerous young and socially disadvantaged groups, where society's promises have proven to be insufficient and unacceptable. It concerns minority groups; those expelled from family, friends and working communities. It concerns lonely and elderly people, who feel estranged from society. [...] In relation to these groups, Christiania should be regarded a social experiment which aims to equip the individual with the prerequisites for a meaningful existence.[8]

Within Christiania, the reaction to the idea of 'the social experiment' varied. But at the time of its conception, it undoubtedly suited all parties, generally embraced as a powerful and effective notion, rendering to the community certain legitimacy. Balancing the political tensions between revolutionary and reformist social visions, the idea of the 'social experiment' rapidly gained in importance, for good and for bad. Offering a certain space for manoeuvre, the notion also placed the Freetown in a somewhat awkward position as hostage to an all the more ubiquitous welfare state. While 'the social experiment' for many of the Christianites indicated radical and limitless creativity, from the perspective of social politics it suggested new forms of tolerant yet monitoring day-to-day governing. From the perspective of the authorities, 'the social experiment' formed part of a problem-solving rather than inventive strategy, in relation to which 'the laboratory' at any time would be called upon for 'results'.

This call for results happened earlier than expected. In the autumn of 1973, a new Liberal government took office; a shift which enabled the ultra-conservative Fremskridtspartiet, (the Progress Party), to force a decision about closure of the Freetown. The decision was taken in April 1975, and the date of eviction was set as 1 April 1976. As early as May 1975, the Ministry of Defence had therefore urged Christiania to present a plan for the clearance. In reply, Christiania had instead carried out a number of required building improvements and in December 1975 also handed in a summons against the State for ignoring the Freetown's acquired status as a 'social experiment' (see René Karpantschof's chapter in this book). 'Christiania started as a violation of the law — as all relevant revitalisations in the history of societies', wrote the Christiania lawyers. 'But the state accepted and legalised Christiania'.[9] Accordingly, it could not be considered compatible with a civil rights system to encourage an experiment embracing several hundreds of people, only to immediately dismiss, ignore and disavow it.[10]

In response to the attempts on behalf of the authorities to incorporate the new settlement into its own social welfare rhetoric, the Freetown, however, played out an unpredictable repertoire of socio-aesthetic experimentation including 'agit prop'-inspired theatre, gay burlesque (see Cathrin Wasshede's chapter in this book) and interventionist buffoonery, attracting significant media attention. These aesthetic activities were not at all marginal caprices, but contributed to a situation where the presuppositions for evaluation, and thus for finalisation of the social experiment, continuously changed.[11]

When documentary filmmaker Poul Martinsen invites the typical Hansen family for a televised evaluation of the social experiment, it is thus far from a neutral litmus test. Instead, as the camera wedges its way into the everyday life of the Freetown, masked by the presence of the Hansens, it also changes the conditions for the experiment as such. Considering the specific set-up, the films did not simply depict and assess the social experiment in relation to a given normality. Instead, by selecting the Hansens and arranging their stays, Martinsen and his team developed a specific setting allowing for the 'typical' or 'recognisable' to be played out against the 'marginal' or 'estranged'. What the *Diary* and the *Return* present is thus not a document of an authentic situation or a historical course of events. It rather operates within a preformatted stage, or a 'semi-speculative frame', where the normal or typical has a key role.[12]

As such, the films form yet another experiment, the subject matter of which is the question of how to create a common perspective of the 'real'. The documentaries address this issue through a focus on positions, actions, or angles as they are acted out in day-to-day dealings. In this sense, they actualise what Michel Foucault in his philosophy of exclusion and inclusion described as the 'micro-physics' of power and knowledge; a 'modern' dynamics of power working through continuous 'end point' evaluation against standards or norms. A micro-physical dynamics is thus a power dynamics, in relation to which the individual body and the local situation is constantly inscribed in a (visual) 'field of documentation';[13] a synonym of which would be 'the everyday'.

Documentary Projections and Everyday Life

The question is then how such an everyday micro-physics is played out in documentary practice, or more specifically, in the 'formatted documentaries'[14] of Martinsen. The question is also how this affects the experimental everydayness of the Freetown. A historical answer would take as its starting point the close affinity between documentary filmmaking and the emergence of 'everyday life'. It is not incorrect to claim that the notion of the everyday constitutes the floating label for the sphere of minor whereabouts articulated through modern mediating technology. Film, it seems, naturally captures 'the ordinary'; everything from people leaving their work place to the whirl of leaves stirred by the wind.[15] As such, the moving image brings the trivial into common consciousness. As the discourse on everyday life develops, especially after the Second World War, it is certainly influenced by this new and mass-mediated visibility.[16] Yet, the everydayness emerging on the screen is not simply a passive representation, but a political shifter; a socially active figure dislocating focus from structures of power to spaces of mobilisation and change.[17] Thus understood, 'everyday life' is the 'micro-space' where ordinary acts such as chatting, cooking, fixing water pumps, singing or throwing stones at the police takes place; in short a space where representational practice is acted out, invented and reinvented.

Accordingly, rather than a capture of or an outlook onto everyday life, documentary film could be understood as an integral part of it. As Bill Nichols, principal theorist of documentary puts it, even though there is a strong mutuality between the documentary and 'authentic' everyday life, it is not a representational relationship. Rather, the documentary unfolds as 'a practice of authentication',[18] and as such constitutes a rhetorical claim to realism and relevance, which should not be confused with the 'real'. Thus dependent upon documentary 'authentication' for its emergence, everyday life is rather an effect of the use of certain modes or representational formats. These modes include such aspects as camera positioning, framing of subjects, directing of performance, and sequencing or editing of footage; all of which according to Nichols present the 'axiographic' scheme of the documentary.[19]

Mainly operating through what may be called a conventional, 'expository'[20] documentary format, the camera in Martinsen's films is disguised, first and foremost used as an instrument, blending in with the happenings in front of it and subjugated to the goal, which is that of exposing a topic and giving a report. There is also an affinity between the camera perspective and the commentator's or narrator's voice, which is equally neutral and anonymous, even when it occasionally leaves its external position, addressing the family members directly. At these instances, the framing is simple and the camera frontally positioned so as to emphasise the disinterested and impartial onset. This establishing of a self-evident point of view is specifically obvious in the evaluating sequences, often talking-head shots, where the family members reflect upon their experiences, for example in their own living room in Hedehusene.

While the voice-over in both films sometimes crosses the border and enters the plot, the opposite is also frequent, as the testimonies of the family members are elevated to the commentary level, often further sustained by overview images, giving the statements an analytical distance. The neutrality is also reinforced through the chronological 'diary' format, which renders to the films a self-evident temporality, the flow of images and sounds constituting a natural analogy with quotidian, day-to-day living.[21]

At times, however, this expository mode is shifted for a more subjective form of expression. Occasionally, the camera interferes in a more intimate way, closing in on happenings or tracing movements, almost seeking bodily contact, all in order to create a more emotional sense of uncensored presentness, a heightened atmosphere of embeddedness. In Martinsen's films, this mode — at times achieved with handheld camera — is used in many of the more intimate, indoor sequences, such as those depicting the social activities of cooking or having dinner, or in the sequence at Nemoland, where controversial issues, such as weapons and violence are being discussed. Paradoxically enough, this 'direct' or 'close' mode also has an intensifying and dramatic effect, in the *Diary* most notable in the Fredens Ark scenes, where the camera explores the darker corners of the Freetown along with dogs and drug addicts. In the *Return* this mode is applied in the intimate everyday sequences at the hairdressers or in the bath house, but also in the more confrontational passages depicting encounters with drop-outs or politicians. The most 'direct' sequences in the films are, however, the riot sequences, partly consisting of imported, shaky and rough amateur footage, which in the *Return* fills the double function of authentication and dramatisation.

The most explicit gesture, used by Martinsen, however, concerns the performance of the protagonists. The authenticating power of the films first and foremost emanates from the fact that the typical Hansen family plays themselves; that they re-enact all the minor actions and social relations of the everyday. When in a rooftop shot we see the family, as they meander through the Freetown, perched on a red tractor, it is certainly not an unprompted happening, but a highly stylised 'masquerade of spontaneity',[22] planned and directed for dramatic and rhetorical purposes. This very specific kind of acting imbues the two films, affecting the tension in the kitchen, at the dinner table or in the plenary meeting. Irrespective of how messy the social experiment, we immediately spot the ordinary Hansens, who through their presence provide us with a space, where the 'recognisably "real" interacts with the dramatically "irreal"'[23] The ordinary is made to perform for us, and in this specific case in an extraordinary and experimental everyday setting.

When the *Diary* was shot, in the mid-seventies, this accentuation of everydayness through the use of non-professionals represented an emergent mode in cinematic and televised documentary. The inspiration for Martinsen was most certainly the ciné-ethnographic tradition[24] and perhaps more specifically Paul Watson's BBC production *The Fam-*

ily, broadcast in 1974, a television series following a working class family in Reading on their daily ventures, thus offering to the similarly family-centred television audience an entirely new potential for access and assessment of their own ordinary lives.[25] In the same vein, Martinsen's films present a mix of objective — or looking *at* — and subjective — or looking *through*; in their acting themselves, the Hansens appear as both objects and subjects, through their familiarity rendering the extraordinary recognisable, at the same time dramatising their own typical roles, narratives and identities.

The Everyday Staged

Without doubt, the documentaries about the family Hansen's visits to Christiania provide a rich source of information for the understanding of the Freetown as a social experiment in everyday life. Taken together, the two films present a spatio-temporal mapping of the experimental from the perspective of the norm, as such providing basic data for navigating the wider Christiania discourse. The first of the two films in particular, with its close-ups of everyday challenges, also managed to change the course of events in favour of the contested community.

Yet, what also becomes evident, especially when comparing the two films, is that the notion of 'everyday life' is transient, and that much happens in twelve years. While the *Diary* in 1975 was very successful in its staging and authentication of everydayness, to the extent that it became a weapon in the battle for the Freetown's further existence, the *Return* twelve years later did not manage to make the headlines or change public opinion in at all the same way.

In retrospect, it is obvious that what Martinsen staged as a *Return* was neither a return to the same alternative scene, nor to the same media landscape. Although the close affinity between the social experiment and the mass-mediated field of documentation was still strong — or perhaps even stronger — it had undergone some decisive change.

The emergence of Christiania was already, initially, intimately related to its appearance in the media. Its very formation, dated 26 September 1971, was staged as a documented performance which was then covered in the daily press. With the explicit goal to reconstitute or reappropriate daily life, Christiania already rested on what could be described as an authenticating desire for 'a performance that is not a performance';[26] a realism that is not reality; or an everyday life that is not simply a trivial 'everyday'. Martinsen takes this as the starting point for his project, through the family Hansen skilfully extrapolating this desire so as to coincide with a more general craving for a meaningful existence. In the case of the *Diary*, Martinsen also manages to reach the general Danish public in their living rooms; at the time a quite homogeneous audience watching one and the same monopoly transmission, and bringing to the act of viewing related expectations and assumptions of a similar kind.

While the *Diary* in this respect offered a degree of identification and intimacy, which at the time was unrivalled on Danish television, the *Return* was aired in a totally different media landscape where the expectations of phenomena such as 'family', 'experimentation' or 'everyday life' had changed. And even though in 1988, reality TV and docu-soaps were not yet ordinary fare, an increasing dramatisation of the ordinary and fictionalisation of news had placed new demands both on the articulation of the everyday and on the formatting of the documentary. And if in 1975 there had been a self-evident constituency of viewers, the situation twelve years later was different.

What the 'moralities' of the Hansen family and their acquaintance with the Freetown teach is that a social experiment with the everyday always also requires a representational or documentary experiment including a reconsidering of the micro-physical 'formats' for communicating, disseminating and sharing experience. This is an issue most present in the Hansen story and also in the story of Christiania at large.

ALTERNATIVE VISIONS OF HOME AND FAMILY LIFE IN CHRISTIANIA: LESSONS FOR THE MAINSTREAM

Helen Jarvis

> It's a very good life to live with friends and neighbours around. It is very different [from other Copenhagen neighbourhoods] [...] I think if I was living in an apartment alone somewhere with a young child I'd go nuts. Here alone with a child it is very easy.[1]
>
> It's one thing that makes it very difficult to leave Christiania, that you only have to go to the shop to buy milk and you meet friends and you might then share a meal with them... this feeling... that you belong. That's very hard to give up.[2]

The picture of an alternative way of life that is painted of Christiania usually calls attention to the political struggle with a Danish state bent on 'normalising' this autonomous community and the prime downtown site it occupies. We less often hear about the creative initiatives and collective support Christianites routinely engage in to resolve the multiple threads of their home-work-parenting identities. In mainstream discussion this is popularly known as the project of 'work-life reconciliation'. This chapter contributes knowledge and understanding of everyday work-life reconciliation in Christiania by focusing on creative home-making practices, including those rooted in collective reciprocity. Much has been written about Christiania's influential cultural institutions; such as Pigegarden (Girls Guard), Solvognen (Sun Chariot) light and music theatre group, and the annual free Christmas party for the homeless.[3] Less has been written about some of the more mundane institutions and practices which influence everyday life.

Mainstream reconciliation, or, more typically, the anxiety and stress of never achieving that elusive 'balance', is closely associated with hypermodern time-space coordination. It involves making a living (or managing transfer payments) while striving to feed, clothe and care for the family; get children to school and social activities and; to reconcile this with affordable housing, transport and the extra pairs of hands needed to help make all this function to schedule. Hypermodern coordination routinely involves sophisticated information and communication technologies. Yet, rather than to slow the pace and ease the tensions of complex time-space choreography, these technologies generally serve to stretch the distances and shift the timing of multiple commitments, so that more activities can be scheduled more intensively into each day. Arguably, it takes a strong sense of common purpose and creative use of time and space in order to resist these pressures to speed up and intensify the treadmill of existence.

Ethnographic observations of ordinary routines and social support networks have been used by the author in previous research to uncover the 'secret life' of the city; those aspects that are neglected in official data collection and policy responses but which, ironically, are not a secret to each of us in our everyday lives.[4] This chapter employs a similar approach to consider the questions whether, and in what ways, the Freetown cultivates a more harmonious, creative and just means of coordinating home, work and family life. The expectation is that the unique social and material conditions of collective living in Christiania go some way towards fulfilling long-standing feminist family-friendly ideals — such as those of the Nordic 'New Everyday Life' housing and community project. This vision highlights the neglected significance of a 'social architecture' to correspond with the priority usually given in male-stream planning to the design and layout of the material architecture.[5] The discussion below animates this idea by attending to the 'soft' as well as 'hard' infrastructure at work in Christiania.

The questions at the heart of this research seek not only to uncover the 'secret life' of Christiania's humanistic pace and rhythm, but also to expose the 'arrested development' of mainstream individual private dwelling. In 1903, Charlotte Perkins Gilman observed a depressing 'tyranny' in the replication of myriad routine domestic tasks in millions of separate homes.[6] Today, a striking feature of household composition in Denmark is the growing proportion of one-person households and one-parent households: 65 per cent of Copenhagen's population live alone, typically inhabiting homes designed to the idealised standards of owner-occupied single family dwelling.[7] In public health circles there is growing concern for the mental health risks of a lonely society.[8] Although international surveys consistently place Denmark high on the 'happiness scale' of self-proclaimed contentment, disparities are increasingly evident between income groups and generations.[9] In particular, the residential property market is perceived by young people to represent a 'private party' for which the entrance fee has become so high they feel indefinitely excluded from joining.[10] By contrast, Christiania's 'public party' provides a home to many people who would not otherwise 'belong' in any public or private space.

A significant but neglected story of the countercultural movement that inspired Christiania was distaste for the emphasis on privacy and personal attachment to material possessions attributed to the conventional Western nuclear family and home.[11] Parallels can be drawn today with new social movements of 'down-shifting' 'compacting' and 'voluntary simplicity.'[12] This quest for new and alternative models of home and family life is attracting renewed attention and it is no longer the preserve of a 'hippie fringe'. The high cost of social isolation and underutilised domestic space and amenities has led planning practitioners and environmentalists to consider new ways of fostering shared public space and mutuality through daily social interaction in close-knit residential arrangements.[13] A popular discourse has rallied around the convivial and self-reliant ideals of an 'urban village'. As an intentional community, as a 'micro-nation' of sorts, Christiania can be viewed as a 'laboratory for testing and demonstrating new ideologies and social structures'.[14] It is defined by collective values (notably the absence of private real estate), shared (car-free) physical space and non-hierarchical consensus governance. This 'laboratory' provides a rich source of inspiration for architects and planners looking for more progressive, humanistic solutions to the problems of isolation and exclusion noted above. Significantly, Christiania's collaboratively designed *Green Plan* was awarded the Initiative Award of the Society for the Beautification of Copenhagen in November 2006. The plan received positive endorsement from the Local Agenda 21 Society because of its sustainable goals and democratic, participatory design process.[15] Crucially, the alternative local infrastructure cultivated in Christiania facilitates not only social networks of mutual support and concern for the environment, but also circuits of innovation, learning, resistance, doing, being and becoming. These circuits can be progressive or they may serve to inhibit new ideas, exclude certain groups or prevent change. It is important to recognise that alternatives are not necessarily superior to the structures and institutions they replace. At the same time, *the process of constructing an alternative* in itself provides a critical benchmark against which to reflect on taken for granted mainstream assumptions.

Data Collection and Analysis

This chapter draws on first-hand ethnographic observations from a fortnight spent living as a researcher in residence in the community of Christiania.[16] This community case study was selected and conducted as part of a larger, multi-site international, comparative study of intentional community and collective living. Data collection included 14 interviews (9 recorded and transcribed verbatim) together with visits (by invitation) to many different types of dwelling and casual encounters and conversations with visitors and residents. The interview quotes which are included in the discussion are selected to illustrate and represent significant themes which emerged from the complete body of data: conversations; observations; existing research; and interviews. Subject identities are protected by the use of a two-letter coded pseudonym. The research approach draws on a fine-grained reading of dwelling and area types and the arrangement and use of shared and private spaces from site visits as well as from a review of existing research and publicly available archives. A detailed picture is pieced together of the infrastructures of daily life in Christiania; in the built environment, across the social institutions and in the local moral cultures of shared space and collective action.[17]

Infrastructure of Daily Life

All aspects of daily life function according to an infrastructure which can be enabling or constraining. Location and affordability typically determine access, but additional social and cultural factors influence whether, and how, different groups actually engage with the networks and flows that pulse through the city. Like the streets, tunnels, water pipes and fibre-optic cables we are familiar with in the built environment, this infrastructure has a material quality, but institutional regimes and moral codes also serve as 'soft' conduits that convey local knowledge and routine practices of living. An example of a 'soft' conduit would be the journeys and arrangements parents make to chaperone young children to kindergarten or primary school and the social interactions which occur at fixed times of arrival and departure at the school gate.

The concept of an integrated 'infrastructure of daily life' encompasses all that it takes in a practical sense for individuals and families to 'go on' from one day to the next. This integration brings multiple economies into consideration (formal and informal, cash in hand work, transfer payments, domestic food production, do-it-yourself construction and maintenance, reciprocity and the economy of regard of unpaid care-giving and emotion-work),[18] alongside systems of governance and the projects and amenities normally taxed as a 'public good' in urban planning. This approach benefits the sub-municipal scale of autonomous community studied here by moving beyond the partial, fixed infrastructure of state engineering and taxation. This approach acknowledges a hugely significant, but highly gendered, infrastructure of constraint including, for example, normative behaviour in parenting, communication, tolerance, privacy and obligation. In the case of Christiania, this allows us to explore the role and sustainability of a 'soft' infrastructure of shared space and collective endeavour; that which may be expected to cultivate alternative (inclusive and democratic) models of home and family life.

In conventional urban structure, 'materiality' is evident in the distribution of fixed assets such as homes, schools, shops and transit stops. Access is mediated to a large extent by market competition. In Christiania, an alternative material infrastructure is shaped by the absence of a real property market (individuals have the right to occupy but never to own or benefit financially from transferring the rights of their home or business premises to someone else), alongside a powerful culture of 'do-it-yourself' construction (largely unrestricted by building codes or planning regulation) and local decisions agreed by consensus in monthly meetings for each of the 14 geographic areas into which Christiania is divided. At the same time, the community has invested considerable sums, from the General Fund (Common Purse), in the maintenance of the grounds, modernisation of the sewerage system, provision of public toilets and a comprehensive garbage collection and recycling enterprise. Christiania is known as 'a place where nothing goes to waste.'[19] For example, the community has won prizes for its garbage collection, recycling and composting: because all the garbage is sorted, the municipality collects the end products free of charge, saving the community money and reducing its carbon footprint; the goal is to maximise re-use, only recycling what cannot be re-used.[20]

The matrix in Table 1 presents a holistic approach to the complex, intersecting infrastructure of daily life. The format takes into account the existence of multiple economies, as compared with the partial view offered by narrow monetary definitions, identifying in turn the assets that individuals and families typically have to work with to achieve various projects and goals. Assets (listed in the left-hand column) are the means by which households avoid and/or adapt to crises and make adjustments to life-course transitions such as childbirth, retirement or long-term limiting illness. Assets are categorised in diverse ways by different authors, but the main categories include physical or productive assets, financial assets, human capital, social capital and political capital.[21] In the matrix developed for Christiania, assets relating to the unpaid work of social reproduction assume greater importance compared with mainstream society. Intersecting with individual household assets are the 'hard' and 'soft' infrastructure networks and flows (identified in the top row) which emanate variously from communal provision, participation in direct democracy, the shared use of space and collective action which may be political, cultural or simply involve reciprocal co-operation between neighbours. It is important to bear in mind that Table 1 does not represent a 'shopping list' of progressive innovations: assets and infrastructure intersect in ways which may be advantageous or problematic for the individual and/or for the community.

Institutional regimes encompass all manner of regulation, from that functioning within the household (who does what, where, when, with whose moral authority), to that of the state and the extent to which it regulates behaviour and subsidises private markets.

Christiania's self-governance is practised through a series of meetings, each with its own content and function: the Common Meeting, the Area, Treasurers', Economy, Business, Building, Associates' (workshop and business cooperatives) and House Meetings, all lubricated to a considerable extent by the daily debate which goes on privately as well as in Christiania's public space (the 'soft' infrastructure noted in the right-hand columns of Table 1).[22] The Common Meeting determines the annual budget of the Common Purse and the monthly rent that each adult resident has to pay (equivalent to about 250 euro): a system of social assistance is available for those who get into financial difficulty and are unable to pay the rent each adult must pay, so 'membership' is not restricted by income. The Common Meeting also deals with negotiations and cooperation with the Danish state as well as national and international advocacy groups; with the Contact Group acting as go-between.

The Area and House Meetings are pivotal to housing allocation and what would be defined elsewhere as 'tenure'. Residents invest their own money and labour in their homes and are unable to withdraw that value when they move out or to another property but, equally, they could not be evicted unless they broke one of the few rules of residence.[23] A similar measure of transparency and security is not true of the allocation and transfer of 'occupation rights' (and thus to a large extent 'membership') when a dwelling becomes available. Access to a vacant dwelling is not restricted by income, as it would be in Copenhagen, but instead the transfer of occupation is determined by the Area Meeting or, in the case of rooms available in large houses, at the House Meeting. There are competing pressures; to accommodate the estimated 200 third-generation children, some living in extended families, with many wishing to establish independent homes nearby; and to introduce 'new blood' — activists and creative entrepreneurs willing to militate the effects of an ageing community. When new people do gain entry it is through an organic process; 'hanging around here, they get part-time jobs here; they borrow someone's house while they're travelling and get by in various ways.'[24] Thus, vacant rooms tend to be allocated through unequal social capital — such as friendships with residents of a partic-

Table 1: Matrix illustrating the intersecting infrastructure of daily life in Christiania (examples are selective rather than comprehensive).

Asset Type	'Hard' infrastructure	'Soft' infrastructure	
	Material and institutional	Shared space	Collective action
Political: representation	Direct democracy; large venues for Common Meetings	Public spaces for impromptu public events	International 'brand' of Freetown
Productive: work equipment, secure tenure, housing, basic utilities and services	Absence of real-property; adults pay rent/subscription plus meter-regulated rates for water and electricity; machine hall; Green Hall; post office; recycling station	The 'traffic group'; the playground group (and other voluntary groups); social responsibility promoted through participatory governance	Separation of waste (cardboard, paper, batteries etc) by individuals, households (checked by the recycling group) reduces the cost of waste management
Re-productive: unpaid domestic work	Children's facilities (organised by age); **see photo 1;** bath house; laundry (and services)	Opportunities for shared meals and communal dining; shared childcare	Large unwanted items (scrap metal, car parts, furniture) made available for easy re-use (as a central freecycle); **see photo 2**
Human capital: spending on education and preventive healthcare, qualifications, life experiences, training and skills	Sundhedshuset (health clinic); Herfra og Videre (Upwards and Onwards, CA consultancy and social office); cultural societies	Skills and ideas exchanged in the process of home construction; co-operation between neighbours	Entrepreneurial initiatives; festivals; circus; music; theatre; artistic endeavours

Labour: the terms and conditions of income generating activities (work-life balance)	Workshop space paid for on a rate based on turnover; businesses operate within cooperatives; opportunities for tele-working and micro-enterprise	Community jobs (e.g. bakery, gardening, laundry, machine hall) allocated a common wage	Voluntary work such as in the information office or conducting guided tours — raises money for community projects
Social Capital: networks through which people access jobs, credit, help in times of need (two-way reciprocal relations)	Ugespejlet (the Weekly Mirror free newspaper); posters and graffiti; Christiania Radio; community website	Participation in Area Meetings; area working parties; regular social interactions	Sharing information and knowledge; helping each other to build and maintain homes; exchanging tools and skills
Financial: savings/ debt	CA Fund; Løn (local currency — largely symbolic, sold to coin collectors)	Area Meetings consider shared concerns for building maintenance and local improvements	Efforts to create alternative livelihoods to the capital/carbon economy
Natural/Ecology: access to clean air, water, land, green space recreation	Car-free landscape; gardening group; human-scale development	Little scope for permaculture/self-provisioning (poisoned soil)	Green Plan; consensus on adapting and recycling buildings

Photo 1: Extensive children's facilities include playgrounds for all age groups. Photo: Helen Jarvis.

Photo 2: The 'Put-and-Take' community recycling facility for household goods. Photo: Helen Jarvis.

ular area or being widely known for civic engagement in the community project. While there have been attempts to formalise the criteria for the transfer of tenancy the point to stress here is the popular perception — that informal practices reveal a degree of favouritism and internal selection.

Aside from the formal collective institutions and the few explicit rules (no hard drugs, no weapons, no stealing, no biker-gang insignia), the most influential circuits of local knowledge and norms of behaviour function through collective rituals, festivals, music and theatre performances and an everyday entrepreneurial politics of sanctuary for creative expression and experimentation. One example would be the variety of opportunities for shared or communal dining. It is widely recognised in the literature on intentional community that shared meals that neighbours prepare and sit down to eat together are the 'glue' that binds community together: some go so far as to say that 'communities that dine together align together.'[25] The best-known communal eating place in Christiania is Fælleskøkkenet (the Communal Kitchen) which functions both as a low-budget café and a free 'soup kitchen' at certain times of the week. More widely there exist informal arrangements; either in large houses that function as communes (for instance Stjerneskibet, the Star Ship, which is a form of hostel), or ad hoc among friends and neighbours who take turns to cook a shared meal. Another example would be the table settings of the up-market restaurant Spiseloppen (the Flea) which illustrate another sort of institutional arrangement: on one side tables are set for commercial service (4-star tourist rates); the other side is plainly furnished with unreserved refectory tables and benches for Christianites who can buy a 'house meal' for a nominal payment to eat alongside any other Christianite who cares to show up. The idea is similar to that of the 20th century Central Kitchen Buildings which eliminated the need for individual cooking space by serving family meals for communal dining.[26] In principle, communal dining cultivates social capital, reduces the burden of unpaid (feminised) domestic work and reduces energy consumption. In practice, on the occasions observed, this communal dining arrangement appears not to cater well for families with young children. This is possibly because the restaurant setting imposes 'formal dining behaviour' on the stressful task of feeding a reluctant or easily distracted child. Arguably, it is important not to romanticise the many opportunities for social interaction in a small community such as this. Scope to retreat from inter-personal conflict and to protect cherished intimacies of family life is as important to wellbeing as is a sense of purpose and belonging.

By now it should be apparent that the infrastructure of daily life in Christiania (as indeed in other close-knit community settings) incorporates tacit moral codes concerning, for instance, sharing, participation, innovation, tolerance and freedom from authority. Arguably these tacit codes are the least easily conveyed by the matrix in Table 1. Consequently, discussion now turns to consider the process and practices of home-making in Christiania, using this as a way of uncovering the taken for granted moral codes, local cultures and conduits of learning involved.

Junk Playground Hygge

The story of Christiania's origins are well known: prior to squatter-activist occupation, local residents pulled down the fence at the corner of Prinsessegade and Refshalevej to allow their children access to the 'hidden' green space beyond. It can be argued that the 'free space' movement, which Christiania has come to epitomise,[27] coincides with the 'pro-play' and 'free play' ideals that generated what we call adventure playgrounds today. This is not to infer that the serious political struggles of Christiania are in any sense a game or pretend-reality. Making this connection seeks to highlight instead the entrepreneurial and experiential qualities of 'place making' that are denied by conventional notions of urban planning.

The Danish landscape architect Carl Theodor Sørensen coined the term 'Junk Playground' in 1931 in recognition of what he saw, from children playing on building sites and wasteland, as the benefits children gained, experientially, from having autonomy to create their own place in the world. The vision of Christiania as an autonomous space for those excluded from the mainstream (whether by income or life-choice) echoes the claim Sørensen made in the 1930s; that children living in modern apartments who are denied 'free play' should have alternative access to interesting and adaptable space, in relative seclusion, away from authoritarian gaze:

> a junk playground [is] an area, not too small in size, well closed off from its surroundings by thick greenery, where we should gather, for the amusement of bigger children, all sorts of old scrap that the children from the apartment blocks could be allowed to work with, as the children of the countryside and in the suburbs already have. There could be... planks and boards, 'dead' cars, old tyres and lots of other things. Of course it would look terrible.[28]

When the Bådsmandsstræde Barracks site was first occupied there were approximately 150 existing buildings, including the rare, half-timbered, Commanders House (baptised Fredens Ark/the Peace Ark), 17th and 18th century powder magazines on the bastions, a large indoor riding arena (Den Grå Hal/the Grey Hall) and a smaller riding house (Den Grønne Hal/the Green Hall). These historic buildings, which now have conservation status with the Slots- og Ejendomsstyrelsen (the Palace and Properties Agency), were unused and very run-down when squatters took up residence in 1971. The following years saw the original buildings incrementally modified and upgraded and more than 100 new buildings added. By 1975, the resident population was 850–900, similar to what it is today.[29]

The scale of the project of home-making cannot be underestimated. As one example, the Christianite MK describes the evolution of the home she took over, with her then boyfriend, in the late 1970s — from the concrete shell of a chemical store to the light, bright, compact open-plan space she lives in with a subsequent partner today. She differentiates the process of making a home 'as a place to live' from simply squatting:

> When I said we built this place I mean it wasn't fit to live in; there were holes in the walls; we had to re-build it, gut it and restore it, there was just a concrete floor, we put floors in, moved the entrance. We were the first who took it over as a place to live in — but there were others before us who just crashed here… slept here on hammocks in the building as it was. So they just dossed down, squatting. In those days the standards were — we just had a couple of milk crates and a plank of wood as a table; that was normal.[30]

From its early days, do-it-yourself home construction, renovation and maintenance reflected two potentially colliding extremes of Danish society. On the one hand was an experimental, constantly evolving, entrepreneurial quest for freedom — *flere fristeder* (more Freetowns): a retreat from authority, individualism, private ownership and mass-market merchandise. On the other hand was a yearning for authentic being-and-belonging — *hygge*: broadly translated as simple, natural and 'cosy'. From the outset in Christiania the unspoken rule was that buildings were to be adapted rather than torn down and this shaped the aesthetic that exists today.

Nestled behind a long graffiti-clad fence, Christiania benefits from a wild and whimsical seclusion. The significance of separation is not that of a 'gated community', where the fence defends a private enclave, but rather it signals the transition to a liminal (vibrant, transformatory) state:

> where the possibility exists of standing aside not only from one's own social position but from all social positions and of formulating a potentially unlimited series of alternative social arrangements.[31]

This liminal (betwixt and between) space opens up alternative heuristic possibilities (nomadic mind-sets) that are marginal to, or transgress, the mainstream (see also Christa Amouroux's chapter in this anthology). The social interactions that arise are not 'predicated upon sameness but upon the commonality of feeling' — like that of the outsider, 'cast adrift from the mainstream, and as one estranged'.[32] In this context, the liminal metaphor usefully describes the shared space and social time that exists between private 'shelter' and public 'encounter'. Wilderness and whimsy are also apparent in the absence of street lighting and signage: to follow directions to a particular home in Den Blå Karamel (the Blue Candy), for instance, is like reciting a poem or a fairy-tale; right at the thicket of willow, up by the rope swing, look for a pirate ship. Those who require a standardised system of footpath signage and house number sequence should venture no further!

Whereas the junkyard playground ethos is best interpreted as the absence of order, there is parallel evidence of exquisite care and craft skill — where qualities of *hygge* are celebrated in the local culture of home-making. Christiania flouts not only urban policies but also aesthetic conventions.[33] The power of the 'free space' is evident in the opportunity it presents as a conscious antidote to the 'place marketing' witnessed in commercial gentrification. In contrast with the mass-mediated consumer-based material aesthetic of 'anywhere' urban design, Christianites have effectively embraced a post-material interpretation of reclaimed, reused, home-made authenticity. In mainstream society, *hygge* is typically manifest in a café culture of shared snacks and a home décor involving the selection and display of boutique candles. Beyond this 'look', the intention is to evoke a timeless release from hypermodernity. In Christiania, this intention is interpreted ideologically, as a project of moral, political and ecological achievement; making a home, literally, from salvaged materials and time-honoured craft skills. Self-build is a way of reclaiming from 'experts' and 'commerce' the intimate significance of habitation. One resident of a self-built rural dwelling recognises that when outside observers do not share this affinity to the project of home-*making*, they seek to impose 'order' on what they perceive as chaos:

> My grandmother was here the other day and she's never been here before but she came to see [the baby] and she says, oh, it is so messy here, it's very messy. She didn't like the lack of order and lack of modern conveniences. She didn't like the cosy sort of look. For me this is cosy—not so square—but she thought it was all so messy.[34]

Parallels can be drawn between difference in subjective experiences of dwelling, and the discrete ways that the state and Christianites inscribe the natural landscape with meaning through contrasting discursive acts of imagination.[35] Over the past four decades, claim and counter-claim has been made concerning the 'natural state' and right to access this historically important 'green lung of the city'. While the Palace and Properties Agency's notion of a recreation park imagines a 'tidy' and tamed landscape of cut grass, preserved ramparts and open vistas, Christiania's *Green Plan* embraces a wild and 'unruly' nature as representing, in part, the frontiers of an experimental post-material future. A long history of similar conflict over the 'right to the city' and contested geographic imaginations is well rehearsed in the literature on urban parks. The battle over People's Park, in Berkeley, USA, for instance, shares some similarities with Christiania in this respect.[36]

The instinct to 'nest' (as one Christianite described it) is a powerful one that has resulted in some spectacular architecture and inspired efficiencies of interior space-planning. A variety of dwelling types and living standards has taken shape over the 14 areas. Some variation reflects differential private assets (the influx of conveniences in households with one or more good income) while some traces the literal and ideological path which leads away from the noise, commerce and human traffic of Pusher Street to the slower pace of living in self-constructed rural eco-dwellings. The Christianite HA explains how the choice to live simply is facilitated in large part by having shared amenities (laundry and bathhouse/sauna) within easy walking/cycling distance.

> In the Milky Way we were 80 people, in big buildings. Here we are 23 or so, not even that, living in little houses, scattered in a very rural area. Here we are very primitive. We none of us have bathrooms or washing machines and we share a compost toilet. It is our choice. We've decided that we should live simply.[37]

Fluid Families

The 'soft' infrastructures of adaptation, mindfulness, and reclaiming that characterise *hygge* in Christiania extend beyond home-making to all aspects of family life and cultures of parenting. A frequently told story among those who have raised families in Christiania is one of fluid family living arrangements. In the study, Christianites GA, MK, TT, TN and ER (four mothers and one father) each claim that living in Christiania enabled them to negotiate the consequences of separation, divorce, single-motherhood and transition to a blended family arrangement in more flexible, humanistic ways than they believe would have been possible 'outside' in mainstream urban social structures:

> I came to live here together with my boyfriend in 1974… we went on to have two children… and that was back in the time when we had no electricity and we had no water inside the house, so we had to carry water in and waste out; we had no toilet either, so that was tough. We had a stove with chopped wood so a lot of our time was taken up with all those everyday things. It was hard but we chose [that way of life]; and it gave us time to be with the children when they were small. When the children were 7

> and 3 their father and I separated and I went to live in another place. We both wanted to stay in Christiania; we wanted to stay close to each other for the children, so Christiania made it possible for us to separate but still to raise the children together. We stayed good friends so we didn't have those fights in that way.[38]

This story uncovers a paradox in the way social capital and networks of reciprocity function in this communal setting. On the one hand, CT and GA describe a rich infrastructure of support for 'women without fathers for their children' managing collectively in Børneengen (the Children's Meadow); as a place where 'you just open your door and there are people everywhere [to] make food and eat together, the children played together'. On the other hand, most Christianites define themselves in terms of what they are not (conventional, mainstream), subscribing to individual scope to 'do one's own thing.'[39] In this way, enduring relationship ties are to some extent undermined by a tacit code of experimentation and greater tolerance and support of diverse family forms. This is not to say that the moral code has been reversed: heterosexual couples who choose to raise children in 'nuclear' households are no more absent from Christiania than they are the monopoly of mainstream society. The point to make is that the infrastructure of daily life appears to lubricate relationship transitions and reduce the acrimonious fall-out of separation in a situation where collective attachments (and opportunities for co-parenting) militate against over-reliance on primary relationships alone.

The culture of do-it-yourself home-making suits fluid family composition in part because individual dwellings can be adapted or allowed to 'grow' in a way that is not possible with conventional housing market models. Again, scope for adaptation varies according to the assets of the dwelling type and location occupied. For example, Christianite CT describes a simple form of 'grow house' adaptation that, since the state now restricts all building development, is a thing of the past:

> Some years ago, what started with all the wagons; when they drove the small wagons in they would say 'one more wagon', then later would come the second, and the third... they start to build up and out like this because along came another child and this is how so many of the houses began, as one wagon at the start, and now they have been built up over many years.[40]

One form of dwelling adaptation that is still possible occurs through a reallocation of living space in consultation with the area meeting. TN has lived in Christiania for 31 years. She has moved between a number of different areas (from the rural fringe to Christiania City) moving between shared houses, first on her own, then living with a boyfriend, then as a couple with a child and now as a single mother. Until recently, her cleverly partitioned circa 50 sq metre living space provided combined quarters for mother and daughter, including a bathroom in one corner and small kitchenette in the other. Conditions were cramped and TN recognised that she and her daughter sometimes needed space apart. At the Area Meeting she requested that she be allowed to take over a spare room belonging to her elderly neighbour — as a separate sleeping space — even though access required her to walk past her neighbour's bathroom. She gained this additional space at no extra cost (rent is levied on each adult at the same rate irrespective of living area) though she is responsible for heating, lighting and maintenance. In other cases the floor space of individual dwellings have been increased or reduced by shifting the walls separating rooms/apartments in sub-divided buildings: for example creating two apartments out of three when a middle room became vacant. In each case, proposed adaptations went before the Area Meeting to be decided by consensus.

Hostile Habits of the Heart

The social and material networks and flows that shape daily life in Christiania are not always benign or indeed sufficient to combat persistent inequalities. While it is evident from Table 1 and the discussion above that practices of home-making and parenting are less constrained by conventional capital assets (housing, utilities, income and savings/debt) than is the case elsewhere in Copenhagen, inequalities in social capital can assume increased significance. In particular, the emphasis that direct democracy places on face-to-face oral communication puts those who lack these capabilities (whether through hearing/speech impairment or timid orientation) at a disadvantage.

Christiania operates without apparent 'leaders' and eschews a fundamental ideology: it is made up of many discrete interest groups that live together, in conflict as well as cooperation, rather than individuals committed to being part of a bigger group. Different communication practices are talked about and experienced in ways that generate positive and negative reputations. Over time, these discursive practices alter the tone and effectiveness of participation. Consensus rests with unanimous agreement among those present at the Common Meeting rather than as a majority vote of all residents. To have any influence on a course of action it is necessary not only to attend the Common Meeting but also to engage in the lengthy, repetitive and frequently hostile mode of communication.[41] Direct democracy, as Christianites readily admit, takes time: it operates at a slower pace and requires many more lengthy meetings than does representative democracy.[42] In effect, the infrastructure of governance itself (the when, where and how mechanisms of participation) shapes the composition of those who actively feel involved. For example, Common Meetings begin at 8pm and they run late into the night. This practice excludes those who are caught up in the temporal constraints of child-care (notably, but not exclusively, single mothers) or those who would compromise their ability to make a living if they went without sleep (see Amy Starecheski's chapter in this book).

The Christianite TN admits that she rarely attends the Common Meeting because she is intimidated by the tone of debate whereby 'a group of drunks in the corner shout a lot and it is quite chaotic and exhausting because nothing is decided or resolved'. CT explains that she finds it easier to discuss the really contentious issues with other women rather than in the open meetings. This reflects the way women-only meetings have mobilised in the past to resolve conflict and to escape the 'angry, hostile and negative' way of communicating opinions which characterises direct democracy in the Common Meeting. By contrast, communication and participation in the women's meetings involves 'taking care of each other' and focusing on the practical business of daily life. From her own experience, CT argues that those men representing the 'old guard' who 'monopolise' the Common Meeting:

> are more about rejecting the outside than they are creating a new inside. They are so angry, so negative; they always want to go back to what it was like before; whereas most of the women here are more practical and for them it is easier to go elsewhere and discuss something else — and we have done that several times — holding women-only meetings.

While the women's meetings do not carry the weight of consensus, they contribute a vital form of participatory democracy. Moreover, previous success in helping the community take positive action at times of crisis has gained respect for commanding a 'moral achievement'. As GA explains:

> Throughout the history of Christiania when life has become intolerable the women have got together and sorted out a practical way forward — and it will be so again.

The importance of social capital to daily life in Christiania is witnessed not only with respect to structures of governance but also basic livelihood. This returns us to the perceived lack of transparency in the allocation of vacant dwellings introduced above. RM is typical of the young 'hidden homeless' in Christiania; he has a part-time job in Christiania City and pays rent to live in the community but he is house-sitting in the absence of a room to call his own. He explains that while the networks of information through which he learns about vacant dwellings function well (for instance notices posted in the free weekly newspaper *Ugespejlet / Weekly Mirror*); the tacit rules and bureaucratic practices employed by different local areas to decide who may or may not move in remain 'murky'.

The sub-heading 'Habits of the Heart' employed in this chapter originally stems from a cultural analysis of North American society where it is used to emphasise the way people talk and what this says about their moral commitment beyond individual self interest.[43] The authors argue that contemporary social problems are not only structural (relating to 'hard' political and economic infrastructure) but also cultural (relating to 'soft' infrastructure). A similar argument is made here for the specific case of Christiania with respect to the relative presence or absence of an ethic of care in local cultures of home-making, family life, governance and livelihood.

Concluding Remarks

This chapter draws attention to a number of unmistakable distinctions, as well as many less tangible ones, between visions and practices of home and family life in Christiania, compared with other Copenhagen neighbourhoods. The concept of 'hygge' has been used to draw attention to the mutuality, conviviality and tolerance that make Christiania 'difficult to leave' and 'a good life to live' — especially for parents with young children. There is evidence that this mode of living shields Christiania from the hectic pace and brashness of the outside world, emphasising instead an intimate scale of shared space and collective endeavour. It sheds light on creative initiatives and partnerships that deliver collective solutions to individual problems. In many situations this demonstrates the positive benefits to society and the environment of greater emphasis on sharing; of pooling efforts and resources. In other instances it reminds us of the need and desire many individuals and families have to retain scope for intimacy and privacy, expressed in temporal and spatial practices of home-making, alongside opportunities for reciprocity in managing routine practices of daily life.

Returning to the questions posed at the beginning, caution needs to be exercised in claiming for Christiania's unique infrastructure of daily life a more harmonious, creative, and just means of resisting hypermodernity in reconciling home, work and family in a collective setting. On the one hand, the absence of owner occupation, as well as routine opportunities for social interaction in shared public space arguably cultivates a powerful local culture of reciprocity, tolerance and trust. On the other hand, individual experience of coping (and struggling) are shaped to a considerable extent by unequal access to networks and flows of local knowledge and social capital, including structures of governance. Christiania is home to far greater variety of dwelling types, fluid families and diverse practices of home-making than would ever be possible in mainstream urban society today: it is by studying this creativity, adaptability and entrepreneurship that we have most to learn.

In conclusion it is important to consider what lessons Christiania offers planners and environmentalists concerned to cultivate mutuality and conservation in mainstream urban public space. How is it that Christiania can provide a place for people to make their own home, where Copenhagen pointedly does not; those people who do not 'fit' or those whose unpaid caring work goes unrewarded? When asking these questions it is important to unravel everyday realities from romanticised imaginations. While the infrastructure of daily life allows diverse groups of Christianites to realise alternative visions of home and family life, an ethic of care fails to thrive in current practices of direct democracy. There are nevertheless lessons to be learned for cities in the mainstream where the care-less competitiveness of hypermodernity is unsustainable.[44]

Finally, this chapter is written at a time when people within and beyond Christiania, indeed people all over the world, are busy getting ready to celebrate the community's 40th birthday. A huge party is a fitting way to celebrate — even as Christiania remains at the crossroads of an unknown future. The mood may be a little sombre for a party: forty years of siege and struggle has resulted in overwhelming weariness. Nevertheless, a party is possibly the best way to illustrate the true (multiple economic) value of 'free space' and the creative culture of innovation it represents. The original hankering for a 'junk playground' still resonates today in the call for alternative visions of home and family life with space and time to flourish — for those who would otherwise have neither home nor family in the city at all. Change is inevitable but as the Christianite TT reminds us: 'consider how many people there are and then it's incredible what we've been able to achieve; and we do always… incredible things happen all the time'.

BØSSEHUSET — QUEER PERSPECTIVES IN CHRISTIANIA

Cathrin Wasshede

> 'Bøssehuset, it sounds a bit scary. Is it about sex or what?' The first thing I saw was the torso with the big dick. 'Do I dare to go inside?' But then I thought: 'Just do it. I just have to do it.' I opened the door and came inside. They were rehearsing a Christmas show and I started working with Christmas decorations.
>
> *Gay activist in Bøssehuset*

Bøssehuset has existed almost as long as Christiania; it started in 1973, two years after the Freetown was established, when some gay men moved into the building Karlsvognen. From 1976 it was the permanent home for Bøssernes Befrielses Front (The Gay Men's Liberation Front, from now on BBF). The quote above is a piece of a story about the first contact a gay man had with Bøssehuset.[1] It highlights some of the many different faces of Bøssehuset. The 'torso with the big dick' is a sculpture with a fountain, placed in Bøssehaven (The Gay Garden), outside Bøssehuset. Another gay man in Bøssehuset claims that this fountain has been demolished many times. He understands those demolitions as expressions of heteronormativity, but is at the same time eager to claim that people in Christiania are very open and sweet and that he *never* has been harassed in Christiania because of his homosexuality. Yet another gay man tells me that the fountain never has been *actively* demolished, but instead used in rather careless ways; for example as a stand for fireworks. According to him this is an ongoing process over the years and not an act of homophobia or heteronormativity.

The reason why I open this text with reflections on this fountain with the big phallus is that it works as a symbol, a materialisation of the gay *male* character of Bøssehuset. The phallus is also the logo for Bøssehuset. In the logo it is placed in the buttocks of another human being.[2] I found it interesting that lesbians, bi- and transsexuals were officially included in Bøssehuset as late as in the middle of the 2000s. Another interesting thing is Bøssehuset's absence in research on Christiania. In spite of its position as one of the most well-known and most visited gay culture scenes in Copenhagen, Denmark and the south of Sweden — by both gay and straight people — it has not been viewed as a subject interesting enough for researchers. When it comes to Christiania's self-presentation, on websites, pamphlets and books, Bøssehuset is mentioned, but not highlighted in the same way as for example Solvognen (the Sun Chariot) and Christiania's Pigegarde (Girls Guard). My main interest in this chapter is to look at the relation between Bøssehuset and Christiania, including lesbians as well. Do gay people have experiences of heteronormativity in a 'free' — and maybe queer — place such as Christiania? If so, is it the same sort of heteronormativity as in the wider society or another kind? Why is there a gay house in Christiania? By which needs is it motivated? Queer is a word with many connotations. It was a word that was used to insult people that were sexually off the norm, it was captured by queer activists in New York in 1990 and it has ever since been elaborated both theoretically and politically. It is anti-normative, especially anti-heteronormative. Queer politics often use humour, parody and provocation when staging resistance. Key words are 'transgressing', 'destabilising' and 'performance'.[3]

In the following I will, as a background, say something about the early history of Bøssehuset, and after that I will discuss gay people's relations to (other) Christianites, the relations between lesbians and Bøssehuset and the relation between Bøssehuset and the Danish national organisation for homo-, bi- and transsexuals. I will also briefly touch on the issue of HIV/AIDS and its effects on Bøssehuset and the people engaged in it.

History of Bøssehuset

On Bøssehuset's website one can read about the history of Bøssehuset and BBF from 1971 to 1982.[4] The historical documentation site is filled with photos and details from the past. The tone is quite self-embracing; they write about successes and triumphs during the years, but they also reveal problems they have had, for example conflicts around ideology, leadership and the use of 'women's clothes'. In the following I will present an overview of this early history, divided into phases.

The first phase is constituted by the birth of BBF and is described as a period with lots of activity and ideas. BBF grew out of a demonstration in 1971, held in memory of Stonewall[5] and arranged by some members of Forbundet af 1948 (national organisation for homosexuals),[6] as a response to the experienced need for more direct action. From the beginning, BBF met every Monday and Bøssehuset's activists still do.

The next phase is distinguished by expansion and crisis. In 1972 BBF activists started to join the Thy Camp, which is a big yearly summer camp, following in Woodstock's footsteps, and organised workshops, performances and introduction meetings there. Thy Camp seems to have been one of BBF's most important recruiting places.[7] When BBF in 1973 participated in a broadcast — which later was printed in a book called *Mænd, det svækkede køn*[8] (*Men, the weakened sex*) — they had a sort of breakthrough in society; they were invited to present information about gay liberation at a large number of schools. According to their own storytelling on the website they were the first in Denmark to provide information about homosexuality in schools.[9] Another milestone was the publishing of Bent Jacobsen's record *Bøsse.*[10] BBF gained many new members. In spite of — or due to — this, BBF experienced the same problem that many groups in the women's movement did; disagreements, endless discussions and schisms. They tried to handle this by striving for more firm structures and a common base.

The next phase, of which settling in Christiania is a significant event, is characterised by cultural approaches and performances. When BBF, in the spring of 1976, moved to Bøssehuset in Christiania this was celebrated with a big torchlight procession through the city, escorted by the police. From then on this was the permanent home for BBF. Later that year BBF produced its first theatre performance. Another cultural-political activity arranged by BBF was Bøssekaravanerne (Gay Men's Caravans) that travelled round Denmark in rented buses, visiting small cities, where they gave theatre performances and information about gay liberation and made direct actions.

1980, which is the starting point for the next phase, is described on the website as the year when BBF 'commits collective suicide and arranges its own funeral under festive forms'.[11] Some of the members became more active in Forbundet af 1948, some were more engaged in the work of Christiania. The only thing that went on was a choir called Bøssekoret (The Gay Men's Choir).

In 1982 the deadlock came to an end and the Monday meetings were taken up again. The new phase started off with the forming of Bøsserup's Pigegarde, as a part of Copenhagen Carnival. After that a theatre scene was built in Bøssehuset and the choir performed 'Melodi Grand Prix', which resulted in one thousand visitors during a period of ten days. In 1985 the first Frøken Verden (Miss World Contest) was held — a tradition that went on for many years. Bøssehuset had become a very important place for gay culture, not only for Denmark, but also for people from all over Europe.

Gay People in Christiania

In Christiania the idea of freedom of the individual is central. 'Live and let live' is a motto that embraces a very tolerant attitude towards other people and their personalities and ways of living. As long as you behave decently — which in Christiania means that you do no harm to other people and that you fulfil your undertaking — you are worthy of respect. One of the gay men I interviewed put it like this: 'As long as you are not violent, as long as you don't misuse people, as long as you behave decently at your level, it is okay. And we do that here. And people say their meaning.' Another gay man says that Bøssehuset has always been a sanctuary for him and that you don't need to be 'smart', you can just be relaxed and 'yourself'. It is obvious that he talks about both Bøssehuset and Christiania as a whole. The mixture of people is highlighted as something positive: 'I like the mixture of minorities [...] the alcoholic [...] no, they smoke too much hash, but they are *a part* [included]. They are welcome.' Because of this ideology, where everyone is allowed to live her/his life as s/he wants to, I think it is interesting to highlight the possible occurrence of heteronormativity.

The gay men in Bøssehuset that I have interviewed all claim that they have never felt harassed due to their homosexuality in Christiania, rather the opposite: 'I have never met a person here that is negative towards me. They actually don't bother. You are just here', one of them says. In relation to a story about an 'Olympic Game' that Bøssehuset arranged at the end of the 1970s, another gay man says that the Christianites often go to Bøssehuset to have a really good laugh. It is a place where good laughs are expected. At the Olympic Game they were all dressed up in elegant women's clothes and competed in a 100-metre race in stiletto heels, English waltz and handbag tussle. In the story told by the gay man the point is that even people such as the Bullshit biker gang were amused by the *fisselettes* (sissies, I return to this epithet later in the chapter) in Christiania:

> Suddenly we discovered that there were like ten bikers in full uniform and we thought: 'Here we are in women's clothes and dancing English waltz and everything. Okay, if they come and beat us, they do.' [...] But nothing happened. Quite the contrary; they were about to die of laughing. They had the most amusing afternoon they have had for years and years.

At the same time he says that the pushers in Christiania are not always free from homophobia. Sometimes they shout at gay men in women's clothes, and the word 'bøsse' is the worst they can come up with when they want to offend each other. Another gay man — who has been living in Christiania on several occasions, altogether six years — also says that the Christianites like Bøsssehuset and are happy for it. But when asked about heteronormativity in Christiania he almost shouts: 'Yes there is!' The thing he brings up is the repeated demolition of the fountain with the big phallus in Bøssehaven that he has heard about. Besides that, people are really cute, he says. But when talking about heterosexual men, he is deeply convinced that they are the same in Christiania as everywhere else. I try to understand what he means and ask him a lot of questions about this, but it is hard to catch it. He says it is about the gender, about masculinity, and makes a loud and raw sound to illuminate this. I propose the word *macho* to describe it, but he rejects that. Instead he says that they are good at working and that they are relaxed. I then propose the word *hippieman* and he agrees quite distractedly. He talks instead about the clothes; the way that heterosexual men in Christiania dress in a relaxed way and don't care about fashion. Maybe the reason why he brings this up is that he himself is very interested in fashion and likes to dress in 'nice, proper clothes'. He describes himself as vain and continues: 'I am a too proper lady, too conservative to live here. It is a bit too much gum boots and such things here.' Another thing he brings up is that even though there is a more open atmosphere in Christiania, it works the same way as things do on the 'outside'. One example of this is, according to him, that people live in their own 'small boxes' in the same way as the villa owners do on the 'outside'.

Two of the interviewed men talk about how demanding the open and tolerant ideology is. The gay man who has been committed to Bøssehuset for 15 years, but never lived there, answers my question asking if he would like to live there as follows:

Interviewee: I don't think I could let go.
Cathrin: What is it that you should let go?
Interviewee: Myself as a person. There are some things that you should work with. [...] I really need to be by myself. I live alone and I love the place I live [...] a nice apartment and all that, you know. And I have Bøssehuset when I need it. I think it is a good balance. I am not a hash smoker, I only smoke hash for comfort, on special occasions. [...] I don't need to be in only one place. I want Christiania, I want Bøssehuset, I really want our dear gay community, but I also want my lovely colleagues and their hetero world. I like to connect things with each other. I think it would be too limited, but I don't know if it would be like that if I moved here. I don't know.

Another gay man, who earlier has lived in Christiania for several years, tells me that Christiania demands open mindedness from you.

Bøssehuset has participated in many activities in Christiania. According to Ole Lykke, Christiania resident since the late 1970s, they are among the most devoted and hard-working Christianites. One example of this is their participation in the Junk Blockade in 1979, when Christianites threw all the heavy drugs out (see Tomas Nilson's chapter in this book). Another example is that they have been part of *Valborg*—Christiania's election list for the municipality—with Bøsselisten (The Gay List).

An interesting aspect of the Freetown and homosexuality was exposed in an article in *Ordkløveren*, a Christiania magazine, in 1977.[12] In this article homosexuality was defined by the author as a bourgeois phenomenon and as a sign of sickness—a product of the capitalist society in the same way as drug addiction. The main argument was the classic one: since homosexuals are supposed not to reproduce the human species, it is unnatural. The author did not want to punish the homosexuals, but to prohibit people from spreading what he called 'lies', such as claiming that homosexuality is natural and should be equated with heterosexuality.

Of course this article ought to be understood in its context; it is written at a time when homosexuality still was a psychiatric diagnosis. It was not until 1980 that it was eliminated from the Danish register of sicknesses. But still, it is interesting to reflect a bit over this phenomenon. In a place like Christiania, where the freedom of the individual and the collective community is so fundamental, and where a place such as Bøssehuset exists, it is noteworthy that homosexuals still could be regarded as mentally ill. Important though, is that members of the editorial board in the following issue very clearly distanced themselves from the article. Many people had contacted them and asked why they gave space to such a standpoint. The editors argued that *Ordkløveren* existed for Christianites and that the man who wrote the article was a Christianite. Besides, if he had this attitude towards homosexuality, it was a part of, and a problem for, Christiania. In the editors' answer they used such strong words as 'fascist', 'male resentment' and 'heterosexual rubbish' to describe the author and his text. In the end they ironically thanked him for not wanting to punish them.[13]

In another issue of *Ordkløveren* in 1976, a man who identified himself as bisexual, wrote an article about the oppression of homo- and bisexuals in Christiania. He claimed that people were afraid of being called homosexuals and being laughed at. To avoid this they suppressed their so-called feminine characteristics, such as emotions and human love. He continued:

> How often do we see two men dancing tight together in Christiania's restaurants? Almost never. How often do we see two men kissing each other passionately? Never, because the surroundings do not allow it, and the surroundings are us, you.[14]

The author of the article further writes that in the past, he used to smuggle men into his house during the night and make sure they left before people in Christiania had woken up. Once he danced and kissed with another man at the dance hall Loppen (The Flea). After that he felt like no one dared to meet his eyes. He also noticed how people became stiff when he physically touched them. The reason why he stayed in Christiania in spite of this experience of homophobia was that he considered Christiania a better place, more conscious, than the wider society. So he came out and tried to make the Freetown a better place for homo- and bisexuals, a process that went very slowly though, according to him: 'But you can still very easily feel oppressed in the Freetown.'[15]

His story is quite different from those of the interviewees who claim that they never have been met negatively in Christiania. This can be related to the difference in time; the article was written in 1976 and the interviews were conducted in 2010 and 2011. The climate around homosexuality has changed. Another possible reason for this difference is that Bøssehuset and gay people were more *explicitly* political in the 1970s than they are now, at least if you listen to the gay men I interviewed. Two of the interviewees, active in Bøssehuset at the time of the interviews, actually reject the idea of seeing sexuality as something political: 'That is private, you know. Not that you can't talk about it, but I can't understand that people can get pissed about others having a different sexuality.' They both talk about the importance of equal rights and human rights as something central and taken for granted: 'Of course we shall have the same rights. It's nothing to talk about, if we should or should not. We shall just have it!' Politics are boring according to one of them. But when he reflects on the theatre play he is participating in at the moment for the interview, he finds out that it is utterly political. And still fun to do. This is central. It has to be fun. If it is fun and creative, if politics is passionate, it is worth doing it.[16] As I see it, this is a central feature of queer politics. Another aspect of this 'de-politicisation' is the individualisation process. The phrase 'the personal is political' seems to be less central for the activists in Bøssehuset today than in the 1970s. Sexuality is, listening to those gay men, considered a personal and individual thing — and *not* a political one.

Over the years, Bøssehuset has, according to their website, also participated in direct actions organised by other groups that were part of the overall left-wing movement in the 1970s. For example they participated in support demonstrations and other activities for the squatters in Nørrebro in 1976; the squatting of the Swedish embassy as a protest against the eviction of the squatted block *Mullvaden* in Stockholm in 1979; and a demonstration — including a hunger strike — at the Iranian embassy as a protest against the assassinations of homosexual men in Iran. When participating in 1st of May demonstrations they had a banner that said: 'Down with the Dick Imperialism'. There were lots of other activities together with the left-wing movement and the organisation the Mandebevægelsen (the Men's Movement), such as seminars, workshops, camps, leaflets, information at schools and the magazine *Seksualpolitik* (*Sexual Politics*).

Bøssehuset as a (Gay) Cultural Institution

Bøssehuset's status in Christiania is closely related to its role as an important cultural institution. Christianites, as well as people from all over Copenhagen, Denmark and the south of Sweden, have enjoyed — and still enjoy — the many theatre plays, performances, cabarets and film festivals that have taken place in Bøssehuset, or been arranged by Bøssehuset.

Through the whole period, so-called women's clothes and attributes have played a central role in Bøssehuset's cultural and political activity. Many of the gay men — probably not all of them, but those that I have met and heard about — call themselves *fisselettes*. *Fisselette* is a Danish word for 'sissies' or 'wanton women'. Etymologically, it probably comes from the word *fisse*, which means cunt. A *fisselette* is a man in women's clothes who has feminine attributes, with a stereotypically feminine manner. He is not pretending to be a woman and he does not want to pass as a woman. He is not even a drag queen, since the drag queen often tries to be as 'authentic' as possible. The gay men often combine the feminine attributes with a beard and are eager to show that they are 'men'.

Even back in the 1970s, when BBF visited schools to inform about gay liberation, they dressed in women's clothes, used music and theatre because 'the lectures were too boring', as one gay man expresses it. It was a way to 'pep them up' and it became 'more and more a strategy' to achieve their political goals, he says. In 1976 there was an article in *Ordkløveren* about feminine gay men, in which the author claimed that they made a common cause with Rødstrømperne (Redstockings, the Danish women's movement).[17] He argued that the wearing of high heels, make-up, long painted nails, big hats, ostrich feathers and women's clothes was feminism, since it challenged the gender roles:

> Probably heterosexuals get red rashes all over the body when they think of or meet homosexuals, since they consider gay men as men that betray the man's role. Gay men refuse to be men. What is a man? A man is first and foremost characterised by the fact that he has acquired, through his socialisation and function in society, power and hegemony over women, children and nature. Besides, it is his duty to manifest power over as many other men as he can. If a man thinks that this 'power' is something natural, something he has the right to, we call him a dick imperialist.[18]

According to the article, a man wearing feminine attributes showed that he was gay and that he had given up his male power. The author continued by declaring that this exposed the fact that this power was not natural; a fact that in its turn made men unsecure and put the male power in danger. I find this analysis interesting because it is almost identical with Judith Butler's theories about drag, written fifteen years later.[19] Parodical performances of femininity or masculinity show that you make fun of them and of the idea of a true essence of identity. It becomes obvious for the observer that femininity and masculinity are not natural, but constructed and illusionary. Dissonance between any of the three levels; anatomical sex, gender identity or gender performance, actually unmasks and destabilises the heterosexual matrix. It is through using what Butler calls the ambivalent space, that we can change dominant norms and systems.[20]

In the article the author was obviously responding to criticism when he wrote that feminine gay men did not oppress women. On the contrary, the strategy was to provoke and eliminate the gender roles through making the feminine features grotesque and maybe combining them with a full beard. He wrote that they embraced the characteristics that men imposed on women in order to make women sexual objects. The criticism that I assume he was responding to is made visible in the interview I conducted with a lesbian Rødstrømpe in Kvindehuset (The Women's House) in 2010. She claims that she is not interested in that kind of politics — she even implicitly hints that it doesn't qualify as politics — because as a radical feminist she has thrown all that feminine stuff out. She actually talks about a correct uniform for a true feminist that includes working trousers and no feminine attributes: 'It is the uniform I think is appropriate for a feminist. I don't think she should have long finger nails and stuff like that'. I would however argue that even if the genders that are performed in drag, fisselettes, cross-dressing and butch and femme, can appear stereotypical and conservative, they can be subversive in that they denaturalise sex/gender, put them in new contexts and push the limits of them.[21] Of course not all gay men embraced this strategy. In 1973 Bøssehuset had 20 activists from HAW (Homosexual Action West Berlin) staying in Christiania. On Bøssehuset's website one can read that Bøssehuset's activists learned about the use of make-up and drag as a political strategy from the German activists. This is said to have led to some disruption in Bøssehuset, but later that year gay men from Christiania were giving out leaflets on Strøget, some of them dressed in skirts.[22]

In one of the interviews, a man is very careful to stress that he is *not* a drag queen, but a *fisselette*. A *fisselette* is, according to him, a man who dresses in women's clothes, and that is not the same as trying to look like a woman. He explains this by saying that he has kept his moustache and his beard when dressing in women's clothes for performances. Another gay man also talks about the use of women's clothes and beard, in connection with the word *fisselette*:

1. Christiania in a global perspective.

2. 'Christiania's Common Law'. Photo: Håkan Thörn.

3. Building materials depot, featuring mannequins. Photo: Amy Starecheski.

4. Circus visit Christiania. Photo: Amy Starecheski.

5. Anette and Britta. Photo: Amy Starecheski.

6. Rasmus and Carsten. Photo: Amy Starecheski.

7. Nils at home in Christiania. Photo: Amy Starecheski.

8. Christiania history mural. Photo: Amy Starecheski.

9. The Peace Arc / Fredens Ark. Photo: Signe Sophie Bøggild.

10. Lisa. Photo: Amy Starecheski.

11. Tata at work. Photo: Amy Starecheski.

12. Ole at home in Christiania. Photo: Amy Starecheski.

13. Christiania garbage truck. Photo: Amy Starecheski.

14. Lisa and Eira. Photo: Amy Starecheski.

15. Photo: Anders Lund Hansen.

16. Photo: Anders Lund Hansen.

17. Climate Bottom Meeting, December 2009. Photo: Håkan Thörn.

18. Funeral ceremony at Climate Bottom Meeting, December 2009. Photo: Håkan Thörn.

19. Grave at Climate Bottom Meeting, December 2009. Photo: Håkan Thörn.

20. Girls Guard in the Metro. Photo: Nils Vest.

21. Girls Guard EU march. Photo: Nils Vest.

22. Girls Guard's cheerleader Ramona Macho and drummer Lis. Photo: Nils Vest.

23. Girls Guard, Christianshavns torv. Photo: Nils Vest.

24. Allan at home in Christiania. Photo: Amy Starecheski.

25. Birthday party 2010. Photo: Cathrin Wasshede.

26. The world's safest café. Photo: Håkan Thörn.

27. Winter flowers. Photo: Håkan Thörn.

28. Winter message. Photo: Håkan Thörn.

29. Stupa. Photo: Håkan Thörn.

30. Post Office. Photo: Håkan Thörn.

31. Inside Post Office. Photo: Amy Starecheski.

32. Mural. Photo: Håkan Thörn.

> It was a weapon we used. To emphasise that we were different. We kept the beard. Because when we walk around in our ordinary clothes we look like quite ordinary people. We used it as an instrument for struggle; to dress like women and at the same time being men. And continue to be men.

To combine the dress or skirt with a beard seems to be a strong symbol for radical gay and gender politics.[23] Through dissonance between anatomic sex and gender performance they unmask the heteronormative gender system.

Bøssehuset has arranged several Frøken Verden (Miss World Contests) for gay men. It started off in Bøssehuset but, an interviewee tells me, when it became so popular that people crawled up on ladders to peep through the windows, it was moved to Den Grå Hal (the Grey Hall) in Christiania. The interviewee says that it was not a drag show, but a personality contest. When it became more like a superficial fashion contest they dropped it: 'Then we did not want to do it anymore […] It lost its magic.' During the interview with the lesbian Rødstrømpe, she tells me about how lesbians were asked to perform as bodyguards at a contest in Den Grå Hal. She laughs when she talks about the sissy gay men and the butch lesbians and says: 'We support each other'. This very year, 2011, when BBF, as well as Christiania, celebrates its 40th anniversary, Frøken Verden has been resurrected. On Bøssehuset's website one can read that the misses — who can be of all genders — are said to come from the 'homo underground'[24] and that:

> The show is probably the most outrageous drag monster contest. The show is a parody of the world's beauty contests and the drag shows in the gay milieu […] Even if Frøken Verden mostly is about having fun, it is also a gender- and sexual political comment on a body-fixated world with stereotypical beauty ideals and gender roles, both inside and outside the gay milieu, in the best self-ironical spirit of Bøssehuset.[25]

Another important thing that Bøssehuset has engaged in is Christiania's Pigegarde (Girl's Guard). Pigegarden's history started in 1982 when

Bøssehuset participated in the Carnival of Copenhagen with something called Bøsserup's Pigegarde. A *pigegarde* is a uniformed marching women's orchestra, and Bøsserup is a small village in Denmark. Christiania's Pigegarde was active between 1991 and 2003 and was, according to one of the interviewees, for the 'ladies of Christiania'. The epithet 'ladies' included, according to him, heterosexual and lesbian women and gay men. I ask him if there were any heterosexual men participating, but he did not think so. Another gay man who was part of Pigegarden however says that heterosexual men have participated in Pigegarden. Christiania's Pigegarde was a well-known phenomenon for people all over Copenhagen. They marched in the streets, in front of the castle and Folketinget (the parliament) and other places such as Bakken (a well-known amusement park with a zoo). When they performed they were always political, both in their uniforms and in their texts. One example is the use of timers on their shoulders, which symbolised the fact that the ladies had enough. Another example is their creation of Kvindeligt Opløsnings Forbund (Female Association of Dissolution), who in connection with the Danish referendum on the EU Amsterdam Treaty in 1998, marched under the motto 'Close your eyes and think of the Fatherland — we vote blindly'. They wanted to contribute to 'the general voting psychosis' and marched with white blind sticks, sunglasses and toilet paper with EU flags on their heads.[26]

Several performance groups that experiment with gender attributes have existed in or visited Bøssehuset over the years, for example at Din Salon (Your Salon); Ask Helga, Schwanzen Sänger Knaben and Aupair Outrair, just to mention a few. During the 1980s Bøssehuset performed some cabarets related to the HIV/AIDS crisis, something which I return to later in this chapter.

When talking about Bøssehuset, the two interviewees who at the time of the interviews were active in Bøssehuset, both almost exclusively mention its role as a cultural institution. When I ask one of them what he would do if Bøssehuset did not exist, he first answers by talking about his acting and that he maybe would not be able to play theatre any more. After that he says: 'My life would be more boring. Bøssehuset has really pushed my limits as a human being. I have learned more about the necessity of accepting people as they are'. And again he returns to the significance of Bøssehuset as a cultural institution: 'It is fantastic to be part of an underground movement, an off-off-Broadway-thing, it is *marvellous*'. The other man also talks about Bøssehuset mainly as a cultural institution, a theatre. When he came there he was a student actor. He highlights how Bøssehuset's cultural character makes it easier for other people to go there. For example he mentions that his own parents have visited Bøssehuset to watch performances.

Lesbians in Bøssehuset

Over the years Bøssehuset/BBF has co-operated with lesbians and the Lesbisk Bevægelse (Lesbian Movement). In 1975 BBF held a meeting for students at the University of Copenhagen together with people from the Mandebevægelsen, the women's movement and Lesbisk Bevægelse. At a big bøsse party at Loppen in Christiania in 1978, there was a performance by *Søsterrock* (Sister rock), Denmark's first feminist women rock band, and many people from Lesbisk Bevægelse were there.[27] A lesbian cabaret took place in Bøssehuset in the 1970s and the lesbian Rødstrømpe who I interviewed claims that lesbians were always welcome to use the Christiania milieu. Bøssehuset was the place if you wanted to have really big parties, she says. She was playing music and having fun at Bøssehuset when they celebrated the 100th anniversary of International Women's Day in 2010:

> It was not purely a women's party, it was a mixed party and the gay men were there and they were dressed up in women's clothes. It was a very funny mix of real left-wingers, anti-fascists and members of Femø [a summer camp for women/lesbians related to Kvindehuset — the Women's House — in Copenhagen, author's remark] and then the gay men.

Even though lesbians had been part of Bøssehuset over the years, they did not really feel included, according to a lesbian living in Christiania:

> Bøssehuset [...] we did things for them, came to some parties, but we were not a part of it. Sometimes it was mixed parties, which I came to. Or theatre, they could use some stands for decorations. No doubt they had great respect for us.

Even though she uses the pronominal 'us', she later says that she was the only lesbian in Bøssehuset for long periods. One of the gay men mentions other individual lesbians who have been participating for some time — for example a woman who provided light and sound for the performances. When I watched a video of performances in Bøssehuset in the 1980s, I do however see a lot of women actors on the scene, even more women than men.[28]

Even though the lesbian woman never felt as if she was a part of Bøssehuset, she claims that it has been important to her. Maybe this is related to the fact that she never found a lesbian community at Christiania. Instead she had Kvindesmedjen (the Women's Smithy) which, besides its function as a workshop and apprentice place for female smiths, was a kind of feminist community. She describes it in very ambivalent terms: both as a strong women's group; a breeding ground for long-lasting friendships, and as a heterosexual nuclear family and craftsmen community. Further she claims that the women in Kvindesmedjen were almost exclusively heterosexual — some of them, according to her, even wanted Kvindesmedjen straight — and at the same time she tells me that there were two other lesbians in Kvindesmedjen who had a love relationship with each other. In a way she leaves them out of her account: 'I was among hetero women. No, there was a lesbian couple, but they were not political about it. Or I just did not see it.' She says she did not know the 'few lesbians' that lived in Christiania. It seems like it is only the politicised lesbianism that counts and is made visible. Besides, this ambivalence, where the gay or lesbian identity and community is downsized, can also be about privileging the community of Christiania and the identity as Christianite over the gay/lesbian ones. This may be due to the fact that Christiania is often under big pressure and therefore needs people to identify with and struggle for it, and it can also be due to heteronormative attitudes in Christiania. Bøssehuset on the other hand, was very explicit with its function as a community for gay men. A physical place, a community and an identity were offered — and therefore we have gay men in Christiania. This was never the case for lesbians — and therefore they 'do not exist' in Christiania. Silence, in this sense, entails invisibility. Still, many lesbians seem to have felt partly included in Bøssehuset.

The lesbian interviewee characterises lesbians in general as sometimes 'too serious, analytical and academic' compared to the funny, queer and humorous gay men. She says: 'The gay men were funny and did not pose that many questions to the heterosexual community, in that serious lesbian way, if you understand.' A central thing in this is that Bøssehuset's queerness probably was more fitting in Christiania. Christiania is kind of queer in itself, since it challenges many norms and since the politics is characterised by parody, humour and carnival. At the same time, the articles in *Ordkløveren* and the history of BBF point in another direction; the gay men *were* posing questions to the heterosexual community, at least to men and masculinity. Why is it that those questions are seen as less serious and less challenging than the lesbians'?

One of the gay men points out that the lesbians had Kvindehuset (The Women's House) in the city to go to, as a reason why they were not included in Bøssehuset. Besides it was BBF that formed Bøssehuset — and they were obviously gay men. Even though it has been separatist — my word, no one uses it to describe it — women, hetero as well as lesbians, have always visited Bøssehuset, mostly as guests, enjoying the shows and the company, or as crafts(wo)men helping with practical work. They were however not allowed to the Monday meetings. This was changed in the middle of the 2000s when lesbians, as well as bi- and transsexuals, were officially included in Bøssehuset. One of the gay men discusses this in the interview:

> In 2009 or something, we started Din Salon [Your Salon] and suddenly we began to invite women. And we had Den Røde Tråd [The Red Thread, a women's musician group], and all the others. And we made several women get on the stage, and there were some men who said 'what are we going to do with all those women?' And I say: 'hello, women are also human beings.' If we are to move on again, we can't close the door, we can't say no. We need more people who wish to do the things that we wish to do. And we will do it together.

The words *move on again* expose something that another gay man told me: that Bøssehuset had a crisis around 2006 — at the same time that they decided to officially include lesbians, bi- and transsexuals. Even the words *we need more people in* expose this. Of course one can question my interest for this earlier lack of inclusiveness; why should lesbians be part of something like Bøssehuset? They are not gay men. Maybe my question should be: Why isn't there a lesbian house in Christiania?

AIDS in the 1980s

During the 1980s Bøssehuset was heavily stricken by HIV/AIDS. One gay man I interviewed tells me about this period and he returns several times to the fact that people died. When he counts the names of those who survived, he only comes up with four names. In the beginning they didn't know how HIV was passed on:

> It was completely insane. In the beginning we didn't know how it was passed on for example. We didn't know anything. It was a process that went on for ten years and people died and died and died and died and died. [...] It was really, really, really many people that died. We went to many funerals.

One significant funeral was that of Nelly Nylon; who was described by the interviewee as 'a big political talent' and 'a magic person', as well as the person who started the Frøken Verden personality contest. At the end of his life, Nelly lived in a gay collective called Konesumpen (The Wife Trash) in Christiania, and the funeral ceremony for Nelly took place in the Freetown. Photos from that occasion were published in a magazine called *Press.*[29] This is an example of Bøssehuset's deep anchorage in Christiania.

Even though the activists in Bøssehuset lived under significant pressure due to HIV/AIDS, they had a great time, the interviewee says. They produced theatre plays, had parties and spent a lot of time together. One play was called *Intet nyt fra Pestfronten* (*From the plague front, nothing new*) and it is described as rough, in a way that mirrored the daily life:

> It was so rough! It was like: you went to the hospital in the afternoon and bathed your dying friend's forehead with a chilled sponge and then you went to Bøssehuset and partied all night long. [...] It [HIV/AIDS] diminished the work force, but I don't think it diminished our lifestyle. Because there was nothing to do. We could nevertheless have fun [laughs].

As a family they took care of each other — a phenomenon well known in gay groups and research.[30] In the interview it is described as follows:

> It was very characteristic that we used BBF to make new families. Those people became very much our families. Some of us were thrown out from our families [of origin] because they really didn't want such a child.

An interesting aspect of the 'family' and the drawing up of boundaries is that the risk of being infected is supposed to be kept inside the gay men's group. At least if one listens to the HIV-positive gay man I interviewed. He says that since he got HIV he has never had sex with heterosexual men, because he does not want them to be infected. I am a bit surprised and ask him several times about his motive for this. He states that as a gay man you are always aware of the risk when you have sex with another man, it is somehow a part of the parcel. But when it comes to heterosexual men, you just don't expose them to this: 'A gay man knows very well that it is one of the *conditions* of being gay. And it's not a condition for a heterosexual man.' According to him it is an ethical question. This ethic is among other things related to the fact that heterosexual men are supposed to become fathers, he says, even though he himself is a father: 'But that is something else. It's a limit that I don't want to cross. It's one thing when you infect each other because you have gay sex [...] but with a heterosexual man [...] it is just too *dangerous*.' The words *each other* explicitly show that the gay men group is clearly defined and separated from other groups of people. It is exclusive.

Bøssehuset's Relation to Forbundet af 1948/ LGBT Danmark

Bøssehuset and BBF have an ambivalent relation to Forbundet af 1948/ LGBT Danmark. On the one hand they want to connect and cooperate with them, for example by celebrating Stonewall and participating in the board of Forbundet af 1948, but on the other hand they distance themselves from them. In the beginning they used Forbundet's place for their meetings. One of my interviewees explains this use of place by telling me about how hard it was in Christiania in the beginning, with building work, heating and other things that were 'too troublesome for such beautiful *fisselettes*'. The critique of Forbundet af 1948/ LGBT Denmark is, as I see it, about the different political practices. The most important difference is about organisational structures. In BBF and Bøssehuset they have a flat and rather anarchistic organisation, with the self-consciousness raising groups and the cultural activists at its heart. Forbundet af 1948/LGBT Danmark is a more traditional association, with a board constituted by chosen representatives. Their work is mainly directed at lobbying, changing laws and counteracting discrimination. Of course it also works as a social meeting place and over the years they have, among other things, arranged support groups, parties, school information and have contributed to the change in people's attitudes towards homosexuality. Besides the organisational difference, they use different political strategies. BBF marked this difference as early as 1971 by making a spontaneous demonstration after the one arranged by members of Forbundet af 1948. They wanted more direct action. As I see it, one of the characteristics of the content and form of BBF/Bøssehuset's politics at this time was what we today call queer. It is about challenging norms, pushing limits and provoking in a parodical, humorous and subversive way. Having fun is central. In another interview the picture of Forbundet af 1948/LGBT Danmark as traditional and boring is modulated: 'There has been a lot of theatre as well. I know they did a lot of things in earlier years, when they were more provocative.'

When talking about the — for me — surprising fact that Bøssehuset participated in Copenhagen Pride for the first time in 2010, one gay man tries to explain why it didn't happen before: 'We didn't want to be in that piss, that commercial thing [...] MTV [...] the shows are too bad [...] and people think that the politics they offer, the messages they come with, don't concern us.' Bøssehuset's activists were however received by the Pride people with open arms and, as it seems listening to the interviewee, the activists from Bøssehuset liked it a lot. He talks about it in terms of a coming out process: 'Now it is time to come out of the closet again. Now Bøssehuset just has to come out again.' Bøssehuset promoted Christiania's probably most used slogan: 'Bevar Christiania' (Save Christiania) when participating in the Pride march.[31]

Concluding Remarks

Bøssehuset is a political-cultural institution almost as old as Christiania itself and it has played a central role in the Freetown's existence. A lot of people have visited the performances that have taken place there. The activists in Bøssehuset have been some of the most committed to Christiania and the struggle for the Freetown. It is quite remarkable that this fact is not at all reflected in the research on Christiania and not enough in Christiania's own material.

Central to Bøssehuset's activity during the years was their queer strategy. They have used, and still use, parody, humour and provocation as important features of their resistance to dominating norms. At first glance it may be argued that Bøssehuset has been transformed from being very *political* in the 1970s to become more of a *cultural* institution from the 1980s and on. But as is evident when looking at social movement practices in general, such a distinction between politics and culture is questionable.[32] Culture and sexuality are political, and vice versa. In the 1970s, Bøssehuset's activists used cultural strategies and methods to achieve their goals, and nowadays they still engage in political issues, as for example in one of their latest theatre plays, 'Titus Christianus', where they deal with war and power.

BBF's and Bøssehuset's relation to Forbundet af 1948/LGBT Danmark is and has always been ambivalent. Solidarity with Forbundet af 1948, need for their help and critique against their politics, exist side by side. The gay liberation movement has been enriched by Bøssehuset's humorous and parodist strategies and the other way around; it is possible that Bøssehuset has been able to be critical and radical *because of* the gay liberation movement and its achievements. This is an analytical and empirical question to explore further: is it possible to work in a queer, opposing, deconstructing and 'in-your-face' way without a struggle for human rights, such as protection in laws, acceptance/tolerance in society, access to medical care etcetera? Is it possible and/or desirable to skip that aspect?

An interesting aspect of the phenomenon queer is its position in time. We usually consider queer as something that was born in 1990 in New York, when some activists broke out of the Pride festival and exposed their rage and militancy, and which later on has been more and more distinguished by its provocative and parodist aesthetics and forms.[33] Looking closer at the practices, strategies, contents and ideologies of BBF's and Bøssehuset's political/cultural work, it seems like some things in the 1970s already were queer — before queer as a political and academic field even existed.

The gay *male* character has been strong in BBF and Bøssehuset. It is however important to be careful with how story telling works. The phallus symbolism and the official exclusion of women in Bøssehuset do not seem to mean that there were no women there. The interesting thing is the ambivalent position that the lesbians (as well as bi- and transsexuals) had; they were a part of the gay community at the same time as they were not a part of it. Maybe this is changing now, when lesbians, bi- and transsexuals officially are included and can go to the Monday meetings. Only the future can tell us about what this implies when it comes to political/cultural strategies in Bøssehuset.

It is obvious that the context for the phallus is central. Put together with the word imperialism it symbolises patriarchal power. When used in the gay men's own garden it is a sign of humour, provocation, sexuality and community. It is experienced and used in different ways: as a collective identity symbol, as a queer and fun sign of men loving sex with other men — and maybe loving their own sexual organ; a parallel with the way in which parts of the Women's Movement worked with the speculum to get women to like their own vagina[34] — and as a symbol for men's domination in a capitalist and imperialist society. What does it mean to lesbians to be part of an association that has the phallus as its logo? An interesting question is if it would be possible for gay men to be part of an association that had a vagina as its logo/symbol.

The phenomenon of HIV/AIDS works in two directions regarding inclusion and exclusion processes. On the one hand it breaks all boundaries, since everyone can be infected. It is, so to speak, inclusive. On the other hand it seems to strengthen the boundaries around the group of gay men. They are a family that takes care of each other; they bury each other, party together and as one of my interviewee says, even keep the risk of transmitting the disease between themselves. In this sense the disease is exclusive.

In this chapter, I have called Christiania 'queer in itself', as a way to understand Bøssehuset's good relations with Christiania/other Christianites. Of course such a statement depends on how you define queer. What is queer about Christiania? Mostly it is the strategies, the political practices. The Freetown uses the device of turning things upside down and deconstructs and questions things that are taken for granted. Humour, parody and performance are central to this provocation, as is sometimes the use of dirty, abject things like the toilet paper on Pigegarden's heads or the dog poops on their shoulders.[35] Through this means they destabilise and confuse things and orders. Christiania opposes dominating norms, showing that another way of seeing and doing things is possible. The part of the concept queer — an important part — that is about opposing *hetero*normativity is however not included in Christiania's self-representation. This does not mean that Christiania is a homophobic environment — even though there are a few stories about that as well. But it implies that homophobia is not seen as an important political field to work with. So — is Christiania queer or not?

‘WEEDS AND DEEDS’ — IMAGES AND COUNTER IMAGES OF CHRISTIANIA AND DRUGS

Tomas Nilson

> Christiania, the narco-swamp, is a stinking boil, and is contaminating large areas in the Øresund region... The unrestricted handling of drugs in Christiania is no longer only a Danish problem but a concern for the whole of the Nordic region.
> Esse Petersson, Swedish MP (Folkpartiet/the Liberal Party), December 1981[1]

> [I]n the Freetown everybody can do as they please as long as they do not cause problems to others: get completely wasted or take acid five weeks in a row.
> Keld Løvetand, Christianite, April 1973[2]

> Let us get the criminality out of hash, because a lot of the money that comes in, they end up at the mafia, or at war and weapons, and a lot of other things, so let us grow some more hemp and get the green light for it — then everything will be much better.
> Olga, Christianite, November 1997[3]

The quotes above are images of Christiania’s relations to drugs, but very different ones: first external images — the ascribed ‘outside’ images — and then internal ‘counter’ images, Christiania’s own perceptions. In this chapter I will discuss such images and their relations to each other via a case study of the 1982 public debates on Christiania and its relations to drugs. That year, strong demands for a complete closure of Christiania came from the neighbouring countries in the form of political pressure, anti-drug rallies and a media drive — all based on the assumption that Christiania had turned into a stepping stone to drug addiction for Nordic youth. Also in Denmark, a strong anti-Christiania rhetoric existed, carried by political parties on the right-wing, such as the populist Progress Party (Fremskridtspartiet), the Conservative Party (Konservativt Folkeparti) and the Christian Democrats (Kristeligt Folkeparti), and outside of parliament, the demagogic European Workers Party (EAP, Europæiske Arbeiderparti).

But the case also deals with the internal images of drugs in Christiania: the 1982 'Love Sweden Tour' is important in that respect as it was a deliberate attempt to counter images of the Freetown as a 'drug nest' and instead show the 'real' Christiania to the outside world. This is an example of the many actions launched by Christiania through the years in its own struggle against a stigmatisation of the Freetown that more or less reduced its identity to a drug haven. In addition to this, Christiania's own 'drug struggle' included actions based on a distinction between 'soft' and 'hard' drugs: 1) the fight against the use and sale of hard drugs in the Freetown; and 2) the campaigns to legalise hash.

The year 1982 is chosen because it represents a *critical discourse moment*, a moment of intensified public debate and mobilisation, in the story of Christiania and drugs.[4] It provides especially illustrative and significant examples of the different views and images created in connection with Christiania's relations to drugs that have been put forth in public debates ever since the birth of the Freetown — and which are exemplified in the quotes at the beginning of this chapter.

According to the American political economist Kenneth Boulding's classic account, every image is a combination of facts, values and emotional expressions stuck together with actions, advocated by different actors.[5] Relating this to the production of 'drug images', American sociologists Craig Reinarman and Harry Levine use the concept of *drug scares* to label periods when antidrug initiatives, legislation and hype gain increased recognition and legitimacy. Drug scares are phenomena in their own right, separated from the use of drugs and problems associated with illegal substances. Drug scares have occurred several times throughout history, for example the 'War on drugs' launched in the USA in the 1980s.[6] During drug scares, drugs (often a particular one) are blamed for a variety of different types of social problems, and links are made between that drug/those drugs and certain subordinate groups in society — segments of the working class or underclass, immigrants, ethnic minorities or youth gangs — and in the process both drugs and groups are *scapegoated*.[7] Events during 1982 contained elements triggered during a drug scare: a drug (hash) and a group (the Christianites) became targets for intense critique, mobilisation and stigmatisation.

The case study will be put into a broader context of Christiania's drug struggle during its 40 years of existence. Before introducing the case study of 1982, where the different images are discussed and analysed, I will first give a brief overview of the relations between drugs and Christiania through the years. Further, after the concluding analysis of images and counter images, a short epilogue accounts for the present state of the drug issue in Christiania in the context of the Copenhagen gang wars.

Setting the Scene — Drugs in Christiania 1971–2011

The outlook on life within Christiania has always been liberal — what the individual chooses to do is pretty much his/her own concern.[8] But almost from day one such a stand became untenable, especially concerning drugs. The drug scene in Christiania evolved rapidly — it went from mostly private use to large scale pushing involving large amounts of cash. This development was viewed critically from both within Christiania and by actors on the outside.

The separation of drugs into two kinds — the *soft* drugs, such as hash, and *hard* drugs, such as heroin — has been the traditional way in Dan-

Pusher. Drawing by Leah Robb.

ish drug policy, which made it considerably more liberal than the other Scandinavian countries. Sweden and Norway have much tougher legislation in place. Since 1969 possession of soft drugs has not been an offence in Denmark; and there is a different scale when it comes to the Penal Code compared to other Scandinavian countries. In Denmark, crimes related to hard drugs have stiffer punishment attached than offences regarding soft drugs, while in the other Scandinavian countries, soft drugs carry the same penalty as other drugs.[9] There, hash is considered a so-called *gateway drug*, a stepping stone to the use of hard drugs.[10] Hash is according to such reasoning an *introductive* drug, while in Denmark hash is considered an *alternative* drug, used instead of hard drugs.

1971 to 1979 — the dilemma of freedom unlimited

At one of the first Common Meetings (which govern Christiania), a resolution was adopted stating that Christiania 'as an alternative community, cannot under any circumstances allow commerce in drugs'.[11] Obviously, at that time, the sale of drugs had become a problem concerning the whole of Christiania. According to a leading Christianite, Per Løvetand Iversen, there was an increase in sales of drugs in Christiania, despite earlier resolutions.[12] Not long after the resolution was passed, an article in the Christiania periodical *Ordkløveren* voiced criticism of the ongoing drug business within Christiania. To be a pusher in Christiania should not be possible, the writer stated, and suggested that all dealers (and users of hard drugs as well) should be expelled.[13] At the same time there seems to be a relative consensus, 'that the only acceptable drug to use is hash and the only acceptable way of dealing is between friends'.[14] This is an echo of an earlier statement that said that inhabitants should 'earn as little as possible [from drug dealing] and [...] clamp down hard on all other dealers [...] that sell other stuff than *harmless* hash'.[15]

In August 1973 another Common Meeting was called. Again the drug problems were in focus. In spite of earlier resolutions and subsequent actions against drug dealing, it was still an ongoing business. Now, the proclamation read, it was time to take a harder stance. If the rules stating that no dealing in hard drugs, and no making of profit through hash dealings, were breached, the guilty party would be reported to the police and then be evicted from Christiania. The existence of Christiania was at stake and every autonomous area must obey these rules and also face the consequences of breaking them.[16]

As is evident, the content of the first resolution on a total ban of drug dealing quickly eroded during the first years, but only the sale of hard drugs, or selling soft drugs in order to make profit, are condemned. When it comes to making profit the critical remarks should be seen in light of a certain 'zeitgeist' — a rejection of the modern consumerist society that left-wing/alternative groups were so critical of.

Right from the beginning there were however also mixed opinions regarding drugs, which separated Christianites into different groups. Christianite Børge Madsen claims that a huge gap had opened up between activists and the pusher group as early as the 1970s, mainly along the lines of profits, but the divide was getting increasingly sharper during the 1980s when the hash market started to become more autonomous (see Christa Amouroux's chapter in this book).[17]

The last years of the 1970s saw a lot of the leading activists depart because of disillusionment with drugs. Christiania ran the risk of going down the drain because this 'brain drain' of activists. A growing sense had started to emerge among many Christianites that drugs put the whole existence of Christiania at risk; and they were no longer prepared to accept that as a consequence.

Struggle against hard drugs and visions of legalisation

The Junk Blockade is an event that has gone down in Christiania folklore as an important (and perhaps rare) moment of almost complete unity. In 1979 the inhabitants of Christiania decided on a blockade in order to rid Christiania of heavy drug dealers and users. The latter were given the choice of leaving or participate in rehabilitation. The 40-day-long blockade was successful and a permanent ban on hard drugs was imposed (see René Karpantschof's chapter in this book). In a sense, as Christianite Ole Lykke points out, the blockade was a critique of the ultra liberal way of living.

But only a few years later, this particular problem resurfaced again. In the early 1980s the biker gang Bullshit gained a foothold in Christiania and started cornering the drug market. After a lengthy and quite violent power struggle, involving the Hells Angels, Bullshit left Christiania in 1987; and was dissolved. As a result, several rules were established, such as no gang-related regalia, no violence, no weapons and no dealing in hard drugs, and were explicitly expressed in the Common Law.[18]

The acceptance of soft drugs in Christiania was linked to campaigns to make them legal in Denmark. The legalisation movement in Christiania was centred around 'Free Hash', a group of people that publicly put forth arguments about positive impacts of smoking hash, and ultimately sought to legalise hash. Their motto was 'Fight narcotics — allow free hash'. From that movement sprang *Hampebladet*, (the *Hemp Sheet*), a glossy paper that was started in 1980. In the first issue, the editors proclaimed that first and foremost the paper was about 'hemp, hash and smokers', and little space would be devoted to other kinds of drugs. Plenty of reasons for supporting the movement were outlined, such as various 'good' cultural and medical reasons to use hash; and the argument that legalisation would curb the smuggling of hard drugs.[19]

After the Bullshit gang left in 1987, a renewed drug struggle took place in Christiania — in 1989 Christiania fought outside dealers and a wall was built closing off the main entrance to Pusher Street. In 1992 the police started a lengthy campaign against drugs in order to rid the Freetown of hash. It lasted for 16 months, during which Christiania's claim that it was not a place for hard drugs was confirmed by the police's searches. Simultaneously, the police started to act with more force and in 1994 Amnesty International even felt inclined to report on police brutality (see René Karpantschof's chapter in this book).

The hash hearings

In the late 1990s a renewed campaign for legalisation of hash was launched by Christianites. To legalise hash was of course an old wish for a number of Christianites, but a more serious approach began in 1997 with the 'hash hearings'.

In total four 'hash hearings' were held between 1997 and 2001, three of them initiated by Christiania, one called by different committees in the parliament, where Christiania's strongest defender in the 2000s, the Red-Green Alliance (Enhedslisten) argued for the legalisation of hash. In these hearings, the medical, cultural and social implications of smoking hash were discussed by a number of scholars, politicians and artists. Mobilising experts in support of its political campaigns was a method that had been used by Christiania before to good effect.

The closing down and re-opening of the Pusher Street hash market

A key element in the new Normalisation Plan launched by the Liberal-Conservative government that came into power in 2001 was to increase efforts to rid the Freetown of hash. This came into effect through intensified police activities in Christiania, emphasising zero tolerance, and in 2004 the Pusher Street hash market was closed down. In connection with this the Danish National Museum bought one of the 'hash stalls', characteristic of the Pusher Street hash market, and put it on display, presented as part of the Danish 'cultural heritage'.

The consequences of the closing down of Pusher Street were exactly what the defenders of Christiania's hash market, and even the police, had predicted. It only moved the drug dealing to other places and created new problems for the police when a violent drug war broke out in the Nørrebro district as different gangs fought each other for control of the lucrative hash market. But just a couple of years later Push-

Pusher Street hash stall. Drawing by Leah Robb.

er Street was in business again.[20] In 2011, the hash business is back to 'normal' in Christiania; even the characteristic hash stalls, in which different brands of marijuana and hash are on open display, are to be seen along Pusher Street.

1982 — the Year of the Leaf

The situation around New Year 1981–82 was that the drug scene in Christiania had rapidly developed into a rather large-scale operation, turning over huge amounts of cash. The drug scene had also deepened the divide inside the Freetown, which caused concern among many of the leading Christianites. Further, in the beginning of 1982 Christiania was viewed as the cause of almost every drug-related problem in Scandinavia. Demands for closure came from both within Denmark and from neighbouring countries, resembling the scenario of a drug scare. In parliamentary debates in Denmark and Sweden, during meetings of the Nordic Council and in the context of an anti-drug mobilisation in Sweden, it became clear that the Freetown was under severe threat as demands were made that it urgently needed to clean up its act to avoid risking sanctions or worse — closure.

Close Christiania! — Sweden mobilises

'Close Christiania!' This demand was put forward at an anti-drug rally in Malmö in January 1982. According to the organisers, the National Committee against Alcohol and Drug Addiction (RFMA), Christiania had become a commercial centre for drugs, where hash was sold openly by hundreds of dealers and where the legalisation movement in Denmark had its strongest support. The organising panel included politicians, members of the police force and social workers from both Sweden and Denmark.[21]

Meetings of this kind were commonplace in the beginning of 1982: set up by the same type of organisations, participation by a like-minded group of actors, and with the same kind of streamlined anti-Christiania rhetoric. At such a meeting, a Nordic conference held in Malmö in February, once again demands were raised that Christiania must be closed.[22] One of the speakers, Rune Gustavsson, the former Swedish Minister of Social Affairs (the Centre Party/Centerpartiet) and the leading anti-drug politician in Sweden at the time, was somehow pessimistic though — 'It will probably take a long time before the Swedish and Norwegian demands are met', he said. And even more disturbing to Gustavsson was the fact that Denmark had refused to accept a common Nordic approach aiming at co-ordinating national drug policies: 'I have been to Christiania and saw for myself how hash is openly sold. It was a deplorable sight, an environment with a lot of down and out drug users and small children. We must continue this debate with Denmark'.[23]

To one of the other Swedish anti-drug organisations RFHL (the National Association for Aid to Drug Abusers), closure of Christiania also seemed the only appropriate thing. In an editorial in their journal *Slå tillbaka!* (Fight back!) in autumn 1981, it is pointed out that to demand that Christiania itself clear out the sale of hash is not an option because it is totally unrealistic: in a Danish society with more than 400,000 hash smokers, and a very liberal attitude to hash, who would believe that Christiania, 'the stronghold of hash and the legalisation movement', would become free of hash — 'anyone realises how empty such a claim sounds'.[24]

Representatives of the police force and the social authorities in Sweden also voiced similar fears. Superintendent Sven Fehrm of the drug squad declared that he had noticed a steady increase in young Swedes travelling to Christiania to obtain hash, not only for individual use, but in many cases also to bring drugs back to Sweden for the purpose of reselling them. The main blame for this was, according to Fehrm, the excessively liberal view on hash in Denmark. Tougher punishment ought to be introduced to deter people from using drugs. Personally he would like to see Christiania closed.[25]

According to social authorities in Sweden, a huge proportion of the drugs available in the south of Sweden emanated from Copenhagen, especially through the open sale of hash in Christiania.[26] In 1982, Swedish social workers in Copenhagen and Malmö echoed such sentiments: the numbers of young Swedish drug addicts in Copenhagen was rapidly increasing, and the same went for Malmö. One of the social workers interviewed by a Swedish newspaper even said that because of the proximity of Copenhagen, 'we fear a future of mass abuse of hash if something radical is not done'.[27]

Local politicians in the south of Sweden also viewed Christiania as a social problem for Malmö — their ever presence at anti-drug rallies during this period gives such an impression. One of them, the head of the social department in Malmö, believed that 'many young people from Malmö get caught in addiction after visits to Christiania', and according to his information '70–80 per cent of the Christiania population make a living out of selling drugs and committing crime'. While he admitted that harder drugs than hash seldom were found in the Freetown, he assured that 'the inhabitants will benevolently direct you to pushers outside of the Freetown' in order to find such drugs. Just like the above-mentioned superintendent, the preferred solution to this local politician was to close Christiania.[28]

The image put forward by anti-drug organisations, the police, the social authorities and the odd politician resembles that of a stigma, where Christiania is reduced to 'drug problems'. The recommended action was closure, accomplished by applying pressure on Denmark to change its (too) liberal stand on drugs.

A somewhat different actor on the anti-drug scene at this time, active both in Sweden and in Denmark, was the European Workers' Party (EAP), in spite of its name a small right-wing group connected to the LaRouche Movement in the US. The party was extreme in its hard stance against drugs, and adhered to the 'War on Drugs', that since the early 1980s had been the Reagan administration's preferred stand.[29] At least since 1979, EAP, through the organisation the Anti Drug Coalition (ADK) and its journal *Stoppa knarket* (*Stop drugs*), had been trying to get Christiania closed. EAP's image of Christiania was dire. The party claimed that the Freetown constituted an ideological centre for 'storm troopers who do not obey any laws', recruited via hash and large drug parties — 'bill boarded all over Copenhagen'.[30] According to Christianite Ole Lykke, EAP had staged a campaign against Christiania in autumn of 1981, with demonstrations and daily hand-outs at Strøget in central Copenhagen, demanding the immediate closure of Christiania.[31]

The Swedish debate in parliament

The question of Christiania and drugs had also been raised in the Swedish parliament. As early as October 1981 Esse Petersson (Folkpartiet/

The Liberal Party) posed a set of questions to the Minister of Social Affairs; one of them concerned what steps the government was prepared to take to curb what he described as 'the extensive inflow of drugs to Sweden, which chiefly emanates from uncontrolled selling in Christiania?'[32] By asking this, Petersson wanted the Swedish government to force its Danish counterpart to take action.[33] The subsequent debate in the parliament shows a rather united front on Christiania and drugs, one that goes well beyond party politics. The prevailing stand was that political pressure on the Danish government had to be applied in order to stop drugs being sold in the Freetown.

As earlier mentioned, drug policies in the Scandinavian countries have traditionally been coordinated towards zero tolerance and total prohibition — with the important exception of Denmark. In the Swedish debate, Christiania was commonly used as the incarnation of this less strict drug policy.

The perceived 'soft' stand on drugs in Denmark was something that concerned quite a few of the Swedish members of parliament (MPs), simply because it was deemed to have negative implications for Sweden. Several parliamentarians said that Sweden had to focus on how to change the different attitudes on drugs that existed in Denmark. And in doing so, a policy of interference might have to be adopted. According to Karin Söder, the Minister of Social Affairs (Centre Party), letting Swedish opinion on drugs be known to the Danish parliament is not a case of meddling in internal business — it is rather a sign of international solidarity. Inga Lantz from the Swedish Communist Party (VPK) was even more adamant in her opinion: because drugs from Christiania are flooding Sweden, Sweden has to interfere in what essentially is a Danish internal issue.

Interfere, but in what ways? One preferred strategy — the dominant one — was to somehow make the Danes see the rational value of adhering to a common Nordic drug policy. Karin Söder explicitly stated that the Danish government did not observe the Nordic convention on drugs — they simply could not when large amounts of hash were being sold openly in Christiania. She also said that the interpretation of the convention differed between Denmark and Sweden, especially when it came to hash. Christiania then, was not *the* main problem, even though it served as a 'shop window', and was likely to be a stepping stone to drugs. It was according to Söder merely a symptom of the (warped) attitudes to hash in Denmark, which constituted the major obstacle. To others, like Petersson, Christiania *was* the main problem, being the drug centre of Scandinavia; where drugs were sold to Swedish young people, who then got stuck in addiction and crime. Further, it harboured the heart of the Danish legalisation movement, and therefore posed a major threat to Swedish drug policy.

The action that the majority of the participants in the debate recommended was to influence/persuade the Danish government to change its stand on drugs to a tougher one, and by doing so the problem of drugs in Christiania would indirectly have to be solved by either (Danish) law and order measures or in some other way. But some, like Petersson, were more critical and demanded more direct intervention — closure.

The rhetoric of the debate was clearly framed in a mix of *worries* for the wellbeing of Swedish young people and pent-up *anger* towards the perceived 'soft' Danish position on drugs.[34] One might add *incomprehension* as well. The Social Democratic MP Grethe Lundblad confessed during the debate that she really did not *understand* the Danish stand on drugs, which she was certainly not supportive of.[35]

The issue clearly seemed to have a *regional* twist as many of the most vocal and most critical politicians taking part in the debate either originated from southern Sweden or represented constituencies in the south. They often claimed to have first-hand experience of the effects of drugs — Rune Gustavsson for example, who repeatedly maintained that hash in that part of the country originated from Christiania and its open market.[36]

The Nordic Council: further critique

Political discussions on Christiania were also held at a Nordic level: first at a meeting of the Nordic Council of Ministers in Stockholm, which was followed by a meeting of the Nordic Council in Helsinki.[37] The first occasion was an extraordinary meeting of the Nordic Council of Ministers in Stockholm in February 1982 called on Swedish initiative, because of a perceived drug situation claimed to be 'alarming'.[38] In the press, there were speculations on a showdown between Denmark and the other Scandinavian countries regarding demands to close Christiania. But in the press statement issued after the meeting, demands for closure were not mentioned.[39] The Swedish minister of Justice, Carl-Axel Petri, even claimed that Sweden did not issue a formal demand for closure because 'we don't believe that would solve the drug problems in the Nordic region'.[40] The Swedish ministers further explained that Swedish opposition to Christiania had indeed been voiced but that closure was out of Swedish control as the matter was an internal Danish affair. The part regarding the formal demands was correct — neither the Swedish government nor the parliament had ever officially called for Christiania to be closed; it was MPs, such as Gustavsson and Petersson (along with politicians at a local level) who had embraced the idea during rallies with anti-drug organisations, and the press had simply tagged along and ascribed such intentions to politicians in general.[41]

In March 1982 the scheduled meeting of the Nordic Council took place in Helsinki. One issue on the agenda was the creation of uniform and efficient drug prevention measures in Scandinavia — a proposal presented by individual members, signed among others by Rune Gustavsson.[42] It had already been discussed at the Stockholm meeting, and was to be founded on the principles agreed there: first not to accept *any* kind of drugs (that is not for medical use), second to increase available resources and to intensify cooperation among police and customs, and third to see to it that uniform legislation on drugs was introduced. The other part of the debate was dedicated to the reply by the Danish

Minister of Justice on the question put by Sweden on how to handle the drug problems in Christiania. The debate was intense and differences of opinion became obvious — not only between different countries but also between political parties from Denmark.[43]

When it came to the member proposal, different solutions were suggested during the debate. The Swedish delegation (and the Norwegian) wanted to synchronise Nordic drug policies in order to get compatible legislation in place — either by streamlining Danish legislation towards a Swedish/Norwegian mode or ensuring that already existing laws and regulations were also adhered to in Denmark. The latter was emphasised by Rune Gustavsson. He argued that a stricter implementation of existing laws must be enforced, not only as a way of ridding Christiania of drugs — Gustavsson said that if everybody were to accept the principles decided on at the Stockholm meeting, 'the open drug dealing in Christiania would have been dealt a death blow'. But a fully implemented legislation would also have a deterrent influence on people, especially on young people. Gustavsson's bottom line was simple — it was unacceptable to have an enclave (Christiania) were it was easier to obtain drugs than in other places in Scandinavia. This view was shared by the Norwegian representative, Christian Christensen of the Christian Democrats (Kristeligt Folkeparti), one of the signatories of the member proposal.[44]

The Danish group of MPs were defined by an internal divide: the left-wing supported rehabilitation and the right-wing the law and order alternative. Some of Christiania's defenders argued that the solution to drugs in Christiania was social rehabilitation, not tougher legislation. The proposal for closure was also countered by another familiar response: that the problem would only move to another place. According to Bernhard Tastesen of the Danish Social Democrats, drugs are present everywhere. He argued that Gustavsson

> […] and other Swedish MPs just have to look out the window from the parliament building in Stockholm and watch the dealings at Sergels Torg, where not only hash […] but also much stronger stuff is sold, without anyone being able to stop it.[45]

Margrete Auken from the Socialist Party (Socialistisk Folkeparti) also emphasised that the Swedes used double standards, stating that she found that 'Swedish hypocrisy sometimes is matchless', considering that Sweden has as many users of hash as Denmark, and to her knowledge, they were not all in jail — so much for the deterrent effect of tougher legislation. Tastesen further remarked that while Gustavsson criticised the sale of hash in Christiania, he had never mentioned that hard drugs had been successfully prohibited by the Christianites since 1979.[46]

One incident highlighted the perceived double standards of the Swedish argumentation. At the meeting Ole Henriksen of the Danish Socialist Party showed a piece of hash he had purchased in Stockholm — and was subsequently arrested. The stunt was reported as 'a scandal' in the Swedish media. Henriksen however explained that he wanted to expose the double standards concerning hash that he felt the other Nordic countries were guilty of, as hash was easily available in the other countries too. He also stated that he had not just bought the hash as a protest against the Swedish inquires, but also to make the point that hash is not as dangerous as hard drugs and therefore should not be treated the same way.[47]

Henriksen's sublime act of insubordination got mixed receptions from his colleagues. Norwegian delegates criticised Henriksen and the Danish stand: in their bantering about a 'new moralism', stemming from especially Sweden, Danish politicians were unable to see the seriousness of the use and selling of hash. The Danish delegates from the right-wing, especially members of the Progress Party, were also critical of Henriksen's stunt, while delegates from the socialist camp supported him.[48] Ultimately, the critique leveled at Henriksen boiled down to the different views on hash: as an illegal and harmful drug or as a drug more or less equal to alcohol.[49]

From the reply to the initial Swedish inquiry by the Danish minister of Justice, Ole Espersen (Social Democrat), it was evident that he was under tremendous pressure to adhere to demands to clean up the hash market in Christiania. He said that Denmark would try to bring the drug business in line. He further stated that he understood the Swedish criticisms and the underlying fears, but found them exaggerated. For example, he did not trust figures showing that most of the hash in Malmö emanated from Christiania (figures of 90 % had been put forward).[50]

The Danish response — the media and experts strike back

In Denmark, Nordic demands that 'interfered' in Danish domestic affairs were met with anger, and the media immediately struck back. Sweden in particular was singled out. 'Close Sweden' was the eloquent title of an article in the influential Danish daily newspaper *Berlingske Tidende*. In the article, written by Mogens Berendt, Sweden was seen as the main culprit, the Big Brother of Scandinavia, intolerant and bigoted — a nation where everything was forbidden. To close Christiania would not solve the drug problem, just make it invisible — according to Berendt the common Swedish way of solving problems.[51]

A large number of articles criticising Sweden in accordance with Berendt's article, were published. For example, in two articles written by the Danish journalist Flemming Røder, the Swedish government was accused of meddlesomeness, ignorance and of simplifying matters. In the first article, published in the Danish tabloid *Ekstra Bladet*, Røder claimed that Swedish authorities uncritically relied on biased and incorrect information provided by EAP and the Danish narcotic police, ignoring information from Swedish social workers stationed in Copenhagen.[52] If consulted, they would have told a different story of conditions in Christiania regarding drugs — that Swedish heavy drug users residing in Denmark had left/got kicked out of Christiania as an effect of the stricter policy adopted after the Junk Blockade in 1979. The notion of Christiania as a place where innocent young people are seduced into drug use — a quintessential assumption of the Swedish official rhetoric — Røder found oversimplified and untrue: '[if] only we close Christiania, we will get no more hash users, that's what they say. Reality is not that simple'.[53] Instead he shifted the blame back to Sweden, saying that it was young people who were victims of a failed unemployment policy, and therefore already down and out, who ended up in the Freetown.

In the second article, published in *Dagens Nyheter*, the largest morning paper in Sweden, Røder's critique continued but was more directed towards what he labelled Swedish *propaganda* against Christiania. He provided several examples of highly exaggerated statements on Christiania, from the media, the police force and from medical doctors and psychologists. This concerted verbal baiting was according to Røder to blame for the demands to close Christiania. A picture of Sweden as a trying meddler in other people's businesses was again laid down — maybe Sweden should export all its 'know-how of bans and control', Røder suggested.[54]

Berendt's and Røder's articles are just some examples of a Danish fury that had been sparked by the Swedish critique and the demands to close Christiania. In articles and in TV and radio shows, the media expressed their anger, and in letters to the editor, the general public did the same. Denmark stood united by a sense of not being willing to let others meddle in internal affairs, not least Sweden.[55]

The Danish debate in parliament

In the Danish parliament (Folketinget), Christiania was also the subject of debates during 1982 — one held in March, the other in November.[56] In both debates, drugs were a key topic, which was discussed in rather heated manners. Among the critics were the Centre Democrats (Centrumdemokraterne), who made reference to the Nordic Council's critique against Denmark's 'tolerance' of the hash market in Christiania.[57] One of Christiania's fiercest critics in the debates, Agnete Laustsen of the Conservatives (Konservative Folkeparti), did however make clear that she thought that there was no need 'to engage other countries' in this business. She then went on to state that when 25,000 Swedes come to the Danish city of Helsingør in a day because they wish 'relief from their own society' and create heavy problems by drinking too much, the Danes try to solve that in a good neighbourly spirit — and so should Sweden regarding the hash problems in Denmark.[58]

In the first debate, the Minister of Justice, Ole Espersen, and Minister of the Environment, Erik Holst, both from the Social Democrats, had to clarify their stand on Christiania. Espersen said that even though the Conservatives and their ideological allies used available statistics on drug arrests in Christiania as an indicator of the general drug scene — in order to paint a grim picture of Christiania — he refrained from doing so as the material lent itself too easily to speculation. According to Holst, the numbers presented by parties on the right-wing were highly exaggerated. Both he and Espersen however agreed that the hash market in Christiania had to go. But, as Holst put it — the government then had to reach out and help Christiania solve the prevailing social problems because 'they are present in the larger society as well'.[59]

Most fiercely opposed to Christiania during the debate was Knud Lind of the Progress Party. Christiania was to him lawless, — 'a mecca for hard drugs ... a refuge for drug dealers.'[60] Christiania had 'made a mockery' of all efforts to stop drugs and related criminality that were executed in the neighbouring countries — 'what help is it to wash one's children if they just run over to the neighbour to roll around in his filth?'[61]

The second debate took place in November, and was caused by a proposal by the Progress Party to close Christiania. They were supported by the Conservatives, the Liberal Party (Venstre) and the Centre Democrats.[62] To these parties, Christiania represented a failed social experiment and a living proof that crime pays — drugs and drug dealing are the sad results of having had Christiania around for ten years. Birgith Mogensen of the Centre Democrats even argued that Christiania financed its whole existence from 'the sale of hash and other forms of criminality', and if such activities could be abolished, Christiania 'would simply go bust'.[63]

The Love Sweden Tour — Christiania goes abroad

In an extra issue of Christiania's weekly *Ugespejlet* (the Weekly Mirror) in February 1982, Christianites were invited to a Common Meeting to discuss ways to respond to the fact that, as the writer put it — 'the Swedes have for almost half a year given Christiania a hard time'. According to him, this pestering had reached its climax in December 1981 when all the parties in the Swedish parliament demanded that Christiania ought to be closed. As shown above, no politician or political party (at least not in Sweden) had made such official demands, but the claim nevertheless mobilised Christiania's forces.

The solution that Christiania came up with was a charm offensive, aimed at Sweden and the Swedes, called *The Love Sweden Tour* (Ælsk Sverige). The ultimate aim of the tour was to present Christiania 'as we want it to be, despite pressure from the outside'. To create an opportunity to show all the other aspects of Christiania, it would bring art exhibitions, music and theatre performances, parades, slide and film shows and public lectures, and would visit Lund, Stockholm and Gothenburg for almost two weeks.[64] The tour was timed to coincide with the scheduled extra meeting of the Nordic ministers in Stockholm.

The origin of the tour was an idea for an art exhibition in Lund. The initiative had come from Swedish sympathisers, one of them the owner of an art gallery in Lund, who found the current anti-Christiania drive offensive and exaggerated. Ole Lykke and a fellow Christianite went to see the owner of the gallery, and on the way back they had the idea to expand the exhibition into a much larger manifestation. During a frantic three-week period everything was arranged: the programme, the financing, the transportation and all the necessary permits from local authorities. Then, only a few days before 100 Christianites in two buses were to embark, a phone call from Lund changed the plans. According to Ole Lykke, there had been a meeting in Lund, attended by people from the university, the libraries and the police, where it was opted against allowing such a manifestation to take place — with 20,000 'vulnerable' students in town, a 'massive Christiania effect' could not be risked. All the prior arrangements were called off, except the parade, the debate at one of the libraries and the exhibition, which anyhow was to take place at a private establishment. In retrospective, this decision to call off large parts of the programme was clearly a result of the ascribed image of Christiania that persisted in Sweden during early 1982.

Eventually, the tour got started, and left for Sweden. At customs in Limhamn, the special narcotic unit (equipped with dogs) was waiting for the two buses from Christiania. After an hour-long search, which eventually did not reveal any drugs, the Christianites were allowed to continue towards Lund. But, as one of the customs officers said — 'we did not dare to just let them in. Imagine if something was to happen in Lund'.[65]

In Lund, the carnival, described in one of the local papers as colourful and amusing, with nice music and songs that accompanied the message 'no drugs in Christiania', gained little attention.[66] Ole Lykke's view is that the delay at customs in Limhamn caused the schedule to fall apart, and since the shops were closed, almost no one watched the parade that went through central Lund.[67]

The arrival of busloads of Christianites was of course deemed highly newsworthy. The dominant image of Christiania in certain Swedish papers at the time was one of suspicion. In *Kvällsposten* (the *Evening Post*), a Malmö based tabloid, the Christianites were described as inhabitants of the 'infamous' Freetown, embarking on a 'missionary' trip to erase rumours of Christiania being the biggest drug dealing centre in Scandinavia. According to the paper, customs officials had prepared themselves well for the 'invasion' of Christiania, and even though no drugs were found, the paper dryly noted 'not this time'.[68] As registered, the language used was very much biased and well in line with the official view.

In Stockholm, the next stop on the tour, agreements had been reached with Kulturhuset (the House of Culture) to host an exhibition that would counter the claims made against Christiania during the last six months. A parade would also take place, planned to coincide with the meeting of the Nordic Council of Ministers, and a combined theatre and cabaret show was scheduled as well — two nights at the alternative theatre Narren (the Jester) and one night at Medborgarhuset. But just as in Lund, some of the arrangements were cancelled. The main reason that the event at Kulturhuset had to be called off was fear of violence. The Swedish branch of the political party EAP had threatened to conduct daily demonstrations outside Kulturhuset if the exhibition was held.

Ole Lykke recalls his surprise at the extent the Swedish alternative movement was relying on state or municipal subsidiaries, and a fear that showing any kind of understanding towards Christiania could lead to those being cancelled — 'everyone was so nervous because of this… it was really an established fact that Christiania meant drugs. If you only mentioned Christiania, you were an advocate for drugs… the whole thing was so square'.[69]

One thing that struck Ole Lykke was the lack of interest showed by the Swedish newspapers when the Christianites finally arrived in 'the lion's den' — the Swedish capital. Not a lot of publicity was created, and Christiania had no money to purchase advertising space either. This fact of course affected attendance figures at the shows: at Narren almost nobody came, and at the larger Medborgarhuset, few people attended.[70]

When the papers actually wrote something after the activities and shows had been performed, it became clear that the 'anti-Christiania sentiment' was first and foremost rooted in the southern part of Sweden.[71] *Kvällsposten*, the Malmö tabloid, described a march staged outside parliament in Stockholm in derogatory terms: according to the paper, the Christianites were rigged out and resembled more a travelling circus than demonstrators with something important to say.[72] But when the leading morning papers in Stockholm, the conservative *Svenska Dagbladet*, and the liberal *Dagens Nyheter*, ran articles on the Love Sweden Tour, they lacked the smugness of *Kvällsposten's* reports. For example, *Svenska Dagbladet's* article on the march outside of parliament reported on happy painted faces, music and catchwords in the sunny streets of Stockholm. The Christianites even resembled minstrels of old times when they stopped outside Rosenbad to sing, according to the report.[73]

The show at Medborgarhuset caused some commotion. Right from the outset a contingent of plain clothes police from the drug squad were present. According to *Dagens Nyheter*, they were there to demonstrate their dislike of Danish drug policy. Mats Hulth of the Social Democrats, vice mayor for Social Affairs in Stockholm, said that he could understand that Swedish police felt provoked when 'those people come here and spread propaganda' for something (drugs) that is fought on a daily basis in Sweden. Later during the show, social workers on emergency duty were called in. Rapports of hash being smoked in the premises had to be investigated as there were several young children among the Christianites. Though none of the rushed-in social workers detected anyone smoking hash, it was decided that children should not be allowed to dwell in such an environment — 'where hash is accepted' as one of the social workers put it, according to *Dagens Nyheter*.[74]

Then the tour left for Gothenburg. The exhibition was hosted in a museum/gallery, housed in the premises of an old public bath (Renströmska Badet) in Haga, a centrally located old working-class district which at the time was a space for alternative culture in Sweden's second city; a few years earlier activists in Haga and Christiania had formed the 'Freetowns in union'. In Gothenburg, the Christianites decided to go small: no theatre shows and no public lectures and debates, only the exhibition and a parade. The exhibition then ran for three or four weeks.[75] In contrast to Lund and Stockholm, the press hardly paid any attention at all, perhaps because the Christianites themselves had decided to keep a low profile due to prior experiences.

In Gothenburg a statement was issued by a group of Christianites relating to the ongoing debate on, and critique against, Christiania because of its hash market. The group stated that it wished to solve the problem with drugs in a realistic way (read legalisation) and not by 'forcing hash back to the tough mafia-controlled supermarket of drugs again'.[76] The continuation of the statement — that politicians and social workers have given up trying to solve problems created by economic structures and a failed social policy — is of course a critical account of those who believed in disciplinary and legal measures instead of social rehabilitation.[77]

Conclusions — Images and Counter Images

In 1982, the issue of Christiana and drugs was intensively debated in both Denmark and Sweden: in parliament, at anti-drug rallies and in the media. Anti-Christiania feelings were running high, mostly due to the drug issue. The images and counter images visible during 1982 are of several kinds — the opponents of Christiania shared a basic set of assumptions, which resembled those used during a drug scare, a deliberate set of measures to scapegoat certain drugs and certain groups in society. But in some cases the opponents' arguments differed considerably, while the supporters of Christiania — who were to be found almost exclusively in Denmark — largely argued along the same few lines.

In perspective, the images produced by *the anti-drug organisations*

Poster for Love Sweden Tour. Photo: Håkan Thörn.

in Sweden was fairly one-sided: two basic assumptions founded their rhetoric — to make no difference between soft and hard drugs ('a drug is always a drug') and that hash is to be seen as a gateway drug, the stepping stone to addiction. Implicit in the latter part is an act of seduction, where especially 'innocent' young people were at risk. Crime was seen as a result of addiction, and consequently hash must be regarded as a huge societal problem. Christiania was singled out as a drug centre, where drugs were easily available and from where they flooded Sweden, especially the southern parts. The solution to the conceived problems was closure of Christiania. But it is not clear what actors to blame for providing drugs — instead the more fluid metaphor 'the drug market in Christiania' was used. *The police force and the social authorities* in Sweden also acknowledged the image ascribed to Christiania by the anti-drug organisations.

Swedish (and Norwegian) *politicians* shared the same critique of the drug scene in Christiania (but not necessarily of Christiania itself) but foremost expressed an interest in putting an end to the spread of drugs from Christiania to their own countries. To officially demand closure was not regarded an option, even though this was on the Norwegian Christian Democrats' agenda. Instead politicians sought to influence, and in the long run change (bring in accordance), the conceived 'too liberal' Danish drug policy. That was, at least in Sweden, a common stand among all the parties in parliament. The fear of young people getting stuck in drug abuse was echoed here as well — several bills explicitly stated that this was something that had to be prevented.

The level of engagement in the issue of Christiania and drugs was stronger with politicians from/representing the southern parts of Sweden, than others. That anti-Christiania feelings seem to have been stronger in the southern parts of Sweden is also manifested in *the media*, where the Malmö tabloid *Kvällsposten* led the campaign against the Freetown, while Stockholm morning papers were more detached in their reports.

The Danish critique/support of Christiania has of course a longer history than in the rest of Scandinavia. Christiania had been the subject of several debates in parliament even in its first ten years of existence, two of them in 1982. The 'for and against' Christiania in these debates, also when it comes to the drug issue, was clearly divided along the right-left axis (see Håkan Thörn's chapter in this book). The Progress Party in particular was extremely aggressive in its critique, arguing that Christiania created misery for young people who were seduced by the dope lifestyle. Their criticisms mainly emphasised terms of law and order: 'breaching the law', 'selling illicit drugs', 'exporting an illegal lifestyle'. This is a clear example of a drug scare, and how it functions. The Progress Party (and other parties that sympathised with their attitudes to Christiania) used the question of hash as a way of stigmatising the Christianites, and their lifestyle. Key to this strategy was avoiding making any distinction between pushers and other Christianites in order to instead cultivate a general image of a culture of lawlessness and drugs dominating the Freetown.

The main *defenders of Christiania*, the socialist parties (including the Social Democrats) did not sympathise with the open sale of hash, but chose to defend Christiania by de-linking the drug issue from the Freetown, instead emphasising that drugs were a general problem for Scandinavian societies that had deep social roots and called for pro-active social politics. The *Danish media* in 1982 in a sense indirectly provided support for Christiania, as they directed its attention not to Christiania, but to the Swedish critique against the Danish position on drugs, accusing the Swedes of double standards.

Christiania's own drug struggle, including its attempts to counter the images of their antagonists, is pretty well summarised in an episode during the Love Sweden tour. At the march outside parliament in Stockholm, Christianite Zig Zag is said to have repeatedly shouted 'there are no drugs in Christiania'. When the reporter then asked her 'what about hash?', she answered 'of course, but we do not consider hash a drug'.[78]

Epilogue — Rock Against Gang War

On 18 July 2009, Christiania organised a festival titled 'Rock Against Gang War' (Rock mod bandekrig). Its key theme was the ongoing war over the control of the drug market between gangs in Copenhagen. This issue was however linked to the many sided controversy around the hash market on Pusher Street, with speeches and statements by leading Christianites. Christianite Klaus Trier Tuxen, long-standing activist in Christiania's own Free Hash movement, and leading candidate to the city council elections for the Pot Party in Copenhagen, argued that:

> In reality, it is the state that has blood on its hands, because it is its foolish prohibition of cannabis that now is to blame for the blood in the streets. The present, extremely violent condition is also a consequence of the fact that the government launched an attack on Pusher Street a couple of years ago and the result is all too obvious today: Written in Blood.[79]

The only way to solve the problems of crime associated with hash is thus to legalise it, declared Tuxen, who ended his speech in a way deeply characteristic of the spirit of Christiania's Free Hash movement: 'let us smoke a joint and wish that soon hash will be free'.[80]

Britta Lillesøe, here representing Christiania's Cultural Association, gave a speech in the form of an open letter to the Danish government, titled 'Money is the strongest drug'. She emphasised that the Pusher Street hash market represented a reasonable alternative to the conditions that had caused the gang war:

> Here, a certain control is exercised, so that hard drugs are excluded from the market. That is why it is possible to sell cannabis in Pusher Street, while keeping it separate from other and harder drugs. You cannot be sure that this praxis exists in other parts of the country, where trade is much more hidden. If the government still chooses to go back in time and try to hide the problems by stopping the open hash market in Christiania — without at the same time legalising and de-criminalising the drug — the problems will start to tower seriously.[81]

In a sense, Rock Against Gang War in many respects summarised Christiania's four decades of 'drug struggle': the attempts to counter stigmatisation of Christiania as a 'drug nest' by staging cultural performances; the persistent resistance against hard drugs; and the campaigning for a legalisation of hash. When compared to the way that the issue of drugs was framed in the 1970s, there is however a significant shift of emphasis, which also reflects changes in the discourse on drugs in the surrounding society, as for example expressed in the debates in the Danish parliament (see Håkan Thörn's chapter in this book). While drugs to the political right were always an issue of 'law and order', the discussion on (soft and hard) drugs in the 1970s was nevertheless always linked to a discussion of social issues: social problems were the reason why people became addicted to both alcohol and hard drugs. Even the arguments for the legalisation of hash linked up with such a discourse, as it was argued that it was non-addictive and brought people together in a society defined by feelings of alienation and isolation. In the 2000s, the social dimension is largely absent; whether drugs are discussed in Christiania, the press or in the parliament, it is first and foremost embedded in a discourse of criminality and gang wars.

NORMALISATION WITHIN CHRISTIANIA

Christa Simone Amouroux

Since the squat's founding in 1971, Christiania's citizen-activists[1] have been responding to and resisting dominant narratives of normalcy and, more recently, rejecting the state's right to radically alter the spatial, political and social organisation that Christianites have built over the past forty years. The Normalisation Plan[2] in Christiania demonstrates how states attempt to manage citizens through various strategies of control such as privatisation, urban renewal and forced expulsions. In response, Christianites create contending narratives and engage in oppositional practices that range from graffiti to organised peaceful protests. 'The Normalisation Plan', as defined here, is an example of a historically situated spatial and discursive strategy of control initiated in 2001 by Anders Fogh Rassmussen's Liberal Party (Venstre) to manage the unruly 'Freetown'. The Normalisation Plan represents a certain set of logics, a way of conceiving of community, property, social relations and political organisation, which Christianites argue is in opposition to the 'Christiania way' of living, organising, imagining and building. The result is a collision of contending narratives concerning the rights of citizens; the meaning of ownership; the connection between identity and spaces.

As a point of departure, this chapter focuses on normalising processes within Christiania. In the following narratives, Christianites discuss tensions in their community and through these narratives attempt to define boundaries of belonging and the Christiania way. The differences between activists and the pushers, the contentious issue of young Christianites squatting Christiania houses, and other conflict moments help us understand the internal social and political terrains in Christiania. Through these moments of strife — political, spatial, and social — I note how normalisation is recreated in the exclusionary practices, contending narratives of belonging and spatialised practices of exclusion that delimit 'right' from 'wrong' and enforce the logics of the Christiania way. These contentious moments help us understand how normalisation is produced politically, spatially and socially.

I conducted several years of ethnographic research over a period of time in Christiania (1996–2004) and these visits have provided me with a range of examples of how normalisation takes place within Christiania.[3] These tensions between activists and pushers, generational strife between youth and elders over the future of the community, the rights of youth occupancy, and the logics of spatial and social organisation symbolised by Christiania houses, are demonstrative of how normalisation is created, engaged and resisted within Christiania.

External Normalisation

The Normalisation Plan is short-hand for a state generated strategy of control that attempts to manage the Christiania area and justifies this through 'common sense' notions of fairness (paying taxes), responsibility (private ownership) and public good (access to public spaces). Normalisation, as the state employs it, is meant to bring Christiania into an 'equal' relationship with the rest of Copenhagen and Denmark, more generally. Under the leadership of Anders Fogh Rasmussen, the Danish state rationalised its management role and created a development plan for the area. In doing so, certain logics and taken-for-granted notions were employed: citizens should pay taxes for property; property should be privately owned rather than cooperatively managed; squatting is an 'unfair' use of public space. These assumptions about rights, citizenship and property inform the state's strategy of privatising Christiania's commonly owned housing, reordering the space to make it more 'public' by creating a recreation and parking area, and building market housing. This is accomplished through overt tactics of power such as evictions, relocations and demolishment but also supported by logics and rationalities of order and control that find their basis in policing the limits of 'acceptable' and enforcing discipline to order this unruly space.

For Christianites, the Normalisation Plan is an overt, state-generated strategy of spatially reordering a 'problematic space' in order to effect social and political changes desired by the post-welfare state. It is also an example of a Foucauldian strategy of normalisation because the subtle logics and overt practices informing the relations of power (often referred to in Christiania as 'bulldozer politics') are presented as givens or 'common sense'. The post-welfare state relies on logics of a rational use of public space, privatisation as the way to manage public space, and private property. Several authors deal with the issue of external normalisation in this volume, but this chapter argues that internal normalising processes must also be situated in relationship to the external normalisation initiated by the Danish government (see Håkan Thörn's chapter in this book).

During my research it was apparent that external normalisation was shifting, and in some cases intensifying, the internal divisions between groups such as the activists and the pushers. External normalisation informs internal normalisation as the pressure from the 'outside' informs power relations within Christiania. So, even though this chapter deals predominately with internal normalisation, it is important to recall the interrelated dynamics of power relations as the state sets terms and Christianites respond. The following sections discuss the complexities of internal normalisation and the problematics of belonging, space and identity in Christiania.

Normalisation and Foucault

Foucault used the term normalisation to draw our attention to the contingencies of power in the modern disciplinary society, and to counter the idea that modern societies' logics are absolute truths. Foucault's notion of normalisation demonstrates that contingent and historically specific modes of being are naturalised and then made into common sense norms, categories and practices. Foucault argued for subtlety, contingency and historical specificity of extant regimes of knowledge and offered normalisation as a way of understanding how progress narratives, categorisations and scientific discourses order society and that these logics of order are inscribed in spaces such as factories, schools and prisons.

One question this chapter wrestles with is: How is Foucault's notion of normalisation enacted in Christiania? Normalising practices of bodily control are evident in, for example, the policing of Pusher Street where running, photography and hard drugs are prohibited (see René Karpantschof's chapter in this book). Running is prohibited because large dogs, trained to attack thieves or interlopers, are agitated by quick movements on 'the street'. Photography is prohibited because pushers don't want outsiders — tourists and cops — to document their illegal activities. Hard drugs are prohibited, though sometimes sold clandestinely in cafes, on Pusher Street. Cannabis is acceptable and other 'hard' drugs such as heroin are deemed 'bad' due to Christiana's problematic history with heroin, addicts and the decline of the community due to the infiltration of organised crime (see Tomas Nilson's chapter in this book).

Foucault argued that a self-disciplining subject was created through the organisation, control and surveillance of space and control of the body. I am particularly interested in the intersection of spatial strategies of control and narratives of normalcy because they intensified during the third phase of my field work in 2003–2004.[4] Within Christiania, how are logics of knowledge, power and belonging organised and explained? For instance, what is the Christiania way; how do belonging and identity manifest in spaces; how are spaces politicised and policed? I draw on Foucault's notions of normalisation and discipline, as spatialised processes, to better understand how certain logics of power are inscribed into spaces such as houses; how differences are created in the categorisations and labelling of pushers versus activists; and how narratives of belonging and exclusion are used in relation to Christiania's young people.

Relations of power seem to emerge most clearly in hierarchical power relations that are supported by specific knowledge formations, but daily practices, informal knowledge, spatial arrangements, and rationalities also subtly craft subjectivities, delimit right from wrong, and manage difference. My focus is on normalising logics and practices, and how these manifest in Christiania.

Spatial Normalisation

Pusher Street

According to Foucault, normalisation is created through a range of disciplinary apparatuses that instantiate 'the subject', who is disciplined into being by restricting bodily movements in carefully constructed spaces of control and surveillance.[5] The most famous example of the spatialisation of control is Jeremy Bentham's Panopticon, a potent symbol of self-discipline and spatial control:

> This enclosed, segmented space, observed at every point, in which the individuals are inserted in a fixed place, in which the slightest movements are supervised, in which all events are recorded, in which an uninterrupted work of writing links the centre and periphery, in which power is exercised without division, according to a continuous hierarchical figure, in which each individual is constantly located, examined and distributed among the living beings, the sick and the dead — all this constitutes a compact model of the disciplinary mechanism.[6]

The Panopticon orders life through the extreme control of bodily movements in a confined space, and Foucault uses this as an example of how discipline becomes a 'mechanism' which is internalised and, thereby, generative of a modern subjectivity. As he explains:

> It is an important mechanism, for it automatises and disindividualises power. Power has its principals not so much in a person as in a certain concerted distribution of bodies, surfaces, lights, gazes; in an arrangement whose internal mechanisms produce the relation in which individuals are caught up.[7]

As I mentioned earlier, Pusher Street is a great example of how bodily movements are constrained by tacit relations of power and overt rules governing conduct. Taking photos, unless you are a known Christianite, is a potentially dangerous proposition. Large signs, graffiti on walls, show a camera with a red slash through it. I have heard of tourists whose cameras were torn away and then smashed on the street.

Normalisation within Christiania occurs with a spatial control that orders and then categorises. Foucault suggests that ordered spaces can transform unruly and undisciplined bodies (prisoners, children, squatters, etc) into 'willing' and disciplined subjects. In Christiania, a disciplining power is spatialised, but also instantiated in narratives of what it means to be an activist or a pusher, an insider or outsider. Once defined, these categories help to delimit action and generate subjectivities.

For Foucault, normalisation permeates society in part through the standardisation of spaces. Spaces become structured using logics of scientific systems of evaluation, production, and investigation. Bodies operate in highly ordered spaces and subjectivities are transformed into coherent, self-regulating subjects. Foucault argues that discipline and control are achieved, in part, through the regulation of bodily rhythms that are controlled through the use of timetables that regulate embodied practices; repetition and regularity create the basis for the commonsense; and order is buttressed through the pathologisation and criminalisation of others. These various apparatuses and accompanying knowledge encourage subjects' complicity in their self-regulation. Foucault's normalisation is about noting the ways in which foreclosures, silences, and limitations are instantiated in spaces, knowledge and practices.

Christiania is organised into areas where access to housing is closely managed by residents and it is enclosed by a wall that has two main entrances in order to control the flow of people leaving and entering (see Helen Jarvis' chapter in this book). During my fieldwork, lookouts were stationed at six entrances. Hired by the pushers, their job was to assess threats to the hash market; whether or not undercover police or other 'problematic' people were entering Christiania. I saw a 'lookout' ask a young man who he was and where he was from. The lookout was assessing this man's background — undercover cop, potential threat, etc. And the threat of violence in this exchange was palpable. Christiania is not a Freetown for everyone. The enclave community is policed by residents and has spaces that are designated private and public, dangerous and safe, open and closed.

Belonging to Christiania: squatting a squat

> Field notes — May 2004:
> Outside my window I hear the banging of boards as the squatters who have taken over Karlsvognen's basement reorganise and remove the stuff that is stored there. Palle is very angry because three young men have come 'illegally' into his house. While the neighbours agree that Palle and Karen should be allowed to decide who lives in the building, they also stress the issue of space. Karen and Palle live together and share a hundred square metres of space, while the basement, which is equally large, is used only for storage (Palle stores his delivery van there and other materials from his private business). The neighbours explain that something productive has to be done with the house and basement.

During my fieldwork in 2004 I lived in Karlsvognen, a three-storey building that once housed military officers on the first floor and, until 1932, stables for horses on the ground floor. The massive building was taken over, like many others in the Mælkevejen area (The Milky Way), in the early 1970s and turned into politically active spaces where up to thirty adults and many visitors lived, partied and worked. As the years went by, Karlsvognen's residents slowly moved out and those who stayed took over the remaining space, expanding their bedrooms and transforming living spaces into workspaces. I lived with Karen and Palle on the second floor. There were three bedrooms, a workshop and a 100-square-metre living room.

Over thirty years after the house was squatted, three of Christiania's young people argued that the house was in decline, so they began to move into the basement, systematically removing the basement's contents and placing boxes, building materials, props, machine parts and various scrap at the side of the house. They emptied the contents of the basement without permission and began the process of renovating the basement.

They built a deck where they could socialise and present themselves in public as the new occupants, added a new door and lock, and set up a living space with a couch, TV and mattresses on the floor. They planned to divide the basement into a three-bedroom apartment. These 'invading' Christianites, as Karen called them, argued that the basement was just storage for Palle's 'junk' and it should be converted into living space. They pointed out that cars are not allowed in Christiania, but Palle stored his delivery van, which is the basis for his removal and delivery business, in the basement.

The squat of a squat or the 'invasion', as it is referred to by Karen and Palle, generated a community-wide dialogue on the rights of young Christianites to live in their community, which has very limited available spaces for the next generation (often housing becomes available only after someone dies, or moves out). The other issue raised by the squat was the rights of current residents — Karen and Palle — to decide who lives in their house. An interesting dialogue occurred between the adults and youths who squared off with contending narratives of belonging and rights.

On the narrative of 'belonging' and 'rights': the three youths argue that as Christianites they have a right to live in the community where they were raised. Since there are very few spaces available to young people they decided to squat Karlsvognen as a form of internal social protest and to highlight their generation's rights. The response from Christiania's adults ranged from sympathy for their plight as homeless young Christianites to deep concern that the social order would be disrupted if other houses were squatted. The anti-squat, counter narrative was based on upholding Christiania's rules of residence (current residents need to agree and invite you to live in their area). Since Karen and Palle did not allow the three to live in the basement, the Common Meeting (Christiania's general assembly of consensus decision making) said that the young men should have handled it differently (i.e. asked for permission). The youths countered that permission was sought but denied, so they took action just like their elders had done so many years before when they formed Christiania. Karen argued that they were denied access because the basement was not suitable for living with its small windows, and that Christiania's 'children', as young people are referred to, should leave Christiania as a rite of passage.

Karen suggested to me that it is good for the young to leave the community and live in the city for the experience because they are so 'protected' in Christiania. Karen explained, 'They are too protected here and need to see what life is like outside'. I asked: What will happen if all the young people leave? Who will carry on the 'traditions' of Christiania? Will it turn into a conservative, old folks home as some have suggested? Karen just smiles weakly back at me. She goes on to explain that the basement is not fit for living; the windows are too small and the basement is not a healthy place for young people to live; a familiar argument and the same one that the government used to try and justify Christiania's closure in the 1970s. It is an argument (health and safety) that the government is still using to rationalise the normalisation of the area and the removal of certain houses. The youths responded with indignation, pointed out this hypocrisy and instead took action. Their occupation highlighted a double standard. Their 'elders' used the same logic of exclusion that the government used in 1971 and, continues to use, when trying to justify evicting residents: lack of acceptable sanitary conditions, poor ventilation, illegal occupation, etc.

The youths remained defiant, contacted the national newspaper *Politikken* to discuss their grievances in a national forum and they continued to build their version of a Christiania 'dream'. Karen and Palle responded that they were too 'weak' and needed help to remove the interlopers (i.e. a forced eviction process that has occurred in Christiania over the years when residents band together to evict an undesirable). So, the three youths remained, and Palle and Karen eventually came to tolerate their new neighbours.[8]

Karen realises that her house is 'dying' and that the young Christianite squatters are just following in the footsteps of their elders and are directly confronting the need to create space for the next generation. Karen explains that squatting is not allowed in Christiania, and continues in response to my concern that her stance is hypocritical, 'people here are sensitive to criticism and are always on the defensive'.

Christiania's young people are engaging in the same practices and logic that their elders did in the 1970s. This is an example of how logics are normalised, but also contested. In Christiania, squatting is now prohibited. Once founded as a squat, the community developed to exclude the practices upon which it was based. The young people contend that, as Christianites, they also have rights; the right to live in their community. It is during conflict moments that normalised logics are contested and engaged.

Social Normalisation

The pusher house

The pusher house sits along the 17th century military embankments built by King Christian IV. It was occupied by a pusher, one of the many Christianites arrested during the 'Clean Sweep' police operation in 2004, which attempted to close down dealing in Pusher Street.[9] The house is an original design, and the artwork reflects the owner's artistic interests, budget, and abilities (this structure has also been targeted by the state because it was built without permission on the embankments). Many of the homes that have been built along the canals are considered architecturally innovative and creative expressions that are representative of a 'Christiania' aesthetic. Often, however, well-maintained or 'new' pusher houses have become emblematic of Christiania's problems. These houses symbolise the wealth and power of pushers who are able to invest large sums of money in their modern, extravagant homes. Activists argue that Christiania houses should be ecologically friendly, low-cost, well-maintained and artistic, and not modern pusher houses (the degree of care and maintenance given to houses is expressive of the level of personal commitment to Christiania). Activists align themselves with the anti-consumptionist and communal approach, and so accuse pushers of excessively transgressing Christiania norms because pushers have a reputation for purchasing expensive cars, and furnishing their houses with large screen TVs, loud stereo systems, and other high-end consumer goods.

The development and economic prosperity of Pusher Street enabled a class of Christianites to develop who were much wealthier than most Christianites who refused to sell cannabis products. When Pusher Street was 'closed' by the pushers in 2004, it was Europe's largest outdoor cannabis market and generated millions in profits. These profits allowed the pushers to build and furnish homes that clearly symbolised their wealth but also marked their difference. Many of these structures are noticeable because of their new appearance, high quality materials, and modern building style. Rather than artistic, piecemeal, eclectic structures created over the years, the pusher houses were described as 'not Christiania' (see also introductory chapter in this book).

Ida,[10] a long-term resident of Christiania and self-defined 'intermittent activist,' identified the pusher houses as 'other.' She would point them out and say, 'There is a pusher house,' and remark, 'We do not like these houses, and only in weak areas are pushers allowed.' Pushers are excluded from 'strong' areas because of their perceived lack of commitment to the community values and the community's refusal to accept 'black money'.[11] By contrast, Pusher Street is referred to as a 'tough area' because the threat of violence and control give 'the street' an oppressive feeling; movement and purpose are surveilled and managed. Indeed, locals' routes through the community often intentionally avoid Pusher Street and the centre where 'the tourists go'. This self-regulation of bodily movements, as an everyday practice, is an example of how identity (activist versus pusher), space (Christiania versus Pusher Street) and belonging (authentic versus inauthentic) are normalised. Like their houses, the pushers' spatial control of Pusher Street — the economic centre — differentiates them from activists. Still, pushers are socially isolated and often marginalised because they lack the right community values. This marginalisation is marked spatially because their homes are located in 'weak areas' where political will and the strength to exclude them is lacking, and their control is centred in Pusher Street; the problematic space.

Pushers are represented using several interrelated narratives of belonging and spatial constructions. 'Pusher houses do not fit into Christiania.' Ida made this remark as we passed a brightly decorated, brand new, red summer cottage near her house. 'A pusher girl owns this house. I do not like it. It is a summer house and it does not belong in Christiania.' Nearby another summer wagon, built by a long-time resident, does not threaten the cohesiveness of the community's identity as an oppositional space because it is an old, established structure that is not 'fancy'. By contrast, the pusher girl's house is a new, expensive, pre-fabricated house that looks like an upscale summer cottage. This small red house sits alongside the water in a remote but coveted area of Christiania. The cottage is conspicuous because of its pre-fabricated newness, and desirable for its remote location. New furniture and abundant toys lay strewn about the rose-filled yard. A white picket fence conjures images of idyllic village life, but it also contrasts with the nearby houses, many of which are run-down and cluttered with trash.

According to activists such as Ida, the pushers — like their houses — ostentatiously display their wealth. They do not fit in. Newness and wealth symbolised by material goods such as large-screen TVs, leather sofas, and new bathrooms contravene an ethos of anti-consumption, ecologically friendly houses, and an ethic of hard work and simplicity. Pushers are aligned with the 'outside' culture where wealth and greed are said to predominate. Pushers have a 'gangster mentality' and do not — as another activist Ditlev summarises — 'give a shit' about Christiania, but 'just come here for the money'. Specific houses symbolise the pusher identity (such as the Info House, or the pusher girl's cottage), and like Pusher Street have now become sites for state intervention. Pushers, and the spaces they occupy, have come to represent the problems with Christiania and why the state threatens to close it down. And for many activists these houses and Pusher Street are a constant reminder of what divides and weakens Christiania. In response, normalising rhetorics are employed along with spatialised practices to differentiate 'good' Christianites from 'bad'. Pusher houses and activist spaces define relations of power and control in Christiania, and these logics regulate how spaces are occupied, moved through, and who belongs.

The Christiania Way

In general, homes that are acceptable to the activists are 'green buildings'; ecologically friendly, green, artistic buildings. Good Christiania homes and gardens are often cooperatively maintained, and designed to have limited impact on the environment (see Helen Jarvis' chapter in this book). Most trash is composted, and excessive consumption is frowned upon. Reclaimed or found materials, building supplies, and self-made objects are preferred building materials.

A house called 'Air-condition' is located in the area called North Dyssen which is on the periphery, far away from the problems and difficulties of the central area, where most pushers live and work. Ida comments on the ethos of communal ownership, humble living standards, and commitment to Christiania in Air-condition that differentiates them from the indecent, excessive materiality of the pusher girl's cottage. Air-condition lacks the newness of the pusher cottage, the ostentatious display of consumer goods. Openness, care, preservation, communal living, and anti-consumption form the basis of the Christiania way and an activist's identity. It is also used to justify Christianites' use of the area. Houses should be hand-crafted, well-maintained, and nurtured not for personal use, but for the benefit of the entire community. Whereas the pushers are seen as radical individualists performing the rituals of modern capitalist society, activists see themselves as individuals working together to preserve Christiania. Radical individuals take from the community while cooperative individualism works to support the community.

Pushers and activists

I mentioned to Ida that I thought Christiania is run by a small group of elites, and I asked if people would be angry to hear this. She gave me one of her flat stares and stated very matter-of-factly, 'Everyone knows it's true'. There is a front guard and a designated spokesman for Christiania and, as Ida pointed out, substantial power lies within the Economy Meeting, where a small group controls the flow and distribution of Christiania's money. Generally, power resides with those who have worked over the years to take it over and 'it is not very democratic'. The front guard of Christiania tends to be those who have the longest residence, and who have 'fought' for Christiania. Their 'cultural capital' allows them to speak for the community and they are self-identified activists for whom preservation of the Christiania way often places them in opposition to pushers who are seen as taking from rather than giving to the community.

According to Pierre Bourdieu, 'cultural capital' represents the collection of non-economic qualities, such as family background, social class, and varying investments in and commitments to education that influence social success.[12] Bourdieu distinguishes several forms of cultural capital. The 'embodied state' is directly linked to and incorporated within the individual and represents what they know and can do. As embodied capital becomes integrated into the individual, it becomes a type of *habitus* and therefore cannot be transmitted, unlike education. The 'objectified state' of cultural capital is represented by cultural goods, material objects such as books, paintings, instruments, or machines. These can be appropriated using economic capital and symbolically using embodied capital. Bourdieu argues that the various forms of cultural capital are ultimately used by the individual to gain economic success and social prestige. In the case of Christiania, cultural capital describes the personal attributes the community generally views as favourable, attributes that confer respect from other community members and allows for participation/power in the social processes. Anyone can speak in Christiania, but to be heard, to have your opinions regarded by others, requires acceptance from the community. Perception of personal worth varies. For example, activists are more likely to evaluate one's worth based upon contributions and work for the community, while the pushers will consider your group affiliation.

The cultural capital necessary for full political participation in Christiania stems from several factors. Foremost is the perception of commitment. Further, the longer one lives in the community and contributes to it, the greater the cultural capital and the more credibility one has. With duration comes a sense of commitment to Christiania. Therefore, age and commitment are the essential forms of cultural capital.

I interviewed an activist named Tata before the closure of Pusher Street. Tata runs a shoemaking workshop and has been living in Dyssen for over twenty years. She has two children and is originally from Italy. Her studio sits on a quiet dirt road a few minutes' walk from the 'centre' of Christiania. A small round sign with an old-fashioned lady's boot hangs outside. I entered Tata's shop on a calm, sunny summer day. The small hallway was dark but immediately opened into a large, spacious, white-washed and airy room. Animal hides hung on a trellis-like structure, and to the left was an elevated platform where Tata designed her custom shoes.

Customers have their feet measured and then cast. After deciding on the style and colour of the shoe, Tata creates a pair of customised shoes which cost 300–1,000 US dollars. Tata explained that customers come from all over Copenhagen to this small shop, and she reminded me that her shop does very well.

During this interview in 1998 Tata revealed the complex and fraught relationship within Christiania between activists and the pushers. The pushers argued that Christiania was served by the 'free hash' movement, which is a politicised resistance to the criminalisation of cannabis (see Tomas Nilson's chapter in this book). However, as an activist Tata was concerned about the cost to Christiania of the 'free hash' movement. She explained, the pushers came from outside, used Christiania to sell (make money) but called it a political statement of resistance.

Tata discussed some of the central problems facing Christiania. She explained that people came from outside to sell, and this external influence brought problems to Christiania. The 'outsiders' did not have the same connection to Christiania and 'just take' from the community because, Tata explained, they were only interested in making money. As a result, the expansion of the market resulted in increased police oppression and state intervention. In response, Christiania's common economy refused to use 'black money'; illegal money would have provided even more justification for the state to close Christiania.

Tata: People come from outside and sell. The hash market has grown. We had a Common Meeting because of the increasing pressure from the police. Legalisation is a current idea. And they (the pushers) justify their presence with the political reason that they fight for legalisation.

The pushers keep hard drugs out […] supposedly. Is it worth it to have them out there to keep out hard drugs? And they add to the life of Christiania. In general the pushers are peaceful […] most of them are nice people […] friendly […] but I mind that there are so many of them. It makes a sort of imbalance in the community. They are very powerful. They are not on the outside. The last ten years […] there are other types of people. They are not cosy people. They are businessmen […] more heavy criminal background.

Christa: How do they have power in the community?

Tata: They stick together and take care of their interests. They create a community within a community.

Christa: Do they have power over your life?

Tata: I think they have because it is impossible to make a decision about their market. They are too many […] it is impossible to decide how to reduce their numbers. Nobody knows, but I guess that there are 25 per cent of the people involved in the drug market. The atmosphere is heavy because they have to have this hidden life. You can't ask people how they earn their living: 'How it is going? How are you doing?' The good things (about Christiania) are that we know each other and that we can be strong together […] strength of the social relations […] the fact is that I am rich — although I am not rich. I am only rich because I have so many resources around me. Christiania is a good place for children to grow up.

Tata asserts that Christiania is divided into two powerful groups, but that the pushers have more influence because of their money, and they control decisions regarding the hash market and create a 'community within a community'. Other Christianites suggest that the pushers are 'not cosy', but criminals who are willing to use force in order to protect their stake in the highly profitable hash market. Tata uses metaphors of 'insider' and 'outsider' during our conversation to highlight, as many Christianites do, those who belong to Christiania and those who do not; those who simply come to take and make a profit.

I asked her to identify the characteristics that distinguish 'real' Christianites from the rest:

Christa: What is it to be a Christianite other than living here?

Tata: To have a wish to build something different. To have a wish, a dream of being active in your own life and more in control of your own life. One person said that we are here because 'we don't fit outside'. No, but when you hear of people who don't fit outside that means they really don't fit outside. There are people who really couldn't live outside, usually because they have alcohol problems or psychological problems.

Christa: Does the lack of property ownership keep people here?

Tata: It is a small part. They stay for better reasons than that. It is one of the factors that keep people here. It is hard when you have spent your whole life here. It is hard to leave. The Christiania laws (Grundlov) are understood. The rules are a process, our democracy is a process, and we have not found the right formula to live with each other because things change constantly [...] And many people ask if Christiania changed since the beginning, 'Of course', and we have no philosophy that we have written down and each day brings a new solution. We are not socialists, we are not anarchists, we are not communists, and we are not capitalists. What are we? We

> don't define it and that is good. The undefined community is a definition in itself [...] if you stick to it [...] yes [...] but if you just let go and just change with time [...] so we have no line to follow [...] so we look at one problem at the time.

Another activist, Ditlev, discussed the tensions between the pushers and activists in the following interview conducted during my visit in 1998. Like Tata, Ditlev had lived in Christiania with his family for over fifteen years. He came to Christiania with the hope of creating a new life and realising his ideals of a utopian, consensus-based community. Over the years he had become disenchanted with the internal politics, but remained hopeful that Christiania would offer an alternative model, a counter-point to the dominant modes of thinking. He envisioned Christiania as a model for people who visit to imagine another way of life.

Ditlev and I discussed some of the obstacles facing Christiania. This interview took place several years before the Normalisation Plan was implemented. At the time of our conversation, Pusher Street was still the commercial centre of Christiania, which Ditlev characterised as a fraught and politicised space dominated by grim, dangerous adult males and their overly large and aggressive dogs.

During our morning conversation we sat in his house in Dyssen, a remote area of Christiania near the water that is often referred to as a suburb. Sitting at his kitchen table, I watched as Ditlev turned on the propane to light the small stove in his cluttered, small kitchen. The water boiled as we sat together at a rough wooden homemade table. There were books and papers everywhere. Ditlev is a carpenter by training, but has built a side business developing alternative forms of dispute resolution and travelling around Europe to discuss Christiania's consensus-based decision-making (see Amy Starecheski's chapter in this book).

The house has only a few, small ground floor windows and is somewhat dark on the first floor, having been transformed from a former military storage building for several adjacent residences. Ditlev lives with his girlfriend and their three children. It was a cosy but crowded space, but they had built a magnificent, well-lit study and bedrooms on the second floor. The study had two large desks, computers, and row after row of book shelving, and even more books and papers lay on the floor. I mention these details to point out several things. First, the building Ditlev lives in, which is two storeys high and several metres long, has been divided into several separate living spaces, but each house is not owned but rather borrowed. Several families and single people live together in this building and share responsibilities for the common grounds and maintenance of the structure. Each space has been renovated by the resident, many who have lived there for thirty or more years. Second, I want to point out that Ditlev and many of the people I spoke with in Christiania are activists whose daily life is a politicised one. With the help of activists such as Ditlev, Christiania introduced its own currency in 1995 and tried to establish a means of generating an internal barter economy. The currency has been marginally successful, but represents an attempt to formalise the already active internal market.

Ditlev and Tata explain that they work to improve their community through various projects that include 'going outside' and talking to researchers in order to educate people about Christiania. This often entails a complex process of dispelling commonly held assumptions and misunderstandings about Christiania such as the level of criminality, the illegality of the squat, the perceived misuses of state resources, and the notion that Christianites do not pay taxes or rent. When Ditlev or Tata discuss Christiania they may choose to emphasise the utopian vision of Christiania as a counter-cultural haven. Either way, Christianites are often asked to narrate their community and, thereby, justify their choices to live there. This narrative often begins with their decision to live a 'different way' and therefore to engage in a highly politicised life where politics intersects with home, work, and daily life.

Christa: Do you think that privatisation will come to Christiania?

Ditlev: No. No. It is a part of the agreement that we can't sell the houses. It means that we are users of this area. Christiania is a user of this area and we are just a user of this house. The mentality and the values of Christiania have developed against the economy, therefore nobody owns anything. You can't speculate and because of the collective structure you can't own them, and you can't earn a lot of money. You move to Christiania not to earn a lot of money. It is because of a dream. Money is not a central thing in Christiania. [...] Of course it is a tool. It is a need but not a central thing. For very few people money is a central thing. But of course, if the community is not functioning then people turn into themselves and to money because it is too difficult. [...] Our values have developed in opposition to money and ownership. We don't own the houses and because of the collective organisation of the workshops, we don't own them either. [...] Christiania [...] thought in ideas and dreams. In making new things. I think that is the most necessary thing that we need to be more economically realistic. We still have to remember the old values and use money as a tool and not as the central thing in our community.

Ditlev responds to my questions by saying that Christiania will not be privatised because common ownership has historically been part of Christiania's agreement with the government; the buildings are legally owned by the state, and the self-built houses cannot be sold. He firmly believed that Christiania had an indelible right to use the area because that right was supported by a legal agreement (the Christiania Act was however overturned under the Normalisation Plan). The Christiania Act had provided bare and provisional rights to use the area, and because this agreement had been renewed over the years, many Christianites felt that their longevity and connection to the space would ensure their future rights to remain.

Ditlev's rejection of privatisation is common among activists who emphasised that living in Christiania is a political choice not based on mainstream values of accumulating wealth. As he says, 'You do not move to Christiania to earn a lot of money. It is because of a dream. Money is not a central thing in Christiania'.

Our conversation turned to the possibilities of generating new ideas and change in Christiania:

Christa: Well, it seems like ideas are happening but very slowly.

Ditlev: I think all this hash and the criminality and the police are putting a blanket over the whole thing, and squashing the life out of it. In the 1970s the hard drugs drove out a lot of the good people. Because it was too hard, too much, too much fighting. So, I think if we didn't have all this hash and all this criminality there would be much more energy for these ideas.

Back in 1998, Ditlev would have preferred that the pushers leave because their interest in making a lot of money diverges from the 'Christiania way'. However, in response to internal conflicts and the debates generated by the Normalisation Plan, Christianites have begun to reflect on the two major issues facing their community: the division between the activists and the pushers, and the threat of privatisation. Although long-term differences have separated the pushers from the activists and subsequently created dynamics of internal normalisation, the state's intervention is also causing a re-evaluation of these differences. For Ditlev, the Normalisation Plan has begun to significantly impact the community by creating an opportunity to generate a new Christiania politics and sense of collective cohesion:

> Christiania is a pearl that provides room for a good life. Both for those who live in the Freetown and the many for whom Christiania is a symbol of a free and more meaningful life. But the beauty and the possibilities to develop the Freetown in a viable direction are threatened from without and from within. The state rolls forward with its *normalisation politics* that is founded on the idea that everything should be rule-driven and made for money. The criminalisation of the hash market has contributed to the fact that money, threats, violence, and political control are the dominant factor in the Freetown. Last but not least, Christianias several political and organisational difficulties mean that Christiania cannot develop its local and global potential as a Free State and social experiment. Christiania's contribution to another world is possibly frayed at the edge.

For Ditlev, the intensification of the state-led normalisation created an opportunity for Christiania to develop its own political agenda, to solidify its consensus decision-making, and to build a transnational social movement network because the issues facing Christiania have become more complex. Despite his earlier contention that the pushers were 'squashing the life out of Christiania', the police pressure to close Pusher Street and the subsequent arrest of many pushers in 2004 has forced Ditlev to rethink the internal divisions that so easily placed blame on the 'criminals' who were in Christiania 'just for the money'. Rather, Ditlev highlights how internal normalisation, which found its basis in the divisions between activists and pushers, is being transformed. The internal normalisation processes that marked the division between the activists and the pushers, are now being reordered, in part, due to the state's efforts to reorganise and control the community. Activists like Ditlev, who were adamantly in opposition to pushers, are now reconsidering how relations of power are constructed in Christiania so that normalisation, far from a subtle or covert process, can be — under certain historical and political contexts — hotly debated and actively contested.

Turning to a conversation with Bjørn, a young Christianite whose mother Ida is a long-time resident, I explore how normalisation is resisted. Bjørn was one of several persons under twenty whom I spoke with. He lives in Dyssen, the countryside of Christiania, in a small cosy wagon surrounded by a garden and overlooking a beautiful lake. As Bjørn said, 'I can have garden parties, entertain friends and take the canoe on the water if I want. I am here for the nature.'

Bjørn expressed dissatisfaction with the Christiania way and the rhetoric of equality. He chose to question his elders' philosophy of equality, fairness, and openness, so his criticisms were largely disregarded. Although he is a second-generation Christianite, his youthfulness prevents him from full political participation. Bjørn lacks the cultural capital necessary for full political participation in Christiania and this stems from several factors. Foremost, his lack of commitment and length of stay: age and commitment to the community are essential forms of cultural capital and Bjørn lacks these. This is a complicated dynamic because other young people feel disenfranchised from political involvement. Finally, Bjørn was isolated because he was a 'talker' rather than a 'doer'. Bjørn never committed to Christiania because he cannot accept the community's ideals, because he felt that the underlying inequalities and overt contradictions are ignored and never addressed. Unlike many of the older activists, Bjørn did not buy into the rhetoric of community involvement, building a dream, or the anti-state positionality. He wanted a nice, inexpensive place to live and he was not invested in Christiania because it was no different from the neighbourhoods surrounding Copenhagen. He felt Christiania had 'fake ideologies'.

Bjørn: Communism like this has two problems. If the person gets ambitious or says, 'I don't want to', what are people going to do?

Myself, I have broken no official rules. I pay my rent. I don't damage anything. I haven't beaten up on anything or anybody. So they got no choice but to let me stay because, if they threw me out over purely personal and ethical reasons, would they be any better than the state? So they can't do it.

Bjørn referred to the dominant rules within Christiania, which he has not broken. Although there is no legitimate reason to throw him out, he resists by openly criticising Christiania's philosophy of social equality. Because of his open, hostile questioning of their philosophy, other Christianites have chosen to ignore him. His antagonism places him in a fraught situation because other 'weak' Christianites (unconnected individuals who lack a strong social base) have been thrown out in the past. Bjørn is careful not to provide a justification for that type of action.

Bjørn: And since I say 'go away, go away', their only choice is to ignore me and that only serves to increase my contempt. Like a child sent to bed without supper. When he realises that he can't get any supper, he says, 'Fine'. Therefore, their only choice is to ignore me.

Christa: So they don't try and do anything positive to bring you back in?

Bjørn: Of course. Of course they do. But nobody likes to bring up these subjects. It is not a nice subject. You really, really have to be stupid not to see the faults, not to see the problems, not to see the contrasts. Nobody likes to bring it up so, therefore, it is hard to bring a person back in. Especially when we talk about it, I hit all the sensitive nerves. So, it is pretty hard.

By ignoring or de-legitimising his criticisms and questions, Bjørn argues that other Christianites simply want to deflect his criticisms. 'What? Do I need to live in Christiania for ten years before anyone will listen to me?' In Christiania we favour those 'Who are known. Who have given back to the community.'

Conclusion

Narratives and practices of Christianites are used here to explore how normalisation is a spatial and social process, but one that is also contested. The tensions between the pushers and activists, young people and elders, insiders and outsiders, and the state and Christiania demonstrate the complexity of normalising processes as they occur at a specific historical moment and in a specific setting. This strategic reading of Christiania's social dynamics focused on critiques and contentious engagements and, as such, it occludes many other stories. However, the narratives offered by Karen, Ida, Tata, Ditlev, Bjørn and the young squatters are meant to reflect how normalisation is created, engaged and resisted.

Although normalisation within Christiania was the focus of this chapter, external normalisation and internal normalisation are intertwined. The external pressures from the state inform narratives of legitimacy and belonging within Christiania. While the state uses specific political logics and taken-for-granted notions to justify the Normalisation Plan, Christianites also employ logics of belonging that attempt to delimit insider from outsider. As Foucault pointed out, scientific discourses are employed to naturalise and discipline, and in Christiania, logics of belonging are used to justify their occupation of the area.

'Insider' and 'outsider' spatialise normalisation and narratives of belonging — 'pusher' and activist' — enforce 'the Christiania way,' which relies on certain taken-for-granted notions. Just as the prisoner is disciplined by the fear of the overseer in the Panopticon, spatial normalisation in Christiania acts to modify the body's movements — avoiding Pusher Street — or separating legitimate spaces (activist spaces) from illegitimate (pusher houses). Practices are normalised through the alteration of daily routines that seek to avoid conflict or subtly contest 'the street's legitimacy' as a central space of control within Christiania. Spatial normalisation also defines the boundaries of belonging such as insider or outsider, and pusher's versus activist's houses so that space and narratives of belonging and exclusion are intertwined.

Social normalisation also works to create exclusions and to define the boundaries of belonging; I used the example of a 'pusher house' to explain how spatial and social normalisation are intertwined. Pusher houses and activist spaces help to define power relations and map spaces of exclusion and inclusion so that identity and belonging become spatialised.

Bjørn's commentary captures the complexity of normalising processes in Christiania and how dominant modes are contested by younger Christianites. Bjørn, like the young squatters, openly challenges exclusions that are supported by, what they argue, are contradictory narratives of belonging. Rather than accept the Christiania way, Bjørn openly criticises what he sees as 'hypocrisy', whereas the young squatters use the same narratives of belonging to justify their actions to take over the basement of *Karlsvognen*.

Normalisation begins with spatial control that orders and then categorises. Orderly spaces transform unruly and undisciplined bodies into 'willing' subjects. The disciplining power is instantiated in construction and regulation of structured spaces. Populations are created, then targeted, and finally (self-) controlled. According to Foucault, normalisation permeates society through the standardisation of spaces. Spaces become structured around formal scientific systems of evaluation, production, and investigation. Bodies and subjectivities are transformed into coherent, self-regulating subjects. Bodily rhythms are controlled through the use of timetables that regulate embodied practices; repetition and regularity create the basis for the common-sense; and order is buttressed through the pathologisation and criminalisation of others. These various apparatuses and accompanying knowledge encourage subjects' complicity in their self-regulation.

Foucault's normalisation is about noting the ways in which foreclosures, silences, and limitations are instantiated. In Christiania, normalisation emerges initially as the state's desire to control space. Privatisation will allow the state to regulate which citizens have a right to live in the city centre. Both subtle and overt forms of normalisation are present. The pushers' arrest and reorganisation (closure and policing) of Pusher Street are two examples of overt forms of spatial control and I have discussed subtler forms of Foucauldian normalisation, such as the rift between the activists and the pushers.

Normalisation is a fascinating theoretical concept because it allows us to discuss the 'unspeakable', that which is taken for granted or accepted as given, natural or self-evident truths. As I argue, it is during conflict moments that normalisation becomes contingent; the historically specific instantiations of relations of power that inform social relations, shape knowledge, and police spaces. Christiania is an interesting space to discuss how normalisation operates, but also how it is negotiated, resisted and reformed.

CONSENSUS AND STRATEGY: NARRATIVES OF NAYSAYING AND YEASAYING IN CHRISTIANIA'S STRUGGLES OVER LEGALISATION

Amy Starecheski

Some Common Meetings (fællesmøden) at Christiania are not very well attended: when the matters to be decided are routine, the meeting is small. But when something truly important is being discussed, hundreds of people gather in the only space large enough to hold them: the Grey Hall (Den Grå Hal). This massive building, originally constructed as a riding arena for the Danish military, has a soaring roof, crisscrossed by wooden beams, and gigantic paned half-moon windows. When Christianites have gathered recently to decide whether to accept or reject proposals that they legalise their community, it has been packed, sometimes night after night, by arguing, listening, debating residents.

Almost every Christianite has a story to tell about the legalisation process of the last seven years, in which Christiania has struggled to decide how to deal with the Danish state's demand that they legalise their property ownership and bring their homes in line with all Danish codes and laws. Since 2004, the right-wing government has presented Christiania with a series of ultimatums, each insisting that they accept the newest proposed legalisation plan or face eviction and demolition. In the face of these yes or no questions, Christiania repeatedly responded with ambiguous maybes until, in June of 2008, they finally said no to the state's plan. One would expect Christianites' stories of this period to describe the intermittent home demolitions and battles with police, the symbolic violence of being forced to number their homes and name their streets, or the ongoing courtroom conflict, and they do. But, surprisingly, their most vivid stories are about the more private dramas of their unusual internal decision-making process.

To many outsiders, the forty year-old squatted Copenhagen neighbourhood of Christiania is known as 'the hippie town', a great place to buy hash, see music and art, or go for a quiet bike ride, but Christiania also deserves to be known for its radically democratic form of decision-making: consensus democracy. Some other recent social movements that have used consensus to make decisions in large groups have developed complicated apparatuses to structure their process, including affinity groups, spokespeople, hand signals, multiple facilitators, and often the option of using modified consensus when the group is stuck.[1] Christianites, on the other hand, just talk it out, or try to. Eight hundred to a thousand people live in Christiania, and when they have a major decision to make, they all have to agree. The meetings where they try to do so are extraordinary.

Recent historical and ethnographic studies of participatory democracy in social movements, such as David Graeber's *Direct Action: An Ethnography* and Francesca Polletta's aptly titled *Freedom is an Endless Meeting: Participatory Democracy in American Social Movements,* have argued that direct democracy is not merely a prefigurative practice, but has also functioned as an effective strategic tool. Both activist and scholarly discourses tend to dichotomise strategy and direct democracy. They assume that hierarchical structures are the most effective ways to organise strategically, while direct democracy is mainly of use in building community and facilitating personal growth within movements. This popular wisdom asserts that when an important decision needs to be made, voting and the influence of clear leaders will allow it to be made most effectively and efficiently. Consensus democracy is then seen as a luxury, which becomes a hindrance when the stakes are high. The works of Graeber and Polletta challenge these assumptions, showing that the use of a consensus process for decision-making can help movements to develop novel tactics and deflect attempts at co-option. Christianites' narratives and analyses intervene directly in this debate: some think that their consensus process is one of their main assets in negotiating effectively with the state, while others see it as a liability, a holdover from the 1970s that actually allows structural power inequalities to flourish clandestinely, limiting both strategic efficacy and democratic decision-making.

It is true that consensus is the traditional way of making decisions at Christiania, in place as a structure of governance almost since the community was created. Therefore, it does not make sense to say that Christianites chose consensus as a *conscious strategy* to enhance their effectiveness in this most recent round of negotiations with the state. This chapter will be examining, instead, whether consensus democracy *functioned strategically*, in terms of furthering the group's stated goals. At Christiania, consensus has undoubtedly been most strategic for those who have not wanted to negotiate a legalisation plan with the state, or have rejected the agreements offered. The use of consensus has allowed them to stall under the cover of democracy, refusing all deals while appearing to engage in the negotiation process in good faith. Because the consensus process insists on attention to marginal and minority voices, and forces the group to seek creative compromises, it has also produced innovative ideas. Christianites' refusal to vote has protected them from being divided and weakened, and the powerful sense of unity created when Christianites have managed to agree has sustained many participants through a stressful process. However, the more common experience of ongoing, unresolved conflict has exhausted many others. For those Christianites who wanted to reach an agreement with the Danish state at any cost, consensus has been an obstacle to reaching their goals, and those individuals are far more likely to see consensus as unstrategic. In the case of Christiania, consensus may be a strategic and powerfully effective way to say no, and is an effective shield from co-option. However, with such an informally structured process and a large and diverse group of people, it appears to be difficult to use consensus to agree on a positive course of action.

This chapter is based primarily on sixteen oral history interviews I recorded with Christianites,[2] most of which are archived at Christiania.[3] Oral history is founded on a premise of 'shared authority' which begins in the co-construction of the narrated account.[4] Like the consensus process, oral history practice privileges a collaborative model of meaning making. The oral history interview is designed to allow the interviewee to provide an initial structure for the narrative, blending anecdote and interpretation, the personal and the political, to tell both what happened and why.[5] Social movement research benefits from an engaged approach that attends to the theories and analyses produced from within movements, and oral history is an ideal method to elicit these interpretations.[6] While I also interviewed people who had not been deeply involved with the negotiation process, this chapter primarily draws on my interviews with 'activists,'[7] who have participated intensively in the negotiations with the state and in Christiania's internal debates. Oral histories with these activists provide a unique insight into how the consensus form has shaped Christiania's response to fluctuating pressure from the Danish government. The rest of this chapter will provide a close reading of these activists' accounts of three critical moments in their decision-making process, culminating in the final decision to say no to the proposed legalisation. Christiania's activists' stories of these moments allow me to investigate the intersections of strategy and consensus, and to illuminate the informal rules and structures that characterise Christiania's consensus process.

The Sending of the Flute Player

At times during the past seven years, Christiania has been deeply split between 'naysayers' who reject the terms being offered by the government's representatives, and 'yeasayers' who want to move ahead with legalisation as proposed by the Danish government, and that was the case when Daniel Jensen (a pseudonym) moved into Christiania. He had been coming to Christiania since 1996, when he was 16, and moved in after a period of intense involvement with the squats in Nørrebro, a diverse neighbourhood in Copenhagen known for its large immigrant population and recent riots in defence of squats (see René Karpantschof's chapter in this book). To him, Christiania and other autonomous spaces provided a way to 'manifest what you want from the future, what your dreams are' and he got involved in part because he felt that it was one of the only movements actually trying to oppose the right-wing in Danish politics after 2001. What Jensen found when he started attending Common Meetings, in the midst of one of the most intense periods of decision-making, surprised him:

> I thought that the yeasayers, they would be really scared and like, 'oooh, the government is going to come,' and the naysayers would be brave, and having this heroic look in their eye, 'We're standing here…!' But it wasn't like that. *Everyone* was *totally* fucking scared of each other. […] And the naysayers were afraid of the yea, and vice versa, and they were just paranoid.
>
> And I just remember one guy standing up in the middle of everything at one point and saying, just totally out of the debate, just saying (hippie voice) 'What if we answer the state by just sending this guy out to play the flute?'
>
> And that just stopped everything. People were just like […] just looked at him. And he was not afraid. He was the only person at the meeting that wasn't scared, and he just said that [laughs]. And it ended up that that was actually our answer to the state.[8]

Expecting a traditional press conference, the Danish media was instead presented with a masked jester, accompanied by a flutist, who expressed Christiania's frustration with the state's ultimatum through an interpretive dance. In front of a stunned audience, he leaped like a frog, threw cash into the air and, in a grand finale, ripped open his cape to reveal a Christiania T-shirt. This sending of the flute player in 2006 is one of the moments that comes up repeatedly in Christianites' narratives of the legalisation process, and several narrators use this story as a vehicle to present their analyses of Christiania's political life. Jensen's story illustrates several of the widely acknowledged benefits of a consensus process: an openness to tactical innovation, and to minority voices that might otherwise be marginalised by a majority vote.[9] While some may claim that consensus represses the conflicts from which new ideas arise and that 'a demand for consensus as a creative force is thus a contradiction,'[10] I argue that in this case and in others, consensus democracy facilitates innovation because it empowers minority voices and requires creative solutions to overcome differences. Conflicts cannot be repressed; they must be dealt with. Yet this same decision could also be read as an illustration of the failure of the consensus process to reach a decision on a difficult and complicated issue. Rather than making a 'real decision,' this line of argument would go, Christianites sent a flute player, a joke, as their answer to the state. However, everyone I talked to, naysayers and yeasayers alike, loved it when Christiania sent the flute player to respond to the state's ultimatum; their voices filled with joy and pride when they talked about it.

When I asked Lisa Madsen, an artist, one of the main organisers of Christiania's popular circus, and another recent resident, if she had any specific memories of Common Meetings, she also remembered a time 'from the yes/no period':

It was a really ridiculous period, and it ended up really beautiful but I remember many moments of just sitting thinking: this is absolutely ridiculous. We're trying to find a yes or a no and we know that we cannot take any of them really because if we say no we are, so to speak, doomed, in their eyes. If we say yes, we just sold ourselves to the devil.

What did happen, at the end, which I remember as a really beautiful happening, was that we decided to give them an answer in the way that *we* want to give an answer. Which is not sending letters and writing it, black on white, but we have our jester. He has a mask, and he has a cane, he's also the fortune-teller in here, and he calls himself Duke Lighting. He made a dance […]

I think that was a really good move. And then we also of course said, 'we say yes to development, and we say yes to this and this and this,' but we never said yes to their idea, cause it's a ridiculous idea.[11]

Rasmus Blædel Larsen is another Christianite who shared fond memories of the flute dance. He has had an on-and-off relationship with Christiania for almost his entire life: he was first brought to Christiania as a baby, by his hippie parents — his first recollection of the place is 'a vague hazy memory of running around naked with my ass bare, being 3 or 4.'[12] When we talked he was working at the Christiania post office, and was counted among the 'activists' of Christiania, although he would not define himself that way. He, too, remembers the sending of the flute player as a formative moment in his relationship with Christiania:

So the first ultimatum from the Ministry of Finance was totally unacceptable. That was in November 2006, and we made a reply, which was beautiful, which was the best reply we could have given and one of the things that makes me proud to live here. We had a professional jester make a dance for them. It was a beautiful dance. It was choreographed by a couple of people out here and a guy was playing the flute […] It was just totally absurd and still it had symbolic gestures to show what we thought of their proposal.

This symbolic gesture was made at a particularly sensitive point in the negotiations with the Ministry of Finance's Palaces and Properties Agency (Slots- og Ejendomsstyrelsen, the branch of government newly charged with managing Christiania) and after a period of intense debate within Christiania. Some background is necessary to understand this moment in time: In June of 2004 the Danish parliament had ratified a new Christiania Law, which mandated that Christiania be divided into three parts, normalised, legalised, and developed, while its 'alternative social structure' should be preserved.[13] Christiania as an organisation had initially resisted direct involvement in these governmental deliberations about its future, but the threat of being left out of the implementation process for the new law led residents to change their minds. In a Common Meeting on 1 August 2004 those who wanted to negotiate with the state prevailed, and Christianites selected members of a 'negotiation group' who would be charged with opening a dialogue with the Palace and Properties Agency on Christiania's behalf. This was a departure from their previous mode of organisation, in which a longstanding 'contact group' dealt with the state in all of its manifestations, but was not empowered to negotiate (see Håkan Thörn's chapter in this book). It seemed to be a small shift towards a more representative and less direct form of self-government, and some might consider it 'the first step towards "normalising" Christiania.'[14]

Ole Lykke, Christiania's de facto historian and a long-time resident, saw the creation of the negotiation group as a significant moment in the struggle over process, which has characterised Christiania's recent negotiations with the state. He introduces consensus as both the process for deliberating and a contested point in the negotiations:

> In my mind the negotiation group was part of the Christiania Law. The state didn't want to negotiate with the contact group, or any kind of structure or any kind of political organisation that Christiania came out with. They wanted a negotiation group that had a mandate to negotiate *on behalf of* all Christiania. So that's been a problem in this whole process, that

> even if the state thinks, 'OK this is the negotiation group, we can negotiate with these guys,' these guys don't have the mandate from Christiania to say, 'OK, now we'll do this, this, and this' and then go back [to Christiania] and say, 'This is decided.' They have to go back and say, 'Do you want this?' and when people say no, you know [...] So this is like the Indians, that the US came and said, 'OK, who wants to negotiate? You and you and you,' so now you sell the land. There's a clear parallel there.[15]

The decentralised organisation typical of squatting movements has long been an effective tool against state co-option: without leaders who can negotiate to legalise squatted buildings it becomes far more difficult to make a deal.[16] Lykke also makes a connection between Christianites' struggle to control land and the dispossession of American Indians. He notes, as have scholars studying state formation,[17] that indigenous groups which have representative leaders who can be convinced to transfer collectively controlled land to the colonisers in exchange for power within the new regime can be more vulnerable to colonisation than decentralised societies. Consensus developed at Christiania 'partly in order to stand strong and united against the enemy and to ensure that society did not split the group via a "divide and conquer" strategy.'[18] It is clear in this and other accounts that Christiania's decision to accede to the state's demands and create a negotiating group was, either intentionally or not, misleading: the Palace and Properties Agency proceeded as if the negotiation group was empowered to accept or reject an agreement, whereas the understanding within Christiania was still that any deal negotiated by the group must be approved by consensus in the Common Meeting.[19]

However, the negotiation group was given a mandate within which they could negotiate. This mandate is important; it provides an explicit and concise articulation of Christiania residents' goals within the negotiation process, agreed upon through consensus. I realised just how important the mandate was when, during an interview in 2010, a recent resident who has been involved with the negotiation pulled out his wallet and removed a creased piece of paper to read me the six points: Christiania must be preserved as a whole, be allowed to choose who lives there and be protected from capitalisation of housing; they must maintain a diverse population and consensus-based self-government. He carried them with him everywhere, and had for years.

With such a diverse group of people, with admittedly varying goals and needs, it becomes difficult to define strategy, and thus to evaluate the strategic efficacy of the consensus process. The articulation of shared goals in this mandate can provide a point from which to measure Christiania's success in the negotiations, based on whether the goals have been achieved, or perhaps whether their achievement has at least not been foreclosed. However, it is essential to remember that even though there was consensus on it, the mandate does not actually represent *everyone's* goals. There are people within Christiania who dispute the legitimacy of the Common Meetings entirely, and there are those who would vehemently oppose some elements of the mandate (see Helen Jarvis' chapter in this book). For example, there is a minority whose goal is to own their own homes individually, and even to capitalise on them.

Finally, it is important to note that the Palace and Properties Agency has its own interpretation of this same mandate. To the points listed above they add, most tellingly: 'legalise the area,' 'participate in the development of local plan,' and 'produce the basis for building new buildings.' Consensus and the ability to choose residents do not appear on the Agency's list of Christiania's negotiation aims.[20] In fact, the Palace and Properties Agency explicitly condemns consensus as a practice in which 'responsibilities melt into air,' and demands that Christianites give it up.[21] As Ole Lykke notes, consensus is not merely a structure within which decisions about legalisation are made at Christiania, it is itself an object of the negotiations, one which is contested in part through representations of those negotiations.

During the twenty-six month period from August 2004 to September 2006, the negotiation group met with the Palace and Properties

Agency and other involved parties to develop a plan for how to implement the Christiania law in a way that could satisfy both Christiania and the Danish state. On 26 September 2006, on Christiania's 35th birthday, the Palace and Properties Agency delivered the state's proposal, along with an ultimatum. It made clear that Christiania had only two options: to say yes, and implement the plan, or to say no and have the plan implemented without their consent. As Rasmus Blædel Larsen put it, 'The threat from the state was that if we didn't take that proposal they would just come and bulldoze the whole squat — they wanted us to believe that we had only two options.'[22] The plan clearly conflicted with several of the mandates from which the negotiation group had been working: Christiania would be divided into three units, each of which would have different structures of governance, and available housing would be allocated by lottery — Christianites would have no say in the choice of their neighbours. A common housing association would own most of the housing, and residents would rent their homes from the association. But it was still not easy to say no to this deal — Christiania had eight Common Meetings in as many weeks and finally on 15 November gave their reply.[23] It was in the last of these meetings that the idea of the flute player was born.

The Palace and Properties Agency maintains a timeline of the negotiations with Christiania on their website. Each twist and turn in the process is described in some detail; the entry for November 2006 is uncharacteristically terse: 'Christiania replies with an answer that is neither a yes or a no.'[24] Faced with an ultimatum, and a dichotomy, Christiania's consensus process yielded a third way, both in the flute dance, and in the idea of saying yes to negotiations, but no to the plan.

A De Facto No

The threatened bulldozers were not forthcoming, and from November 2006 to June 2008, Christiania continued to say maybe to the state's legalisation plans. The Palace and Properties Agency timeline lists a series of deadlines: February 2007, March 2007, April 2007 and June 2008, and depicts Christiania first asking for 'clarification and elaboration of the state's offer,' and then 'requiring further clarification on the agreement,' following which 'the Minister of Finance Thor Pedersen bemoans this in a letter to Christiania.' After all of this deliberation, Christianites finally state 'that they cannot approve the agreement as they still have significant reservations.'[25] I would not be the first to note that 'deadlock had long been Christiania's best defence.'[26] It may continue to be, and consensus facilitates this kind of stalling. While the ponderous slowness, and even potential for deadlock, in consensus-based decision-making processes is often cited as a weakness, here it could be seen as an asset.

None of the proposed plans allowed Christiania to achieve the goals of the mandate with which they had entered the negotiations. Christianites again seemed faced with an impossible yes/no choice, holding their own futures, and the future of their world-famous collective endeavour, in their hands. It was paralysing. Rasmus Blædel Larsen puts it best:

> It is a difficult and mind-wrenchingly naked condition for anybody, any individual, in control of his or her life — here we were eight or nine hundred people with not only our individual or collective future to gauge, but the whole fucking dream and sacred ground-thing that our community represented to millions of people around the world. It all made every mindful Christianite doubt what was *actually* the best way — many of my friends had good arguments for saying yes, and I think the deadlock more than anything else reflected the very real and powerful inability to decide what the implications were.[27]

Christiania said maybe in part because many people honestly did not know what the right thing to do was. By saying maybe, they kept the door open while waiting for conditions to somehow change in their favour: perhaps there would be a change in government, or they would win one of the many court cases they had lodged against the state.

Hulda Mader, a member of the contact group since 1989 and a strong naysayer, sees stalling as strategic, and consensus as a vital tool in Christiania's negotiations with the state:

> Sometimes it's awful but it's been enormously helpful in our dealings with other systems, because they hate it, they *simply abhor* consensus democracy, and that's the beauty of it. So, I think it's great.
>
> Every time they say, 'Oh we think you should do this,' we say 'Yes'. They say 'Can we make an agreement?' and we say, 'No we have to go back and talk to the Common Meeting and the meeting says no and we come back and say, 'They said no'. And they get angry and we say, 'We can try again'. Decisions can take months, which is good for us and very bad for them. Their system cannot deal with stuff like that. They cannot deal with people who can say no, not to their face but just by action. It's not outright disobedience, but they think it is but they cannot [...] because we always say, 'Yes, we will do that and we will go back and listen to what people say, yes, and we will try' [...] That's how we got the snail down at the front [a sculpture of Christiania's mascot] because there was one politician who said, 'When we have closed down Christiania the snail will again be the slowest'.[28]

Because Christiania's consensus process is framed by the ideal of democracy, so dear to the Danish state, the state cannot punish, or even vigorously condemn, the disobedience consensus engenders. Christiania is able to resist, while seeming to comply, and Hulda Mader believes that this 'helped [them] until now quite a lot.' However this 'them' is an often divided group, and it is undeniable that deadlock and stalling have disproportionately favoured the naysayers, as Ole Lykke explains:

> It was a strategy to drag out the meetings. That was a really crucial thing making the meetings hard [...] People who don't respect the process, they can just drag out and drag out and we're getting closer and closer to the [deadline on the] 11th, and if we surpass the deadline they have won, even if they are a minority because then the state will say, 'OK, you didn't make it, we do what we like'.[29]

Clearly, not all Christianites are as positive about the consensus process as Hulda Mader. Githa Iversen is one of many frustrated Christianites who have been actively working to transform Christiania's consensus process and make its structure more formal. She came to Christiania in 1980 as a teenager because she loved the dance parties there, and stayed to raise a family with her husband, Allan Lausten. When the right-wing government was elected in 2001, Iversen decided that she was going to defend Christiania. However, she also decided that she would have to make sure that Christiania was worth defending, so she got involved with initiatives to reform the procedures through which available living spaces are allocated and rents assigned and, after a frustrating period as a member of the negotiation group, she also took on the consensus process. During the long process of meetings and debates in 2007, Iversen was one of the most outspoken yeasayers: she wanted to accept the deal, and she has a clear analysis of why Christiania eventually decided to reject it. Her story shows that consensus at Christiania is not simply a process of patient listening, creative thinking, and thoughtful compromise, but is also shaped by aggression and violence in ways which, she believes, undermine its democratic premises entirely.

> These Common Meetings, they're *just terrible*, and I don't think there's democracy at Christiania – – Many people are afraid to talk in front of a large audience, especially in Christiania, because if you say things which are not popular, people start shouting at you and become very aggressive in a way, and they interrupt you. You have to be really, really strong. In this way it's not democracy. It's just those that can stand this pressure, those that can stay up for a long time during the night, for instance. Those who can speak, they're the ones who – – […] And I think it's not fair.[30]

To Christianites, it is crucial, as Iversen's quote and Hulda Mader's comment above show, for the consensus process to be legitimised as democracy. Iversen and others frame their critiques of it within these terms — when the process is not working, it is 'undemocratic.' The traditional democratic ideal at Christiania is not, however, the practice of contested elections (as in a representative democracy), but is rather a form of direct, participatory democracy in which every person can speak, be heard, and thus have input into the decisions made. With a few other people, Githa Iversen developed a plan to improve the fit between this ideal and Christiania's real practice. They put people in smaller, randomly assigned discussion groups at big meetings, so that people would feel more comfortable talking and would be encouraged to compromise by discussing issues with people they did not already agree with. There would be clear agendas and time limits and careful facilitation.

Githa Iversen's efforts represent only one part of an ongoing effort towards reform. Christianites also formed, and funded from their common purse, an ongoing working group to rethink the consensus process, with an emphasis on learning from their long history of practicing consensus. This group met weekly for eight months during the decision period, and even brought in consultants to teach workshops in decision-making. Based on their discussions, they developed a model of facilitation that might allow for broader participation on Christiania's consensus process, but few attended the meeting called to present the plan, and it was never adopted by the Common Meeting facilitators.[31] In the past few years, there does seem to have been a shift towards more tightly facilitated meetings, and a closer connection between the Common Meetings and the small-scale discussions that happen in local area meetings (see Helen Jarvis' chapter in this book). It has been a while, for example, since a meeting has gone on all night, and the days when 'there used to be lots of people talking *a lot* and some people screaming in the back and some people sitting smoking pot in the back so we couldn't breathe' may be receding.[32] Githa Iversen worked hard to push these changes. She even encouraged voting, making an explicit move from direct to representative democracy.

During the past seven years, as Christianites have repeatedly struggled over yes/no decisions and deadlines imposed by the state, the idea of trying some kind of voting has been raised several times. In the period in 2007, when Christiania was most deeply divided, voting in an 'advisory referendum' was tried twice. According to activist and vocal naysayer Allan Lausten, yeasayers wanted a vote because they could see that at that moment they had a majority, but that they would never win through consensus. A secret ballot was used, but the results are debated: according to some sources, so few people participated that the results were considered worthless,[33] while others claim that most people voted.[34] In another attempt at resolving the deadlock, Christianites tried dividing up spatially, with yeasayers going to one side of the room, naysayers to the other, and the undecided remaining in the middle. Lausten describes the scene as Christiania physically split: 'It was amazing. People were spitting on each other. It was really wild.'

It was clear at this point that there was indeed a majority who wanted to take the deal: Allan Lausten estimated that perhaps 40 per cent were in favour, 30 per cent opposed, and 20 per cent undecided. (As always, some people, perhaps 10 per cent, did not participate at all.) If Christiania had voted at this point, it seems certain that they would have accepted the government's offer. However, by all accounts this process did not lead Christiania any closer to consensus, and it was unclear how Christiania could legitimise a major decision made by voting, when no consensus could be reached on whether or not to vote. Hulda Mader says that 'it was quite bad at that time, people got really angry at each other, and there were really bad feelings, and it felt like Christiania was splitting and fragmentising.'[35]

In the aftermath of the advisory referendum, Githa Iversen attempted to facilitate a massive meeting of five hundred people on 22 March 2007, in which Christiania tried once again to reach consensus on how to respond to the complicated deal being offered. While she wanted to have a strict agenda and a focused discussion, the meeting 'went totally chaotic'. One man punched another before the meeting even started, and no one did anything about it; all her efforts to regain control failed, and she blamed it on the drug pushers (see Christa Amouroux's chapter in this book), who in some ways had the most to lose from legalisation:

> Christiania was split in two: it was like a yes and a no group. The pushers, they were kind of like saying no because it would ruin their business, or whatever. And if we did not take any decisions, it would be a no. So it was kind of like, in my reality, they were interested in just obstructing the meeting. So one of these guys he had, inside a blanket, he had these racquets or something, carrying a *weapon* into a *meeting*. I heard that afterwards, and I just got so angry.[36]

The next morning, exhausted after a late night and an early morning getting her children sent off to school, Githa Iversen picked up the phone to find Reuters media on the line, and without thinking much she told them what she thought: that the pushers were obstructing the process, and keeping the majority of Christianites from accepting the deal. Within hours she was being quoted all over the world as a 'spokesperson' for Christiania; by the end of the day the Danish media had interviewed Allan Lausten too, and the divided spouses were all over the news. Iversen had broken a rule about keeping internal Christiania negotiations private, and she had angered the pushers. They called a meeting that night to try to throw her out, but she did not attend. Feeling her life was threatened, she briefly retreated to the countryside, and had to force herself to begin attending meetings again soon after that. I asked her how, then, the process had ended, as the deadline loomed:

> After this specific meeting, which was very crucial for me, but not for everybody, there were maybe eight meetings more, like almost every day, because there were no decisions taken. And there were less and less and less and less and less people. I actually went to many of these meetings and I was at the last meeting which was until three o'clock in the night, and we were 30 people, and this is supposed to be democracy.

This last meeting happened at the end of March, and resulted in another ambiguous answer from Christiania: a 'yes with conditions'.

The Miracle Meeting

Finally, in June of 2008, Christiania definitively rejected the much-clarified and elaborated agreement. Christianites, when asked to talk about the legalisation process, often told vivid stories about the meeting where this decision was made, and the series of meetings leading up to it. Many described it as a pinnacle of unity for Christiania, and a transformative personal experience. Allan Lausten, a naysayer, is one of these people. He and Githa Iversen have raised three children in Christiania, and he has been involved with squatting in Copenhagen for thirty years. Their self-built home is a showplace featured in several books about Christiania. Lausten was a member of the negotiation group, and says that he knew a year before the final proposal was produced that he would not support the deal: 'From my point of view, no way! *I* will not support it. I think it's like lunatic; it's like madness.' Half of the negotiation group, he reported, felt the same way.[37] Here is Lausten's story of how the decision was made to finally reject the deal:

> When we had this meeting I was running, together with somebody else, we were three guys, we were actually a small group who was running the meeting. We were the meeting … How do you say?
>
> Amy Starecheski: Facilitators?
>
> Allan Lausten: Facilitators, yes, exactly, that's the word. We were the ones. And when you choose to be up there you also have a fantastic opportunity, not to control the situation, but you have to be the one who's, 'How should things develop? What should we increase? What should we give less energy?' And of course you cannot decide anything but you can kind of help the situation.
>
> And it was amazing. *It was amazing*. We were these guys and we said, 'We're going to do this. We're going to take responsibility that *we* are the ones who's gonna bring this to an end. Whatever it's going to be, we'll take

this to an end.' And the contact group accepted that we took the responsibility. They said, 'OK we have full trust in you guys, we support you. We know that this is not the best deal but if Christiania wants it then we're gonna go for it' ... But we didn't really hope, and we didn't believe in it, so we didn't fight for it. We'd fight for something different, and what was it we would fight for? Pah! We don't know. But it was *certainly* not that deal we had there [...]

So we went to this meeting and [...] the deal was signed up, and it was, phew, a pile of paper like this [gestures with hands — two feet tall] with papers, with deals. I mean so incredibly much work. The state spent more than 25 million crowns to do this deal. Then you don't think about what *we* spent, you know? We spent a lot of money, but the time? Ha! We spent like 150 million time in this deal [...] And it ended up in this small blue book, you know. 'You just have to sign down there and everyone will be happy'. Ha!

And we took this: 'Does anyone really believe that this is a good deal? And this is what we can go for in the future [...]?' People said no. OK. Poof. Throw it away. So, we have two months. We have spent like five years now. We throw the fucking five years away. What are we going to do?

Allan Lausten went on to describe the intense process, over the next two months, during which Christiania crafted their own plan for their future. For him, this was one of the highlights of his experiences at Christiania, a time when people genuinely came together to do something productive and creative for their community, and it provides an example of consensus working to create a positive vision, rather than just saying no. His account illustrates the powerful role of facilitators in Common Meetings, and the meticulous way in which this power should ideally be managed by those who hold it. Lausten notes that others agreed to give him this power, to allow him and two other men to take on this responsibility. While he makes it clear that he facilitated the meeting with a certain outcome in mind, he repeatedly asserts that he would have supported any decision made.

Christianites' accounts of this particular meeting are especially valuable sources for those seeking to understand how consensus works, and is supposed to work, at Christiania. Consulata Blanco (or Tata, as she is called by everyone) came to Christiania from Italy in the 1970s, married a Dane, raised her family there, and is now a grandparent. She runs one of Christiania's thriving businesses, crafting handmade shoes in a sky-lit workshop just outside of Christiania's downtown, and has been involved in negotiations with the government for decades. Tata Blanco's story about that decisive meeting, and her analysis of Christiania's consensus process, highlight some of the complications of using consensus in such a large group. She says, 'I think consensus is a terrible way to make decisions between 800 people,' and that

> it's a hell to make a decision sometimes, because we stick to this consensus thing that is wonderful and possible in some occasions, but completely impossible in others. But we *stick* to it, so I think sometimes we stick too much to old things ... We choose the lowest common denominator, and that's the bad thing about consensus, you always choose the lowest. And that can be boring. Boring! 40 years and we still fight with the state ... And that's because of the consensus, that we cannot make good decisions.[38]

But her story of the meeting at which Christiania finally decided to say no is just as permeated with a sense of transcendence as Allan Lausten's:

> Sometimes it's just obvious for everybody. And sometimes a miracle happens, and all the gods are with us. So when things have to be done, at the last moment we always find a solution. It wasn't hard to decide to say no. That's very easy, actually, it was lucky that we all thought so. It's not difficult to say no. It's more difficult to say yes to something, in this case ... There was a group of young people, with a leader, for that day, or for that moment, not a leader but one who speaks for –
>
> Amy Starecheski: A spokesperson —
>
> Tata Blanco: Yes, a spokesperson. And she said, 'I represent this group of young people'. They were there, and they were many. And they also said why they think we should say no, even though they wish that we could reach some kind of political agreement. But they had talked together and they had decided that we could not say yes to that. And that kind

> of, not influenced, but established for sure that we should say no. And it was very touching to see the young people, our children stand there and tell how they felt about it. It was very strong, it was a very strong moment for everybody.

Christiania emerges here as an almost ideal Arendtian public, in which free subjects come together to make decisions, using rhetorical power to persuade each other.[39] Of course, as Githa Iversen, Tata Blanco, and others point out, access to this rhetorical power is limited to those who can stay up late at night, who can stand up to the jeers of their opponents and perhaps even threats of physical violence. Rhetorical power can inspire people to rally behind a choice that most people already agreed with, or it can sway the group in a way that some would say undermines the democracy which consensus is meant to promote. The line between these two effects is fine and permeable. Later in our interview, Tata Blanco says:

> What makes [consensus] very undemocratic, actually, is that the decision is made because somebody has a very good speech about something and we say, 'yeah, yeah, that's good!' So if you can speak your mind, you will have much more influence than people that cannot speak their mind, and that's very bad … When the structure is so loose, then there will be a hidden power group. It's just not official, but there is, and I can see it in Christiania.

Yet when I asked her if the story she told before, about Ella Forchammer (the spokesperson for the young people) persuading the group to say no, was an example of this kind of undemocratic abuse of rhetorical power, she said:

> Not with her. No. But it's an example of how just talking, the charisma of some person can influence, yeah. And sometimes it's great. It's not a problem with people that do it in some occasions, in the right occasions, but if people just do it always, because they want the power, or things have to be the way they figure. And we have a few persons that are so strong.

Tata Blanco draws the line clearly: effective use of rhetoric from time to time by an individual is acceptable; it is the long-term amassing and consolidation of political power through speech-making that warps democracy. Her narrative illuminates some of the values that underlie consensus for her. Blanco carefully avoids the use of the word 'leader' when describing Ella Forchammer, for example. And she demonstrates the value placed on compromise when she categorises people for whom 'things have to be the way they figure' as those who should not be allowed to control the decision-making process.

Activists and social scientists interested in consensus have long recognised that emergence of a hidden power group within loose structures is a potentially problematic phenomenon. Jo Freeman's famous essay on 'The Tyranny of Structurelessness' was written in the early years of the second wave of American feminism as a critique of supposedly 'structureless' groups, such as the friendship-based consciousness-raising groups that characterised parts of the women's liberation movement at that time.[40] Composed almost forty years ago and circulated in underground movement publications for two years before it appeared in a sociological journal, it is still an important reference point for activists trying to use consensus in their organising. In fact, the working group on consensus discussed above translated and read it as part of their process.[41] Freeman argued that all groups have structure, and that groups intended to be structureless actually just disguise informal structures with complex implicit rules. Because they are difficult to examine and critique, these informal structures tend to reproduce the social inequalities of the broader society, such as racism, classism and sexism. Christianites' narratives address the existence of this hidden structure and hint at its composition.

Andreas Winther (a pseudonym) tells the same story as Tata Blanco, from a different angle: from the point of view of young people. He got involved at Christiania because, as a radical leftist, he wanted to defend this enclave of resistance to private property. Before he moved to Christiania he put up posters around the area exhorting: 'No sale, no rental, no shared ownership' but now he sees the choices differently. Winther has come to recognise that Christiania is already privately owned, by the state, and that it would probably be preferable for a foundation controlled by residents to own the land. As a resident, he says he has to be responsible in a new way, to the group and the real politics of defending one's home. He was opposed to the deal being offered to Christiania in 2008, and he also tells the story of Ella Forchammer's powerful speech, from quite a different perspective:

> I would like to tell you about one of the things that I have been part of in Christiania's Common Meeting, which was manipulating, big time. But it was loyal to Christiania, and it was about this [question of] what to say. And people, some said yes and some said no and there was no common feeling. We had some meetings in a youth group in Christiania where all the kids who grew up out here and us who moved in here, we were together 30 people, 40 maybe. And we met up and said, 'OK, this idea, or this law, or this proposal, is not good enough. But it's important that we keep this negotiation running, and it is important that we come up with something.'
>
> And then we made this speech from the youth. Just at the right time, we had one of the girls get up and we had this agreement that when she got up we would, all the young people would get up around her, and we went up there 30, 35, 40 people. Some of them did not participate in the meetings before, they just see that all their friends went up here so they went too. And we went up there and Ella said that you could see all these parents that was getting gray in the hair, small teardrops in the eyes and so on. Because it was just, this was working so good. And we ended up saying no to the proposal, and we will make a new proposal for [the state] ... But that was manipulation, and we did that but we talked about it and talked about how what we're doing is manipulation but it's OK because now we're doing this for Christiania.[42]

Winther's insider view gives an example of how groups can use rhetoric to influence the consensus process, and illustrates the micropolitical practices through which consensus actually works. In these accounts, we can see the implicit rules of Christiania's informal structures become explicit. Blanco and Winther's narratives illustrate the power of a skillful blending of public, rational rhetoric ('We need a political solution, but this deal is no good'), affective and relational discourse ('We, your children, the future of Christiania, implore you to say no'), and performance (standing up as a visible group). These activists' analyses of this moment provide insight into how it was intentionally constructed, how it was received, and how it meshes with the unwritten rules of Christiania's public discourse. Like Blanco, Winther distinguishes between acceptable manipulation and unacceptable manipulation. He notes specifically that this group formed in response to this particular moment, and does not represent a sedimented power structure, and that they explicitly discussed the issues raised by Blanco: when is it OK to use rhetoric to manipulate? Like Tata Blanco, he makes it clear that Forchammer was not speaking just for herself; 'they were many'. His story confirms that Forchammer was not a leader, but a spokesperson.

Conclusion

Oral history is always about the relationship between the past and the present. The stories about consensus Christianites told me in the summer of 2010 are certainly different from those they will tell if Christiania is destroyed because they refused prior compromises, just as these memories will undoubtedly change if a new government allows them to reopen negotiations under more favourable terms. Yet through these accounts — of the decision to send the flute player, the stalling of the process, and the unified decision to refuse the Danish government's offer — we see that consensus does appear to be strategic on several levels. Consensus has indeed, at least at times, facilitated the emergence of new ideas and strategies. While Christiania has often been divided, consensus has kept these splits from being manifested in decisive action, and it has provided a few moments of transcendent unity. The rich affective content of these stories illuminates the enduring power of these moments, as well as the deep pain and frustration that comes from a failure to find agreement. Consensus has also allowed Christiania to stall without appearing to be disobedient, because both Christiania and the Danish government depend on a language of democracy for legitimacy. For naysayers, more than others, this stalling was strategically effective.

As Jo Freeman most famously noted, there is a certain potential for tyranny in purportedly structureless organisation. Making the implicit structure explicit, as in these interviews and this analysis, then can become an inherent part of a process of reform. In these oral histories it becomes clear that what might initially appear to be chaotic meetings are actually shaped by some immanent rules of engagement: rhetoric is acceptable, even necessary, but not if used to accumulate power; spokespeople are expected, leaders frowned upon; a facilitator need not be neutral, but must be willing to accept the decision of the group. Rules do not, of course, translate unproblematically into behaviour, as Githa Iversen's story illustrates. Most participants recognise the disjuncture between the ideal of direct, participatory democracy and the informal structure that determines who can participate in meetings, and attempts to reform the process are ongoing: Iversen has stepped back, but others are still working on the project. The meetings in the Grey Hall will continue, and will continue to be lively, at least for now.

CHRISTIANIA AND THE RIGHT TO THE CITY

Anders Lund Hansen

> […] the right to the city […] is not merely a right of access to what the property speculators and state planners define, but an active right to make the city different, to shape it more in accord with our heart's desire, and to re-make ourselves thereby in a different image.[1]
>
> David Harvey

Christiania is notorious for its everyday struggles and activism. In the following section, I will share *one* moment in Christiania's long history of struggles that I experienced as a Researcher in Residence in Christiania. Early Monday morning on 14 March 2007, the police arrived and demolished the Cigar Box (Cigarkassen), a small one-family house located on the ramparts in an area named Midtdyssen in Christiania, only to see it rebuilt the next morning. It was the first time in Christiania's history that the authorities annihilated a building in Christiania. According to the Danish state's Normalisation Plan, the building was an 'illegal structure' with 'illegal inhabitants' (homeless people). The demolition was followed by street battles between activists and the police. The Danish state took action despite the fact that a court decision on these issues would be announced a few days later. Five days after the events a decision was announced — in favour of Christiania.[2]

Wanted: Political Goodwill and Commitment!

On Tuesday morning, 15 March 2007, the Cigar Box reappeared as a phoenix from the ashes, less than a day after the police had demolished the building. 'Come again!' read a three-metre long red banner that was

Map adapted from Christiania's own alternative community plan. The X shows the location of the Cigar Box.[3]

lashed to a tree. The house was approximately four by two metres in plan and three metres high. It was constructed of wood pallets, laths and veneer sheets. It was a solid construction that even had a small annex by the water with the inscription: 'The reconstruction team strikes again'. The idea of the annex was to signal, 'when they tear down a house — we will build two houses', explained a young woman. The main house had an awning that said, 'Welcome'. The sign was made 'in honour of the helicopters' explained the activist who painted the message. Inside the house all was neat and well lit. There was a fixed bench and a picture hung on a nail on the wall. Most striking was the 'fireplace' with painted flames creating warmth in the otherwise chilly time we live in.[4]

The Cigar Box's new 'fire place', with its painted flames — creating warmth in the otherwise chilly times we live in. Photo: Anders Lund Hansen.

The evening before, 25 to 30 activists — most of them in their twenties — completed the action. They worked throughout the night with great enthusiasm. Meanwhile, street battles took place in the neighbouring area of Christianshavn (where I live) between the police and supporting activist groups. Many activists were arrested, among them my neighbour's son. I was drawn towards the place that started the day's events. I offer the following account of the events of the night to give an impression of the people, their efforts, and their convictions as they rebuilt the Cigar Box:

The reconstruction is well in progress when I arrive. Tools are changing hands and building materials are being brought into use. The warm May evening is full of a positive energy that stands in stark contrasts to the street battles fought half a mile away. As darkness falls, power cables and halogen lamps are retrieved and work continues. 'It was damn good, we were here early,' says a man around thirty years of age to his friend while opening a Tuborg beer. Both are dressed in white carpenter's pants and they confirm that they are professional craftsmen. They report: 'We said very quickly that such and such a small solid house could be constructed. Everybody accepted the plan and now you can see that it works.' Both men are satisfied with their efforts. People at the building site talk about the government, police violence and the normalisation of Christiania.

Activists are working eagerly on the rebuilding of the Cigar Box. Photo: Anders Lund Hansen.

'Does anyone here live in Christiania?' asks a young girl who is helping out by coordinating the construction work. 'Yes, here,' says a man in his 40s. 'We need some building materials. Do you know where we can find something we can use?' The request is coordinated and dealt with. Later, I am told by a Christianite who participates in the work that several activists are previous Children's House (Børnehuset) children. Water, cola, beer, coffee, tea and sweets are being fetched. Later, there is someone who tries to get some food for the whole group: 'Is there anyone who'd give their number out, so I can call and see if you are still here?[5] It may take some time to get the food.' Two or three activists volunteer their number. One suggests getting hold of a joint. But this proposal is refused, the group feeling that 'a high activist is a slow activist.'

The atmosphere is good, though people are aware of the situation's seriousness. 'Just imagine, maybe we will get arrested? Do you think this is illegal?' a young woman wonders. People talk about Christiania's building stop and the implications of the action. An activist approaches the site: 'Does someone want to replace one of the guards who has been sitting down the road and kept an eye on the police for some hours now? One of them would like to be replaced.' The group has a clear awareness of the event's historical potential, and it is clear that taking part in the evening/night's events is a considerable action to add to any activist's CV. References are made to Byggeren, a similar action in Nørrebro (the northern part of the city) in the 1970s and 1980s, and people take pictures and films.[6]

The next morning, the building was finished. The morning highlighted the imaginative, colourful decorations and unambiguous words, which effectively expressed what the night's action had been all about: 'Wanted: political goodwill and support!'

During the day, Christiania's press office made sure that the nationwide media got wind of the story. A significant number of reports covered the rebuilding effort, but the vast majority of the headlines focused on the street battles, barricades and burning cars in the surrounding

The Cigar Box — rebuilt, 15 May 2007. Photo: Anders Lund Hansen.

neighbourhood, Christianshavn. In isolation, the rebuilding of a small wooden house may not seem significant. But the action could be regarded as an active politics of scale — an important *symbol* of Christiania's proactive fight for its 'right to the city'.

In this chapter I will shed a critical light on two very different appropriations of the concept the 'right to the city' in Copenhagen.[7] First of all, property rights have been the most dominating right to the city throughout the history of capitalism and were at the core of the 'neoliberal revolution' launched by people like Margret Thatcher and Ronald Reagan three decades ago. Cities throughout the globe have become important spaces for neoliberalism and entrepreneurial urban politics, more accommodating towards investors and developers. Proactive city governance uses Thatcher's TINA acronym to suggest that There Is No Alternative to the global neoliberal uneven growth agenda — and thus also the norm in today's post-political Copenhagen; where Christiania is fighting *against* normalisation and *for* their version of the right to the city. This brings me to the second appropriation of the concept of the right to the city. Christiania has since its genesis four decades ago been executing a very different right to the city. From the initial squatting of the area to today's collective rights to the land and housing. Through the example of the rebuilding of the Cigar Box, I have presented one moment in the long history of struggles. I argue that collective activism, dedication, improvisation, art, humour and politics of scale are important elements in Christiania's 40-year fight for the right to the city. I use this example as leverage for a general discussion of the multi-scalar battles over space that go on in cities throughout the globe. The broader intent of this chapter is to discuss Christiania's fight for survival as part of general urban space wars; i.e. as a larger scalar reconfiguration of the geographical and social embodiment of political and economic powers.

Urban Space Wars, Gentrification and the Right to the City

> Urban territory becomes the battlefield of continuous space war, sometimes erupting into the public spectacle of inner-city riots [...] but waged daily just beneath the surface of the public (publicised), official version of the routine urban order (Zygmunt Bauman).[8]

From the cellular to the planetary scale, the battlefronts are many and varied. The urban scale is no exception. Urban transformation processes, from the normalisation of Christiania and urban renewal of Vesterbro in Copenhagen to the construction of the Expo in Shanghai and the gentrification of Lower East Side and Harlem in New York, take the form of space wars: a deliberate and systematic creative destruction of the very fabric of urban space. Demolition of spaces for 'the other' and construction of borders to control who is inside and who is outside have been common practice among city builders for millennia. Walls and weapons of force, furthermore, remain essential aspects of space wars — causing 'wounded cities' and 'urbicide'.[9] Space wars, however, are more than physical destruction, fortifications and military hardware.[10]

Zygmunt Bauman describes how processes of globalisation entail increased struggles over space.[11] Bauman uses the term 'space wars' in his analysis of how the modern state increases its demand for control over space. New tools are constantly forged to establish 'objective' units of measure and maps are used to avoid local subjective interpretations of space. The processes of modernisation of our societies have according to David Harvey inherent elements of 'creative destruction', 'be it gentle and democratic, or the revolutionary, traumatic, and authoritarian kind'.[12] This tendency can be recognised in the creation and destruction associated with urban change — and is a very real part of the obstacles that Christiania is facing. But why use such a heavy metaphor as space wars? The Greek meaning of a metaphor is to 'transfer' or 'carry something across', and the metaphor of 'space wars' brings a critical perspective to the study of urban transformation processes and uneven development. Urban space wars are not abstract distant phenomena. They are a very real part of the everyday life of many people — in Denmark too. Space wars are, however, more than police barricades and NIMBY (Not In My Back Yard) resistance.

The term 'space wars' is related to the processes of 'gentrification', which cover the upward socio-economic shift that some areas go through.[13] Should the Danish government choose to realise its plans to sell the properties in Christiania, and thus commodify space, the gentrification debate can enlighten us about some of the challenges that Christiania is facing. Traditionally the gentrification debate has focused on decaying working class areas near city centres, such as for example Vesterbro in Copenhagen, where middle and upper middle class people moved to the neighbourhood, leading to the displacement and eviction of existing residents.[14] Processes of gentrification have deep historical roots and are geographically widespread.[15] Discussions have often revolved around cultural[16] and economic[17] arguments, and the majority of case studies up until the beginning of the 1990s were conducted in cities 'occupying strategic positions in the international urban hierarchy'.[18] One vein in the debates has paid tribute to the complexity of the process, a debate that sometimes fails to remember the root causes of gentrification.[19] As Eric Clark reminds us, these root causes are: commodification of space, polarised power relations, and a set of fictions that strategically naturalise the drive to conquer space.[20]

Another tension in the debate is the 'emancipatory city' versus the 'revanchist city' thesis.[21] The prior perspective argues that 'social mixing' is a positive outcome. Peter Byrne for instance concludes that gentrification can improve the economic opportunities for the urban poor.[22] Furthermore, this positive vision can be recognised in recent hype around the 'creative city'. The popular argument, articulated by Richard Florida, is that businesses and people move to the places where the creative urban environments are.[23] Accordingly, 'people climate' is important for the branding of cities, and gentrified neighbourhoods are seen as magnets attracting the 'creative class'. From this perspective, it makes economic sense for the city to facilitate gentrification. 'Good' governance targets deprived neighbourhoods for (state-led) gentrification in order to emancipate the creative potential of the city.[24] The gentrifiers are seen as the embodiment of global cultural and economic flows — an emerging global elite community equivalent to the creative class.[25] Forces of global capital accumulation, shifts towards neoliberal urban governance and increased interurban competition during past decades have led to a 'nouveau-bourgeois war for talent', causing increased struggles over urban space and sweeping displacement of people.[26] In his book *The Revanchist City*, Neil Smith identifies how the logic of the market, the state and police force produce unjust conditions for the urban poor and other socio-economically weak groups while serving the upper classes to 'reclaim' the city'.[27] Smith analyses the flip-side of gentrification:

> As new frontier, the gentrifying city since the 1980s has been oozing with optimism. Hostile landscapes are regenerated, cleansed, reinfused with middle-class sensibility; real estate values soar; yuppies consume; elite gentility is democratised in mass-produced styles of distinction. So what's not to like? The contradictions of the actual frontier are not entirely eradicated in this imagery but they are smoothed into an acceptable groove.[28]

According to Neil Smith, uneven development is today increasingly organised around the nexus of global and local.[29] The 'glocal' rhythms of capitalism and urban governance formed by competition between cities translate into uneven development — segregation, exclusion and 'space wars'.[30] A focus on space wars sheds critical light on urban renewal — especially in a Scandinavian context where gentrification is given little public or political attention and researchers on urban issues often gloss over the connection between urban renewal and gentrification. As Eric Clark suggests, this may in part be due to the successes of the Scandinavian welfare state, which is often seen as a guarantor of socially just planning.[31]

Urban transformations in Copenhagen have, however, involved many legal battles that are being fought over urban space. The Danish slum clearance policies of the 1980s created very real battlefields between the state and its residents. In particular, Byggeren (a playground with self-built constructions, referred to earlier in this chapter) in inner Nørrebro became the epicentre of battles between the police and people fighting for their right to the city (see René Karpantschof's chapter in this book). The protests were primarily directed towards the municipality's large-scale demolition scheme for the area; but the battles could also be interpreted as a reflection of a broader class struggle for social justice.[32]

There are tendencies in European, and especially Scandinavian, literature on 'urban renewal' to claim that the North American urban conflict rhetoric is highly exaggerated and theories developed in a North American context cannot be transferred to Scandinavia. In this view, Scandinavia supposedly has superior planning legislation and rent regulation that prevents the kind of urbanism practiced in North American cities. Our study of the consequences of recent urban renewal of the urban neighbourhood of Vesterbro in Copenhagen, however, suggest that the urban renewal policies can be seen as smooth — even stealthy — tactics to kick-start gentrification. And I will argue that the normalisation plans of Christiania should be seen in this context.[33] Henri Lefebvre saw the emancipatory potentials associated with the creative destruction of the three-dimensional (material, ideological-institutional, symbolic-affective) multi-scalar processes behind *the production of space.*[34] His book *The Urban Revolution* is both a diagnostic of how urbanisation has become a worldwide process, but also an analysis of how the processes of urban transformation offer opportunities for marginalised social groups to claim 'the right to the city', through space wars.[35] Lefebvre does not use the term 'space wars', but he talks about how revolutionary claims can be turned into social surplus and political decision-making articulated through struggles over space. Christiania is an excellent example of such a struggle. The Danish government's plans to 'normalise' Christiania threaten the existence of the community. One of the objectives is a revanchist strategy to gain control over the area through privatisation of the common land of Christiania. The potential enclosing of Christiania is not happening without a struggle. These struggles not only take the form of violent street battles, but are also fought at a more subtle policy level. As one Christianite states: 'It [the government] is grinding us down slowly. They realise that using bulldozers is not a good idea. Bureaucrats are good though: they work! And suddenly it [Christiania] becomes a 'nice' area — and damn boring. I can't stand niceness!'[36]

New Urban Imperialism: Accumulation by Dispossession

These social processes, however, are not new. 'Primitive accumulation', the process of separating people from their land and thereby their means of providing for themselves was essential in kick-starting the capitalist system.[37] It undermined the ability of people to provide for themselves and prevented them from finding alternative survival strategies outside the wage-labour system. In this light, space wars constitute a fundamental element in the invention of capitalism itself. Karl Marx emphasises that the process is anything but idyllic and illustrates how force was an integral practice of primitive accumulation.[38] The term primitive accumulation embraces a wide range of processes. According to David Harvey, these involve:

> [...] the commodification and privatization of land and the forceful expulsion of peasant populations; conversion of various forms of property rights (common, collective, state, etc.) into exclusive private property rights; suppression of rights to the commons; commodification of labor power and the suppression of alternative (indigenous) forms of production and consumption; colonial, neo-colonial and imperial processes of appropriation of assets (including natural resources); monetization of exchange and taxation (particularly of land); slave trade; and usury, the national debt and ultimately the credit system as radical means of primitive accumulation.[39]

David Harvey argues that the theory of over-accumulation and of capital's tendency to exploit 'spatio-temporal fixes' to overcome crises is central to the understanding of the new (urban) imperialism. Furthermore, he introduces the term 'accumulation by dispossession' and suggests that the practices of 'primitive' accumulation constitute an ongoing process. He argues that 'all the features of primitive accumulation that Marx mentions have remained powerfully present within capitalism's historical geography up until now'.[40] In countries like Mexico and India, for instance, displacement of peasant populations and the creation of landless populations have increased during the past three decades. Moreover, privatisation of global environmental commons (land, air and water), public assets and intellectual property rights constitute new waves of 'enclosing commons'. Resistance to this process forms the core of the agenda for many of the participants in alter/anti-globalisation movements.

On the urban scale, privatisation and liberalisation of markets have been part of neoliberal politics for decades, generating new rounds of dispossession.[41] I find the term 'accumulation by dispossession' very useful in grasping how space wars constitute an integral part of the capitalist space economy and new urban imperialism. The term is highly relevant for the understanding of the structural pressures that Christiania is facing in recent years, because it illuminates elementary mechanisms behind contemporary urban change. According to geographer Richard Walker:

> Real estate is a critical dimension of internal imperialism… When San Francisco and other Bay Area cities wanted to expand their business, industry, transportation or housing, they eagerly conquered new space by such devices as filling in the bay, bulldozing hillsides, and even removing the dead outside the city limits to claim the cemeteries. After World War II, the downtown real estate operators looked to the surrounding neighbourhoods, potential office and commercial space — that is, if the people and old buildings could just be removed. This development marked the era of 'urban renewal' projects that devastated historically working class, poor neighbourhoods around downtown San Francisco […] driving out many of the poor and people of colour. That process of internal conquest continues to this day […] leaving many more homeless.[42]

Walker uses the term 'internal imperialism' to characterise 'the internal conquest' in cities. But are the real estate investments really that local today? In prior research I have looked more closely at the 'globalisation' of fixed capital investment.[43] I would argue that greater sensitivity towards contemporary scalar dynamics of urban change reveal the new urban imperialism as simultaneously 'internal' and 'external'.

Investors, financiers, real estate agents, developers, local politicians, the state and local social groups are all powerful combatants in the struggles over urban space. Processes of specific battles among specific actors over concrete places and times lead to specific urban outcomes. However particular and unique, these socio-material topographies are heavily influenced by the structural characteristics of the capitalist space economy. Neil Smith identifies a series of shifts that crystallise a new stage in uneven development. In this new stage, the geographic dynamic of uneven development has shifted from national and regional economies to the nexus between global and local.[44] The geographical scales of human activity are the product of changing economic, political and social activities and relationships, and are to be understood as something different than the traditional distinction between urban, regional, national and global. Smith shows us how the transformation of the global political economy since the 1970s has involved a restructuring of the scales on which different kinds of political, economic, and cultural activities are organised. This has, according to Smith, led to 'a profound transformation in the entire geographical framework of capitalist accumulation'.[45] Following some of the same ideas, Saskia Sassen suggests that a new, as yet informal empire is emerging 'that might eventually evolve into a grid of imperial and sub-imperial cities'.[46] The OPCE (Businessmen's Organisations of Capital Cities) resolution, *Make the growth engines work!*, regarding the capital cities and regions of Europe, confirms the tendency towards stronger urban regions:

> [M]ost of the metropolitan areas in the EU are the growth engines of their surrounding regions and of their countries. They help to lift other regions to a higher economic level and help through this the EU to reach the goals of the Lisbon process — making Europe the most competitive region of the world.[47]

Christiania — a Contested Space

Not surprisingly, Christiania is a prime target for the current 'cultural battle' launched by a Danish right-wing government that came into power in 2001. The government's plan is to 'normalise' Christiania;

the central objectives are to close down the cannabis market,[48] register and legitimise the building stock, and to abandon the principle of joint ownership of the land in favour of individual rental contracts and private property rights. A neoliberal revanchist strategy stamped by the logic of a new urban imperialism, the design is to make way for gentrification, to harvest huge land rents (development gains) and attach the 'economically sustainable'[49] population and displace the socio-economic week population — or the 'trash' as the former Head of Planning in Copenhagen calls this group of people.[50]

Since the establishment of Christiania, Copenhagen has generally experienced a huge transformation. The Danish government has not only strived to 'normalise' the Freetown, but also to build a cross-border growth region together with southern Sweden to meet the global and local challenges of 21st century urban transformations. This is also emphasised by Copenhagen Capacity, the capital's booster organisation:

> Copenhagen has one of the world's best business environments. [...] The investment and business climate is world-class, combining low corporate taxation and a highly educated workforce with an international outlook and an outstanding quality of life. This is why Copenhagen is open for business. But Copenhagen is 'Open' in many other ways too. Whether you are seeking cultural experiences, shopping, enjoying the city's quality of life or a great place to live, Copenhagen is open for you, which is reflected in the city's new brand: 'cOPENhagen — open for you'.[51]

The central actors on the urban political scene perceive Copenhagen as a node in the European urban system, and as a growth engine for all of Denmark. In this process the most powerful actors in the region have invested heavily in creating an identity for one whole region — the Øresund region — by linking Greater Copenhagen and the region of Scania (Skåne) in southern Sweden. Major investments include a motorway and railway bridge over The Sound, expansion of the international airport, a new subway line connecting the downtown with the airport, a new 'city tunnel' in Malmö facilitating train services between Scania and Copenhagen, and new major urban development projects such as Ørestaden, Holmen (next to Christiania) and Havnestaden. Other material manifestations include symbolic works of architecture, such as the Turning Torso in Malmö, the Ark (Arken), the new Museum of Modern Art, and the Black Diamond (Den Sorte Diamant), the new waterfront annex to the Royal Library, a new concert hall in Ørestaden, and a new opera house on the harbourfront in Copenhagen. The opera house is a 'gift' to the city from Mærsk Mc-Kinney Møller, the owner of a major multinational (shipping, oil, airline etc.) corporation, and the most powerful capitalist in Denmark. As a powerful actor in what Cindi Katz calls the age of vagabond capitalism, Mærsk Mc-Kinney Møller offers gifts rather than pays taxes.[52] The gift offers convenience because the donor decides what to give — and it is not polite to complain about a gift.

Other material manifestations of the 'new economy' include the newly built environments for the main actors (the information technology, finance, insurance and real estate sectors), including luxury hotels, restaurants, conference centres and shopping malls, such as Fisketorvet on the harbourfront, and luxury housing and publicly financed renewal of inner city housing to attract the 'new middle class', the employees of the 'new economy'. These processes of gentrification, generated by public policy, entail the displacement of inner city residents who do not fit in the 'new creative economy' and Copenhagen's 'world-class business climate' aspirations.[53] The city is thus open to some people while closed to others. In light of this changing urban scene, Christiania is under considerable pressure.

Christiania: a Space for Urban Politics

As in many other western cities, landscapes of urban slums produced by economic restructuring and disinvestment characterised the inner city areas of Copenhagen in the beginning of the 1970s. It was in this context that the Slumstormers (Slumstormerne) squatted the area on 26 September 1971, and since then they have used it as a platform for the development of an alternative urbanism. What started out as a squatter occupation of an abandoned military compound in central Copenhagen, covering more than eighty-five acres, has developed into a home for almost nine hundred inhabitants.[54] Through continuous struggles, Christiania remains a laboratory for new modes of urban design, democracy and social and environmental justice.

It is now a socialist/anarchist/liberalist urban social experiment (a success has many parents) that attracts tourists, students, artists, architects and social scientists who come to experience and study this extraordinary urban setting.[55] What are the ingredients that have made Christiania into such a unique place? And how can other places be inspired by Christiania as an antipode to contemporary post-political urbanism? Environmental — physical as well as social and physiological — awareness and responsibility have been an integral part of Christiania's value basis and urban praxis from the outset. Through continuously experimenting with ecological buildings, biological wastewater treatment systems, alternative energy, a 'car-free city' politics, recycling stations, compost systems, using rainwater for flushing, composting toilets, Christiania seeks to reduce the ecological footprint of the neighbourhood. With this comes a social responsibility implemented in the form of the Upwards and Onwards (Herfra og videre) programme, which is a social support service provided in collaboration with Copenhagen municipality's social services, employment services and health system, Christiania's own Health House (Sundhedshus) and other parties that are relevant in solving often complex social problems (see also Helen Jarvis' chapter in this book). Furthermore, 'culture' is seen as the cohesive force in Christiania, where different ages, genders, ethnic and socio-economic groups are working and living side by side. The ideal is to develop a 'feeling of belonging' for all groups, through for example jointly developed rituals and cultures around Christmas, funerals, baptising, meetings, democracy and much more.[56] Far from being perfect, the experiments to improve the environments in the Freetown have, over the years, served as inspiration for its surroundings.

The neoliberal urban strategies behind the production of 'New Copenhagen' are applied to Christiania through the discourse of 'normalisation', that is, the 'legitimisation' of its building stock and the 'privatisation' of its common lands.[57] Christiania's struggles for the right to the city are multi-scalar and multi-facetted. The recent main strategy, a court case against the Danish state, in which Christiania claimed squatter's rights, was lost in the High Court in the spring of 2011. There is, nevertheless, a long tradition of alternative local politics and art practices. Best known are the actions created by the theatre group the Sun Chariot (Solvognen) from 1969 to 1982, and from 2006 (when the group resurrected as the theatre group Thrundholm Bog). Some famous events include the invasion of the Native Americans at *Rebildfesten* (the celebration of Danish-US relations) in July 1976 and the Guantanamo happening in July 2006.[58] As a possible counter strategy to the government's gentrification strategy, the idea is to transform Christiania into an independent non-profit rental housing association and a foundation for small businesses. The future will show if a marriage of the special forms of anarchism we find in Christiania and the reformed socialist practice of Danish non-profit housing organisations is a viable solution for Christiania. Co-option and misrepresentation constitute key challenges in this context. Internal turf wars, reflecting the wide spectrum of income, age, gender and ethnic diversity that is a main ingredient of Christiania, and other communities who are fighting for their right to the city, could potentially divide and destroy the community.[59] On the other hand, the roots of Christiania's struggles can be compared to tenant struggles against urban renewal and gentrification, the environmental justice movements and struggles against suppression of rights to the commons. Seen through the lens of David Harvey's concept of accumulation by dispossession, these struggles resonate very well with many of the struggles that form the agenda of participants in alternative globalisation movements.[60]

It would be nice if one could identify a 'Christiania doctrine'—a magical formula that could be used in the strife for a more democratic and just city. However, it is impossible to present a comprehensive account of Christiania's forty years of insights into activism, alternative living and fighting for their right to the city. I have instead shared *one* moment in Christiania's history that I experienced when I lived in the community as a Christiania Researcher in Residence (CRIR) in May 2007. Since 2004, the locally supported and driven CRIR programme has offered residency for artists and academic researchers who are interested in generating important knowledge about Christiania (www.crir.net). The programme has sponsored more than forty projects on a variety of themes (see the introductory chapter in this book). Visiting scholars and artists share their work and experiences through different modes of representation, including books, articles, photo, film, performance, and seminars; contributions that highlight Christiania's uniqueness and some of the general obstacles that the community is facing. Hopefully, the collective efforts of these people can contribute to a better understanding of this unique alternative urban community.

Conclusions: Christiania and the Right to the City

The Freetown Christiania has from the outset been organised around collective ideals. The social climate in Copenhagen in the fall of 1971 was full of criticism for the 'established' society's mode of organisation and behaviour, and Christiania was founded in the pursuit of a self-governed society where people can unfold freely while remaining responsible to the community'.[61] In contemporary neoliberal times, however, the concept of freedom is connected to free market logic; private property rights and growth are superior to all other versions of the 'right' concept imaginable. The protection of 'human rights' is today's political and ethical response to the question of how we achieve a better world. Often these rights, however, are linked to individual and property-based rights. They do not challenge the hegemonic liberal and neoliberal market logic, and related legal and government structures. Market utopianism, furthermore, persists despite the recent economic crises. In *A Brief History of Neoliberalism*, David Harvey suggests that in the event of a conflict between the health and well-being of financial institutions and people, financial institutions will win every time.[62] He also proposes that under neoliberalism government resources are primarily used to create a good 'business climate'. Throughout the world, shrinking governmental resources are increasingly redirected towards the support of business' needs at the expense of social budgets — often imposed through a 'shock doctrine'.[63] Neil Smith recently stated that neoliberalism is dead, dominant and defeatable, but reminds us that a dead rattlesnake 'can still strike, and neoliberalism, however dead, remains dominant'.[64] But is it defeateable? And can we learn from alternative urban communities like Christiania?

Historically, there are examples of alternative concepts of freedom and human rights based on collective ideals. The Scandinavian labour movement or the 1960s civil rights movement in North America have had global influence on the development of a rights discourse and practice, based on collective rather than individual ideals: freedom was thus sought through collective principles and practices. The discussion of 'the right to the city' inscribes itself in this tradition. Christiania is an excellent example of a struggle by marginalised social groups to claim the right to the city.

In this chapter I have shed a critical light on two very different visions of the right to the city. First of all, private property has been the dominant right to the city throughout the history of capitalism and it has been at the core of the 'neoliberal revolution'. Cities throughout the globe have become important spaces for neoliberalism and an entrepreneurial urban politics that accommodates investors, developers and the so-called creative class.[65] Those in charge of city governance use Margaret Thatcher's TINA acronym (There Is No Alternative) to support neoliberal policies and make them the norm in a post-political city.[66] And this is also the case in 'cOPENhagen' where Christiania is fighting *against* 'normalisation' and *for* a very different right to the city, that is, a collective right to land and housing. Through the example of the re-building of the Cigar Box, I have presented *one* moment in a long history of struggles. I suggest that collective activism, dedication, improvisation, art, humour and practicing a politics of scale are important elements in Christiania's forty-year struggle for the right to the city — and may still be important elements in a future 'system change'.[67] The Danish government's plan to 'normalise' Christiania, however, threatens the existence of the community. One of the central objectives is to abandon the principle of joined ownership of the land in favour of private property rights and free market forces. A neoliberal strategy designed to harvest a profit and make way for a (generalised) gentrification of the area. I suggest that the politics of 'normalisation' has to be understood as part of a larger scalar reconfiguration of the geographical and social embodiment of political and economic powers — where ordinary people are being dispossessed of their collective right to the city.

Notes

INTRODUCTION

1 See Social Democrat Kjeld Olesen's opening statement in the debate (Folketingstidene 1974:6236–7).
2 Arbejds- og Socialministeriet (1973).
3 A slightly different experience was however encountered by Jacques Blum in the 1970s, see further below.
4 (www.crir.net). Here is a selection of CRIR project themes and titles as recounted by Anders Lund Hansen, member of CRIR: self-government and self-policing; a comic strip, 'What is the Mystery', published in *Ugespejlet* (the *Weekly Mirror*, the local newspaper); the repair of a mural painting; social perspectives on new housing areas; video art; a search for *The Perfect Location*; a documentary film entitled *Our heart is in your hands*; a dance performance named *Half Machine*; gaps in the political economy of Christiania's land — Christiania as a space of hope; the practice of 'ownership' in Christiania; the relations Christianites have to the pictures often shown of Christiania in the media; gentrification; the dogs of Christiania; space wars; lessons from Berlin; how to rebel in a society that is already in a state of rebellion?; democracy; social justice; surveillance of government buildings, symbolically redressing the balance; *You Film Us, We Film You*; a quest for Utopia; Christiania's symbolism; paths through utopias; paradise; a location-sensitive model for a future history museum on Christiania; GNH — Gross National Happiness; sleeping in spandrels; high on life; movie on the residents' relation to the rest of Copenhagen; 'Bevar Christiania'; conceptualising the 'ecosocial'; creative Copenhagen; community experiments in collaborative homes and lifestyles; public space.
5 For a full bibliography of books, articles and reports on Christiania (both academic and non-academic), see Christiania's homepage (www.christiania.org).
6 C.f. Smith (1996) and Lees (2002).
7 Løvetand Iversen (1972:5). All quotes in the introduction translated by the editors.

[8] The competition, named 'Christianshavn og det fremtidige Christiania', had been commissioned in April 1974 and two of the proposed plans came in at first spot.

[9] Accordingly, Rasmussen gave his royalty to *Støt Christiania*.

[10] Tingbjerg had been planned and built by him according to modernist principles of space and freedom, but after some time Rasmussen changed his opinion. He then came to view Tingbjerg as an antithesis of good living: its inhabitants were 'governed by time plans, adjusted to fit institutions, whose purpose was to control them from the cradle to the grave', Rasmussen (1976: 34).

[11] Rasmussen (1976:87) and Rasmussen (1976:83).

[12] Rasmussen's lecture was first printed in *Politiken* (11/2 and 12/2 1977).

[13] Rasmussen (1977:4).

[14] Blum (1977:9).

[15] Ibid.:9.

[16] Blum and Sjörslev (1977:151–2).

[17] Balvig (1979:103).

[18] These three groups are according to Madsen further differentiated. For example, Madsen argues that there was a group consisting of young workers that unconsciously were part of the social dissociation process, as they started to build autonomous working places in Christiania. Yet another group was according to Madsen hit by social deroute. They had serious social and drug-related problems and were often part of the squatter groups since they needed places to live.

[19] From the beginning state-led camps on different Danish islands, for families and young people, later on organised autonomously by grass-root movements.

[20] Juhler et. al. (1982:258).

[21] Ibid.:262.

[22] Conroy (1996:18).

[23] Ibid.

[24] Karpantschof and Mikkelsen (2002:122).

[25] Dirckink-Holmfeld and Keiding (2004).

[26] Ahnfeldt-Mollerup (2004:56).

[27] Ibid.:61.

[28] In 2003, 60 % of the 900 inhabitants had elementary school as their highest degree (Christianiaudvalget 2004).

[29] Kvorning (2002:132).

[30] Ibid.:132.

[31] Maria Hellström Reimer has also published two articles, in which she further develops key themes in her dissertation; Hellström Reimer (2009); Hellström Reimer (2011).

[32] Hellström (2006:5).

[33] Ibid.:308.

[34] Doron (2006:212).

[35] Miles (2008:1). The other examples are: Economy, Pennsylvania, Arcosanti, Arizona, Cambridge Cohousing, Massachusetts and ZEGG, Belzig.

[36] Nielsen, Dehs and Skov (2005:6).

[37] Bøggild (2005:68).

[38] The title of the project is 'Veje til bevaringsstrategier for et anderledes byrum' (Ways to preservation strategies for a different urban space), which was also the title of the first book from the project (Riesto and Tietjen 2003).

[39] Tietjen, Riesto and Skov (2007:26).

[40] Arnfred (2007:253).

[41] Ibid.:253.

[42] Karpantschof and Lindblom (2009); Karpantschof and Mikkelsen (2009) and Karpantschof (2009).

[43] The article has also been published in the Danish political science journal *Politica* (Midtgaard 2007b).

[44] Midtgaard (2007a:312).

[45] Ibid.:312.

[46] Haga was a space for alternative culture between 1970 and 1990, but is today largely gentrified. In the project we are interested in finding out about the similarities and differences between Christiania and Haga as spaces for alternative culture; as well as regarding the way they have interacted with urban restructuring processes in the two cities — and with each other. In the 1970s, there were interaction and co-operation between groups in Christiania and Haga, and an informal association called 'Fristeder i forening' (Freetowns in union) was formed. On Haga, see Thörn (2010).

1 This chapter is written in continuation of my previous studies of Christiania and other Danish squatter communities, which again involve other academic works, which are referred to in these studies (Karpantschof 2009a, 2009b; Karpantschof and Mikkelsen 2002, 2008, 2009; Mikkelsen and Karpantschof 2001). One work, though, must be highlighted here: Jæger, Olsen and Rieper (1993), as it presents a very thorough analysis of the relations between Christiania and the state 1971–1993. Further the chapter builds on various official files, Christiania's own story-telling and statements, opinion polls, a newspaper database made for the occasion and more, cf. notes and list of references. I thank the former Christianite Preben Smed and Christianite Ole Lykke for reading and commenting on the chapter.

2 Christiania (1971). Translation by Conroy (1995).

3 Quoted from Jæger, Olsen and Rieper (1993:43).

4 In December 1975 Christiania had responded to the threat of eviction with a summons against the state for breach of agreement with the argument that by recognising Christiania as a social experiment in the first place the state had already 'given the green light for an experiment with an alternative way of life.' The case ended in the Supreme Court 2 February 1978 with the decision that the Christianites had no strictly legal right to use state territory.

5 The margin of uncertainty in the polls is illustrated by the fact that when the Gallup institute, used in Figure 2, in January 1978 measured a small majority of 40–35 per cent *against* Christiania, another institute, the AIM, in that very same month came up with a small majority of 41–39 per cent *in favour* of Christiania, cf. Jæger, Olsen and Rieper (1993:50).

6 Gallup 1976, cf. Figure 2.

7 Gallup 1975, 1976, cf. Figure 2.

8 Balvig (1979), quoted from Jæger, Olsen and Rieper (1993:50).

9 "Fed eller færdig", *Information* 29/9 2001.

10 BZ: a phonetic abridgement of the Danish word for squatting

11 Folketinget (7/6 1989); Forsvarsministeriet (1991).

12 Jæger, Olsen and Rieper (1993:165).

13 *Berlingske Tidende* editorial 27/9 1991.

14 *BT* editorial 20/4 1991.

15 Gallup 1996, cf. Figure 2.

16 Christiania (2004).

[17] Christiania 13/11 1971.

[18] *Politiken* editorial 28/9 1996.

[19] *Berlingske Tidende* editorial 26/9 1996.

[20] *Jyllandsposten* editorial 28/9 2001.

[21] Pia's Ugebrev, www.danskFolkeparti.dk/Ryd_Christiania_.asp

[22] Like many other countries Denmark experienced a *cycle of protest* from around 1968 until a general demobilisation in the late 1980s followed by a period with comparable few protests in the 1990s. Since 2002, though, it seems that the Danes have returned to the streets with new and increasing numbers of demonstrations. See also figure 1 in Karpantschof and Mikkelsen (2008).

[23] Forsvars- og justitsministeriet (2003); Forsvarsministeriet (2004); Folketinget (2004).

[24] Forsvars- og justitsministeriet (2003).

[25] *Jyllandsposten* editorial 2/2 2004.

[26] Christiania (2004).

[27] *Berlingske Tidende* editorials 4/8 and 8/5 2003.

[28] *Jyllandsposten* editorials 2/8 2003 and 2/2 2004.

[29] *Information* editorial 10/1 2007 and *Ekstrabladet*, editorial 14/3 2004.

[30] *BT* editorials 15/4 2003 and 6/1 2004.

[31] Forsvarsministeriet 31/3 2004.

[32] Gallup 1996, 2003, cf. Figure 2.

[33] Gallup 1996, 2003 (cf. Figure 2) and an opinion poll by Analyseinstituttet Rambøll published in 'Voldene skal blive', *Jyllandsposten* 7.11.2006.

[34] *Ekstrabladet* editorial 15/1 2004.

[35] Opinion poll by ACNielsen AIM published in Ugebrevet Mandag Morgen 34, 6/10 2003.

[36] 'Film: Betjente som bøller', *Berlingske Tidende* 3/3 2008.

[37] Slots- og Ejendomsstyrelsen (Sept 2006).

[38] Christiania (2006).

[39] Slots- og Ejendomsstyrelsen (Dec 2006).

[40] Christiania (2007); Finansministeriet (2007).

[41] Christiania (2007); Finansministeriet primo april (2007).

[42] *Politiken* editorial 10/1 2007.

[43] A sympathy proved by a series of opinion polls on the Youth House issue 2006–08 that — somewhat surprisingly, considered the many violent protests — virtually all turned out in favour of the youngsters (Karpantschof 2009a).

[44] 'Christiania advarer regeringen mod konfrontation', *Nyhedsavisen* 27/6 2008.

[45] Editorial in *Jyllandsposten Vest* 4/4 2007.

[46] Slots- og Ejendomsstyrelsen (2009).

[47] Overall, the most peaceful period in 1971–88 was also the period with, in general, the most Christiania-hostile popular attitudes and the most insecure relationship with the state compared to the following period 1989–2011, which had significantly heavier riots (that escalated in earnest and became a returning phenomenon from 1989) but nonetheless clearly more popular support and better agreement with the state. So the riots themselves didn't seem to damage Christiania decisively and on the contrary may in fact have obliged the public and the politicians to take a stand in a way that often turned out advantageous to Christiania — which a close study of the relations between spectacular clashes, public opinion and political acts during the Youth House struggle suggests could very well be the case, cf. also note 43.

GOVERNING FREEDOM

[1] Quoted from Hellström (2006:32), who quotes from Traimond (1994:40). Translation by Hellström.

[2] Ludvigsen (2003).

[3] Arbejds- og Socialministeriet (1973:2). All translations from Danish are made by the author.

[4] Ibid.:3.

[5] Fox (2010:4).

[6] The title of the book (Rasmussen 1993) is *From social state to minimal state (Fra socialstat til minimalstat).*

[7] Folketinget (2003:1–2).

[8] I would like to thank Henrik Gutzon Larsen and Cathrin Wasshede for valuable comments on the draft version of this chapter.

[9] For a complete list of all of the 22 debates on Christiania in the Danish parliament between 1974 and 2004, see the reference section in this book.

[10] Foucault (2007: 240). In the 2003 Christiania debate, the Conservative Party actually cites a sentence from the law of Jutland (Jyske Lov), which is also quoted above the entrance to the Danish parliament: 'The land shall be built by the law' (Folketinget 2003:27).

[11] Foucault (2004:240).

[12] Ibid. The two quotes in this paragraph are from p. 240.
[13] Foucault (2007:18)
[14] Foucault (2008:64).
[15] Folketinget (2003:1).
[16] Gramsci (1971:263).
[17] Karpantschof and Mikkelsen (2008).
[18] Thörn (2006); Rothstein (1992); Jæger, Olsen and Rieper (1993).
[19] Arbejds- og Socialministeriet (1973:1–2).
[20] Wacquant (1999); Franzén (2005); Keith and Pile (1993); Smith and Katz (1993); Thörn (1997).
[21] 'A rats' nest' (Folketinget 1981/2:3716); 'a lawless district' (Folketinget 1981/2:3744), both the Progress Party in a 1982 debate. 'A place where people get inspiration', the Social Democrats in the 1974 debate (Folketinget 1973/4:6235); 'an experiment', the Socialist Party in the 2003 debate (Folketinget 2003:1).
[22] In his book *Urban Utopias*, Malcolm Miles (2008) maps alternative settlements around the world (including Christiania), but none of them can compare to Christiania in the sense I am discussing here.
[23] Hellström (2006:309).
[24] Folketinget (1973/74:6259).
[25] Ibid.:6241 and 6366–7.
[26] Ibid.:6257 and 6374.
[27] Ibid.:6266.
[28] Ibid.:6357.
[29] Ibid.:6257.
[30] Ibid.:6356.
[31] Ibid.:6262–3.
[32] Ibid.:6368.
[33] Ibid.:6273. In an open letter to Inge Krogh, Christianite Peter Thiel gave his version of what happened, stating that he was lying in his bed with his girlfriend and her daughter, reading a fairy tale, when the door suddenly opened and 'a little old lady stood on the doorstep'. According to Thiel, they asked Krogh to sit down on the bedside. And it was only in the evening of the day of the parliamentary debate, that he realised that 'it was you Inge Krogh, who sat on the bedside listening to fairy tales'. Quoted from Rasmussen (1976:95).
[34] Folketinget (1973/4: 6254).

[35] Ibid.:6351.

[36] Ibid.:6364.

[37] Most frequently mentioned are Professor of Architecture Stein Eiler Rasmussen, criminologist Burt Kuchinsky, and Tine Bryld, advisor for the Social Board.

[38] Ibid.:6367.

[39] Ibid.:6277.

[40] Ibid.:6359.

[41] Ibid.:6267.

[42] Ibid.:6254.

[43] Ibid.:6235.

[44] Elklit and Pedersen (2003).

[45] According to Elklit and Pederson (2003), the 2001 election manifested a deepening of the same structural tendencies that were expressed in the 1973 election.

[46] Borre (2003).

[47] The term 'new politics' is in political science associated with Roland Inglehart (1971). I am using it in a broader sense, referring not just to changing values and voting patterns, but also to the new social movements (Thörn 2006). For a discussion on these changes in a Danish context see the special issue '30 år efter Jordskredsvalget' (30 years after the Earthquake Election) of the Danish journal *Politica* (no. 4, 2003).

[48] The Socialist Party got more votes than in any election since First World War, while the Conservatives had their best election in 25 years, Elklit and Pedersen (2003).

[49] Borre (2003:439) and (2003:433).

[50] In the 1974 debate, the Danish Communist Party argued that those who claimed that Christiania's alternative lifestyles were part of the class struggle were wrong, because in order to struggle you need 'organisation, knowledge and discipline', and that 'those who fear Christiania on these grounds, can probably relax', Folketinget (1973/4:6277). The Communist Party was however one of the founders (together with the Socialist Worker's Party/Sosialistisk Arbejderparti, and the Left Socialists) of Enhedslisten in 1989.

[51] Folketinget (1987/88:2313).

[52] Thörn (1997); Hellström (2006).

[53] Folketinget (2003: 6361)

[54] Folketinget (1973/4/5:3241).

[55] Ibid.:3188 and 3141.
[56] Borre (2003:439).
[57] Borre (2003).
[58] Ibid.
[59] Folketinget (1991/92:352).
[60] Borre (2003).
[61] Fogh Rasmussen (2002).
[62] Folketinget (2002:23).
[63] Both these demands were made by Ulrik Kragh; on collective use of property, Folketinget (2004a:1); on consensus democracy, Folketinget (2004b:4).
[64] Folketinget (2003:31).
[65] Ibid.:1.
[66] Ibid.:26.
[67] In the 1991 debate, after Brusgaard of the Progress Party argued that he had felt threatened when visiting Christiania (Folketinget 1991/92:1372), a discussion broke out regarding if, and to what extent, the chairmen of the parties in parliament had actually been to Christiania, who had been there most frequently, and whether they had felt secure or not.
[68] Folketinget (2003:3).
[69] Ibid.:3–4.
[70] Ibid.:20.
[71] Ibid.:11.
[72] Ibid.:3–4.
[73] Ibid.:31.
[74] Ibid.:13.
[75] Gutzon Larsen and Lund Hansen (2008:2433). See also Lund Hansen, Andersen and Clark (2001).
[76] Following a small riot in Prinsessegade on 6 December (during the Climate Meeting), the police chained approximately 100 people to each other (and subsequently detained them) in a long row on Pusher Street in the middle of the night, while a helicopter lit up the street. Interview with anonymous Christianites, 7 December 2009.
[77] Regarding zero tolerance in Christiania see Bryld (1986) and Karpantschof and Mikkelsen (2009).
[78] Folketinget (2002:7). That such an order has been made is also verified in a report by Hanne Bech Hansen, General Commissioner of the Copenhagen Police, Østre Landsret (2008).

[79] Quoted from Ludvigsen (2003:75). Translation to English by Conroy (1995). On 15 May 2003, the advertising agency Propaganda McCann published an ad in the financial paper *Børsen* in support of Christiania, stating: 'Liberalism's fundamental idea actually prospers better in Christiania than in any other place', ibid. (2003:25).

[80] Rasmussen (1993:143).

[81] In the 2004 Christiania Committee's official Action Plan, the three different scenarios presented all involve some kind of privatisation of the property.

HAPPY EVER AFTER?

[1] Rasmussen (1976:35), author's translation. All translations from Danish to English in this chapter are made by the author.

[2] Christianite Allan An Archos at a seminar in Christiania, 22 January 2011.

[3] Inaba (2009:2–3).

[4] Provoost (2006:http://www.eurozine.com/articles/2006-06-28-provoost-en.html).

[5] Wagenaar (2004:9).

[6] Nielsen (2008:56).

[7] Socialdemokratisk Forbund (1945).

[8] Nielsen (2008:58–59).

[9] Steen Eiler Rasmussen in Egnsplankontoret (1947/1993:0).

[10] Bæk Pedersen (2005) and Diken and Albertsen (2004).

[11] Besides participating in everything related to Danish urban planning, and mentoring architects such as Jørn Utzon, Eiler Rasmussen joined international debates as an honorary corresponding member of the Royal Institute of British Architects (1947), visiting professor at MIT (1953) and Yale (1954), honorary member of universities and architectural institutes in Europe and USA, and author of books on English, Dutch, etc. architecture. Simultaneously, the autodidact general's son, high school and architecture school dropout, was a polymath commentating on culture and everyday life, happy to receive the newspaper *Politiken*'s Peanut of the Year, while refusing to become Knight of Dannebrog, Lind (2008).

[12] Steen Eiler Rasmussen's Office (1963:21).

[13] Ibid.:4.

[14] Ibid.:5.

[15] Ibid.

[16] Ibid.

[17] Rasmussen (1976:8).

[18] Ibid.:51–53.

[19] Ibid.

[20] Like most New Town architects Eiler Rasmussen never lived in Tingbjerg. He built his own house in the prosperous Rungsted in Whiskybæltet north of Copenhagen.

[21] Rasmussen (1976:10).

[22] Ibid.:13.

[23] Ibid.:34.

[24] Ibid.:17.

[25] These strategies were first presented by the Lettrists in *Potlach* magazine, 1954–56, Sadler (1998).

[26] Jorn (1947:61–68).

[27] Ibid.:62.

[28] Nielsen (2008:24).

[29] Jorn (1947:63).

[30] Nielsen (2008:26).

[31] Lefebvre (1991:26).

[32] de Waal (20 October 2010: http://www.information.dk/248301)

[33] Scott (1998:111).

[34] Sadler (1998:6).

[35] With this attitude Jorn co-authored *Fin de Copenhague* with situationist anchorman Guy Debord (1957). This 'psychogeographical' publication addressed the industrialised welfare society's confused consumers: 'What do you want? Better and cheaper food? Lots of new clothes? A dream home with all the latest comforts and labour-saving devices? A new car [...] a motor launch [...] a light aircraft of your own? Whatever you want, it's coming your way — plus greater leisure for enjoying it all. With electronics, automation and nuclear energy, we are entering the new Industrial Revolution which will supply our every need, easily [...] quickly [...] cheaply [...] abundantly.' Jorn and Debord (2001).

[36] Sadler (1998:7).

[37] Rasmussen (1956/57:197).

[38] Nielsen (2008:58).

[39] Steen Eiler Rasmussen's Office (1963:5).

[40] Wallenstein and Mattsson (2010:8).

[41] Söderqvist (2008:15).

[42] Tingbjerg's website (2011: http://www.tingbjerg.com/om-tingbjerg/tingbjerg-paa-film.aspx).

[43] David Pinder in Furness (2007: http://bad.eserver.org/issues/2007/78/pinder.html).

[44] As a counter-site or inverted mirror, challenging, representing and subverting all other sites in Copenhagen/Denmark, Christiania seems close to what Michel Foucault designates as a heterotopia — a space of distribution where more principles of organisation and mutual untranslatable spaces coexist contrary to the utopia guided by 'one principle of organisation', Foucault (2002).

[45] Bøggild and Bruun Yde (2010).

[46] Danish Radio (2 August 2010: http://www.dr.dk/P1/Reportagen/Udsendelser/2010/07/07125744.htm).

[47] Christiania (1971: http://www.christiania.org/modules.php?name=Side&navn=Maalsaetning). Translation to English by Adam Conroy.

[48] Fogh Rasmussen (1993).

[49] Fogh Rasmussen (2002: http://da.wikisource.org/wiki/Statsministerens_nyt%C3%A5rstale_2002).

[50] The diplomatic controversy between Denmark and Muslim countries caused by the newspaper *Jyllandsposten* printing a series of caricatures of the prophet Mohammed in 2005.

[51] See the report *Fremtidige organisations- og ejerformer på Christianiaområdet.* The Palaces and Properties Agency (2005:www.ses.dk/da/Christiania/~/.../fremtidige_organisations_og_ejerfor.ashx).

[52] Steen Hvass on The Heritage Agency of Denmark's website (12 October 2007: http://www.kulturarv.dk/presse-nyt/nyhed/artikel/fredning-af-11-bygninger-paa-christiania/)

[53] *Politiken* (10 November 2010: http://politiken.dk/indland/ECE1105353/de-fleste-af-christianias-ulovlige-byggerier-er-lovlige/).

[54] Trier Mogensen (21 February, 2011: http://politiken.dk/debat/signatur/ECE1201242/hippierne-hopper-ind-fra-hoejre/).

[55] Ibid.

[56] Ibid.

[57] Jens Arnfred in Løvenbalk Hansen (25 July 2007: http://www.information.dk/127485).

[58] Albæk (11 August 2010:http://politiken.dk/politik/1033992/loekke-tager-hul-paa-ghettoturn/).

[59] Ritzau (16 December 2010:http://www.information.dk/telegram/254068).

[60] Stig T. Kaspersen in Ritzau (19 November 2010: http://politiken.dk/indland/ECE1113534/andre-ghettoer-siger-nej-til-nedrivning/).

[61] Ritzau (22 February 2010: http://www.information.dk/telegram/225164).

[62] Strårup (24 June 2009: http://www.berlingske.dk/koebenhavn/tingbjerg-bliver-familievenlig).

[63] Gravlund in ibid.

[64] KAB's director remarks: 'Don't call the buildings black spots and ghettos. They are vulnerable housing areas with giant challenges.' Ritzau (22 February 2010: http://www.information.dk/telegram/225164).

[65] I am indirectly referring to architectural historian Wouter Vanstiphout's critical interpretation of the Amsterdam New Town Bijlmermeer's total transformation, a model for 'anti-ghettoisation' efforts like Gellerup's, Vanstiphout (2008).

[66] Bøggild and Bruun Yde (2010).

[67] About Casablanca see Avermaete et. al. (2010). For Caracas see Brillembourg et. al. (2005).

[68] Bøggild et. al. (2010:27).

[69] Popper (1988).

THE HANSEN FAMILY

[1] Translations from Danish to English of titles and soundtrack by the author of this article.

[2] See Edwards (1979:241) and Hellström (2006:54).

[3] The 'intellectual' is in this case the architect Per Løvetand Iversen, during the first years of Christiania's existence one of the key activists and the author of many important articles and manifestos.

[4] The threats against the Freetown generated a significant amount of cultural activity in 1975–76; an LP-record was released with recordings by some of the most popular bands in Denmark; big support concerts were organized; the successful theatre performance *Elverhøj* attracted great crowds, and the writings in support of Christiania by architect Steen Eiler Rasmussen received a lot of attention.

5 See Balvig (1979).

6 The slogan 'I kan ikke slå os ihjel, vi er en del av jer selv', also the title of a song on the best-selling LP record *Christiania*, released in 1975, has been one of the most frequently used catchphrases in the debate.

7 See Krarup (1976); Jæger, Olsen and Rieper (1993); Hellström (2006).

8 Quoted in Krarup (1976:6)

9 Krarup (1976:6); Hellström (2006:52).

10 The case was brought all the way to the Supreme Court, which in february 1978 ruled against Christiania, however, with the extraordinary comment that this judgment was strictly juridical, and that a final decision would have to take political, social and human aspects into consideration, Falkentorp, Hansen, Juhler, Kløvedal and Løvetand (1982); Hellström (2006:54).

11 The most significant of these performances in relation to Martinsen's project was without doubt the remake by the performance group Solvognen (the Sun Chariot) in the autumn 1975 of the national theatre piece *Elverhøj* (*the Elves' Mountain*) by Johan Ludvig Heiberg, which had been written for the National Theatre in 1828. *Elverhøj* had a strong popular appeal, and through the play, Christiania managed to become Elverhøj, a mythical Danish landscape between utopianism, expressive popular culture and experimental avant-garde (Hellström (2006).

12 Ward (2008).

13 Foucault (1977:189); see also Gutting (2010).

14 Holmes and Jermyn (2008:235).

15 Kracauer (1960:ix), evidently commenting on the first documentary sequences by the Brothers Lumière.

16 The major reference is of course Henri Lefebvre and his *Critique de la vie quotidienne*, the first volume of which appears in 1947.

17 See Lefebvre (1947). This aspect of the moving, mass-mediated image as a 'shifter' is obviously highly present already before the war, sociologically as well as cinematographically articulated by Benjamin, Vertov and Ruttman, just to mention a few.

18 Nichols (1991:127).

19 Ibid.:76–103.

20 Ibid.

21 Ibid.

22 Ward (2008:192).

23 Ibid.:193.

[24] One of the most important precursors is in this sense without doubt Jean Rouch's and Edgar Morin's *Chronique d'un été* (France, 1961), which was an attempt to turn the 'ethnographic gaze' towards the ordinary French people, and which set the standards for cinéma vérité. See Jean Rouch (1962/2003).

[25] Holmes and Jermyn (2008). Another important precursor was the American PBS series *An American Family*, broadcast in 1973.

[26] Nichols (2001:193).

ALTERNATIVE VISIONS OF HOME AND FAMILY LIFE

[1] GA, female resident of CA for 28 years, reflecting on life as a single parent in the 1990s.

[2] CT, resident of CA for 30 years, reflecting on life as a single parent in the 1990s.

[3] See for instance Jørgensen (1982).

[4] Jarvis et al. (2001).

[5] Gullestad (1984); Booth and Gilroy (1999); Jarvis (2005).

[6] Gilman (2002); Parker et al. (1994).

[7] OECD (2008); see also Jarvis (2006). Single-person households make up 39 % of Denmark but this figure rises to 65 % for the municipality of Copenhagen. For Denmark as a whole 16 % of households with children are single-parent households (compared with 13 % for EU25 and 24 % in the UK) (Eurostat, http://epp.eurostat.ec.europa.eu/ data retrieved 29.10.2010).

[8] Griffin (2010).

[9] VisitDenmark.Com (2009).

[10] Vestergaard (2006). The research project on which this paper is based received economic support from REALDANIA.

[11] Miller (1999).

[12] Bekin et al. (2005); Jones (2007); Shaw and Newholm (2002).

[13] There is a large and influential literature engaging with the pros and cons of what is widely referred to as the 'new urbanism'. The way that village-like housing schemes are realised in practice is heavily determined by planning regime (Denmark differs from the US for instance) and local housing market (notably the role of tenure, gentrification and the relative power of grassroots social movements). The new urbanism is heavily criticised in academic

debate as a cosmetic and regressive solution to a lack of social and environmental sustainability. Interestingly, the debate in Denmark is re-engaging with classic literature on urban public space; Gehl (2010). See also Lofland (1973). A seminal text on the subject of spatial arrangement for social interaction is Alexander et al. (1977).

14 Forster (1998). It is a matter of opinion whether Christiania can be defined as an intentional community or as an autonomous community but the fact remains that CA is listed on the public on-line directory Fellowship for Intentional Communities, www.ic.org.

15 www.ses.dk; Garbarczyk (2008).

16 The author wishes to acknowledge the Christiania Research in Residence (CRIR) initiative for providing both accommodation and assistance with setting up the research. Particular thanks are due to Emmerik Warburg, Lise Autogena and Anders Lund Hansen. The opinions expressed in this chapter are those of the author and not attributed to CRIR or any other individual interviewed.

17 The homes visited spanned a number of dwelling types and locations; including a large room on a shared floor in Fredens Ark; studio apartments fashioned out of the distinctive acute angle buildings on the rampart promontory; self-built chalets, adapted site-huts and original stone buildings variously situated along the ramparts, in the wooded areas and on the edge of 'Christiania City'. Observations were made by attending public festivals, such as Christiania's 'alternative' Grundlovsdag (Constitution Day), as well as a more intimate community fund-raising event at the Operaen. Much was gained from everyday routines: cycling with my young daughter many, many times the length and breadth of the site; shopping for groceries at the Indkøbscentralen (Shopping Central) and Grøntsagen (the Vegetable); frequenting the community cafés and eating-places; and continually making notes in a research diary. Data collection and analysis derives from the highest standards of ethical conduct for open ethnographic practice. Interviews and photographs were always taken with informed consent. A two-letter pseudonym is used to protect the individual identity of individual subjects. Interviews were transcribed for thematic coding and narrative analysis.

18 Gibson-Graham (1996); Bakker and Silvey (2008).

19 Interview with ER, resident since 1974, lives with partner and child on the edge of Christiania City.

20 Interview with EN, resident and entrepreneur of CA for 28 years; Christi-

anites effectively pay for social public goods normally provided by the municipality, Bates (2009).

21 Rakodi (1999); Beall (2002).

22 Information on Christiania's self-governance is extracted from the *Christiania Guide.*

23 The rural dwelling HA and friends were allowed to move into was made vacant because of a double eviction; the man who lived in the house sold it on to another man and when this came to light both were thrown out of the area — because it is a strict rule that no-one owns or seeks to gain financially from their house. HA and friends secured the house in competition with many others who also wished to have it by hanging around for several years 'building a good reputation'.

24 Interview with EN, male resident living with partner and adult children, resident since 1982.

25 Meltzer (2005).

26 Communal dining was made fashionable in London in the 1930s in the Pritchards' Isobar restaurant which served residents and guests of the Isokon building on Lawn Road, London. The Isokon building was a Le Corbusier inspired experiment in modern living: there was a communal kitchen and restaurant and a range of domestic services made it possible to strip down individual apartments to minimal living space. See alsoVestbro (1992; 1997).

27 Social movements reflecting a youthful zeitgeist typically call for more free space by variously 'reclaiming' public space for anti-capital, anti-consumer expressions (including the free distribution of unwanted goods and holding free public events) and through the temporary or more permanent installation of do-it-yourself architecture, autonomous events and 'happenings'. See for instance Gehl (2010) and Anders Lund Hansen's chapter in this anthology.

28 Sørensen (1935).

29 Midtgaard (2007).

30 Interview with female MK, resident since 1974, living with partner (adult offspring also in CA).

31 Turner (1974).

32 Ibid.

33 Hellström (2006).

34 HA resident since 2003, living in a rural shared house with partner, baby and house-mates.

35 Reinder and van der Land (2008).

[36] Mitchell (2003).

[37] Interview with female HA, resident living with her partner and baby in a shared house.

[38] Interview with TT, female resident since 1978, living alone across Dyssen, with an ex-partner and adult offspring living independently elsewhere in CA.

[39] Amouroux (2006).

[40] Interview with CT, resident of CA for 30 years.

[41] Endre et al. (2010).

[42] Jacob Ludvigsen, disaffected co-founder of Christiania, no longer believes that governance by direct common consensus is democratic because of the breakdown of rules of fair discourse and agreement; quoted in Øberg (2007).

[43] Bellah et al. (1985).

[44] Jarvis (2007).

BØSSEHUSET

[1] Bøssehuset means The Gay Male House. Bøsse is a Danish word for 'gay man', a word that from the beginning referred to a kind of breech-loaded rifle, and was used as an insulting term for homosexual men. I have conducted four interviews with gay people in Christiania: Gay man I in Bøssehuset, 12-08-2010. Not living in CA. Gay man II in Bøssehuset, 12-08-2010. Has been living in CA. Lesbian, 10-01-2011 to 13-01-2011. Living in CA. Gay man III, 21-01-2011. Living in CA. In this text I have chosen not to use personal names as synonyms for the interviewees (which has as an effect that I do not refer to an individual interviewee when quoting). The reason for this is that it would be too easy to disclose the identity of the activists if you were able to follow them through the quotations; and because it is not important to follow one person through the text. They all speak as gay activists in Bøssehuset — or as a lesbian in Christiania — and their personal life stories are not in focus (apart from the HIV-positive man's experiences of the disease and its effect on Bøssehuset). Those interviewees are regarded as 'key informants', which means that they, through their positions and experiences, are 'nodes' in activist networks; and are thus supposed to have an overview of the context I am interested in. Further, I have used Bøssehuset's own website as empirical material, as well as three issues of the Christiania magazine *Ordkløveren*; and a video of performances from Bøssehuset in the 1980s. Translations from Danish are made by the author.

[2] They do have a second logo, which consists of the two classical double gender signs for homosexual men and women, but as it seems, it is not used as frequently as the logo with the phallus. See http://www.flickr.com/photos/15643599@N08/sets/72157602611076477/ and http://www.flickr.com/photos/15643599@N08/sets/72157623008420896/

[3] For an overview see for example Jagose (1996).

[4] After 1982 one can find pieces of 'historical documentation' on the website, but it is not put together on a special site. Most of the information in this section is based on Bøssehuset's website: http://www.boessehuset.dk/. See also the book about BBF and Bøssehuset: *Virkelige Hændelser fra et Liv ved Fronten: erindringer om Bøssernes Befrielses Front* (2011).

[5] See Jagose (1996).

[6] Nowadays named LGBT Danmark — The National Organisation for Lesbians, Gays, Bisexuals and Transsexuals.

[7] Apart from the Thy Camp, BBF was also a part of the whole ø-lejr bevægelsen (the 'island camps movement' in Denmark), mostly in those camps that were arranged by the Men's Movement. See Pérez Skardhamar (2010, part II).

[8] Clausen and Thygesen (1974).

[9] Nissen and Paulsen (13-01-2011).

[10] Parts of this record are available on YouTube, for example: http://www.youtube.com/watch?v=ui9HKf7W7ts and http://www.youtube.com/watch?v=PdwQ2VP6ewA&feature=related

[11] http://www.boessehuset.dk/historiesider/historieside23.htm

[12] *Ordkløveren*, (1977:1, pp. 6–7).

[13] *Ordkløveren*, (1977:2, pp. 6–7).

[14] *Ordklöveren* (1976:8, p. 8).

[15] *Ordkløveren*, (1976:8, p. 9).

[16] See Wasshede (2010a) and Hallgren (2008).

[17] *Ordkløveren* (1976:8). On the Red Stockings Movement in Denmark, see Dahlerup (1998).

[18] *Ordkløveren* (1976:8, p. 14).

[19] Butler (1990).

[20] Ibid.:136.

[21] See Butler (1990:138) and Westerling (2007).

[22] http://www.boessehuset.dk/historiesider/historieside8.htm

[23] In Gothenburg Röda Bögar (Red Gays) did the same in the 1970s, and activists in the extra parliamentary left used the same strategy in the 2000s, see Eman (2000) and Wasshede (2010a) and (2010b).

[24] http://www.boessehuset.dk/FrkVerden.html
[25] Ibid.
[26] *Christianias Pigegarde, Altid Fremad 1991–2001* (2001:15).
[27] See http://www.youtube.com/watch?v=E61IiSj4Ru8
[28] Handed over to the Christiania Archive from Grethe Thy.
[29] *Press* (1993, no. 88).
[30] See for example Svensson (2007) and Henriksson (1995).
[31] See photos from this event at: http://www.flickr.com/photos/15643599@N08/sets/72157624656879883/
[32] See for example Butler (1990) and (1997), Wettergren (2005) and Hallgren, (2008).
[33] See for example Jagose (1996).
[34] See for example Hallgren (1998).
[35] See *Christianias Pigegarde, Altid Fremad 1991–2001* (2001).

WEEDS AND DEEDS

[1] Riksdagen 1981/82. Minutes 43:63. If no other information is given, translations from Swedish and Danish are made by the author.
[2] *Ordkløveren* 29/4 1973. Quoted from Mollerup and Løvetand II (1976:5).
[3] Christianias Kulturforening (1997:118).
[4] On critical discourse moments, see Gamson and Modigliani (1989).
[5] Boulding (1956).
[6] Other examples in the US are the struggle of the temperance movement against alcohol during the 18th century; the opium smoking of the Chinese in the 1870s and the Marijuana Act in 1937, see Reinarman and Levine (1997).
[7] Reinarman and Levine (1997).
[8] This is part of the Common Law of Christiania since 1971, 'where each individual can unfold freely while remaining responsible to the community as a whole', Conroy (1995:8).
[9] Hakkarainen, Jetsu and Laursen (1996).
[10] For different views on the gateway hypothesis, see http://en.wikipedia.org/wiki/Gateway_drugs
[11] Common Meeting 23/11 1971 §6, in Mollerup and Løvetand II (1976).
[12] *Ordkløveren* 13/8 1972. Quoted from Mollerup and Løvetand II (1976).
[13] *Ordkløveren* 11/2 1972. Quoted from Mollerup and Løvetand II (1976).

[14] *Ordkløveren* 27/8 1972. Quoted from Mollerup and Løvetand II (1976:3).

[15] *Ordkløveren* 5/7 1972. Quoted from Mollerup and Løvetand II (1976:3).

[16] *Ordkløveren* 17/8 1973. Quoted from Mollerup and Løvetand II (1976).

[17] Madsen (1979).

[18] Ludvigsen (2003:178–79).

[19] *Hampebladet* (1980:1, p. 5).

[20] One result was even more strained relations between activists and pushers, as Amy Starecheski shows in her chapter.

[21] Flyer announcing the meeting (kept at the Christiania archive). RFMA was a Swedish umbrella for various political, religious, union and women's organisations.

[22] This rally was organised by the national branches of *the People's Action Against Hash*. See *Dagens Nyheter*. 16/2 1982.

[23] *Dagens Nyheter,* 16/2 1982.

[24] *Slå Tillbaka!*, no. 9 (1981:2). In February a united effort by the Lion's clubs of the Scandinavian district to collect money to support anti-drug organisations was launched, *Kvällsposten*, 15/2 1982.

[25] *Politiken*, 16/2 1982.

[26] Nordic Council (1982 II:2396). This is from the debate following on the question posed in October 1981 by the Swedish Minister of Justice, Gabriel Romanus (Liberal Party), to the Nordic Council.

[27] *Dagens Nyheter*, 16/2 1982.

[28] His name was Bengt Hellén and his view was given in an article on drugs in *Sydsvenska Dagbladet*, 16/2 1982.

[29] For a critical review of the LaRouche Movement, see http://en.wikipedia.org/wiki/LaRouche_Movement

[30] This is from a letter to the editor from Ulf Sandmark, representative of EAP, under the heading 'Christiania a threat against democracy', *Sydsvenska Dagbladet* 22/2 1982.

[31] Interview with Ole Lykke 14/2 2010 (by Håkan Thörn).

[32] Riksdagen 1981/82. Interpellation no. 9:125 (15/10 1981).

[33] The subsequent parliamentary debate on the topic of Christiania and drugs was held in December 1981.

[34] Or as Petersson put it: the Danish showed a 'low interest in intervening against drug dealing'. Riksdagen 1981/82. Interpellation no. 9:125 (15/10 1981).

[35] At an anti-drug rally a few months later, MP Rune Gustavsson also admitted to always have been puzzled by Denmark's 'incomprehensible' liberal views on drugs, *Sydsvenska Dagbladet*, 16/2 1982.

[36] See also statements by local politicians (Hellén), officials (Larenius/*Sydsvenska Dagbladet*, 18/2 1982) and social workers (Gardestig/*Svenska Dagbladet*, 20/2 1982) from Malmö on the problems caused by drugs in the southern parts of Sweden.

[37] The origins of the discussion on Christiania at the Nordic Council was the question the Swedish government had posed in October 1981 to its Danish counterpart, asking what it intended to do about the (assumed) drug problems in Christiania, and was itself a reaction to an earlier interpellation by Esse Petersson in the Swedish parliament. Members question E1, Nordic Council (1982: 2396).

[38] At the Nordic Council of Ministers, only the Ministers participated: in Stockholm it was the Ministers of Justice and Social Affairs that debated drugs.

[39] As a comment on this, one heading in *Svenska Dagbladet*, 20/2 1982, simply stated 'Denmark won'.

[40] Accounts of politicians, see *Kvällsposten*, 19/2 1982.

[41] At the height of the debate in early 1982, the Swedish parliamentarian Esse Petersson participated in a Danish TV show debating drugs with other Nordic politicians. He demanded the closure of Christiania and said that a kind of 'low culture' had developed, one that caused people to live at the bottom of society. *Tranås Tidning*, 3/3 1982; *Ekstra Bladet*, 5/3 1982. He shared this opinion with Sten Andersson of the Swedish Conservative party (Moderaterna), who at the debate in parliament spoke in similar words.

[42] The other signatories were the two Norwegians, Christian Christiansen and Asbjörn Haugstvedt, both from the Christian Democrats (Kristeligt Folkeparti), and Bror Lillqvist (Social Democrats) from Finland.

[43] Members' suggestions A 616/s, Nordic Council (1982: 659). As early as 1971 the Nordic governments had issued a recommendation for tighter cooperation in the field of drug prevention. But only a few years later, it was rebuked on the grounds that surveys showed that drug use among young people had decreased and that international cooperation was preferred.

[44] Members' suggestions A 616/s, Nordic Council (1982:312). It is worth noting that no delegate from Finland took part in the debate, even though Lillqvist was one of the signers of the member proposal.

[45] Members' suggestions A 616/s, Nordic Council (1982:302). The case of Swedish double standards had been addressed earlier. According to *Sydsvenska Dagbladet*, 18/2 1982, Jimmy Starth, member of the Danish parliament (no information was provided regarding what political party he represented),

said that the Swedes ought to sweep up in front of their own front door before criticising others. He claimed that at Sergels Torg and in the subway, even a Danish parliamentarian in suit and tie had been offered hash.

[46] Members' suggestions A 616/s, Nordic Council (1982:302, 305).

[47] *StockholmsTidningen*, 3/3 1982.

[48] All the commotion caused by Henriksen can be followed in various Nordic newspapers. See for example *Stockholms Tidningen*, 3/3 1982; *Dagbladet i Sundsvall*, 3/3 1982 (Sweden); *Ny Tid*, 10/2 1982 (Norway); *Ekstra Bladet*, 3/3 1982; *Berlingske Tidende*, 5/3 1982 (Denmark).

[49] *Sotra-Nytt*, 12/3 1982. To leading Danish politicians, like the Prime Minister Anker Jørgensen of the Social Democrats, the whole thing was clear: hash is not comparable to hard drugs. Jørgensen's party comrade, Inge Fischer Möller, also supported such a view when he said that he believed hash to be less harmful than alcohol. Jørgensen made his comment at the Nordic Council, and was immediately criticised by the media and other politicians, both domestic and foreign.

[50] Members' suggestions A 616/s, Nordic Council (1982:313–316).

[51] *Berlingske Tidende*, 14/3 1982.

[52] *Ekstra Bladet*, 2/3 1982.

[53] *Ekstra Bladet*, 2/3 1982.

[54] *Dagens Nyheter*, 20/3 1982.

[55] Both Preben Dich and Jørgen E. Pedersen tried to 'explain' the Swedish reactions to Berendt's accusations (*Berlingske Tidende* 21/3 1982), while Berendt himself wrote an additional article where he discussed the Swedish replies to his original article (*Berlingske Tidende*, 28/3 1982).

[56] The first debate was concluded when a coalition of parties (the Progress Party, the Liberals, the Centre Democrats, the Christian Democrats and the Conservatives) wanted to close Christiania but were defeated in a vote favoring Christiania.

[57] Folketingstidende (1981/82:2402).

[58] Folketingstidende (1981/82:3739).

[59] Folketingstidende (1981/82:3718, 3727).

[60] Folketingstidende (1981/82:3743).

[61] Folketingstidende (1981/82:3745).

[62] Folketingstidende (1981/82:2399, 2400, 2401–03).

[63] Folketingstidende (1981/82:2402).

[64] *Ugespejlet*, 6/2 1982.

[65] *Kvällsposten*, February 1982 Press clipping kept at the Christiania archive in Christiania, without date.

[66] *Arbetet*, February 1982. Press clipping kept at the Christiania archive in Christiania, without date.

[67] Interview with Ole Lykke, 14/2 2010.

[68] *Kvällsposten*, February 1982. Press clipping kept at the Christiania archive in Christiania, without date.

[69] Interview with Ole Lykke 14/2 2010.

[70] Interview with Ole Lykke 14/2 2010. A figure of 200–300 people in the audience was given by the daily morning paper *Dagens Nyheter*, 20/2 1982.

[71] *Sydsvenska Dagbladet* for instance, ran a series of articles on drugs in February/March 1982 titled 'Drugs are spreading' (Knarket sprider sig).

[72] *Kvällsposten*, 20/2 1982.

[73] *Svenska Dagbladet*, 20/2 1982.

[74] *Dagens Nyheter*, 20/2 1982.

[75] Interview with Ole Lykke 14/2 2010 (by Håkan Thörn). Haga had for a long time been contested and was at the time of the Love Sweden Tour partly demolished.

[76] *TT*, 3/3 1982.

[77] *TT*, 3/3 1982.

[78] *Svenska Dagbladet*, 20/2 1982.

[79] *Ugespejlet* (2009:7) (translation by Håkan Thörn).

[80] Ibid.

[81] *Ugespejlet* (2009:6) (translation by Håkan Thörn).

NORMALISATION WITHIN CHRISTIANIA

[1] I use the terms 'Christianite' and 'citizen-activist' to describe the residents of Christiania. Within Christiania, they refer to themselves using a range of terms that include: 'Christianite', 'Christianitter', 'nitter', 'citizen', 'activist' and 'pusher'. The terms 'pusher' and 'activist' are used throughout the chapter depending on the groups' self-identification, whereas the term 'Christianites' refers to the general population of Christiania.

[2] The aim of the Normalisation Plan was to privatise this publically owned space and capitalise on Christiania's unique character and countercultural cachet. The plan also initiated a complex strategy of control that sought to

manage this unruly space and discipline its residents by incarcerating the pushers and slowly displacing Christianites. The first short-term objective was achieved when Pusher Street was later raided and 56 pushers arrested. The second long-term strategy of displacement began with the introduction of a new law. 'The Christiania Act' had afforded residents minimal land use rights, and this provided the legal basis that legitimised communal ownership. When 'The Law to End the Law on the Christiania Area' was introduced, it terminated the squatters' rights to live and build in Christiania; a space they had been improving, developing and inhabiting for decades.

In the long-term, the Normalisation Plan could displace many of Christiania's low-income residents by transforming the area from a self-governing and semi-autonomous squat into a privatised, 'normal' part of Copenhagen. By controlling this unruly space the state intends to re-integrate Christiania back into the formal economy, cripple its underground economy and undermine an autonomous self-government which represents Christiania's 'citizens', who are often poor, marginalised or social drop-outs. In response to critiques that normalisation is a thinly veiled attempt to squash an oppositional political voice, the state boldly explains that normalisation will simply transform Christiania into 'a normal' part of Denmark. The broader implication is that the state's tolerance for Christiania has come to an end. Christiania's normalisation is situated within a shifting political landscape — one that replaces the 'nanny' or welfare state with a minimal state which endorses entrepreneurialism, freedom, choice, and individual responsibility.

3 I divided my interviews into three groups with ties to Christiania that included: 1) current members (short >1 year, medium 2–10 years, and long term <10 years); 2) former members (departed for over one year); and 3) seasonal (students on break) and temporary visitors (musicians, activists and other visitors who visited Christiania for specific events). I conducted approximately 25 taped interviews with a roughly equal number of male and female participants. These semi-structured interviews solicited opinions and thoughts on normalisation and interactions with the Danish state, personal histories, and involvement in Christiania.

4 My dissertation (Amouroux 2007) focused on the spatial strategy of control and reorganisation of space that the Normalisation Plan entails; the reformation of the urban (the organisation of the built environment) through expert, technical, and highly bureaucratic sets of procedures.

5 Foucault (1977) and (1995).

[6] Foucault (1977:197).

[7] Ibid: 202.

[8] Practices and discourses that are used to control space also shape identities: elder, child, citizen, or squatter. Ray Hutchison discusses the productivity of the built environment in this context to argue: 'Urban spaces are created and controlled by dominant groups and institutions; but they are changed and refashioned by the intentional as well as the unintentional actions of everyday life' (Hutchison 2000: xii). Susan Ruddick (1996) argues that in Los Angeles certain groups, such as homeless drug-addicted youths, are racialised subalterns who create spatialised identities in opposition to the normalising gaze of the state. For Ruddick, these new identities emerge within an urban social imaginary where: 'New social subjects are created and create themselves in and through the social space of the city'. Setha Low makes a similar argument: 'Space takes on the ability to confirm identity', (1999:397).

[9] Amouroux (2009).

[10] This name is a pseudonym.

[11] Black money is how Christianites refer to illegal and untaxed income predominately from the hash market.

[12] Bourdieu (1986).

CONSENSUS AND STRATEGY

[1] Graeber (2009); Polletta (2002).

[2] I spent time at Christiania as part of the Researcher in Residence Programme (CRIR), and would like to thank that programme, especially Emmerik Warburg and Rasmus Blædel Larsen, for making this work possible. I would also like to thank all of the Christianites who so generously shared their stories with me. This work was developed in part through public presentations at ABC No Rio and Columbia University's Oral History Workshop series. My travel was generously financed by the City University of New York Graduate Center's Summer Pre-Dissertation Travel Award.

[3] Some interviewees chose to use a pseudonym, and some chose not to make their full interviews available through the archive. Unarchived interviews are called 'ethnographic interviews' to distinguish them from archived oral histories. All quotes are lightly edited for flow and clarity, with any substantial deletions marked by ellipses, and pauses indicated by a double dash. All interviews were conducted in English.

[4] Frisch (1990); Kerr (2006).

[5] Kennedy (2006); Portelli (1991).

[6] Bevington (2005); Juris (2007); Hale (2006); Hale (2008); Sanjek (1987); Mullings (2000).

[7] 'Activists' is a category used by Christianites to indicate those who are politically involved within the normative framework of Christiania's self-government, usually opposed to 'pushers', drug dealers whose political tactics challenge Christiania's ideals of consensus, either through disengagement or the use of violence.

[8] Ethnographic interview with Daniel Jensen (pseudonym), 12 August 2010.

[9] Polletta (2002).

[10] Reddersen (2004:27).

[11] Interview with Madsen (2010).

[12] Ethnographic interview with Rasmus Blædel Larsen, 2 August 2010.

[13] Slots- og Ejendomsstyrelsen (no date).

[14] Chadwick et al. (2007:70).

[15] Interview with Lykke (2010).

[16] Pruijt (2003); Owens (2009).

[17] Scott (2009).

[18] Reddersen (2004:23).

[19] Chadwick et al. (2007).

[20] Ibid.:66.

[21] Slots- og Ejendomsstyrelsen (2004:5), translation by Håkan Thörn.

[22] Ethnographic interview with Rasmus Blædel Larsen, 2 August 2010.

[23] Chadwick et al. (2007).

[24] Slots- og Ejendomsstyrelsen (no date).

[25] Ibid.

[26] Fox (2010:8).

[27] Rasmus Blædel Larsen, personal communication, Feb. 2011.

[28] Interview with Mader (2010).

[29] Interview with Lykke (2010).

[30] Interview with Iversen (2010).

[31] Blædel Larsen, personal communication, Feb. 2011.

[32] Interview with Mader (2010).

[33] Interview with Larsen (2010); Chadwick et al. (2007:89).

[34] Interview with Iversen (2010).

[35] Interview with Mader (2010).

[36] Interview with Iversen (2010).
[37] Interview with Lausten (2010).
[38] Interview with Blanco (2010).
[39] Arendt (1998).
[40] Freeman (1972).
[41] Blædel Larsen, personal communication, Feb. 2011.
[42] Interview with Winther (2010).

CHRISTIANIA AND THE RIGHT TO THE CITY

[1] Harvey (2003a:941).
[2] Another version of this 'report' was published in Danish in *Ugespejlet* (Christiania's newspaper) and the neighbourhood newspaper *Christianshavneren*, June issue, 5, p.4. (http://www.christianshavneren.dk/upl/8962/2007junisíde113.pdf); and in English (Lund Hansen 2010).
[3] Christianias Udviklingsplan (2006).
[4] 'The chilly times we live in' is also a reference to the popular tune 'Det er en kold tid' [These are chilly times] (my translation) by Kim Larsen, who is a very popular folk singer in Denmark. The tune was played loudly throughout the centre of Christiania during this period in May 2007. The Danish Social Democrat Prime Minister, Anker Jørgensen, also used the reference in one of his speeches at the end of the 1970s to characterise the global and national economic crises.
[5] The Children's House is one of Christiania's own 'institutions'.
[6] Some of the events of the day can be seen at: http://www.youtube.com/watch?v=D1qxIEYwMOU
[7] anders.lund_hansen@keg.lu.se. I would like to thank the editors and the participants in the book seminar at Christiania in January 2011 for constructive criticism and suggestions on earlier drafts of this chapter. The financial support of the Jan Wallander and Tom Hedelius Foundation (research grant number W2007-0055:1) is gratefully acknowledged.
[8] Bauman (1998:22).
[9] Schneider and Susser (2003); Graham (2004).
[10] Lund Hansen (2006).
[11] Bauman (1998).
[12] Harvey (2003c:1).

[13] Lees et al. (2007).
[14] Larsen and Lund Hansen (2008).
[15] Clark (2005).
[16] E.g. Ley (1996).
[17] E.g. Smith (1996).
[18] Dutton (2003:2558).
[19] Beauregard (1986).
[20] Clark (2005).
[21] Lees (2000).
[22] Byrne (2003).
[23] Florida (2002); (2005).
[24] Cameron (2003); Slater (2004).
[25] Rofe (2003).
[26] Peck (2005:766).
[27] Smith (1996).
[28] Ibid.:13.
[29] Smith (2005b).
[30] Swyngedouw (1997); Lund Hansen (2003); (2006).
[31] Clark (2005).
[32] Andersen (2001); Harvey (1973).
[33] Larsen and Lund Hansen (2008).
[34] Lefebvre (1991).
[35] Lefebvre (1970/2003); Lefebvre (1996).
[36] Guldbrandsen (2005).
[37] Perelman (2000).
[38] Marx (1990).
[39] Harvey (2003b:145).
[40] Ibid.:145.
[41] Harvey (2005); (2006).
[42] Walker (2005:1).
[43] Lund Hansen (2006).
[44] Smith (2005b); (2008).
[45] Smith (2005b:97). The nation state, geopolitically, with its patent on the means of violence, has traditionally played an important role in the praxis of space wars and imperialism. A classic historical example of the justification of warfare can be found in the German geopolitical idea of 'Lebensraum' in the 1920s and 1930s. In *American empire: Roosevelt's geographer and the prelude to glo-*

balisation, Neil Smith (2003) demonstrates how the concept inspired US global ambitions in the 1940s, seeking American global economic Lebensraum. The shift from the idea of a geopolitical to a geoeconomical Lebensraum is central to understanding Smith's argument — and to understanding space wars and the new urban imperialism. According to Smith, the US-led wars are to be viewed not only as wars on terrorism. Nor did they just want to control the important oil resources. Rather the wars were designed to complete a US-centred globalisation that has characterised the third moment of US ambition since the 1980s (Smith 2003). *The endgame of globalisation*, as Smith calls it, is about gaining global control through *geoeconomic* means — via the long-term installation of neoliberal institutional frameworks (Smith 2005a).

46 Sassen (2004:22).

47 OPCE (2003).

48 In the spring of 2004, without any major violent coordinated resistance from the inhabitants of Christiania, the police closed down Europe's largest open-air cannabis market on 'Pusher Street' where 'pushers' sold their products from 30 booths in the centre of the community.

49 Copenhagen Municipality (2005).

50 Bisgaard (2000).

51 Copenhagen Capacity (2010).

52 Katz (2001).

53 Lund Hansen et al. (2001); Larsen and Lund Hansen (2008).

54 According to Copenhagen Municipality's Statistical Office, 878 people (167 of them children) were registered inhabitants of Christiania on 1 January 2003. Demographically, middle-aged couples dominate Christiania. The average income is DDK 106,000, which is almost half the average income in Copenhagen in general. 33 % are connected to the job market (56 % in Copenhagen in general).

55 Together with the Tivoli and the Little Mermaid (Den Lille Havfrue), Christiania is one of Copenhagen's main tourist attractions.

56 Christiania (2007).

57 Bisgaard (2000).

58 See: http://www.vestfilm.dk/christiania/solvognen/chariotofthesun.html

59 Angotti (2008).

60 Bisgaard (2000).

61 Quote from Christiania's aspirations, formulated in 1971. Quoted in *Christianias Udviklingsplan* (2006). Translation to English by Adam Conroy.

62 Harvey (2005).
63 Klein (2007).
64 Smith (2008:1–3).
65 Harvey (1989); Peck (2005).
66 Swyngedouw (2007).
67 Harvey (2010).

References

Ahnfeldt-Mollerup, M. (2004) 'Christiania's aesthetics - You can't kill us / we are part of you', in Dirckink-Holmfeld, K. and Keiding, M. (eds.) *Learning from Christiania/Christianias lære*. København: Arkitektens forlag.

Alexander, C. et al. (1977) *A Pattern Language: towns, buildings, construction*. New York: Oxford University Press.

Amouroux, C. S. (2007) *Conflict in Copenhagen: urban reconfigurations, disciplining the unruly*. (Unpublished dissertation, Stanford University).

Amouroux, C. S. (2009) 'Normalizing Christiania: project Clean Sweep and the Normalization Plan in Copenhagen', *City & Society*, no 1.

Andersen, J. (2001) 'The Politics of Gambling and Ambivalence: struggles over urban policy in Copenhagen', *Geographische Zeitschrift*, no. 89.

Andreasson, M. (2000) (ed.) *Homo i folkhemmet: homo- och bisexuella i Sverige 1950-2000*. Göteborg: Anamma.

Angotti, T. (2008) *New York for Sale: community planning confronts global real estate*. Cambridge MA: MIT Press.

Arendt, H. (1998) *The Human Condition*. Chicago: University of Chicago Press.

Arkitekten (1975) no. 14 (Stockholm).

Arkitekten (2004) no. 7 (København).

Arkitekttidningen (1977) no. 13.

Austin, T. and de Jong, W. (2008) (eds.) *Rethinking Documentary: new perspectives, new practices*. Maidenhead: Open University Press.

Avermaete, T., von Osten, M. and Karakayali, S. (2010) (eds.) *Colonial Modern: aesthetics of the past rebellions for the future*. London: Black Dog Publishing.

Bakker, I. and Silvey, R. (2008) (eds.) *Beyond States and Markets: the challenge of social reproduction*. London: Routledge.

Balvig, F., Koch, H. and Vestergaard, J. (1976) *Politiets virksomhed på Christiania*. Kriminalistisk institut: Københavns universitet.

Balvig, F. (1979) *Fra slumstorm til folkebevægelse: mediernas betydning i slaget om Christiania*. Kriminalistisk institut: Københavns universitet.

Balvig, F. and Rasmussen, N. (1986) 'Befolkningen, Christiania og politiet', in Vestergaard, J. (ed.) *Sociale uroligheder: politi och politik*. Holte: Forlaget SOCPOL.

Bates, A. (2009) *Christiania: Copenhagen's funky jewel of sustainability.* www.energybulletin.net/node/51038 (downloaded 3/12 2010).
Bauman, Z. (1998) *Globalization: the human consequences.* Cambridge: Polity Press.
Beall, J. (2002) 'Living in the Present, Investing in the Future: household security among the urban poor', in Rakodi, C. (ed.) *Urban Livelihoods.* London: Earthscan.
Beauregard, R.E. (1986) 'The Chaos and Complexity of Gentrification', in Smith, N. and Williams, P. (eds.) *Gentrification of the City.* London: Allen and Unwin.
Bekin, C., Carrigan, M. and Szmigin, I. (2005) 'Defying Marketing Sovereignty: voluntary simplicity at new consumption communities', *Qualitative Market Research: an international journal,* no. 4.
Bellah, R.N., Madsen, R., Sullivan, W.M., Swidler, A. and Tipton, S.M. (1985) *Habits of the Heart: individualism and commitment in American life.* New York: Harper Perennial.
Bevington, D. and Dixon, C. (2005) 'Movement-relevant Theory: rethinking social movement scholarship and activism', *Social Movement Studies,* no. 3.
Blum, J. (1976) *Fristaden Christiania: Slum, alternativ bykultur eller et socialt eksperiment?* Working paper 2. København: Nationalmuseet.
Blum, J. (1977) *Christiania: Freetown, Slum, Alternative Culture or Social Experiment?* Copenhagen: The National Museum of Denmark.
Blum, J. and Sjørslev, I. (1978) *Spirer til en ny livsform: tværvidenskabelige synspunkter omkring alternative samfundsforsøg.* København: Nationalmuseet.
Booth, C. and Gilroy, R. (1999) 'Building an Infrastructure for Everyday Life', *European Planning Studies,* no. 3.
Borre, O. (2003) 'Dansk vælgeradfærd 1960-2001', *Politica,* no. 35.
Boulding, K. (1956) *The Image.* Ann Arbour: University of Michigan Press.
Bourdieu, P. (1986) 'The Forms of Capital', in Richardson, J.G. (ed.) *Handbook for Theory and Research for the Sociology of Education.* New York: Greenwood Press.
Bryld, T. (1986) 'Magtdemonstration - til gavn for hvem?', in Vestergaard, J. (ed.) *Sociale uroligheder: politi og politik.* Holte: Forlaget SOCPOL.
Butler, J. (1990) *Gender Trouble: feminism and the subversion of identity.* London: Routledge.
Butler, J. (1997) 'Merely Cultural', *Social Text,* no. 52-53.
Byrne, J.P. (2003) 'Two Cheers for Gentrification', *Howard Law Journal,* no. 46.

Bæk Pedersen, P. (2005) *Arkitektur og plan i den danske velfærdsby 1950-1990: container og urbant raster*. Aarhus: Arkitektskolens Forlag.

Bøggild, S.S. and Bruun Yde, M. (2010) 'Concrete Hells and Wild Imaginations: the new town and the Freetown in Copenhagen', in Provoost, M. (ed.) *New Towns for the 21st Century: the planned vs. the unplanned city*. Amsterdam: SUN.

Bøggild, S.S., Bruun Yde, M. and Dehn Sparrevohn, S. (2010) 'Der er altid flere perspektiver på en historie', *Arkitekten*, no. 112.

Bøggild, S.S. (2005) 'Christiania/*Christiania*', *Nordisk Arkitekturforskning*, no. 2.

'Bøssehuset's history', http://www.boessehuset.dk/historiesider/historieside1.html (downloaded 13/1 2011).

'Bøssehuset's Frøken Verden', http://www.boessehuset.dk/FrkVerden.html (downloaded 13/1 2011).

Cameron, S. (2003) 'Gentrification, Housing Re-differentiation and Urban Regeneration', *Urban Studies*, no. 29.

Chadwick, J., Kleene, C., Olesen, K., Pedersen, K. and Uusinoka, T. (2007) *Christiania - Consensus or Conflict?: deliberation through consensus building*. Aalborg: Urban Planning and Management, Aalborg University.

Clark, E. (2005) 'The Order and Simplicity of Gentrification: a political challenge', in Atkinson, R. and Bridge, G. (eds.) *Gentrification in a Global Context — the new urban colonialism*. London: Routledge.

Clausen, C. and Thygesen, E. (1974) (eds.) *MÆND. Det svækkede køn*. København: Tiderne skifter.

Conroy, A. (1995) *Christiania: The Evolution of a Commune*. Amsterdam: International Institute of Social History.

Dahlerup, D. (1998) *Rødstrømperne: den danske Rødstrømpebevægelses udvikling, nytænking og gennemslag 1970-1885*. Bd 2. København: Gyldendal.

Diken, B. and Albertsen, N. (2004) 'Welfare and the City', *Nordic Journal of Architectural Research/Nordisk Arkitekturforskning*, no. 2.

Dirkinck-Holmfeld, K. and Keiding, M. (2004) (eds.) *Learning from Christiania/Christiania's lære*. København: Arkitektens forlag.

Doling, J. and Elsinga, E. (2006) (eds.) 'Home Ownership. Getting in, Getting From, Getting Out. Part II', in Doling, J. and Elsinga, E. (eds.) *Home Ownership. Getting in, Getting From, Getting Out. Part II. Housing and Urban Policy Studies* 30. Delft University Press.

Doron, G. (2007) 'Dead Zones, Outdoor Rooms and the Architecture of Transgression', in Franck, K.A. and Stevens, Q. (eds.) *Loose Space: possibility and diversity in urban life*. London: Routledge.

Dutton, P. (2003) 'Leeds Calling: the influence of London on the gentrification of regional cities', *Urban Studies*, no. 40.
Edwards, M. (1979) *Christiania*. København: Informations forlag.
Elden, S. and Feld, S. (2003) 'Editor's Introduction', in Rouch, J. (ed.) *Ciné-Ethnography*. Minneapolis, MN: University of Minnesota Press.
Elklit, J. and Pedersen, M.N. (2003) 'Decembervalget: 30 år efter', *Politica*, no. 35.
Eman, G. (2000) 'Klänningens betydelse för mänsklighetens frigörelse: om den socialistiska gruppen Röda bögar i Göteborg 1976-78', in Andreasson, M. (ed.) *Homo i folkhemmet: homo- och bisexuella i Sverige 1950-2000*. Göteborg: Anamma.
Endre, J.P., Hello, H. and Ketoma, B.J. (2010) *Participation and Sustainability: a common meeting?* Student Project. Roskilde: Roskilde University.
Falkentorp, J., Hansen, D., Juhler, S., Kløvedal, M. and Løvetand, P. (1982) 'Alternative Ways of Life in Denmark', in Miles, I. and Irvine, J. (eds.) *The Poverty of Progress: changing ways of living in industrial societies*. Oxford and New York: Pergamon Press.
Florida, R. (2002) *The Rise of the Creative Class: and how it's transforming work, leisure, community and everyday life*. New York: Basic Books.
Florida, R. (2005) *The Flight of the Creative Class: the new global competition for talent*. New York: Harper Collins Publishers.
Fogh Rasmussen, A. (1993) *Fra socialstat til minimalstat: en liberal strategi*. København: Samleren.
Fogh Rasmussen, A. (2002) *Statsminister Anders Fogh Rasmussens Nytårstale 2002*, http://www.stm.dk/_p_7354.html (downloaded 22/3 2011).
Forster, P.M. (1998) 'Communities and Academics: a developing dialogue', *Community, Work and Family*, no. 1.
Foucault, M. (1977) *Discipline & Punish: the birth of the prison*. New York: Vintage Books.
Foucault, M. (2002) 'Of Other Spaces', in Mirzoeff, N. (ed.) *The Visual Culture Reader*. London: Routledge.
Foucault, M. (2004) *Society Must be Defended: lectures at the Collège de France 1975-1976*. London: Penguin.
Foucault, M. (2007) *Security, Territory, Population: lectures at the Collège de France 1977-1978*. New York: Palgrave Macmillan.
Foucault, M. (2008) *The Government of Self and Others: lectures at the Collège de France 1982-1983*. New York: Palgrave Macmillan.
Fox, P. (2010) 'The Last Stand of Free Town', *The Believer*, June.

Franzén, M. (2005) 'Mellan stigma och karisma: Stureplan, Sergels torg och platsens politik', *Fronesis*, no. 18.
Freeman, J. (1972) 'The Tyranny of Structurelessness', *Berkeley Journal of Sociology*, no. 17.
Frisch, M. (1990) *A Shared Authority: essays on the craft and meaning of oral and public history*. Albany, NY: State University of New York Press.
Furness, Z. (2007) 'Utopia and the City: an interview with David Pinder', *Bad Subjects*, http://bad.eserver.org/issues/2007/78/pinder.html (downloaded 7/1 2011).
Gamson, W.A. and Modigliani, A. (1989) 'Media Discourse and Public Opinion on Nuclear Power: a constructionist approach', *American Journal of Sociology*, no. 1.
Garbarczyk, M. (2008) *What is the Role of Architects in the Current Trend for a Bottom-up Approach of Redeveloping Harbour and Industrial Areas with Culture as Area-life Generator?* Hybrid Buildings, Masters Project, Architectural Studies: University of Amsterdam.
'Gateway Hypothesis' http://en.wikipedia.org/wiki/Gateway_drugs (downloaded 17/3 2011).
Gehl, J. (2010) *Life Between Buildings*. Copenhagen: Danish Architectural Press.
Gibson-Graham, J.K. (1996) *The End of Capitalism (As We Knew It): a feminist critique of political economy.* Oxford: Blackwell.
Gilman, C. P. (2002) *The Home: its work and influence. A reprint of the 1903 edition with an introduction by M. Kimmel.* Walnut Creek, CA: Altamira Press.
Graham, S. (2004) (ed.) *Cities, War, and Terrorism: towards an urban geopolitics.* Oxford: Blackwell.
Gramsci, A. (1929-35/1971) *Selections from the Prison Notebooks*. New York: International Publishers.
Graeber, D. and Shukaitis, S. (2007) (eds.) *Constituent Imagination: militant investigations//collective theorization*. Oakland, CA: AK Press.
Graeber, D. (2009) *Direct Action: an ethnography*. Oakland, CA: AK Press.
Griffin, J. (2010) *The Lonely Society?* London: Mental Health Foundation.
Gullestad, M. (1984) *Kitchen-Table Society: a case study of the family life and friendships of young working-class mothers in Norway*. Oslo: Universitetsforlaget. US distribution, New York: Columbia University Press.
Gutting, G. (2010), 'Michel Foucault', *The Stanford Encyclopedia of Philosophy (Spring 2010 Edition)*, Edward N. Zalta (ed.), http://plato.stanford.edu/archives/spr2010/entries/foucault/ (downloaded 13/2 2011).

Hakkarainen, P., Jetsu, T. and Laursen, L. (1996) 'The Legal Framework and the Drug Control System', in Hakkarainen, P., Laursen, L. and Tigerstedt, C. (eds.) *Discussing Drugs and Control Policy: comparative studies on four Nordic countries*. Helsinki: NAD publication 31.

Hale, C.R. (2006) 'Activist Research v. Cultural Critique: indigenous land rights and the contradictions of politically engaged anthropology', *Cultural Anthropology*, no. 1.

Hale, C. (2008) (ed.) *Engaging Contradictions: theory, politics, and methods of activist scholarship*. Berkeley: University of California Press.

Hale, C. (2008) 'Introduction', in Hale, C. (ed.) *Engaging Contradictions: theory, politics, and methods of activist scholarship*. Berkeley: University of California Press.

Hallgren, H. (2008) *När lesbiska blev kvinnor/När kvinnor blev lesbiska: lesbiskfeministiska kvinnors diskursproduktion rörande kön, sexualitet, kropp och identitet under 1970- och 1980-talen i Sverige*. Göteborg: Kabusa Böcker.

Harvey, D. (1973) *Social Justice and the City*. Oxford: Blackwell.

Harvey, D. (1989) 'From Managerialism to Entrepreneurialism: the transformation in urban governance in late capitalism', *Geografiska annaler*, no. 71B.

Harvey, D. (2003a) 'The Right to the City', *International Journal of Urban and Regional Research*, no. 27.

Harvey, D. (2003b) *The New Imperialism*. Oxford: Oxford University Press.

Harvey, D. (2003c) *Paris: Capital of Modernity*. London: Routledge.

Harvey, D. (2005) *A Brief History of Neoliberalism*. Oxford: Oxford University Press.

Harvey, D. (2006) 'Neo-liberalism as Creative Destruction', *Geografiska Annaler*, no. 88B.

Harvey, D. (2010) *The Enigma of Capital, and the Crises of Capitalism*. London: Profile Books.

Hellström, M. (2006) *Steal this Place: the aesthetics of tactical formlessness and 'the Free Town of Christiania'*. Alnarp: Swedish University of Agricultural Sciences.

Hellström, M. (2009) 'Pusher Street and the Theatre of Emergence', *Scroope: Cambridge Architecture Journal*, no. 19.

Hellström Reimer, M. (2009) 'Den avvikande allmänningen', in Pløger, J. and Juul, H. (eds.) *Byens Rum 1.5*. Juul & Frost Arkitekter in collaboration with Roskilde Universitetscenter, http://byensrum.dk/aktiviteter_presse/documents/ByensRum1-5Web.pdf (downloaded 15/2 2011).

Hellström Reimer, M. (2011) 'Christiania Copenhagen: a common out of the ordinary', in Jorgensen, A. and Keenan, R. (eds.) *Wildscapes*. London: Routledge, *forthcoming*.
Henriksson, B. (1995) *Risk Factor Love: homosexuality, sexual interaction and HIV prevention*. Göteborg: Institutionen för socialt arbete, skriftserien 1995.
Holmes, S. and Jermyn, D. (2008) 'Ask the Fastidious Woman from Surbiton to Hand-Wash the Underpants of the Aging Oldham Skinhead: why not wife swap?', in Austin, T. and de Jong, W. (eds.) *Rethinking Documentary: new perspectives, new practices*. Maidenhead: Open University Press.
Hutchison, R. (2000) *Constructions of Urban Space (Research in Urban Sociology)*. Stamford, Conn: JAI Press.
Inaba, J. (2009) 'Editorial', *Volume*, no. 20.
Inglehart, R. (1971) 'The Silent Revolution in Europe: intergenerational change in post-industrial societies', *American Political Science Review*, no. 4.
Jagose, A. (1996) *Queer Theory: an introduction*. New York: New York University Press.
Jarvis, H., Pratt, A.C. and Wu, P. (2001) *The Secret Life of Cities: the social reproduction of everyday life*. Harlow: Prentice Hall.
Jarvis, H. (2005) *Work/Life City Limits: comparative household perspectives*. Houndsmill: Palgrave.
Jarvis, H. (2006) 'Households', in Douglas, I., Hugget, R. and Perkins, C. (eds.) *Companion Encyclopaedia of Geography*. London: Taylor & Francis.
Jarvis, H. (2007) 'Home Truths about Careless Competitiveness', *International Journal of Urban and Regional Research*, no. 1.
Jorgensen, A. (1982) 'Touring the 1970s with the Solvognen in Denmark', *The Drama Review*, no. 2.
Jorn, A. (1947) 'Menneskeboliger eller tankekonstruktioner i jernbeton', *Arkitekten Ugehæfte*, no. 16-17.
Jorn, A. and Debord, G. (2001) *Fin de Copenhague*. Paris: Editions Allia.
Juris, J.S. (2007) 'Practicing Militant Ethnography with the Movement for Global Resistance in Barcelona', in Graeber, D. and Shukaitis, S. (eds.) *Constituent Imagination: militant investigations//collective theorization*. Oakland, CA: AK Press.
Jæger, B., Olsen, L. and Rieper, O. (1993) *De offentlige myndigheder og Christiania*. København: AKF forlaget.
Karpantschof, R. and Mikkelsen, F. (2002) 'Fra slumstormere til autonome – husbesættelser, ungdom og social protest i Danmark 1965-2001', in Mikkel-

sen, F. (ed.) *Bevægelser i demokrati: foreninger og kollektive aktioner i Danmark*. Aarhus: Aarhus Universitetsforlag.
Karpantschof, R. and Mikkelsen, F. (2008) 'Vold, politik og demokrati i Danmark efter 2.Verdenskrig', *Arbejderhistorie*, no 1.
Karpantschof, R. (2009a) 'Ungdomshusoprøret 2006-2008', in Karpantschof, R. and Lindblom, M. (eds.) *Kampen om Ungdomshuset: studier i et oprør*. København: Frydenlund & Monsun.
Karpantschof, R. (2009b) 'Statens tveæggede sværd: Danmarks nye uropoliti og storbyuroligheder 2006-2008', in Karpantschof, R. and Lindblom, M. (eds.) *Kampen om Ungdomshuset: studier i et oprør*. København: Frydenlund & Monsun.
Karpantschof, R. and Lindblom, M. (2009) *Kampen om ungdomshuset: studier i et oprør*. København: Frydenlund & Monsun.
Karpantschof, R. and Mikkelsen, F. (2009) 'Kampen om byens rum: Ungdomshuset, Christiania og husbesættelser i København 1965-2008 ', in Karpantschof, R. and Lindblom, M. (eds.) *Kampen om Ungdomshuset: studier i et oprør*. København: Frydenlund & Monsun.
Katz, C. (2001) 'Vagabond Capitalism and the Necessity of Social Reproduction', *Antipode*, no. 33.
Keith, M. and Pile, S. (1993) (eds.) *Place and the Politics of Identity*. London: Routledge.
Kennedy, R. (2006) 'Stolen Generations Testimony: trauma, historiography, and the question of "truth"', in Perks, R. and Thomson, A. (eds.) *The Oral History Reader*, 2nd ed. London: Routledge.
Kerr, D. (2006) '"We Know What the Problem Is": using video and radio oral history to develop collaborative analysis of homeless', in Perks. R. and Thomson, A. (eds) *The Oral History Reader*, 2nd ed. London: Routledge.
Klein, N. (2007) *Shock Doctrine: the rise of disaster capitalism*. London: Penguin.
Kracauer, S. (1960) *Theory of Film: the redemption of physical reality*. Oxford: Oxford University Press.
Krarup, O. (1976) *Stævning: Christiania mod staten*. København: Chr. Erichsens Forlag.
Kvorning, J. (2002) 'Copenhagen: formation, change and urban life', in Madsen. P. and Plunz, R. (eds.) *The Urban Lifeworld: formation, perception, representation*. London: Routledge.
Kvorning, J. (2004a) 'Tre by-temaer', *Arkitekten*, no. 7.

Kvorning, J. (2004b) 'Christiania og grænserne i byen', in Dirckink-Holmfeld, K. and Keiding, M. (eds.) *Learning from Christiania/Christiania's lære*. København: Arkitektens forlag.

'LaRouche Movement' http://en.wikipedia.org/wiki/LaRouche_Movement (downloaded 7/3 2011).

Larsen, H.G. and Lund Hansen, A. (2008) 'Gentrification – Gentle or Traumatic?: urban renewal policies and socio-cultural transformations in Copenhagen', *Urban Studies*, no. 45.

Lees, L. (2002) 'A Reappraisal of Gentrification: towards a "geography of gentrification"', *Human Geography*, no. 3.

Lefebvre, H. (1933/2003) 'Mystifications: notes for a critique of everyday life', in Elden, S., Lebas, E. and Kofman, E. (eds.) *Henri Lefebvre: Key Writings*. London: Continuum.

Lefebvre, H. (1970/2003) *The Urban Revolution*. Minneapolis: University of Minnesota Press.

Lefebvre, H. (1991) *The Production of Space*. Oxford: Blackwell.

Lefebvre, H. (1996) 'The Right to the City', in Kofman, E. and Lebas, E. (eds.) *Writings on the City*. Berkeley: University of California Press.

Lemberg, K. (1978) 'A Squatter Settlement in Copenhagen: slum, ghetto or social experiment?', *International Review*, US Department of Housing and Development, no. 1.

Ley, D. (1996) *The New Middle Class and the Remaking of the Central City*. Oxford: Oxford University Press.

Lind, O. (2008) *Arkitekten Steen Eiler Rasmussen*. København: Gyldendal.

Lofland, L.H. (1973) *A World of Strangers: order and action in urban public space*. Prospect Heights, ILL: Waveland Press.

Low, S. (1999) (ed.) *Theorizing the City: the new urban anthropology reader*. New Brunswick, NJ: Rutgers University Press.

Ludvigsen, J. (2003) *Christiania: fristad i fare*. København: Ekstrabladets forlag.

Lund Hansen, A., Andersen, H.T. and Clark, E. (2001) 'Creative Copenhagen: globalization, urban governance and social change', *European Planning Studies*, no. 9.

Lund Hansen, A. (2003) 'Urban Space Wars in "Wonderful" Copenhagen: uneven development in the age of vagabond capitalism', in Pettersson, B. and Clark, E. (eds.) *Identity Dynamics and the Construction of Boundaries*. Stockholm: Nordic Academic Press.

Lund Hansen, A. (2005) 'Rumskrig, nyliberalism och skalpolitik', *Fronesis*, no. 18.

Lund Hansen, A. (2006) *Space Wars and the New Urban Imperialism*. Lund: Lund University.

Lund Hansen, A. (2010) 'Forty Years of System Change: lessons from the free city of Christiania', in Sandberg, L.A. and Sandberg, T. (eds.) *Climate Change — Who's Carrying the Burden?: the chilly climates of the global environmental dilemma*. Ottawa: Canadian Centre for Policy Alternatives (CCPA).

Løvetand Iversen, P. (1972) *Fristaden Christiania som samfundsexperiment: et forsøg på at belyse strukturerings- og bevidstgørelseprocessen i Christiania igennem det første år af dets eksistens*. København: BYT, Forskningsrapport, Byggteknik, Kunstakademiets arkitektskole.

Maagensen, B. (1996) *Christiania – en længere historie*. København: Gunbak og Kaspersen.

Madsen, B. (1979) *I Skorpionens halespids: et speciale om mig & Christiania*. København: Københavns universitet.

Madsen, B. (1981) *Sumpen, liberalisterne og de hellige: Christiania, et børn af kapitalismen*. Holte: Social og Sundhetspolitisk gruppe.

Marx, K. (1990) *Capital*. Vol. 1. London: Penguin.

Meltzer, G. (2005) *Sustainable Community: learning from the cohousing model*. Victoria, BC: Trafford.

Midtgaard, S.F. (2007a) '"But Suppose Everyone Did the Same": the case of the Danish utopian micro-society of Christiania', *Journal of Applied Philosophy*, no. 3.

Midtgaard, S.F. (2007b) 'Fristaden Christiania: normative perspektiver', *Politica*, no. 4.

Mikkelsen, F. and Karpantschof, R. (2001) 'Youth as a Political Movement: development of the squatters and autonomous movement in Copenhagen 1981-95', *International Journal of Urban and Regional Research*, no. 3.

Miles, I. and Irvine, J. (1982) (eds.) *The Poverty of Progress: changing ways of living in industrial societies*. Oxford and New York: Pergamon Press.

Miles, M. (2008) *Urban Utopias: the built and social architectures of alternative settlements*. London: Routledge.

Miller, T. (1999) *The 60s Commune: hippies and beyond*. Syracuse, NY: Syracuse University Press.

Mitchell, D. (2003) *The Right to the City: social justice and the fight for public space*. Guilford: New York.

Mullings, L. (1987) (ed.) *Cities of the United States: studies in urban anthropology*. New York: Columbia University Press.

Mullings, L. (2000) 'African-American Women Making Themselves: notes on the role of black feminist research', *Souls*, no. 4.

Møller-Jensen, V., Sørensen, H. and Thomassen, M. (1975) 'Christianshavn og det fremtidige Christiania', *Arkitekten*, no. 1.

Nichols, B. (1991) *Representing Reality: issues and concepts in documentary*. Bloomington: Indiana University Press.

Nichols, B. (2001) 'The Question of Evidence, the Poverty of Rhetoric and Documentary Film', in Austin, T. and de Jong, W. (eds.) *Rethinking Documentary: new perspectives, new practices*. Maidenhead: Open University Press.

Nielsen, K.L. (2005) 'SAVE som æstetisk og politisk praxis: med udgangspunkt i Christiania', *Nordisk Arkitekturforskning*, no. 2.

Nielsen, T., Dehs, J. and Skov, P. (2005) 'Arkitektur og politik: introduktion til temaet', *Nordisk Arkitekturforskning*, no. 2.

Nielsen, T. (2008) *Gode intentioner og uregerlige byer*. Aarhus: Arkitektskolens Forlag.

Nissen, V. and Paulsen, I.-L. (2010) *Handling gi'r forvandling. Klip af homobevægelsernes historie i Danmark*, www.lgbt.dk/fileadmin/site/om.../Homobevaegelserne_i_DK.pdf (downloaded 13/1 2011).

Omann, S. (2011) *Virkelige hændelser fra et liv ved fronten: erindringer om Bøssernes Befrielses Front*. København: Forlaget Wanda.

Owens, L. (2009) *Cracking Under Pressure: narrating the decline of the Amsterdam squatters' movement*. University Park, Penn.: Pennsylvania State University Press.

Parker, M. and Richards, C. (1994) (eds.) *Architecture and Order: approaches to social space*. London: Routledge.

Parker, M., Pearson, M. and Richards, C. (1994) 'Ordering the World: perceptions of architecture, space and time', in Parker, M. and Richards, C. (eds.) *Architecture and Order: approaches to social space*. London: Routledge.

Peck, J. (2005) 'Struggling with the Creative Class', *International Journal of Urban and Regional Research*, no. 29.

Perelman, M. (2000) *The Invention of Capitalism: classical political economy and the secret history of primitive accumulation*. Durham and London: Duke University Press.

Perks, R. and Thomson, A. (2006) (eds.) *The Oral History Reader*, 2nd ed. London: Routledge.

'Pia's Ugebrev', www.danskFolkeparti.dk/Ryd_Christiania_.asp (downloaded 20/4 2011).

Politica (2003) no. 4.
Polletta, F. (2002) *Freedom Is an Endless Meeting: democracy in American social movements*. Chicago: University of Chicago Press.
Popper, K. (1988) *The Poverty of Historicism*. London: Routledge.
Portelli, A. (1991) *The Death of Luigi Trastulli and Other Stories: form and meaning in oral history*. Albany, NY: State University of New York Press.
Press (1993) no. 88.
Provoost, M. (2006) 'New Towns on the Cold War Frontier', *Eurozine/Lettre*, http://www.eurozine.com/articles/2006-06-28-provoost-en.html (downloaded 10/1 2011).
Pruijt, H. (2003) 'Is the Institutionalization of Urban Movements Inevitable?: a comparison of the opportunities for sustained squatting in New York City and Amsterdam', *International Journal of Urban and Regional Research*, no. 1.
Rakodi, C. (1999) 'A Capital Assets Framework for Analyzing Household Livelihood Strategies: implications for policy', *Development Policy Review*, no. 3.
Rakodi, C. (2002) (ed.) *Urban Livelihoods*. London: Earthscan.
Rasmussen, S.E. (1956-57) 'Neighbourhood Planning', *The Town Planning Review*, no. 27.
Rasmussen, S.E. (1976) *Omkring Christiania*. København: Gyldendals.
Rasmussen, S.E. (1977) *Fristeder i kulturhistorisk og kulturpolitisk belysning*. Gammel Svebølle: Børge Schnack.
Reddersen, J. (2004) 'Self-management in Christiania', in Dirckink-Holmfeld, K. and Keiding, M. (eds.) *Christianias Laere/Learning from Christiania*. København: Arkitektens Forlag.
Reinarman, C. and Levine, H.G. (1997) 'Crack in Context: Americas latest demon drug', in Reinarman, C. and Levine, H.G (eds.) *Crack in America: demon drugs and social justice*. Berkeley: University of California Press.
Reinder, L. and van der Land, M. (2008) 'Mental Geographies of Home and Place: introduction to the special issue', *Housing, Theory and Society*, no. 1.
Riesto, S. and Tietjen, A. (2003) (eds.) *Christiania: veje til bevaringsstrategier for et anderledes byrum*. København: Institut for Kunst- og Kulturvidenskab.
Riesto, S. and Tietjen, A. (2007) (eds.) *Forankring i forandring*. København: Arkitektens forlag.
Rofe, R. (2003) '"I Want to be Global": theorising the gentrifying class as an emergent elite global community', *Urban Studies*, no. 40.

Rothstein, B. (1992) *Den korporativa staten: intresseorganisationer och statsförvaltning i svensk politik.* Stockholm: Norstedts.

Rouch, J. (1962/2003) 'The Cinema of the Future?', in Rouch, J. (ed.) *Ciné-Ethnography.* Minneapolis, MN: University of Minnesota Press.

Ruddick, S. (1996) *Young and Homeless in Hollywood: mapping social identity.* London: Routledge.

Sadler, S. (1998) *The Situationist City.* London and Cambridge, MASS: MIT Press.

Sanjek, R. (1987) 'Anthropological Work at a Gray Panther Health Clinic: academic, applied, and advocacy goals', in Mullings, L. (ed.) *Cities of the United States: studies in urban anthropology.* New York: Columbia University Press.

Sassen, S. (2004) *The Network of Imperial and Sub-Imperial Cities: what does it tell us about the new empire.* Unpublished manuscript.

Schneider, J. and Susser, I. (2003) (eds.) *Wounded Cities: destruction and reconstruction in a globalized world.* Oxford: Berg.

Scott, J.C. (1998) *Seeing Like a State: how certain schemes to improve the human condition have failed.* New Haven: Yale University Press.

Scott, J.C. (2009) *The Art of Not Being Governed: an anarchist history of upland Southeast Asia.* New Haven: Yale University Press.

Shaw, D. and Newholm, T. (2002) 'Voluntary Simplicity and the Ethics of Consumption', *Psychology and Marketing*, no. 2.

Skardhamar, P.L. (2010) *'Det private er politisk': en analyse af et kollektiv, ø-lejre og mandebevægelse i de lange halvfjerdserne i Danmark.* Roskilde: Roskilde Universitet, RUC.

Slater, T. (2004) 'North American Gentrification?: revanchist and emancipatory perspectives explored', *Environment and Planning A*, no. 36.

Smith, N. and Katz, C. (1993) 'Grounding Metaphor: towards a spatialized politics', in Keith, M. and Pile, S. (eds.) *Place and the Politics of Identity.* London: Routledge.

Smith, N. (1996) *The New Urban Frontier: gentrification and the revanchist city.* London: Routledge.

Smith, N. (2003) *American Empire: Roosevelt's geographer and the prelude to globalization.* Berkeley: University of California Press.

Smith, N. (2005) 'Ny globalism, ny urbanism: ojämn utveckling i det tjugoförsta århundradet', *Fronesis*, no. 18.

Smith, N. (2005a) *The Endgame of Globalization.* London: Routledge.

Smith, N. (2008) 'Neoliberalism is Dead, Dominant and Defeatable: then what?' *Human Geography*, no. 2.

Socialdemokratisk Forbund (1945) *FREMTIDENS DANMARK: Socialdemokratiets program 1945*. København: Fremad.

Steen Eiler Rasmussen's Office (1963) *Tingbjerg: forklaring til en byplan*. København: Steen Eiler Rasmussens Tegnestue.

Svensson, I. (2007) *Liket i garderoben: en studie av sexualitet, livsstil och begravning*. Stockholm: Normal Förlag.

Swyngedouw, E. (1997) 'Neither Global nor Local: "glocalization" and the politics of scale', in Cox, K. (ed.) *Spaces of Globalization*. New York: Guilford.

Swyngedouw, E. (2007) 'The Post-Political City', in Boie, G. and Pauwels, M. (eds.) *Urban Politics Now: re-imagining democracy in the neo-liberal city*. Amsterdam: NAi Publishers.

Söderqvist, L. (2008) *Att gestalta välfärd: från idé till byggd miljö*. Stockholm: Adlibris.

Sørensen, C.T. (1935) 'Etagehusets Have', *Arkitektens Månedshæfte*.

Teller, D., Gringmuth, H. and Pinkert, E.-U. (1978) *Christiania. Argumente zur Erhaltung eines befreiten Stadsviertels im Zentrum von Kopenhagen*. Werdorf: Gisela Lotz Verlag.

Thörn, H. (1997) *Rörelser i det moderna: politik, modernitet och kollektiv identitet i Europa 1789-1989*. Stockholm: Rabén & Prisma.

Thörn, H. (2006) *Anti-Apartheid and the Emergence of a Global Civil Society*. Basingstoke and New York: Palgrave Macmillan.

Thörn, H. (2010). 'Proletarians, Proggers and Punks: Haga and a hundred years of social movements', in Holgersson, H., Thörn, C., Thörn, H. and Wahlström, M. (eds.) *(Re)Searching Gothenburg: essays on a changing city*. Göteborg: Glänta Produktion.

Tingbjerg's website: http://www.tingbjerg.com/om-tingbjerg/tingbjerg-paa-film.aspx (downloaded 12/1 2011).

Traimond, J.-M. (1994) *Récits de Christiania*. Paris: Atelier de creation libertaire.

Turner, V. (1974) *Dramas, Fields and Metaphors*. Ithaca, NY: Cornell University Press.

VisitDenmark.Com (2009) 'Meet The Danes: how the Danes have turned happiness into a way of life', *Denmark Magazine '09*.

Vanstiphout, W. (2008) 'A Retroactive Lens on the Bijlmermeer', *Volume*, no. 16.

Vestbro, D.U. (1992) 'From Central Kitchen to Community Cooperation: development of collective housing in Sweden', *Open House International*, no. 2.

Vestergaard, H. (2006) 'Single-family Detached Housing: a branch of paradise or a problem?', in Doling, J. and Elsinga, E. (eds.) *Home Ownership. Get-*

ting in, Getting From, Getting Out. Part II. Housing and Urban Policy Studies 30. Delft University Press.

Vestergaard, J. (1986) (ed.) *Sociale uroligheder: politi og politik*. Holte: Forlaget SOCPOL.

Wacquant, L. (1999) 'Urban Marginality in the Coming Millennium', *Urban Studies*, no. 10.

Wagenaar, C. (2004) (ed.) *Happy: cities and public happiness in post-war Europe*. Rotterdam: NAi Publishers.

Walker, R.A. (2005) *Power of Place and Space: local dimensions of imperial economic and development policy*. http://urbanhabitat.org/node/214 (downloaded 30/3 2011).

Wallenstein, S.-O. and Mattsson, H. (2010) (eds.) *Swedish Modernism: architecture, consumption and the welfare state*. London: Black Dog.

Ward, P. (2008) 'Drama-Documentary, Ethics and Notions of Performance: the "Flight 93" films', in Austin, T. and de Jong, W. (eds.) *Rethinking Documentary: new perspectives, new practices*. Maidenhead: Open University Press.

Wasshede, C. (2010a) *Passionerad politik: om motstånd mot heteronormativ könsmakt*. Malmö: Bokbox Förlag.

Wasshede, C. (2010b) 'Beard and Skirt: gender bending in public space', in Holgersson, H., Thörn, C., Thörn, H. and Wahlström, M. (eds.) *(Re-)Searching Gothenburg: essays on a changing city*. Göteborg: Glänta Produktion.

Westerling, K. (2007) *La dolce vita: trettio år med drag*. Stockholm: Normal Förlag.

Wettergren, Å. (2005) *Moving and Jamming: implications for social movement theory*. Karlstad: Karlstad University Press.

Øberg, A.S. (2007) *Planning Christiania: the urban designer as mediator*. Unpublished thesis; Aalborg University.

OFFICIAL DOCUMENTS

Danish government sources

Arbejds- og Socialministeriet [Ministry of Work and Social Policy] (1973) *Redegørelse vedr. arealerne ved Bådsmandsstrædets kaserne og ammunitionsarsenalet*. København: Library of the Ministry of Work and Social Policy.

Finansministeriet [Ministry of Finance] (2007) *Finansminister Thor Pedersens brev til [Christianit] Britta Lillesøe,* april.

Forsvarsministeriet [Ministry of Defence] (1991) *Rammeaftale af 30 oktober 1991 mellem Christiania og Forsvarsministeriet.*
Forsvarsministeriet [Ministry of Defence] (2004) *Christianiaområdets fremtid – helhedsplan og handlingsplan.*
Forsvarsministeriet [Ministry of Defence] (31/3 2004) *Bemærkninger til Forslag til Lov om ændring af lov om anvendelse af Christianiaområdet.*
Forsvars- og justitsministeriet [Ministry of Defence and Justice] (6/5 2003) *Forsvars- og justitsministerens redegørelse om Christiania.*
The Palaces and Properties Agency [Slots- og Ejendomsstyrelsen] (n.d.) *Negotiations between Christiania and the State.* http://www.ses.dk/en/Christiania/forhandlingerne.aspx (downloaded 15/2 2011).
The Palaces and Properties Agency [Slots- og Ejendomsstyrelsen] (2004) *The Future of the Christiania Area: unified plan and plan of action.*
Slots- og Ejendomsstyrelsen [The Palaces and Properties Agency] (May 2005) *Fremtidige organisations- og ejerformer på Christianiaområdet.* www.ses.dk/da/Christiania (downloaded 23/4 2011).
Slots- og Ejendomsstyrelsen [The Palaces and Properties Agency] (Sep 2006) *Udmøntning af fremtidige organisations- og ejerformer på Christianiaområdet.*
Slots- og Ejendomsstyrelsen [The Palaces and Properties Agency] (Dec 2006) *Uddybning og supplement af statens tilbud til Christianias beboere af 26. september 2006 om udmøntning af fremtidige organisations- og ejerformer på Christianiaområdet.*
Slots- og Ejendomsstyrelsen [The Palaces and Properties Agency] (2009) *Notat: Faktaark om Christiania: Forhandlingerne.*

Danish parliament sources
Folketinget (7/6 1989) 'Lov nr. 399 af 1989: 'Lov om anvendelse af Christianiaområdet', *Lovtidende*, hæfte 60.
Folketinget (31/3 2004) 'Bemærkninger til Forslag til Lov om ændring af lov om anvendelse af Christianiaområdet', http://webarkiv.ft.dk/?/samling/20031/lovforslag_oversigtsformat/l205.htm (downloaded 7/6 2011).
Folketinget (9/6 2004) 'Lov nr. 431 af 2004: Lov om ændring af lov om anvendelse af Christianiaområdet', http://webarkiv.ft.dk/?/samling/20031/lovforslag_oversigtsformat/l205.htm (downloaded 7/6 2011).

Danish parliamentary debates

Folketinget (1973/4) 'Forhandling om forsvarsministerns skriftlige redegørelse af 25 april 1974 for Christianiasagens udvikling' (8 May), in *Folketingstidende: forhandlingerne i Folketingsåret 1973-74*. København: A/S J.H. Schultz Universitets-bogtrykkeri.

Folketinget (1974/5) 'Første behandling av forslag til folketingsbeslutning om ophør av besættelsen av Bådsmandsstrædes kaserne ("Christiania")' (10 Apr.), in *Folketingstidende: forhandlingerne i Folketingsåret 1974-75*. København: A/S J. H. Schultz.

Folketinget (1975/6) 'Forhandling om forsvarsministerens redegørelse af 19 februar 1976 (om "Christiania")' (25 Feb.) in *Folketingstidende: forhandlingerne i Folketingsåret 1974-75*. København: A/S J. H. Schultz.

Folketinget (1975/76) 'Behandling af f. t. finanslov for 1976-7' (30 March), in *Folketingstidende: forhandlingerne i Folketingsåret 1975-76*. København: A/S J. H. Schultz.

Folketinget (1975/76) 'Forespørgsel til forsvarsministern vedr. Christiania' (31 May), in *Folketingstidende: forhandlingerne i Folketingsåret 1975-76*. København: A/S J. H. Schultz.

Folketinget (1977/78) 'Forespørgsel til forsvarsministeren vedr. Christiania' (8 Feb.), in *Folketingstidende: forhandlingerne i Folketingsåret 1977-78*. København: A/S J. H. Schultz.

Folketinget (1978/79) 'Forslag til folketingsbeslutning om nedlæggelse av Christiania' (2 Nov.), in *Folketingstidende: forhandlingerne i Folketingsåret 1978-79*. København: A/S J. H. Schultz.

Folketinget (1981/2) 'Forhandling om redegørelse om den af konsulentfirmaet Møller & Grønborg udarbejdede skitse til Christianiaområdets fremtidige anvendelse' (16 March), in *Folketingstidende: forhandlingerne i Folketingsåret 1981-82*. København: A/S J. H. Schultz.

Folketinget (1982/3) 'Forslag til folketingsbeslutning om nedlæggelse av Christiania' (26 Nov.), in *Folketingstidende: forhandlingerne i Folketingsåret 1982-83*. København: A/S J. H. Schultz.

Folketinget (1983/4) 'Forespørgsel til statsministeren: hvilke initiativer agter regeringen at tage i forbindelse med Christiania? (6 March), in *Folketingstidende: forhandlingerne i Folketingsåret 1983-84*. København: A/S J. H. Schultz.

Folketinget (1984/5) 'Forslag til folketingsbeslutning om Christianias fremtid' (18 Apr.), in *Folketingstidende: forhandlingerne i Folketingsåret 1984-85*. København: A/S J. H. Schultz.

Folketinget (1985/6) 'Forslag til folketingsbeslutning om Christianias fremtid' (17 Jan.), in *Folketingstidende: forhandlingerne i Folketingsåret 1985-86*. København: A/S J. H. Schultz Universitets-bogtrykkeri.

Folketinget (1985/6) 'Forslag til folketingsbeslutning om Christianias fremtid' (15 May), in *Folketingstidende: forhandlingerne i Folketingsåret 1985-86*. København: A/S J. H. Schultz.

Folketinget (1987/8) 'Forespørgsel til forsvarsministeren vedr. Christiania' (19 Nov.), in *Folketingstidende: forhandlingerne i Folketingsåret 1987-88*. København: A/S J. H. Schultz.

Folketinget (1988/9) 'Forhandling om forslag til lov om anvendelse av Christianiaområdet' (26 Apr.), in *Folketingstidende: forhandlingerne i Folketingsåret 1988-89*. København: A/S J. H. Schultz.

Folketinget (1991/2) 'Forespørgsel til forsvarsministeren vedr. Christiania' (31 Oct.), in *Folketingstidende: forhandlingerne i Folketingsåret 1991-92*. København: A/S J. H. Schultz.

Folketinget (1993/4) 'Forespørgsel til justitsministeren och forsvarsministeren om forholdene på Christiania' (20 Jan.), in *Folketingstidende: forhandlingerne i Folketingsåret 1993-94*. København: A/S J. H. Schultz.

Folketinget (1996/7) 'Forespørgsel til justitsministeren och forsvarsministeren: Hvad kan regeringen oplyse om bestræbelserne på at normalisere forholdene på Christiania, herunder at få stoppet kriminaliteten og håndhævet de i samfundet gældende regler om ejendomsvurdering og skattebetaling m.v.?' (26 Nov.), in *Folketingstidende: forhandlingerne i Folketingsåret 1996-97*. København: A/S J. H. Schultz.

Folketinget (2002) 'Forespørgsel til forsvarsministeren: Hvilke planer har regeringen for arealet Bådsmandsstrædes Kaserne (Christiania) på Christianshavn' (9 Apr.), (http://webarkiv.ft.dk/?/samling/20012/salen/f16_beh1_51_22_53.htm) (downloaded 18/4 2011).

Folketinget (2003) 'Forespørgsel til statsministern og forsvarsministeren: Hvad kan regeringen oplyse om planerne for Christianias "normalisering" set i lyset af regeringens tanker om frihed?' (http://webarkiv.ft.dk/?/samling/20031/forespoergsel/f4.htm) (downloaded 20/4 2011).

Folketinget (2004) 'Første behandling af lovforslag nr. L 205: Forslag til lov om ændring af lov om anvendelse af Christianiaområdet. (Ændret formål og ejerskab til området m.v.)' (16 Apr.), (http://webarkiv.ft.dk/?/samling/20031/lovforslag_oversigtsformat/l205.htm) (downloaded 18/4 2011).

Folketinget (2004) 'Anden behandling af lovforslag nr. L 205: Forslag til lov om ændring af lov om anvendelse af Christianiaområdet. (Ændret formål og ejerskab til området m.v.) ' (18 May) (http://webarkiv.ft.dk/?/samling/20031/lovforslag_oversigtsformat/l205.htm) (downloaded 18/4 2011).
Folketinget (2004) 'Tredje behandling af lovforslag nr. L 205: Forslag til lov om ændring af lov om anvendelse af Christianiaområdet. (Ændret formål og ejerskab til området m.v.) ' (18 May) (http://webarkiv.ft.dk/?/samling/20031/lovforslag_oversigtsformat/l205.htm) (downloaded 18/4 2011).

Other official sources

Copenhagen Capacity (2010) http://www.copcap.com/content/us/doing_business/why_copenhagen/copenhagen_-_open_for_business (downloaded 1/6 2010).

Copenhagen Municipality (2005) *Boliger for alle: boligplan for Københavns Kommune 2005-2008. Forslag*. København: Københavns Kommune.

Eurostat (2010) http://epp.eurostat.ec.europa.eu/ (downloaded 29/10 2010).

Egnsplankontoret (1947/1993) *Skitseforslag til Egnsplan for Storkøbenhavn*. København: Byplanlaboratoriet.

Kulturarvsstyrelsen [The Heritage Agency of Denmark] *Fredning af 11 bygninger på Christiania*, http://www.kulturarv.dk/presse-nyt/nyhed/artikel/fredning-af-11-bygninger-paa-christiania/ (downloaded 12/10 2007).

Nordiska Rådet [Nordic Council] (1982). Del II.

OECD (2008) *The Future of the Family to 2030: a scoping report*. Paris: OECD. P.6

OPCE (2003) *Make the Growth Engines Work!: resolution regarding the capital cities/regions of Europe*, board of directors' meeting, Madrid, Monday 5/5.
http://www.opce.org/pagesuk/statements2.htm (downloaded 10/8 2006).

Riksdagen [Swedish parliament] (1981/82). *Protokoll 34 -35 (A/3)*. 24:11-8:12.

Østre Landsret (2008) 15. Afd. Sag nr. B-3803-06.

CHRISTIANIA DOCUMENTS

Christiania (13/11 1971) 'Christianias Målsætning/Manifest'. Christiania's website: http://www.christiania.org/modules.php?name=Side&navn=Maalsaetning (downloaded 15/2 2011).

Christiania (1991) *Christianias grønne plan*. København: Christiania.

Christianias Kulturforening (1997) *Langt ude i hampen. En høring om hamp, hash og kultur*. Christiania: Christianias Kulturforening.

Christiania (2004) 'Eventyret om Christiania'. http://www.christiania.org/modules.php?name=NukeWrap&page=/inc/tale/ (downloaded 7/6 2011).

Christiania (Nov. 2006) 'Christianias svar til Danmark'. http://www.ses.dk/da/Christiania/~/media/Files/Christiania/_5_christianias_svar_til_danmark_20_november_2006_1.ashx (downloaded 7/6 2011).

Christiania (2006) *Christianias Udviklingsplan*. København: Forlaget Ararat. http://www.christiania.org/inc/pdf/caup2006/CAUP_72.pdf (downloaded 22/2 2011).

Christiania (2007) *Christiania som agenda 21 område: et exempel til efterfølgelse*. København: Christiania. http://www.christiania.org/inc/pdf/07_tekst/07_ca_agenda21_folder.pdf (downloaded 1/6 2010).

Christiania (8/2 2007) 'Christianias svar på statens samlede udspil. Christianias Forhandlingsgruppe på vegne af Christianias Fællesmøde'. http://www.ses.dk/da/Christiania/~/media/Files/Christiania/_7_christianias_svar_til_statens_samlede_udspil_8_feb_2007.ashx (downloaded 7/6 2011).

Christiania (31/3 2007) Fristaden Christianias brev til direktør Rasmus Jarlov, Slots- og Ejendomsstyrelsen. Christianias Fællesmøde. http://www.ses.dk/da/Christiania/~/media/Files/Christiania/_9_christianias_svar_31_marts_2007.ashx (downloaded 7/6 2011).

Lykke, O. (2001) *Christianias Pigegarde, Altid Fremad 1991-2001*. København: Forlaget Ararat.

Mollerup, P. and Løvetand, K. (1976) (eds.) *Fristaden Christianias Udvikling. 2.Del. Pusheri og Stoffer*. København: Christiania.

PRESS MATERIAL

Newspapers and journals

Arbetet
Berlingske Tidene
BT
Christianshavneren
Dagbladet i Sundsvall
Dagens Nyheter

Ekstra Bladet
Guardian
Hampebladet
Information
Jyllandsposten
Jyllandsposten Vest
Kvällsposten
Nyhedsavisen
Ny Tid
Ordkløveren
Politiken
Slå Tillbaka!
Stockholms Tidningen
Svenska Dagbladet
Sydsvenska Dagbladet
Sotra-Nytt
Tranås Tidning
TT (Tidningarnas Telegrafbyrå)
Ugespejlet

Radio and television

Guldbrandsen, C. (2005) *Kampen om staden*, Television Documentary, DR1, January 5, 8 pm.
Danmarks Radio (2 August 2010) *Reportagen*: Tingbjerg part 1–5, http://www.dr.dk/P1/Reportagen/Udsendelser/2010/07/07125744.htm (downloaded 7/6 2011).
Danmarks Radio (1976) *Dagbog fra en fristad*, dir. Poul Martinsen.
Danmarks Radio (1988) *Gensyn med Christiania*, dir. Poul Martinsen.

Acknowledgements

First of all we would like to thank those Christianites who openly and kindly have received the authors of this book. Without the active assistance of people like Ole Lykke, Emmerik Warburg, Britta Lillesøe and Nils Vest, the research on which this book is based would not have been possible. An example of this is the seminar held in Christiania in January 2011, when draft versions of the chapters in this book were presented and discussed. In addition to providing the necessary space and coffee for the seminar, Ole, Emmerik and a few other Christianites also contributed insightful reflections on aspects of the Freetown's 40-year history. Special thanks to Ole Lykke, Christiania historian and archivist, who not only helped us to find documents and other material, but is also one of those who have checked the facts in this book.

We the editors would like to thank the contributors, not just for writing original texts, but also assisting in other ways, such as sending photographs and other material. Special thanks to Maria Hellström Reimer, who allowed us to use, and updated, the Christiania timeline originally published in her PhD thesis. Thanks also to Leah Robb for offering some of her drawings for the book; and for making the beautiful cover.

This book has been organised as part of a research project entitled 'The inner city as public sphere: Urban transformation, social order and social movement', based at the Department of Sociology, University of Gothenburg, Sweden and funded by The Bank of Sweden Tercentenary Foundation (Riksbankens Jubileumsfond) and The Swedish Research Council for Environment, Agricultural Sciences and Spatial Planning (FORMAS).

About the authors

Christa Simone Amouroux has a Ph.D. from Stanford University in Cultural Anthropology and is a lecturer at San Francisco State University's Department of Anthropology, where she has taught a range of undergraduate classes on topics such as global cities and urban transformations; race and the history of anthropology; gender and space; the normalisation of city spaces. She has written extensively on Christiania, which was the subject of her dissertation.

Signe Sophie Bøggild is an independent researcher based in Copenhagen. She has a M.Phil. in History of Art, from the University of Copenhagen and a MA from the Department of Visual Cultures, Goldsmiths College, University of London, where her specialist subject was *Geographies*. She researches and writes about urban regeneration, urbanism and post-war modernism for books by Crimson Architectural Historians, Rotterdam, The International New Town Institute, Almere, and the Bauhaus University, Weimar.

Anders Lund Hansen, Ph.D., is an assistant professor at the Department of Social and Economic Geography, Lund University, Sweden. In his dissertation, *Space Wars and the New Urban Imperialism* (2006), recent urban transformations are analysed through the lens of space wars. His present research on East Asian cities is funded by the Wallander Foundation. His latest, co-edited book is *David Harvey: Ojämlikhetens nya geografi* (2011). Since 2008, his has been a member of the CRIR steering committee.

Maria Hellström Reimer is Professor in Design Theory at Malmö University, School of Arts and Communication. She has a Ph.D. in Landscape Architecture with a specialisation in Theoretical and Applied Aesthetics, and is also a practicing artist. Her dissertation *Steal this Place: the Aesthetics of Tactical Formlessness and 'the Freetown of Christiania'* (2006) concerns the vast and complex borderland between aesthetic activism and urbanist practices in Christiania. For the last couple of years, she has been conducting arts-based research.

Helen Jarvis, Ph.D, is a Reader in Social Geography in the School of Geography, Politics and Sociology, Newcastle University, UK. Her authored books include *Cities and Gender* (with P. Kantor and J. Cloke, Routledge, 2009); *Work/Life City Limits: Comparative Household Perspectives* (Palgrave Macmillan, 2005) and *The Secret Life of Cities: the Social Reproduction of Everyday Life* (with A. C. Pratt and P. Wu, Pearson Education 2001). She was Christiania researcher in residence (CR-IR) in 2010.

René Karpantschof has a Ph.D. in Sociology from the University of Copenhagen and is currently Senior Master at Aurehoej High-School, Copenhagen. During the period 1999–2010, he was lecturer and researcher at the Department of Sociology, University of Copenhagen, in the field of social movements and contentious politics. Karpantschof's publications include among others *Kampen om Ungdomshuset. Studier i et oprør* (København: Frydenlund og Monsun, 2009, ed. with M. Lindblom).

Tomas Nilson has a Ph.D. in History from Gothenburg University. He is currently working on the research project 'The inner city as public sphere: Urban transformation, social order and social movement'. His research interests are gender relations within business, studies of masculinities, social network theory and modern politics. His forthcoming book on Swedish political modernisation deals with the peculiar case of the Swedish Liberal Party.

Amy Starecheski is a Ph.D. candidate in Cultural Anthropology at the City University of New York Graduate Center and teaches at Hunter College. She co-directs the Columbia University Oral History Research Office's Summer Institute in Oral History and is co-author of *Telling Lives Oral History Curriculum*. Her dissertation research is with New York City squatters whose buildings are being legalised, focusing on their shifting experiences of property and their historical practices.

Håkan Thörn is Professor at the Department of Sociology, University of Gothenburg. His research mainly deals with social movements and globalisation, and he has written and co-edited several books on these topics, including *Anti-Apartheid and the Emergence of a Global Civil Society* (Palgrave Macmillan 2006; second edition 2009). He is currently leading the research project 'The inner city as public sphere: Urban transformation, social order and social movement'.

Cathrin Wasshede holds a Ph.D. in Sociology from the University of Gothenburg. Her research interests are gender and sexuality, resistance and social movements. Her dissertation, *Passionate Politics: Resistance to Heteronormative Gender Power,* is about the way in which young left-wing political activists in Gothenburg offer resistance to dominating norms around gender and sexuality. Over the period 2010–2012 she is participating in the research project 'The inner city as public sphere: Urban transformation, social order and social movement'.

◄ Continued from front endpapers

1980
The Archer – a dwelling place in Christiania, an internal visionary report is published
Ugespejlet (The Weekly Mirror) appears

1981
The Møller and Grønborg plan
The Post Office opens

1982
CA debate in The Nordic Council
CA organises the Love Sweden Tour
Bikers war: Bullshit against Hells Angels in CA
Bossehuset gains reputation as centre for gay culture

1986
CA presents *Voilà report*

1987
Government forms the Special Governing Group, which presents the draf
One Step Ahead…Christiania
Parliament grants CA 20 million Danish kroner for restoration work
The last Bullshit members leave CA

1988
The Special Governing Group presents the additional draft *Two Ste*
Ahead - Complement
CA rejects funding from government
DR broadcasting of Poul Martinsen's *Return to Christiania*

1989
Police close all pubs; most reopen after getting legal permissi
The Christiania Law
Proposal for local plan. The Christiania Secretariat is formed
The Grey Hall becomes important hip-hop scene

1991
The state presents *The Local Plan*
CA presents *The Green Plan*
CA's Girls Guard is founded
Nils Vest's movie *Christiania You Have my Heart* i
released

1992
Intense police campaign against hash mark

1993
The National Archive establishes special CA archive

1994
CA publishes additional *Developmental Plan*

1995
The first new common building, the Raisin Building (Rosinhuset), is erected in CA

1995-96
Flourishing cultural life: huge concerts in the Grey Hall

1996
CA and the Ministry of Defence present joint development plan

1997
CA's own currency 1 LØN = 7 euro is introduced
CA organises the first of three hash hearings (1997-2001)

1998
New bridge built by German craftsmen over the moat

1980

1990